IT'S ALL ABOUT THE JOURNEY

It's All About the Journey

Finding Peace, Success and Fulfillment
in the Corporate World

Paula Gamonal and
John F. Williams

Writers Club Press
New York Lincoln Shanghai

It's All About the Journey
Finding Peace, Success and Fulfillment in the Corporate World

Writers Club Press
an imprint of iUniverse, Inc.

For information address:
iUniverse, Inc.
2021 Pine Lake Road, Suite 100
Lincoln, NE 68512
www.iuniverse.com

ISBN: 0-595-25958-8 (pbk)
ISBN: 0-595-65465-7 (cloth)

Printed in the United States of America

This book is dedicated to everyone who enjoyed these articles in their original versions on the Ravenwerks web site (www.ravenwerks.com) and honored us by requesting that they be reprinted in a more permanent form.

It is also dedicated to anyone who feels that business is an arena to improve the lives of the people they serve, including customers, clients, and co-workers.

This book also contains articles not published on the Ravenwerks web site.

The trail is the thing, not the end of the trail. Travel too fast and you miss all you are traveling for.

—Louis L'Amour

Contents

Acknowledgements

We'd like to thank

Our parents, who shaped our ideas and paradigms probably more than they ever would have guessed at the time.

- Judy Franco, for being the best Mom a girl could have, and who taught kindness, patience and forbearance.
- Ron Anderson, for being the best Dad a girl could have, teaching that logic and common sense always trump smoke and mirrors.
- Glen Williams, for being the best Dad a guy could have, and one of the two greatest men I've ever known, and taught me more than I can say.
- Betty Edwards, for being the best Mom a guy could have, and who taught me perseverance, math and much other necessary stuff.

Our Children, for teaching us more than we teach them.

- James K. Williams, for figuring out how to fly (literally) and
- Michelle Williams, for figuring out how to fly (figuratively) both having succeeded in spite of the world.
- Michael J. (Mickey) Gamonal, for being an outstanding example of what a 13-year-old kid is supposed to be, and for being a great guy to have around.

Our brothers and sister

- Pat Elliot, for living an inspirational life, and being the best sister a guy could have.

- Randy Elliot, for getting through the impossible and still able to see the silver lining.

- Kevin Anderson, for setting an example impossible to live up to

Our teachers and colleagues

- Paula's Tae Kwon Do Masters Hyusup Jung and Ok Keun Lee, for teaching persistence and clarity, and for making the most esoteric concepts very physical and very obvious.

- John's MBA team at the University of Utah—Bill Hardman, Alison Johnston, Barbara Ray, and Gary Hammond, for epitomizing synergy and rewriting the book on high-performance teams.

- Joe Bentley at the University of Utah for taking the time to give good advice.

- Rick Mead, for showing that a successful executive can still play in a band at questionable establishments.

- Karen Wardle, for cutting through the bullsh** when necessary.

- Muhammad Farooq, for many afternoons at Sweet Tomatoes tossing ideas around.

- Shauna Bona, for connecting with the past and bringing good news.

- The Golden Braid in Salt Lake City Utah, and the Bad Ass Coffee Company in Park City Utah, for supplying much coffee and a suitable atmosphere for poring over manuscripts.

- Dave Ostlund, the best sales guy anywhere.

- Jim Hall, the best customer support and product information guy anywhere.

- The Harley Davidson Company, for inestimable inspiration.

- The Institute of Chartered Financial Analysts of India, (ICFAI) for continued collaboration on various publications and projects.

- Lois Hearn, for consultations on business etiquette.

- Valerie Haas, our publishing assistant

- IUniverse, for great cover art and publication assistance

- Rick Sidorowicz and the CEO Refresher for collaboration and synergy

- Tristin Tabish and KUER radio for the opportunity to publicize the book AND raise money for public radio at the same time

- Aneel Aranha and the Middle East Entrepreneur magazine

- Nikki Mead and the E-Journal

- Dickie and Angel Shannon of Oldies 94.1, for support, encouragement and publicity when Ravenwerks was in its inception.

- Thomas Friedman, for providing fabulous examples of good writing.

- Women In Technology International, the National Association of Women Business Owners, the American Bankers Association for great material and inspiration.

Companies we've worked for and with

- Wells Fargo, Franklin Covey, the State of Utah, Shipley Associates, Syntel, CTG, General Dynamics, Sears, Conoco, Zions Bancorporation, First Security Bank, IBM, and the Georgia Dept. of Transportation (GDOT)

Introduction

There are many people who are refugees of the corporate world.

They view the business environment as a chaotic, unnatural, unhealthy place that they escape from every weekend, or when they retire to a peaceful island in the Bahamas.

John bought a Harley Davidson Heritage Softtail and had it customized, the way John had always dreamed of, and we put several thousand miles on it within the first few months of owning it. One of the unintended (but pleasant) side effects of riding the Harley is that we meet a great many other people that ride motorcycles in national parks, across back roads through rural areas, and other places that we find peace and beauty. Many of the people we meet are doctors, lawyers, engineers and other professional people who are looking for an escape from their 80-hour weeks and the office backstabbing. They want to feel something real, like the throaty rumble of the engine, the smell of gasoline, and the simple challenge of the road.

My father was a systems analyst who couldn't wait to retire from a major utility company. He was tired of the work, the travel, the phone calls late at night. He moved to the middle of New Mexico, near the Continental Divide, to live on a beautiful but rustic piece of property where he couldn't see his nearest neighbors, the phone and the doorbell would only announce family or friends. He didn't even have a computer for several years. It was great to get away from the politics, the paperwork, and the compulsive demands on time and energy.

At the time, society didn't provide other options, now, it doesn't have to be that way.

Variety in life is one thing, escape is quite another. I'm a strong advocate of spending your "spare time" doing something very different from your career. John has his Harley and a number of projects using his hands. I have Tae Kwon Do, and we both love traveling and photography—being tourists in the big, beautiful world. And there have been times when it felt like a necessary escape. But most of the time we enjoy getting back to work. We enjoy our careers, and we enjoy "moonlighting" projects. We stay up late most nights, because we get involved in work, study, and different projects with family or friends. Needless to say, we don't watch much television. But we see this as an expansion of our work, not as an escape from it.

I think it is almost a moral imperative to enjoy what you do for a living. To feel like you're really contributing something to the world, to your customers and co-workers, and to your organization. Human beings are social creatures by nature. They are also goal-driven creatures by nature.

The "secrets," if there any, are alignment between your personal and work life, and enjoyment of the journey and challenges you meet along the way.

Lack of alignment is an issue for many professional people. Often there is a huge gulf between their work life and their personal life. They are different people if you meet them in a business meeting than if you meet them at home on a Saturday morning. They have one set of values and goals while they're at work, and during their daily commute they exchange them for a different set of values and goals at home. To shift gears like that puts an unbelievable amount of stress on a person.

They feel that they have to rush around like crazy, be ruthless with everyone (including themselves) and frantically drive from one objective to the next. They create enemies that they then have to expend energy defending against. They make unrealistic promises out of fear for their positions, and have to work frantically (and drive their staff frantically) to "cash the checks they've written." They find themselves burned out, they feel abused by their company, their co-workers and their clients, their blood pressure goes up, and they find themselves involuntary or voluntary refugees of the corporate world.

It is important to find an organization, and a place within it, where you can exercise and expand your skills. Your own personal motives and values have to be expanded and amplified by the motives and values of the organization. If you have that "line of sight" between your own personal goals, and your team or department's goals, and the goals of the organization, then everything you do seems to be magnified. You get a satisfying synergy that exponentially expands beyond your personal power.

You also have to enjoy the journey and the process of meeting the opportunities and challenges along the way. You have to see your current project as an end in itself, rather than a means to an end. I'll illustrate with yet another motorcycle metaphor. Many people go on vacation with the intention of arriving at a destination and engaging in specific activities there, expecting the end result to be a refreshed, re-energized self. We enjoy the journey—the chance encounters at gas stations and small restaurants and coffee shops. The scenery, sounds and smells of the countryside or small towns we ride through. We've taken some of the same trips between the same two cities by car or airplane and it's a decidedly different experience. We like to motor along back roads at about 40 to 50 miles per hour, enjoying the smell of new-cut grass or fallen leaves, the wind in our faces, the differences in temperature from the bottom of a hill to the top as the thermals rise, the rumble of the engine, and the vivid 360 degree visual experience. We enjoy the journey.

Alignment and enjoyment are not new concepts. This is not a squishy new-age philosophy. Nor is it exclusively an American philosophy. It was embraced by a number of thinkers very different from each other in time and place.

- *Your work is to discover your work, and then with all your heart to give yourself to it.*—Buddha

- *Far and away the best prize that life offers is the chance to work hard at work worth doing.*—Theodore Roosevelt

- *It is your work in life that is the ultimate seduction.*—Pablo Picasso

- *Work is love made visible.*—Kahlil Gibran

You might be reading this so far and saying to yourself, "Yeah, that's great and all, but these people have NO IDEA how HARD my job is!"

That is true. We wouldn't pretend to know your unique experience, and have no intention of trivializing it or simplifying it. The reason we wrote every one of these articles is because one of us, or someone we know, or someone who asked us for help, was experiencing a problem in and needed real-world, nuts and bolts, practical HELP.

Nobody knows what experiences will befall them on any journey. Bilbo Baggins told his nephew Frodo in JRR Tolkien's *The Fellowship of the Ring* that "It's a dangerous business, Frodo, going out of your door…You step into the Road, and if you don't keep your feet, there is no knowing where you might be swept off to." Of course this advice kept neither of them at home, otherwise the world would not have seen four volumes of great literature.

The following articles illustrate ways to resolve different problems. Each article starts with an "opportunity" which otherwise might be called a "problem." Starting by seeing the problem in a positive light, it discusses a possible solution or way to meet the opportunity.

These articles are meant as tools to help you bring sanity, humanity, peace and prosperity to your work life, and each may be of some value in and of itself. But the maximum benefit from any of them is to approach the situation as an opportunity to align your own motives and values with those of your organization, and to enjoy the *journey*.

I really enjoy the tagline of the *Wall Street Journal*—"Adventures in Capitalism," for just that reason. If you approach each day as an opportunity to face some challenges and enjoy the process of unraveling a problem and chasing down a solution, you will be successful. And not just in the material sense, although that naturally follows doing what you're good at. With thoughtful application, you will also find peace and fulfillment from each individual opportunity, from your current job, and from your whole journey through the corporate world.

1. Business Etiquette—More Than Just Using the Right Fork

THE OPPORTUNITY

Business etiquette is made up of significantly more important things than knowing which fork to use at lunch with a client. Unfortunately, in the perception of others, the devil is in the details. People may feel that if you can't be trusted not to embarrass yourself in business and social situations, you may lack the self-control necessary to be good at what you do. Etiquette is about presenting yourself with the kind of polish that shows you can be taken seriously. Etiquette is also about being comfortable around people (and making them comfortable around you!)

People are a key factor in your own and your business' success. Many potentially worthwhile and profitable alliances have been lost because of an unintentional breach of manners.

Dan McLeod, president of Positive Management Leadership Programs, a union avoidance company, says, "Show me a boss who treats his or her employees abrasively, and I'll show you an environment ripe for labor problems and obviously poor customer relations. Disrespectful and discourteous treatment of employees is passed along from the top."

Most behavior that is perceived as disrespectful, discourteous or abrasive is unintentional, and could have been avoided by practicing good manners or etiquette. We've always found that most negative experiences with someone were unintentional and easily repaired by keeping an open mind and maintaining open, honest communication. Basic knowledge and practice of etiquette is a valuable advantage, because in a lot of situations, a second chance may not be possible or practical.

THE SOLUTION

There are many written and unwritten rules and guidelines for etiquette, and it certainly behooves a businessperson to learn them. The caveat is that there is no possible way to know all of them!

These guidelines have some difficult-to-navigate nuances, depending on the company, the local culture, and the requirements of the situation. Possibilities to commit a faux pas are limitless, and chances are, sooner or later, you'll make a mistake. But you can minimize them, recover quickly, and avoid causing a bad impression by being generally considerate and attentive to the concerns of others, and by adhering to the basic rules of etiquette. When in doubt, stick to the basics.

The Basics

The most important thing to remember is to be courteous and thoughtful to the people around you, regardless of the situation. Consider other people's feelings, stick to your convictions as diplomatically as possible. Address conflict as situation-related, rather than person-related. Apologize when you step on toes. You can't go too far wrong if you stick with the basics you learned in Kindergarten. (Not that those basics are easy to remember when you're in a hard-nosed business meeting!)

This sounds simplistic, but the qualities we admire most when we see them in people in leadership positions, are the very traits we work so hard to engender in our children. If you always behave so that you would not mind your spouse, kids, or grandparents watching you, you're probably doing fine. Avoid raising your voice (surprisingly, it can be much more effective at getting attention when you lower it!) using harsh or derogatory language toward anyone (present or absent), or interrupting. You may not get as much "airtime" in meetings at first, but what you do say will be much more effective because it carries the weight of credibility and respectability.

The following are guidelines and tips that we've found helpful for dealing with people in general, in work environments, and in social situations.

It's About People

Talk and visit with people. Don't differentiate by position or standing within the company. Secretaries and janitorial staff actually have tremendous power to help or hinder your career. Next time you need a document prepared or a conference room arranged for a presentation, watch how many people are involved with that process (you'll probably be surprised!) and make it a point to meet them and show your appreciation.

Make it a point to arrive ten or fifteen minutes early and visit with people that work near you. When you're visiting another site, linger over a cup of coffee and introduce yourself to people nearby. If you arrive early for a meeting, introduce yourself to the other participants. At social occasions, use the circumstances of the event itself as an icebreaker. After introducing yourself, ask how they know the host or how they like the crab dip. Talk a little about yourself—your hobbies, kids, or pets; just enough to get people to open up about theirs and get to know you as a person.

Keep notes on people. There are several "contact management" software applications that are designed for salespeople, but in business, nearly everyone is a salesperson in some capacity or another. They help you create a "people database" with names, addresses, phone numbers, birthdays, spouse and children's' names; whatever depth of information is appropriate for your situation.

It's a good idea to remember what you can about people; and to be thoughtful. Send cards or letters for birthdays or congratulations of promotions or other events, send flowers for engagements, weddings or in condolence for the death of a loved one or family member. People will remember your kindness, probably much longer than you will!

Peers and Subordinates

Impressing the boss isn't enough.

A study by Manchester Partners International, says even in this tight job market, 40% of new management hires fail in their first jobs. The key reason for their failure is their inability to build good relationships with peers and subordinates.

Social rank or class is a cornerstone of social interaction in many cultures. The corporate climate in the United States is no exception. People tend to feel uneasy until they've seen an "organizational chart" or figured out who reports to whom. They feel that it is more important to show respect and practice etiquette around superiors than around peers or subordinates.

The current social and economic climate is one of rapid advancement through technology, which make it very possible (and even likely) for a pesky salesman to become an important client, or an administrative assistant to become a manager.

Mergers and acquisitions add to this "class mixing," causing a former competitor to become a coworker overnight.

This can make things awkward if you treat people differently depending on their "corporate standing." If you show respect and courtesy to everyone, regardless of position or company, you avoid discomfort or damaging your chances in any unexpected turn of events.

Having a consistent demeanor improves your credibility. Even the people at the top will begin to suspect your motives if you treat VIPs with impeccable courtesy and snap at counter clerks.

Superiors

The only thing you owe your boss above and beyond what you owe peers and subordinates is more information. Unobtrusively be sure he or she knows what you're doing, is alerted as early as possible to issues that may arise, and is aware of outcomes and milestones.

Never surprise your boss.

It goes without saying that you should speak well of him or her within and outside the company, and give him or her the benefit of the doubt. (Which you would do for anyone, of course!)

International Business

The information in this article is presented from a Western point of view. It is important to note that etiquette in other cultures requires a bit of adaptation and flexibility. If you're traveling on business to a foreign destination, or have foreign visitors here, it is a good idea to learn as much as you can about the culture and make appropriate allowances.

Items to consider:

- Language (learn theirs if possible, but don't pretend to be fluent unless you have many years of study under your belt!)

- Time zones

- Working schedules (a 35 hour work week is customary in much of Europe.)

- Holidays (The Middle East tradition of Ramadan may not coincide with your plans for "power lunches.")

- Food customs (table manners, use of implements, etc.)

Generally speaking, as long as you are trying to be considerate and express an interest in learning, you should be fine. If in doubt, err on the conservative, formal side.

THE WORKPLACE

The remainder of this article is divided into two sections—The Workplace and Social Situations. The division is really for convenience only, since with less formal workplaces and more "business" seeming to take place in social situations now than ever before, the lines get blurred.

Meetings

If a subject is important enough to call a meeting, be considerate of the participants time and ensure that the meeting is well prepared.

- Communicate beforehand—
  - The objective
  - The expected duration (Be sure to observe the ending time scrupulously, unless everyone agrees to continue.)
  - Items expected to be discussed (Agenda)

Often overlooked—be sure to THANK meeting members for their time and participation, and demonstrate (in the minutes or written record, at least) how their contributions helped meet the objective of the meeting. Participants are frequently left wondering if they've been heard or if their attendance and contributions were noticed. Distribute minutes or some written record (no matter how simple the meeting) to all attendees and absentees, with concise but complete descriptions of decisions made and including action items.

Never assign an action item to a person who is not present to negotiate it, unless you absolutely have to. Note in the minutes that the person hasn't been notified, and will be contacted for a final disposition of the item.

The Phone

Always return calls. Even if you don't yet have an answer to the caller's question, call and explain what you're doing to get the requested information, or direct them to the appropriate place to get it.

If you're going to be out, have someone pick up your calls or at a minimum, have your answering system tell the caller when you'll be back in the office and when they can expect a call back.

When you initiate a call and get a receptionist or secretary, identify yourself and tell them the basic nature of your call. That way, you'll be sure you're getting the right person or department and the person you're trying to reach will be able to pull up the appropriate information and help you more efficiently.

When you're on the receiving end of a phone call, identify yourself and your department. Answer the phone with some enthusiasm or at least warmth, even if you ARE being interrupted, the person on the other end doesn't know that! Besides, YOU allowed the interruption by answering the phone.

Make sure your voice mail system is working properly and doesn't tell the caller that the mailbox is full, transfer them to nowhere, or ring indefinitely. Address technical and system problems—a rude machine or system is as unacceptable as a rude person.

You don't have to reply to obvious solicitations. If someone is calling to sell you something, you can indicate that you are not interested and hang up without losing too much time on it. However, you do need to be careful. You may be receiving a call from an insurance or long distance company that wants to hire you as a consultant! Be sure you know the nature of the call before you (politely, of course) excuse yourself.

Personalize the conversation. Many people act in electronic media (including phone, phone mail, and e-mail) the way they act in their cars. They feel since they're not face-to-face with a person, it is perfectly acceptable to be abrupt, crass, or rude. We need to ensure that we make best use of the advantages of these media without falling headfirst into the disadvantages.

E-mail

Make the subject line specific. Think of the many messages you're received with the generic subject line, "Hi" or "Just for you."

Don't forward messages with three pages of mail-to information before they get to the content. In the message you forward, delete the extraneous information such as all the "Memo to," subject, addresses, and date lines.

When replying to a question, copy only the question into your e-mail, then provide your response. You needn't hit reply automatically, but don't send a bare message that only reads, "Yes." It's too blunt and confuses the reader.

Address and sign your e-mails. Although this is included in the To and From sections, remember that you're communicating with a person, not a computer.

DON'T TYPE IN ALL CAPS. IT'S THE WRITTEN EQUIVA-LENT OF SHOUTING, and you appear too lazy to type properly. This is still a written medium. Follow standard writing guidelines as a professional courtesy.

Interruptions

Avoid interruptions (of singular or group work sessions, meetings, phone calls, or even discussions) if at all possible. Most management folks feel free to interrupt informal working sessions of subordinates, but need to realize that they may be interrupting a brainstorming session that will produce the company's next big success.

Always apologize if you must interrupt a conversation, meeting, or someone's concentration on a task. Quickly state the nature of what you need, and show consideration for the fact that you are interrupting valuable work or progress.

Guests, Consultants and New Employees

If you have a new employee, guest, or consultant working at your company for a day, week, or longer, be sure that that person has the resources and information that he or she needs to do the job. This isn't just courtesy, it's good business, since time spent flailing around looking for things is embarrassing to the consultant and expensive for your company.

Give a consultant or guest the same type of workspace as an employee at your company in a similar role. A consultant who is there to do programming should have, if at all possible, the same size cube, type of computer equipment, etc. as an employee programmer would have in your company. This prevents your employees from feeling looked down-upon, and the consultant from feeling singled out or treated as second-rate.

A guest from a regulatory agency will tend to want to know what's "really" going on in the company. By treating him or her like everyone else, (instead of isolating them in a plush office in a far wing, for example) will raise less suspicion and enable them to get the information they need more efficiently.

Appoint an employee to be a 'buddy' to a guest or consultant to ensure that they are introduced around, "shown the ropes," and have someone to help resolve little logistical problems that may arise and cause non-productivity or embarrassment.

Appreciation/Credit

Always pass along credit and compliments to EVERYONE who made a contribution to the effort. Speak well of your coworkers and always point out their accomplishments to any interested party. Appearing to have taken the credit in a superiors' or customers' eyes is the surest way to sabotage a relationship with a coworker.

Dress/Appearance

It can be insulting to your coworkers or clients to show a lack of concern about your appearance.

Being wrinkled, unshaven, smelly or unkempt communicates (intentionally or not) that you don't care enough about the situation, the people or the company to present yourself respectably.

If in doubt, always err on the side of conservative. If you think jeans may be OK for a social event but aren't sure, show up in ironed khakis and a nice golf shirt. If you think a situation may call for dress slacks, wear a dress shirt and tie. If you have any inkling that a suit may be called for, dress to the nines.

Women's clothing is a bit more complicated, but again, err on the side of conservative and dressy.

Always practice impeccable grooming (even in a jeans environment!)

Social Settings

Many impressions formed during a party, dinner or golf game can make or break a key business arrangement, whether or not business is discussed directly. Always carry business cards. Arrive at a party at the stated time or up to 30 minutes later. (Not earlier than the stated time, under any circumstances.)

Introductions

Before an event, use your address book or your "people database" to refresh your memory about the people you are likely to meet.

If you forget someone's name, you can sometimes "cover" by introducing a person you do know first. "Do you know Joe Smith, one of our account reps?" which will usually get the unknown person to introduce him or herself.

If this doesn't work, an admission that you've had a mental block is preferable to obvious flailing around.

Table Manners

These apply to the Americas and most of Europe. If you're elsewhere, do some research beforehand.

The fork goes on the left. The spoon and knife go on the right. Food items go on the left, so your bread plate is on your left. Drinks, including coffee cups, should be on the right. When sitting at a banquet table, you may begin eating when two people to your left and right are served. If you haven't been served, but most of your table has, encourage others to start. Reach only for items in front of you, ask that other items be passed by a neighbor. Offer to the left; pass to the right, although once things start being passed, go with the flow.

CONCLUSION

This is a lot to consider, and there's a lot more out there. Volumes of information have been written on what is right and correct in business etiquette. It's enough to make veterans and newcomers too insecure to deal with people.

Since you're human, (we're assuming!) there will be times when you step on toes, forget an important name, pop off with a harsh comment, or (heaven forbid!) use the wrong fork. We all do. Think about the "outtakes" scenes at the end of some movies where we see how many times it took to get things perfect, even when everyone was performing to a script! This is real life, there are no scripts, and we're all making it up as we go along.

The important thing to remember is that if you strive to make the people around you feel comfortable and valued, you have succeeded whether you're perfectly in compliance with these or any rules you've read.

2. GAAP (Generally Accepted Accounting Principles)—A Primer

THE OPPORTUNITY

In the recent past, anyone with a reasonably good idea could start a business. It was easy to get a venture capitalist's interest even without knowledge of GAAP and its widespread ramifications. You could usually do pretty well in the stock market without knowing the details of a company's financial profile, or how to compare it with like corporate entities. Today, however, business can be rough on the uninformed.

Starting a business, securing capital, investing in stocks, or even evaluating a marketing plan requires more savvy than it did even six months ago. Money is harder to come by, and more stringently controlled. Whether you're a project manager, department manager, a business owner, or an investor, it is now more important than ever to know the basics of accounting, including GAAP—(Generally Accepted Accounting Principles.)

The United States and Japan use GAAP (and very soon most of Europe) for financial reporting and in some cases government reporting as well. It's becoming more widespread in other areas of the world as well.

Japan had its own GAAP, but is in the process of adopting the U.S. version, because it (the U.S. version) is more stringent and in wider international use.

THE SOLUTION

Those with a passing familiarity with accounting know that managers have choices about the way their organizations report income and financial condition. For example, LIFO and FIFO can lead to different net income. With such an array of methods and practices available, what is the meaning of "generally accepted accounting principles"?

Accounting principles are developed methods, practices and conventions used by managers and accountants to prepare financial reports. Generally accepted accounting principles evolve when these methods become widely used. However, there are many widely used accounting principles for presenting classifications of financial information. It is a challenge then to make correct conclusions and judgements based upon the diversity of "generally accepted accounting principles".

Customized GAAPs

As we know, in life there are choices because not everyone's life is the same. Companies of the same industry by choice therefore, tend to create their own GAAP. This concept allows readers of the same industry to compare financial information. This assumes that financial managers are trying to make the playing field "fair" to the uneducated reader. Therein lies the problem. You cannot take a complicated subject and explain it to an uneducated reader. So why is it expected?

GAAP Evolution

Generally Accepted Accounting Principles have varied over time. While originally these were the policies and procedures used in practice, they now refer to the larger body of guidelines for accounting that exist. This larger body refers to the variety of professional and governmental organizations and standard setting bodies that exist such as the APB, FASB, older items from the AICPA "Research Bulletins" and

APB Opinions. Add to this government standards from the GASB and FASAB.

These standards represent the large variety of financial interests that exist in the world and the variety of special representations needed to accurately and fairly represent their financial position(s).

CONCLUSION

Generally Accepted Accounting Principles (GAAP), are merely common methods of measuring and reporting financial data. More specifically, they are a methodology of observing, measuring and reporting the financial data of an entity to those that may be interested such as investors, creditors, or regulatory authorities. The principles are developed from widely used or recognized practices in reporting financial information.

3. A Case for Creativity—Or, How and When to Stick Out Like a Sore Thumb

THE OPPORTUNITY

There is much to be said for being conservative and careful. Finding and emulating role models, developing repeatable processes, and designing every success into a template for similar future successes is a great way to capitalize on efforts. It has been proven over and over again that a great idea is not enough to have a great business. You must also capitalize on that idea better, faster and cheaper than the competition can find out about it.

Initiatives like ISO 9000 have shown the value of having repeatable, documented, standardized, measurable policies and procedures.

In our zeal to replicate and recreate, however, we sometimes lose sight of the fact that everything starts with the ideas, and everything grinds to a halt without them. "Idea People" are hard to find, and sometimes hard to foster in your organization.

THE SOLUTION

Business leaders can develop his or her own creative skills, create synergy (which is group creativity) and foster creative people in their organization without sacrificing the advantages and efficiency of repeatability. On all three levels (individual, team and leadership) creativity can be fostered and encouraged if it's made a priority.

Environment

The first element of creativity on any level is to create an environment of emotional and intellectual safety. Popular wisdom says that "necessity is the mother of invention," and people who faced with impossible situations often come up with remarkable solutions to problems, the vast majority of people are their most creative when motivated but "safe." If you can build a buffer zone between yourself and the problem, it allows you the time and space to go through a creative process.

Fun, humor, trust, and warmth also foster emotional safety that encourages people to take creative risks and share ideas.

Individual

Many successful leaders build time into their schedule to think and plan. They shut their doors and forward their phones for as much as an hour a day to go through their biggest problems and brainstorm solutions. They may do this in conversation with a trusted colleague, or scribble drawings or outlines to develop later.

Although this seems a large investment that doesn't always directly address the day-to-day directing traffic and putting out fires, this practice can be extremely productive and provide a constant supply of new, creative material that is essential to any business.

Teams or Groups

The most basic handbooks on meetings and brainstorming sessions include the admonition not to critique ideas (or idea submitters) in initial brainstorming sessions. The wider and deeper the group "stretches" from conventional thinking, the better the final solution is likely to be once it has gone through the critical processes of weeding, classifying, refining and implementing.

There are other ways that teams or groups can promote creativity among their ranks.

- Respect one another's skills and contributions publicly (inside and outside the group)

- Seek feedback honestly, and don't argue when it is given. (At least not in the same sitting in which it's given. Thinking about it for a few hours allows you to get more out of it, and shows more respect for the person offering advice. Spend time together working on common tasks to build trust.

- Defend those absent (or the ideas of those absent.)

- Assume everyone has good motives unless irrefutably proven otherwise.

Leadership

- Select members of workgroups that are very diverse from one another. This will keep any one individual from being "singled out" as the different one, and will prevent groupthink and complacency.

- Keep workgroups together for at least six months. This allows them to cement relationships and develop rhythms of working together.

- Never publicly criticize an idea or a person offering one, no matter how wild it may seem. Even in private, respect the risk the person took to bring it to you.

Perception

One of the most powerful tools for promoting creative thought is to change one's perspective of the problem. It has been said that if something appears to be impossible, one of the assumptions is wrong. Change the assumptions, and you will often find a workable solution.

Change the frame of reference. Look at the problem from a wider lens of different angles.

Individual

Look at problems from several points of view or frames of reference. One excellent leader I know always encourages input from people. He asks questions and shows interest in the opinions of many people. I suspect that any decision he makes is based on information from four or more opposing sources. He assumes that everyone is telling the truth as they see it, but that truth is very relative to the situation and that person's frame of reference.

Teams or Groups

Often teams become so task—oriented that they narrow down their focus much too soon. In their rush to 'get down to business,' they drill down on the first likely solution and start planning execution before they have adequately investigated the situation and its possibilities. Keeping the inquiry open a shade longer will often reveal higher-quality, more creative solutions. One of the most valued and under-respected skills is the person on the team that asks questions that make everybody groan. Respect that person, and if it happens to be you, have the courage to avoid buckling under—ask that last question and keep them groaning. ("That which does not kill me will make me stronger"—Nietzche)

Leadership

Encourage workgroups and teams to take the time and energy up front to thoroughly research, understand, and plan. There is some risk in not demanding immediate results, but encouraging the "frontloading" process will ensure that the team is doing the right things, rather than simply doing things right. Support their inquiries, encourage questions, and remove roadblocks to obtaining information whenever possible.

Execution

This is the most difficult stage of the creative process—where ideas take tangible form and become a reality. Many people are good at implementation, fewer are good at the creative process, fewer still make the transition successfully and make a good idea a great implementation.

Individual

Once you've developed a wonderful idea or "future state," put the idea on one end of a blank timeline and the current state on the other. Then develop the steps between. What needs to be done to make this happen? Who or what could stand in its way? How could they be convinced to support it? What bureaucratic or organizational elements would have to be changed? How much will it cost? How can you prove it will be worth it? How long will it take to implement?

Use tools that are comfortable for you and for the scale of the idea—a whiteboard may work well for a simple one, more complicated ideas may need a Gantt or Pertt chart.

Teams or Groups

We've successfully done this timeline process with groups of people using sticky notes. We pass out pads of sticky notes to each member of the team, and have them each write one task, obstacle or element on each and stick them on pieces of butcher paper on the walls. These can be classified into larger items and placed in chronological order on a Gantt chart at a later time.

This works wonderfully because the tasks are separated from the person submitting them. Even new groups are less inhibited to point out obstacles and items to be addressed.

Leadership

Implementation of creative ideas is probably the largest challenge to upper level management. Most business leaders have a fiduciary responsibility to their organization to ensure ideas are sound and money is not wasted. This has to be balanced with a respect for creativity and ideas that could improve the company over what may be a very productive status quo. In *Teaching the Elephant to Dance*, author James Belasco noted that many large and successful companies find a reluctance to introduce change is their biggest stumbling block, and often their downfall in competition with smaller, nimbler competitors.

Any change is a risk. The point is to commit only to good risks, but once committed, don't look back. You have more to lose than the idea itself—you are sending a statement to anyone who may be considering forwarding a good idea.

CONCLUSION

Safety, perception and execution are the most important steps in honoring and encouraging the kind of creativity that keeps businesses alive in a changing economy. Following those steps also allows three points of balance for companies to employ standardization and efficiency to bring those ideas into reality better, cheaper and faster.

4. Finance 101—Doing Business by the Numbers

THE OPPORTUNITY

Your business is off the ground, you have money coming in, and money going out. Unfortunately, you're spending more time managing your money than managing your business. If you've ever found yourself-

- Tracking down missing receipts to resolve a discrepancy

- Finding out that a check bounced due to a mistimed deposit

- Doing some embarrassing talking and/or letter writing to repair damage that the (ahem) incident did to your reputation with a crucial supplier

- Trying to figure out whether discounts or promotions are costing more than the revenue they produce

You used to have a difficult time keeping your eyes open in finance classes in college, but now you're considering hiring a full-time accountant just so that you don't have to deal with the finances and can concentrate on what you do best—managing your business.

THE SOLUTION

Unfortunately, although you have gone into business to offer a product or service, the success of your business is, in many ways, measured by the bottom line. Even if you hired a full-time accountant, you would still need to have a basic knowledge of accounting, how it works, and how to apply its basic principles in order to run a successful business.

Implementing a sound financial system, and keeping it as simple as possible, is one of the best possible investments you can make in your business.

Automated Tools

There are a number of products on the market that will do nearly everything for you. An integrated product that connects all of the transactions you routinely do might be the best choice for the novice (or drafted) office manager or bookkeeper to keep track of everything. Make a list of the functions you need before you go shopping, read the reviews, and even "test drive" the product to see if it will actually work for you if possible. Functions that can typically be automated (with a single product or a suite of products) include:

- Estimating jobs

- Billing/Invoicing (Accounts Receivable)

- Budgeting/Forecasting

- Collections

- Making Deposits

- Paying bills/buying supplies (Accounts Payable)

- Financial Reporting

- Tax calculation

Make sure that the product you buy has a way of handling things like discounts, price fluctuations, and other things that affect your business easily.

The advantages to an automated tool include:

• Avoiding costly mistakes

• Recognizing trends and opportunities more quickly because of easy, graphical reporting

• Saving time that can be devoted to other areas of the business

• Peace of mind—the feeling that things are under control and you "know where you are."

• Simplified Filing System

Now you have an online system set up to accomplish every transaction your business does. Unfortunately, all of these digital improvements cannot make the paper behave.

You have inboxes, shoe boxes, filing crates, filing cabinets, and papers in binders with holes punched in them. You devote a lot of time to shuffling all this paper around, but still panic whenever you realize you have to locate a specific piece of paper. How can you make this easier? Disorganization leads to lost money—in the form of:

• Unopened deposits that could be in the bank earning interest

• Unopened or misplaced bills that will incur late fees

• Rebates filed too late or not filed

• Tax exemptions that could be taken that aren't documented well enough to justify

In *The Courage To Be Rich*, Suze Ormon describes the desk in the home office of a physician who is earning $100,000 per year but can't figure out why he's always stretching to make ends meet. The discoveries in that desk are very revealing.

In businesses, good organization and "housekeeping" practices are even more important. Setting up an easy, simple filing system and devoting a little time at the beginning or end of every business day clearing the in-box, filing items, modifying the system to add or consolidate folders is time well spent. The simpler the filing system is, the less expensive and frustrating it is to maintain yourself, or to get help maintaining it.

Always make sure your online system is backed up with the proper documentation, and that the paper documentation is synchronized and up-to-date online.

Knowing When to Seek Help

Lawyers and accountants are very expensive, and with good reason. They can bail you out of some tough situations. Although it isn't as well known, and does not make for dramatic courtroom drama TV, they can also (generally much less expensively) help you prevent a lot of tough situations.

When to See A Lawyer

- To review a startup business plan for potential legal troublespots (or ways to avoid them.)

- When incorporating or making a change to an incorporation

- When reorganizing

- When considering a product or service you haven't offered before and are unfamiliar with the legal ramifications

When to See An Accountant

• To review or help set up an accounting system initially

• Taxes (for anything more complicated than a sole proprietorship, a little of an accountants time might save a lot of yours!)

• Whenever you have a question or something "doesn't seem right."

It's a lot easier to "seek professional help" fix problems or bookkeeping problems when they're small, rather than to wait for confirmation that "this really is a problem."

Conclusion

Getting your financial affairs set up correctly, and keeping them up to date diligently, saves an exponential amount of time in tracking down and resolving problems after they start. Setting up an automated tool that matches well with the way you do business, and setting up your physical (paper) files to match it is not as daunting a task as it was even five years ago. Seeking help when you need to, and when problems are small, is also a good way to save money and headaches—or even avoid potential pitfalls and failures!

5. Tribal Warfare—Dealing with Cliques in the Workplace

THE OPPORTUNITY

Delivering a high-quality, unique product or service to the marketplace sometimes takes a lot of people.

Whether you work for a small company or a large one, most of us work with a lot of different kinds of people on a daily basis—co-workers, customers, suppliers, government regulators, and many others.

In almost every human situation, likes and dislikes, alliances and exclusions start manifesting themselves. You may find yourself dealing with unseen barriers between groups that are reluctant to help one another, don't share information, and sometimes even actively hinder another person or group's success.

Cliques can be based on tenure, profession, social or economic class, race or ethnicity, gender, or any other factor that differentiates people from one another. I've even seen workplaces with a cliques of smokers versus nonsmokers, cliques of coffee-drinkers versus non-coffee drinkers, and Friends watchers (a popular TV show) versus non-Friends watchers!

We all enjoy the camaraderie of people we share an interest or characteristic with, but when cliques become too exclusive, or destructive to those outside the group, the company suffers. Crucial information is mis-communicated or omitted, deadlines are missed, equipment is hoarded, and employees will sit idle rather than help someone from outside the group.

Morale suffers, and turnover increases. All of this is not just wasteful and unpleasant, it is also expensive and potentially lethal if not dealt with.

THE SOLUTION

You can reduce the harmful effects of all types of cliquishness by changing the environment. In some specific cases, it may also be necessary to analyze the nature of the exclusiveness and address them directly with the groups involved. The first step is usually to figure out the nature and extent of the problem.

Cliques in General

People tend to associate with people that have similarities is usually a positive thing. Having a company softball team, for example, is a camaraderie and shared interest that is usually positive and helpful. The people involved share a bond that makes them more comfortable at work because they know each other from another context.

Cliques can become guarded and hostile to outsiders, particularly in environments where clique members band together against what they perceive as a threat.

The popular reality-based TV show Survivor contains good examples of harmful cliques as participants form alliances and "tribes" devoted to preserving one another's interest and systematically voting non-clique members off the island. In William Golding's novel *Lord of the Flies*, a group of British schoolboys stranded on an island form alliances around two separate leaders, Ralph (who is a rules-based, logical person concerned with practical matters of survival) and Jack (who is

more interested in hunting and having fun.) As the boys align themselves with the leader that most closely represents their own leanings
and philosophies, they become more and more savage to one another,
to the extent of killing members of the other group.

Although in a business environment, the behaviors and damage are
much more subtle, the themes are similar. Cliques should become a
concern only when there are negative consequences for people outside
of the group.

Warning Signs

Signs of harmful clique behavior include:

- Critical business decisions taking place without appropriate input
(from people that are not part of the group.)

- Complaints that you can't get ahead in the company unless you're
part of the group.

- Information or equipment being shared freely among the group, but
not to "outsiders."

- Group members getting a noticeably different ratio of promotions,
incentives, bonuses, and other perks than the rest of the company.

- Group members are getting a noticeably different ratio of disciplinary actions, write-ups or complaints than the rest of the company.

Tenure Cliques

Tenure cliques are very common, especially in older companies that are
undergoing organizational change or adapting to new market forces
and technologies.

In these cases, you have a population of employees that have been
with the company for a long time, and who have been trusted with

functions or information and they perceive that that trust is being eroded or taken away by having to share it with people who are automating certain functions that used to be done by a person; or restructuring a department in a way that gives a person less control over the process or outcome than he may have had in the past. The "old timers" may band together against what they see as a threat to their value to the company. They may (subtly or blatantly) oppose new technology, new processes, and seek to undermine the efforts of anyone new to the company or suggesting new methods or ideas.

Professional Cliques

Professional cliques are also very common—in health care, you have the physicians versus the nursing staff; in law enforcement you have street cops versus investigators, in academia you have tenured vs non-tenured staff. In manufacturing you have management versus labor.

This results from people with different knowledge and skill sets, and people who perceive themselves as having invested more in their careers than others.

More skilled or more educated people feel like they have "paid their dues" and should have more influence in decisions than people who are less specialized or who have invested less in the profession.

Economic/Social Cliques

"Classism" exists in almost every society—there is the upper class versus those who are middle or lower class. People go to great extremes to be included in the upper class—they subtly (or not so subtly) display cars, houses, and clothes to prove membership in the elite upper class.

Time Magazine recently ran an article indicating that the most fashionable status symbol among the new rich (most notably, Microsoft "retirees") is to have a charitable foundation named after them.

Business has a long, rich tradition of being the domain of the upper class. Business meetings are held aboard yachts over champagne and caviar, important decisions are made at expensive resorts over a round of golf or skiing. Having money is often seen as a self-evident credential of being a good businessperson or decision maker.

Addressing Problem Cliquishness

Now that you've determined that a clique problem exists, and now that you know something about the nature and extent of the problem, what can you do to contain the problem and prevent negative consequences?

Find causes of anxiety and address them

People act defensively (and form defensive alliances) when they feel threatened. Groups that are facing uncertainty are especially prone to negative clique behavior. In the case of tenure-based cliques, for example, you may want to make it a point to emphasize the importance of the older employees, seek out their opinions, and ensure they feel included in new and ongoing events.

Recognize the need for a variety of people and skills as vital to everyone's success.

When you have a specific problem to solve, appoint a task force of people from inside and outside the clique. For example, to define requirements for remodeling part of a call center, include management and customer service reps on the task force. The reps will have suggestions for the productivity and enjoyment of the largest part of your population, the management folks will have the information on business objectives and cost. By collaborating, they will come up with a better design than management could working in a vacuum. Be aware that this will take longer than the management team would take alone, but the result will be worth it in the quality of the design and benefits to morale.

Publicly (and specifically) recognize the value of all employees.

Use existing institutions, like an Employee of the Month program, or nominations for bonuses, to recognize people who may be outside the group, and use specific examples of how their actions have helped add to the bottom line. For example, nominating a member of the clerical staff and emphasizing how that person's efficiency and cooperation ensure that physicians have accurate and complete information will show how that person is of value to people in the "clique." This draws the attention of the physicians to how much influence a person outside their group can have on their success if everyone works together.

Clarify roles in ways that emphasize synergy and cooperation.

Having groups participate in drafting Service Level Agreements and other items will open a discussion of what people need from one another, and will generally bring a better understanding of one another's roles to the group. People in clerical jobs often complain that management doesn't have any idea how complicated and difficult it is to produce certain reports. By discussing this in terms of a Service Level Agreement, this gives the clerical staff an opening to define what THEY need in order to do the job properly and on time. They may need information sooner from the sources they collect it from, or may need some training on the software they use.

Consider the performance review process.

Are people's performance reviews based solely on the opinions of people within their own group? Does their performance affect other groups? Some companies have what they call 360-degree reviews, meaning that an employee is evaluated from all the way around his "sphere of influence." Ratings are collected from their team members, business partners, and sometimes even customers. By expanding the view of an employee's performance, they realize that they have more than just one group of people to please in order to be considered successful.

Ensure disciplinary actions are equitable.

Discriminating in the way that rules and policies are enforced often leads to ill-will between groups. If you allow the computer programmers to get away with violating the company dress code but crack down on the mailroom staff, there will probably be grumbling in the least—and it wouldn't be a surprise if the programmers are finding their mail misrouted. If there are reasons for the differences—for example, if groups that have more customer contact have a different dress code than back-room personnel, be sure to explain the reasons clearly. Better yet, involve the employees in defining the dress code, making sure that they understand the business objectives.

CONCLUSION

Depending on how entrenched the "clique culture" is, and how much influence you have on the environment and individuals involved, you may have a long, protracted battle on your hands to make your workplace as open, productive and objective as you'd like. It's been our experience, though, that anyone in the company who uses any one of these suggestions will improve the situation at least a little bit, and at least temporarily. Changing the situation permanently will take persistence and a more concerted effort.

6. Making Good Kills—Stopping Projects, Quitting Jobs, Firing People and Other Necessary Endings

THE OPPORTUNITY

If every project and every product your company turns out is a raging success; every person you hire is perfectly suited, and if your every career move turns out to be golden, you don't need to read this article.

For the rest of us, there is the occasional "kill" that has to be made—ending a project, quitting a job, terminating an employee, dissolving a department or a company, or discontinuing a product or service.

Taking risks is at least a passing nod to the possibility that something may go wrong. Although most of us were raised with a "never give up" attitude and feel it's a failure of sorts to admit a mistake or the need for a change, sometimes knowing when to quit (and redirect your energies to other things) is the key to future successes.

When learning a martial art, (or many other risky sports) a good coach will first teach a student "how to fall." Being able to fall gracefully without hurting yourself is the best foundation on which to begin to take risks. The greatest martial artists performances often involve several falls before an eventual spectacular victory.

The CPA Journal Online indicates that more than 300 U.S. firms go out of business every week. It would be naïve for you to think that you (or your company) are immune to failure. It doesn't have to be a poor decision or mistake on your part—a change in market conditions, the actions of a competitor or inactions of a supplier, the behavior (or lack thereof) by an employee, or any number of factors can create a failure situation.

Businesses, or business people, who can "fall gracefully" learn and adapt quickly, and redeploy their resources in endeavors that have greater chances of success.

THE SOLUTION

Go Into Risky Situations with a "Prenuptial Agreement"

Whenever possible, make specific arrangements (as specific as possible given current information) about what will happen if things don't work out.

It's good to go into a new venture with an idea of some possible decision points or "failure points" at which you determine you will not continue; and determine how to go about killing the venture as painlessly as possible.

In formal business plans, informal agreements and collaborations with suppliers and customers, etc., you can usually frame these in a way that retains confidence that things will work out they way you've planned, but outlines a few of the possible situations that might change things for one or more of the parties involved.

Most employee agreements have "separation clauses" or conditions and processes to be followed to make a termination (initiated by the employee or the company) as fair and problem-free as possible.

Having a way to back out of projects, ventures or positions gracefully will preserve options for possible future relationships, or at least prevent some of the worst possible outcomes.

You may want to create a formal document and run it by your lawyer (or legal advisor) depending on the amount of risk you're taking. In many cases, if you're taking out a loan or forming a legal entity, you're required to seek professional help. In smaller, less formal arrangements, a single collaborated document with signatures of both parties might suffice. If in doubt, ask your lawyer.

Don't Let Bad Situations Linger

Most of us were raised with a "never give up" attitude that makes it difficult to kill a project, fire an employee, or walk away from a situation without feeling pangs of guilt.

Some things are worth heroic efforts to keep things going, or, in the best scenario, to turn them around. But unless the potential rewards are great, or there is a matter of principle involved that would shake your core values to abandon; there comes a time when a business situation's drain on your time and energy (and the morale of the people involved!) may be more than it's worth.

If that's the case, it's kinder to resolve it quickly and definitively than to let it slowly succumb to its own inertia.

"I wish they'd just laid me off," said Alan, a dot-com employee that stuck around to "turn off the lights" at a failing company. "At least then I would have had to make an adjustment, get some training, and get my résumé out there. As it is, if I stick around forever, the best jobs in the area will be taken by the other folks in the company who saw this coming."

Admit Defeat

The news media's coverage of recent events should be enough incentive to make it clear that trying to hide a "kill" is a very bad idea.

Make sure everyone who should be informed about the decision is given all of the information they need. There's no reason to shout it from the rooftops, but be sure that you're up to your usual (hopefully excellent) standard of communication and availability for questions from the involved parties. A well-written e-mail or memo; a "town hall" style meeting with the employees involved; or a face-to-face discussion with key people involved is usually called for.

Cut Your Losses

Do some homework on who the "kill" will affect, and how to make the change as easy as possible on them.

If the "kill" involves displacement of people, do your best to ensure that they are given as many alternatives as possible.

Wells Fargo has a "retain" program that provides resources and ensures that employees being displaced from one of its departments has a good shot at finding employment somewhere else in the company. The HR department works with the person to arrange for training, relocation, and other details.

USAA, likewise, has a pool of employees whose jobs have "gone away" for whatever reason. They have one year to find another job within the company without losing their salary or benefits.

The implication is that it's a small world, and the people you're laying off today might be people you will be working with in some capacity in the future. The concept of "good karma" also makes for good business.

If the "kill" involves financial loss, consult a financial professional about the possibilities of writing off the loss on taxes. Investigate the options available to you to finance the loss while putting as little stress as possible on the rest of the organization (or on you personally, if it was your company.

Although many people tend to want to walk away from a loss as quickly as possible to "get on with other things," it pays to do the homework required to tie up loose ends and gracefully resolve as many issues as possible so they won't haunt you later or cost more than you expected.

Don't Rub Salt Into Wounds

Don't dwell on the negative. If someone asks about the failed project, terminated employee, job you quit, or company you dissolved, talk about the positive aspects of it, and keep the negative as simple as possible. "It was a great idea, but the logistics just didn't work out."

If asked for references about an employee you fired, check with the legal requirements in your area. It's usually best to give a minimum amount of information. Most localities require only that you give the dates that the person worked, the job title he held, and whether the separation was voluntary or involuntary.

Volunteering more negative information than necessary is tasteless at best, and may subject you to legal implications at worst.

Move On

There's an old saying that if you fall off a horse, you should get back on it as quickly as possible so that the horse (and more importantly, you) don't become so affected by a negative experience that you're afraid of further risk.

Immersing yourself, your department or your company in a fresh direction or a new project as quickly as feasible. Don't rush headlong into the first plausible idea—remember to intelligently mitigate risk as much as possible at the outset (re-read the section on Prenuptial Agreements if necessary) but recognize that avoiding risk altogether is not only not possible, it's also not a good idea. Great rewards come with great risks.

Intelligently managed, of course.

CONCLUSION

The business world changes rapidly. People and companies should be agile and able to determine appropriate failure points, make "good kills," and quickly recover when conditions make failure inevitable. Refuse to pour time and energy into anything that you're not firmly convinced will work. If something is past that point, assess your options carefully, end the situation gracefully and move on quickly to something you can be passionate and positive about.

7. Core Competencies—Working Smarter, Not Harder

THE OPPORTUNITY

You have a good product, a good market share, good distribution. How do you "raise the bar" and become truly great?

THE SOLUTION

In most cases, greatness doesn't come from doing the same things but trying harder. When you do that, even the combined efforts of all of your people are too diffuse to make much of a difference. Like having hundreds of people pushing with their hands on a brick wall, you spend a lot of energy getting nowhere.

Greatness comes from focus. Having the effort of those hundreds of people translate into a single point of impact, like a single sledgehammer, will definitely have more impact.

Core competencies are "focus points" that funnel peoples' skills and efforts to make a greater effect.

Successful companies often have one main core competency, or a closely related cluster of core competencies that support each other.

What Are Core Competencies?

Core competencies are the key skills, characteristics and assets that your company brings to the marketplace. These competencies, on an organizational level, are a synergistic blending of the core competencies that your people individually bring to work every day.

What does your company do? If you have to think about that more than a second or two, it may be too complicated.

Example company core competencies:

- Excellent Customer Service

- (State, Nation, Worldwide) Information Networking

- New Product Research and Development

- Market Research

- Relationship Development/Outreach

These are obviously very broad competencies that would work for nearly any company. Yours are probably much more specific.

Defining What You Need

After you've determined your unique market niche and the core competencies your company brings to the marketplace, analyze the skills that you need your workforce to bring to the table. It's important that you do this objectively, so try not to think about what you have, but instead about what you need if you had the ideal workforce and time and money were no object. (There will be time enough for reality later!)

Examples of "people" competencies include:

- Customer Service

- Information Technology/Knowledge Management

- Scientific/Creative skills

- Marketing Skills

- Sales Skills

Once you've finished your "wish list," you'll need to compare it to reality.

Measuring What You Have

We can't emphasize enough that evaluating employees must be done in a way that is objective and respectful to your employees. Solicit their help, if you can, in determining the best way to evaluate their skill levels on the core competencies you've identified. Make sure you make this a positive experience. Let them see what they have to gain by making unknown skills known, obtaining certifications or taking industry-standard tests that will make THEM more valuable to the marketplace (yes, you're gambling here that they might take these skills elsewhere, but any time you employ people you should hope they're working for you because they want to, not because of lack of other opportunities.)

Ways of measuring key items include:

- Skills Surveys/Skills Databases

- Performance evaluations

- Certifications

- Tests

- Assessments

Use certifications, tests, and assessments that are standard to your industry wherever possible. That way, you're leveraging someone else's research (rather than devoting time to building your own programs) and you ensure that your employees have an incentive to participate because it gives them something of value.

Filling Gaps

Once you've assessed the competencies of your current staff and compared them to the "wish list" you made in the previous section, you are likely to have some gaps and overlaps. The overlaps may present some opportunities that you haven't thought of before. Using some creativity, you may find ways of enhancing your product, service, or processes to leverage these windfalls.

Filling the gaps you've identified also needs to be done with great tact and respect for your people. Investing in something that helps them contribute more to the company has an inherent value. You will also want to focus on the positive aspects of greater opportunity as the company expands, enhancing their chances for raises, promotions, and bonuses as they help the company succeed.

Opportunities for Developing Current People

- Off-Site Programs

- On-Site Consultants/Workshops

- On-line or CBT training

- Internal Training/Information Sharing

You may find gaps that no one on your current staff has the time or interest to develop.

Recruiting New People

Advertise for specific skills. Rather than advertising for a role ("project manager" or "accounting specialist", for example,) make sure that all of your advertisements also include expectations of core competencies you require in your organization. Even an accountant or programmer must have excellent communication skills if that is what your company values.

Recruit from learning institutions that teach what you need. Their placement centers are always happy to talk to people who value skills that the institution is known for, and are happy to help place their graduates in an environment where those skills will be utilized and appreciated.

Engaging the Focus

Having people with these skills does absolutely no good unless those skills are engaged for the benefit of the company. It's a traditional complaint that companies bring in outside consultants to do a lot of things that their own people could have told them much less expensively.

Andrew Carnegie commented that most of us take the public school and library system for granted, simply because they are free. We tend to value most, the things that we have struggled to acquire and pay for. But some of the best ideas come free. Don't ignore this windfall!

Communicate regularly with your employees, and emphasize the point that you are open to ideas and recommendations. Make sure you give credit where credit is due. You might ask people directly if they've had opportunities to use all of their skills.

Conclusion

Staying ahead of the changing economy is getting more and more diffi-cult to do by working harder. Adapting to changes and working smarter requires specific focus. Focusing on the core competencies of your company is the means to develop that focus. More specifically, you need to determine what core competencies are needed to meet your companies specific goals and objectives. Once this "wish list" of core competencies is developed, you need to identify gaps and overlaps, and resolve the gaps by developing or augmenting your current staff. Continued effort is needed to make sure those competencies and skills are being leveraged by everyone in your company.

8. Good Writing—Old Art Form or New Advantage

THE OPPORTUNITY

Good writing is seen as an art of the past. My (then) nine-year-old son argues that he should not have to learn spelling when there are spell-checkers, and he should not have to learn handwriting when most tasks are done on a keyboard nowadays.

With all of the changes in business in the last five years, people worry about what to skills to spend time and money developing to best position themselves to take advantage of new and emerging opportunities. Corporations are spending extraordinary amounts of time and money on training to learn software applications that will be obsolete in six months.

Very little time and attention is devoted to good writing. It shows. Poorly targeted, gadget-filled website "storefronts" eat up the budgets of small companies and sell nothing. Mass advertisements are dropped in the garbage unopened. E-mailboxes are clogged with worthless, out-dated or unclear information that takes forever to download, and makes it more difficult to find information you need.

THE SOLUTION

Learn to express yourself well in writing.

Although the Web and related technologies offer lots of opportunities to express rich graphic content, graphics are still slower and more expensive to produce, transport and receive than text. Good writing is more important than ever. People expect more information in less time. They expect it to be accurate, professional and easily understandable.

Documents have always served as a way to "freeze" thought for your own use, or to share a thought with others so that they can comment, add to, criticize, or collaborate.

You may need to brush up on the mechanics of spelling, grammar and composition, but in many cases your writing skill can be vastly improved by simple awareness of document basics, and by the appropriate use of different document types. Other than the mechanics of language, writing well is simply a matter of thinking clearly on paper (or in electrons!)

Document Basics

The most common failure point for a document is the author's failure to define one or both of the two key elements—audience and a purpose. Who are you writing to? What do you want this person to do, know and feel as a result of your document?

Everything you write should be focused around the audience and purpose. The form it takes, the way it's conveyed, and the content it carries should be solely determined by the audience and purpose. Many people inappropriately judge business documents by any number of flawed criteria. Never judge the effectiveness of a business communication based on:

• How long it is

• How flowery the language is

- How elegant the stationery

- How many technical gadgets it employs

- Or how well it meets any particular set of guidelines. (Strunck & White, Chicago Manual of Style, MLA Standards, etc.)

The sole measure of any document's success is how well it reaches its audience and how well the audience does, knows or feels what the document intended.

Writing for Yourself

- Journals

- Notes

- Scattergrams

Benjamin Franklin is probably the most famous example of a person who wrote for himself. He carried around a small book, in which he kept his schedule and journal and scribbled musings. This can be as informal as you like—from exploring an idea by drawing a "scattergram" on the back of an envelope on a long plane flight, to keeping a formal journal or planner.

Journals

I find that keeping a journal helps me recognize patterns of thought or behavior in myself and my relationships. Being aware of these patterns helps me make decisions better. If I know that I get restless and flighty every year around June, I might plan a vacation or new challenge for myself around then to keep myself interested. If I know that my son gets stomachaches that coincide with spelling tests, I can help him spread out his study habits so that he's not cramming and building anxiety levels on those days.

Notes

I always take my own notes in meetings, because I generally have a different perspective (and am interested in different information) than the formal minute-taker. I also take notes in classes. Even if I never refer to them again, taking notes or drawing diagrams helps focus my attention on the subject matter and I retain information better.

Scattergrams

I first learned this technique in elementary school, and have seen them described in several books on writing and creativity—I've no idea who first coined the term or started the use of these. Scattergrams are a wonderful way of developing an idea. Brainstorm all over a piece of paper. Write down every thought that comes to your mind on a particular topic, in no particular order. Then, once you have exhausted the topic, switch from a creative to a critical mode of thinking and organize the thoughts into categories. I do this by circling related items with a particular color. Then group and order the categories. You now have a rich outline, rather than a vague concept. This is a great way to develop an idea into a letter, presentation or plan

Writing for Others

- Expectations, missions, goals and objectives

- Agreements

- Status Reports

- Plans and Strategies

- Letters and notes

- Web Sites

- Discussion Groups

- E-mails

Writing for others is often the best, and sometimes the only, way to share ideas effectively, capture added value from people of different skill sets and experiences, and get agreement on terms. These are powerful tools for when you need more than one brain to accomplish a project.

Expectations, Missions, Goals and Objectives

Writing your expectations of a person or situation is an excellent way to explore common objectives and prevent conflicts. When you enter into a business relationship with another person, writing the expectations of that relationship down in a job description, bill of sale, or contract is often done in a very cursory, legalistic way. Making that process more participatory and informal adds a lot of value. Forming a team to meet an objective is a good example of a time when the process of creating a document is almost more valuable than the document itself. We collaborate on mission, goals and objectives so that each person is involved and understands them. Then roles and responsibilities are defined to support the goals and objectives, so that each person understands how what they are doing contributes to the whole. Although this is typically done (and extremely effective) in a business setting, Steven Covey suggests doing this as a family, creating a "family mission statement."

Agreements

Written agreements are very similar in that they can be improved by discussion and collaboration. However, they have a lot value by their very existence. In case of dispute, you can refer to the agreement later and remind both parties of their obligations.

Status Reports

As much as most people hate writing status reports, they are a good opportunity to let people know what you're doing, to ask for help if you need it, and to create a permanent record of your progress that you can refer to later. Never discount the importance of writing them, or of reading them. This is also an excellent opportunity to report measures—how do you stack up, in black and white, to what was expected?

Plans and Strategies

Plans and strategies come one step closer to reality when they're written. A written plan is something you can hand to someone when you need them to participate in, by providing resources, work, or even just ideas. They tend to improve the more they are read, discussed, referred to, and passed around.

Letters and Notes

Never miss an opportunity to write a letter or note to someone. As electronic forms of media become more prevalent, it becomes even more powerful to receive a handwritten letter or notecard from someone with that says "thank you" or "congratulations" or "I was just thinking of you." This is equally effective with everyone you come into contact with—clients, co-workers, employees, customers, friends, and family

Web Sites

A web site is essentially just a document that is delivered by electronic means. It should follow the document basics of audience and purpose. Web sites have the potential to use pictures, color, movement, music, and many other elements. Every element or gadget is a liability, rather than an asset, unless it specifically and materially CONTRIBUTES to the audience and purpose. Unless it contributes, it detracts by adding to loading time and/or distracting the viewer's attention from what you want them to do, know and feel.

Virtual Vinyards, a very successful Internet-based wine and spirits business in the 1990s, attributed the company's success to the warm, clear writing style of Peter Granoff, the sommelier who writes the content for their web-pages and e-mailed newsletters. Graphics may be fun and interesting, but content conveys information, forms relationships, and gives the customer value that keeps him coming back. Granoff indicates that a disadvantage to the Web is the lack of face-to-face contact with the customer, but the an advantage is that "The site allows us to present the full story, in perfect language, about every product we have. The customer can read the history of a particular winemaker or vineyard, learn about the specific taste, and receive a complete description of the taste. It's as if I could sit down at every table and spend as much time as our guests would like."

Discussion Groups

Discussion groups are "collective documents." The audience and author become one in the same, and the purpose becomes a collective one. Participants add their input on a topic, voice their opinions, forward their own agendas, and sometimes change the subject altogether. The most successful discussion groups are those that are focused on a topic that is specific enough to attract a particular audience, and broad enough to support a variety of opinions and inputs.

E-mail

Edward Esber, CEO, Ashton-Tate has said "A computer will not make a good manager out of a bad manager. It makes a good manager better faster and a bad manager worse faster." I would add that a e-mail makes a good communicator better faster and bad communicator worse much more efficiently. It is now possible to very efficiently deliver thousands of copies of appropriate gems of wisdom and vital information, or to deliver thousands of copies of irrelevant, vague meanderings just as efficiently. In his book *Business @ The Speed of*

Change, Bill Gates recommends that all businesses migrate as much discussion, decision, and business in general as possible to e-mail. This does a number of things—it makes it possible to trace the evolution and threads of discussion, it broadens the conversation to more participants than is practically feasible on paper or in person, and documents why certain decisions and actions took place at certain times.

Document Storage

This leads to another topic that is beyond the scope of this article, but worth a mention. Keeping documents in electronic format adds storage and retrieval options never before possible on a large, practical, "business" scale. It was impossible five years ago to locate the notes from a conversation or the details of a transaction that was somewhere in a stack of magnetic tape or in an archive box in a storage unit somewhere. Now, it is possible to locate a detail in seconds.

This new art and science is called "data mining" or "knowledge management" or any of a dozen other names. The point is that any document you write today, is very likely to become that much more valuable because it becomes that much more accessible and reusable.

CONCLUSION

In *How to Become CEO,* Jeffrey J. Fox includes a chapter on the importance of "speaking and writing in plain English."

Billions of dollars in advertising is wasted annually. Billions of human hours are spent doing wrong or unnecessary tasks. Billions of pages of reading matter are never read. Business communications must be precise, complete, and totally comprehensible.

Although people tend to associate good writing more with the Shakespearean Age than the Electronic Age, good writing that targets the audience and accomplishes its purpose is more important than ever.

9. Reinventing the Call Center—Customer Service for the Digital Age

THE OPPORTUNITY

Call Centers have been the human interface point for years in areas like catalog sales and order-taking, telephone solicitation, and post-sale service (complaints and returns.) With the e-commerce boom, call centers have become even more important since they play these roles in organizations that may have no other physical presence or means for human contact.

These days, customer service takes many forms. Customers expect to be able to get the same answers by whatever channel is convenient for them—sending an e-mail, filling out a form on a web-site, calling on the phone, or using an online service.

THE SOLUTION

Focus on the mission—providing real, human, customer service.

The Cadillac company provides a pretty good illustration of how technology and human service are inseparable in the advertisements for the OnStar system on the Cadillac Catera, when they tell their customers—automatic tellers can only count in tens and twenties. Automatic phone systems can only interpret numbers from a keypad. Sometimes you need to talk to a "real person."

This article discusses the basic elements of Customer Service, and then a few of the options available for achieving the level of customer service your business needs and can afford.

The Elements

The elements of good customer service are not hard to determine. Just think about the last time you had a question or problem. What were you hoping for?

The customer wants to get connected with a human being quickly, and this human being would be:

- Someone with good communication skills.

- Someone with a complete understanding of the product or service.

- Someone who listens to your situation and needs.

- Someone intelligent and empowered enough to resolve the situation effectively.

- Someone who treats you with respect.

Quick Connections

This is largely a function of your staffing levels and technology. Besides the sheer volume of calls or information requests you are getting (or expect to get,) you also need to take some other issues into account:

- Are your customers in different time zones?

- Are they consumers that are using your product or service at some time other than business hours?

- Does the volume of calls vary seasonally, or increase at other times (quarter-end, month-end, particular weekday, or particular time of day?)

- Do you have projections about how a particular event or promotion may affect request volumes?

- Do you offer different channels for customers to contact your customer service department?

Customers these days may expect you to be available in a number of ways:

- In person (in a brick-and-mortar location)

- On the phone

- By fax

- By e-mail

- By Voice Response Unit (VRU)

- By interactive form on the Internet.

Take these factors into account when determining your staffing levels and the technology that supports customer communications.

Communication Skills

Your customer service agents may need skills that they haven't needed in the past. Some items to consider:

- Call center agents have not typically been screened for writing ability, but customer service may now require responses by e-mail. Is your staff equipped to respond professionally in writing?

- Are your reps proficient with the equipment they're using? This should go without saying, but bungling transfers, firing off e-mails to the wrong address, and other fumbles can impair your credibility.

- Are you expanding into different geographical/cultural markets that might require different language skills?

Knowledge of Products and Services

- Do your agents have sufficient reference material available to them to answer 90% of the questions they're being asked? (Granted, there will always be some surprises, but you should have the basics down.)

- Is that reference material arranged in a way that they can access it quickly? (Electronically, or at the very least very clear, concise, and well-tagged printed material?)

- Do you have an orientation program that sufficiently prepares agents to respond adequately?

- Do you have ongoing training efforts to ensure agents are current on new material and fresh on old material?

- Do you have some basic proficiency required of agents before they start taking calls?

Listening Skills

- Are agents incentives based on customer satisfaction, rather than sheer volume of responses?

- Are agents actually listening to customers (or actually reading their e-mails,) rather than watching TV, listening to the radio, checking their stocks on the Internet or playing computer games?

Judgment

- Are agents able to solve most customer problems without another hand-off to a manager?

- Are they empowered to make basic decisions, such as customer refunds, returns, replacements or enhancements?

- Do they cross-sell when appropriate?

- Are they incented to match the customer up with the correct product or service for the customer's needs, rather than meeting quotas on a particular item the company is promoting?

Treating Customers with Respect

- Do you monitor calls?

- Are agents trained to deal with various types of challenges, such as angry customers, customers with less than excellent communication skills, etc. in a professional way?

- Is the importance of the customer emphasized in all materials and training programs?

Anticipating Customers' Needs

Your technology, reference materials, and skills required of agents, should constantly be evaluated and modified based on new information. Stay current and be open to react quickly based on:

- What your customers like or dislike about their customer service experiences

- Statistical trends in numbers and types of calls

- What your competitors are doing

- What other customer service departments (outside of your industry) are doing

- What new technology becomes available

You will probably want reports on statistics on the numbers and types of consumer interactions, but you can't burden your customer service agents with also being the census bureau. Use technology to make this as unobtrusive as possible to the agents and to the customer. Never take the same information more than once.

Determine Your Approach—Do It Yourself or Outsource

After reading the preceding material, you may decide that there is so much involved with customer service that you'd rather not handle it yourself. You can devote your time, people, and facilities much more effectively to your actual product or service, and outsource this function.

Even so, the information here is important to be aware of in selecting a firm that will represent your company effectively and be worth what you pay them.

The Options

Years ago, the only way to supply reliable customer service was to have a customer service department, or to have much of your employees' time devoted to customer service, putting product and service design and production tasks second.

I remember working in a florist shop when I was in college. A poster on the wall in the back room listed the priorities:

- Serve Customers

- Serve Customers

- Serve Customers

- Make arrangements to fill existing orders

- Make arrangements to fill display case

- Water plants and clean showroom

There were times (Especially around Mother's Day and Valentines Day) when we had to scramble and bring in extra people to fill existing orders, the display case got pretty bare, and the showroom was an absolute wreck; but my manager had the priorities straight and the shop was the most successful in the city.

Fortunately, there are alternatives these days so that the rest of your business doesn't have to suffer to meet customer service needs.

Virtual Assistants

Virtual Assistants, or VAs, are an ideal solution for microbusinesses. VAs are generally freelance administrative assistants who work out of their homes, generally for a number of businesses. VAs can take customer calls, answer e-mails, check on your web site, and even perform some sales duties.

They all have their own specialties.

Two cautions—

The first involves tax and labor regulations. Ensure that the tax situation is covered for your area. In some cases, a VA may be hired as an "independent contractor" rather than being put on payroll, which saves a great deal of paperwork; but there may be specifics such as where the person works and whether they work exclusively for you or have other clients. Consult your tax advisor.

The second caution is that since this is a part-time arrangement, people tend to be a bit casual about the paperwork, specifications and requirements. Since you may become quite dependent on your VA very quickly, and they may be your single point of customer service, documentation may be even MORE important than when contracting with a firm. Be sure the expectations of this person are well-documented, understood and agreed to by both parties, and have a back-up plan in case your VA lands a more lucrative client or goes on vacation.

Outsourcing

This is often a very cost-effective, and efficient alternative to having your own customer service department. Customer Service firms specialize in their hiring and training processes, and can afford expensive communications equipment.

Internal Customer Service Department

When you must have control over the customer service process, be able to react quickly to changes, and collect information from customers immediately, this is your most direct option.

- You will need to invest in equipment appropriate to support the communication channels you use (telephone routing systems, e-mail, Internet, etc.)

- You will have to devote the time to recruiting and hiring for a traditionally high-turnover market.

- You will need to develop training and reference materials.

- You will have to provide appropriate motivation and incentives.

- You will have to provide physical facilities that inspire a good attitude (when the call center is in a dark warehouse, callers can usually tell the difference!)

Accommodate the demographic groups that are typically available for customer service work, such as students and senior citizens. See Chapter 24 for some useful suggestions for recruiting and motivating young people

CONCLUSION

Happy, loyal customers are your best salespeople, and repeat buyers are much less expensive to find and sell than new prospects. Customer service is probably the most challenging aspect of doing business in the present market. Fortunately, if you develop a good system for this, it is also the most difficult for your competitors to steal or copy.

10. Succession Planning—How (and Why!) To Make Yourself Obsolete

THE OPPORTUNITY

An executive committee sits around a boardroom table, reviewing the last agenda item—replacing a member of the committee that is retiring.

"Sharon is the obvious internal choice." One member indicates a mid-level manager. "She has quite a bit of experience with the company, she has the requisite education, and a very respectable record of success with her department."

"Yes, but if we promote Sharon, there is no one to take her place. Nobody knows her department as well as she does, and the performance of that department is especially critical." Another member says.

"I'm afraid we can't afford to free her up from her present duties. There is too great a risk if that department slips. Our systems are just too specific to train from ground up. It's easier to recruit externally for the higher-level position than it would be to back-fill Sharon's job." The CEO voices, regretfully. "We might as well get started. Let's inform HR and get the process moving."

Sharon may never know about the conversation in the board room, but she'll undoubtedly be puzzled and frustrated at the outcome. Many people never grasp the fact that it's not just their own performance in their job that counts, it's also their promotability—which includes having a way to ensure that their job will get done if they're promoted.

THE SOLUTION

Grooming a replacement runs counter to common sense for some people, but it may turn out to be your best strategy for getting to the next rung on the ladder.

This article assumes that you want to move up within the company that you're currently with. It also assumes that you're ambitious and motivated, but these tactics work for anyone whether they're starting at the mailroom or whether their next jump is to CEO.

The Trap of Exclusive Knowledge

I've heard a woman brag about how valuable she is to the company because "I'm the only one who really knows the payroll system inside and out." The possible outcomes to that type of exclusivity are:

She'll be stuck running the payroll system the rest of her life and be passed over for opportunities for promotion, like Sharon in our example above, or

Her manager will get nervous about the apparent bottleneck of information, and either prescribe cross-training (forcing our payroll specialist out of her exclusive position) or else replace the payroll system with something more generic, where the skill set to run it is not so rare.

The Wisdom of Replacing Oneself

"I've made myself obsolete four times since I've been with this company." Greg, a call center project manager told me. "I started out answering phones. I learned everything I could, as quickly as I could, and was always willing to teach new people. They always had new people sit near me so I could help them." he said. "At the time, it was just a way to make my job more interesting."

He was naturally promoted to the Training department the first time an opportunity was available. He found he had extra time between classes, so he started learning HTML. With some help from the IS department he developed a reusable curriculum he could deploy on the company Intranet that other trainers could use. He adapted it based on their suggestions. The web-based curriculum was much more efficient than the old curriculum, and fewer trainers were needed to teach it.

Greg was promoted to "specialist." Part of his duties included handling calls that were outside certain call center staff's ability to handle. He did some research and found a company that handled complex call tracking. He put a proposal together to buy and implement the software.

When the proposal was accepted, Greg was promoted to Project Manager to oversee the contractors' work on the implementation.

Of course, some education has been required in the process, but his company has happily sent him to classes and workshops. "My boss would rather train me. She knows I'll get the job done. She could hire somebody who already knows the skills but they don't know the company, and may not have the track record I've got."

How To Make It Work for You

Start with your written job description, if you have one. These are almost never the "whole story" of what you do, especially if you've been in your job for any length of time. Modify and add to it to include everything you do. Automate, or at least document, everything you do on a regular basis to make it easier for someone else to follow.

Look around your department for people who are interested in what you do, or interested in moving up. Suggest "walking them through" some of the things you do. Ask them to cover for you when you're on vacation, or if you're busy with other responsibilities.

Don't get too hung up on finding a specific "protégé'," you will help the company, and yourself, more by raising the level of knowledge and proficiency in your department than by finding a specific person to replace you. This way, if that person's plans change (or the company changes them for him or her) you're still covered.

Let your higher-ups know of the arrangement. Let them know of your "protégé's" interests and aptitudes. Suggest some training for them if appropriate. Help them any way you can.

Now that you have some free time (from automating your tasks, and from having some help) focus your time on your next target—look for other ways to use your skills to help the company. This takes some insight, creativity, and some knowledge of your company and your industry.

Talk to your co-workers (and your superiors) and find out what their particular operational headaches are. See if you can find a way to automate the tedious ones or simplify the complicated ones.

Do some research on what your competitors are doing, and devote some creative energy into developing a proposal for a response or counter.

Spend some time communicating with customers—find out what they want and develop a proposal to improve a product or service to better meet the "real" customer needs. (Sometimes things are missed in the market analysis, or the consumer group ends up being different than what you thought it would be.)

CONCLUSION

It takes some courage to walk into your boss' office and say "You don't need me to do what I've been doing anymore." But we've found if you do just that, prefacing a proposal of what you intend to do next, you're likely to get what you ask for. Even if you don't get promoted right away, at least you'll draw attention to your interest, ambition and insight. You'll get a chance to prove yourself on some new responsibilities. Helping people and taking chances are two sure ways to make your work life much more rewarding, and much more successful.

11. Meetings are Boring and Other Myths

THE OPPORTUNITY

You are an unusual person if you have not spent time this week in a meeting and wondered why you were there, or wished you were somewhere else, actually getting something done.

Millions of dollars are wasted by businesses by holding unnecessary meetings, having unclear objectives for meetings, and including people that don't need to be there.

It seems the higher up the "corporate ladder" we go, these time-wasting, frustrating, contentious, non-productive assemblies gobble up more of our time.

THE SOLUTION

There is no excuse for holding (or attending) expensive, pointless, frustrating meetings. Either the meeting itself can be avoided by accomplishing the objective some other way, or the factors that make the meeting expensive, pointless and frustrating can be mitigated.

Know Your Objective

Whether you are calling the meeting or have "been called" to attend one, your time will be spent much more effectively (and your frustration level will be much lower) if you understand the specific objective of the meeting. Unfortunately, many meetings are called without a specific objective. People simply meet out of habit or custom or because they feel it is appropriate.

It is perfectly acceptable to ask "What are we hoping to accomplish here today?" or "How will we know if this meeting has been successful?"

Examples of successful objectives:

- To brainstorm solutions to a problem.

- To take a "checkpoint" on status when there are many interdependencies.

- There is an actual piece of work than can be best be produced by several people with different expertise.

- To kick off or wrap up a project and ensure everyone involved understands the implications.

Don't hold unnecessary meetings

When not to have a meeting:

- Dealing with personnel issues like hiring, firing, negotiating salaries or dealing with disciplinary and corrective actions.

- There is inadequate data or poor preparation. (If you haven't had time to prepare, it is more acceptable to reschedule than to "fake it.")

- The information could be communicated better by some other means. (E-mail, Intranet, telephone, memo, or one-to-one discussion.

- The subject matter is confidential.

- Your mind is made up or you've already arrived at a decision.

- The subject is not important enough to justify everyone's time.

- There is too much anger or hostility in the group and people need time to calm down before they can collaborate effectively.

Have the Right People (and the Right Number) in the Room

The right people are determined by the meeting's objective. Who needs to be directly involved in the task at hand? Who can be informed later? Generally speaking, every person in the room must have an absolute need to be there. Each person added to the meeting adds to the amount of time it takes to communicate circumstances, arrive at mutually acceptable decisions, and move along the agenda.

Each person invited to the meeting should understand his or her role or expected contribution. Typically, we invite people that we "think should be there" but we don't really give much thought to why we want them there or what we want that person to do. Decide in advance what roles need to be filled to ensure you reach your objective and then determine the best person to fill that role.

Meeting Objective	Ideal Number	Roles to Consider
To brainstorm solutions to a problem	Up to 11	• Facilitator • Participants familiar with subject matter representing all stakeholders.
To take a "checkpoint" on status when there are many interdependencies	Up to 7	• Facilitator • Decision makers from the work projects that intersect.

Meeting Objective	Ideal Number	Roles to Consider
Task group/Working session	Up to 5	• Facilitator • Decision makers (business end) • People with technical expertise
To kick off or wrap up a project and ensure everyone involved understands the implications.	Up to 7	• Facilitator • Everyone involved with the project.
To give a presentation or present information	Unlimited	• Presenter • Audience

Stick to the Point

When items are brought up by meeting participants (as they frequently are) it is important to capture them. One of the main benefits of meetings is the synergy and creative thought that happens when people get together to discuss an issue from several sides. However, getting sidetracked makes you less likely to get your objective accomplished in the amount of time you've set aside.

Capture "side items" in the minutes, or set an action item for someone to take responsibility to ensure the "side item" is taken care of.

Follow Rules of Dialogue

Although we've been taught since we were school children that we must play nicely with others, wait our turn to speak, and treat one another respectfully, we've also all been in meetings where those basic niceties get thrown out the window.

Speaking out of turn, interrupting, raising voices, and ignoring points of view robs the individuals involved of credibility and robs the meeting of any potential for synergy.

Having a simple, agreed-to "rules of dialogue" and having a person who is entrusted to ensure it is followed removes an element of fear and frees up the meeting to get work done in the absence of hostility and frustration.

Evaluate Your Meetings and Change to Fit Your Needs

You can do this formally, by passing out a survey form at the end of the meeting, or informally, by simply asking the question—"Did everyone get what they wanted (or needed) out of this session? How can we make the next one better?"

CONCLUSION

Meetings don't have to be frustrating, vague, hostile, and ineffective. By putting some time and effort into preparing for them and considering the factors in this article, you may actually find yourself looking forward to them! The people invited to them may not admit it right away, but they may find themselves looking forward to them, too! (Or at least not dreading them!).

12. Resolving Conflict—And Still Getting Your Way!

THE OPPORTUNITY

If there is anyone who is a major component in your life (spouse, close friend, coworker, boss, or employee) that you never disagree with, it's probably for one of three reasons:

- You are so incredibly cosmically compatible that you have identical thoughts and feelings on every subject.

- One (or more) of you doesn't care about the outcome.

- One (or more) of you hasn't been paying attention.

Since the chances of the first option are pretty remote (and pretty boring!), you're probably dealing with one of the latter two.

We work together because we need a diversity of skills and experiences to draw from to get better results. When everything is going "too smoothly," you have to worry that perhaps that diversity isn't getting expressed or used.

When any two people are working on anything together, chances are there will be conflicts and disagreements. Although these can be disturbing at times, they are often the catalyst for change, growth and greater understanding between you. In professional relationships, that amounts to being the catalyst for change, growth and greater under-standing for the company.

Realizing that conflict is not only inevitable, but potentially a very positive thing doesn't always make it any easier while you're in the middle of it. Here are some suggestions that will help you realize the benefits without the pain.

THE SOLUTION

There are some things you can do to move through a conflict in a pro-ductive way, rather than letting it become time consuming, emotional, expensive and frustrating.

Solve Problems Early

Don't "save up" grievances until a status report or performance review. Resolve them at the earliest possible opportunity. People are more receptive to input on recent events (rather than ancient history) and by resolving it now, it has less time to grow into a larger issue. It also keeps you up fewer nights.

Our memories also have a way of magnifying things—making them better or worse than they seemed at the time.

Decide What's Important

First of all, ensure that the conflict is something worth spending your energy on. Conflict can be an exhausting process, even when it ends well. Don't waste your energy on anything that isn't worth it to you.

Questions you can ask yourself:

• Who else cares about this problem besides me? Why?

• Will I care about this issue in three months? (six months?)

- Is the issue a single item or a component of a trend?

- Is there a legal issue involved? If so, how severe?

- Is there an ethical principle involved? If so, how severe?

- Can you quantify the impact (in dollars, hours, number of people involved, or some other objective unit of measure?)

You may decide that an issue is merely irritating, but not worth a confrontation or negotiation. Don't back down on anything that is important to you, by any objective criteria. But don't make a conflict out of a trivial item.

Isolate the Contention Points

People tend to paint things with a broad brush, especially when they're annoyed. "That project has caused nothing but trouble." Or "I can't stand dealing with that department" or "Everything that person does is abrasive."

Narrow down the contention and put a fence around it. Don't use words like "always" and "never." Discuss only the specific issue, incident or problem that you want resolved now.

Objectives, not Positions

This is the "seek first to understand, then to be understood" concept, as Steven Covey uses it in his "Highly Effective" books. Rather than assuming you're on opposite sides, or positions, on a single issue, make sure you correctly understand the other person's objectives. There is almost always a way that you can get what you need without damaging your opponent.

Use a Two-Stage Approach

This approach can be used for two people, or two parties, with varying degrees of complexity. In either case, you may want to engage a neutral third party, or facilitator, to ensure that all sides are represented fairly and have an "even shake." Agree on the choice of facilitator or arbitrator before proceeding.

First—Solution Brainstorming

Suggest that you spend a limited amount of time (10 minutes to an hour, depending on the complexity or importance of the problem) brainstorming solutions that would work for both of you. Agree that no solution will be adopted or considered a "done deal" until it's been cleaned up and agreed to by both sides. That way neither party feels that solutions need to be watertight before submitting them. Brainstorm on a whiteboard or sheet of paper. Do not edit or even comment on the solutions—this could have a chilling effect on the creativity of solutions offered.

Second—Negotiation

Now take the best solution, or a combination of them, work out the details, and shake hands. Remember that your credibility is on the line to keep your end of the bargain, especially in a sensitive situation like a conflict negotiation.

Physical/Logistical Considerations

These items may seem trivial, especially in an American business environment. Many other cultures recognize the often subconscious effect that the physical arrangements have on the outcome of a conflict resolution session.

- Make sure that the room is arranged such that no one's chair is at the head of a table (except possibly the facilitator's or arbitrator's.)

- Don't sit or stand in front of the door, psychologically barring exit.

- Dress conservatively. Don't wear wild or loud colors, especially in the red or orange family.

- Use a low, moderate tone of voice. Few people know what they really sound like. You may want to use a tape recorder or have a coach help you with modulating your voice to an unabrasive tone.

- Make sure the room is comfortable—not too warm, cold, noisy, or drafty. Such irritants can add to the sensitivity of the participants or cause them to cut the session shorter than it needs to be.

- It is best if both parties sit together, facing the "problem," in the form of a whiteboard, flip chart, or sheet of paper. This helps "objectify" the problem and separate it from the participants.

CONCLUSION

Avoiding all conflict is not possible, or even desirable. The diversity of opinions and experiences you bring to the table have their place, as do everyone else's. The key is to ensure that opinions, even strong ones, have the opportunity to get heard in an environment where they can be useful rather than damaging to relationships. Try some of these techniques. You may want to try them in your personal life as well, with simple problems at first until you gain confidence that they will bring you the results that you want. Then employ them in more complex or heated situations. You'll come out of the conflict with better results every time.

13. Leadership for Non-Bosses

THE OPPORTUNITY

You're accountable for getting a project done, and you need assistance and cooperation from a number of people.

There is a gap, however, between your responsibility and your authority level. Maybe you aren't high enough on the food chain to tell people what to do, or maybe even if you are, command and control is just not your style.

How do you get buy-in, cooperation and assistance from people who don't report to you?

THE SOLUTION

No matter how high up the corporate ladder you are, you will find yourself interacting with groups of people that you need to influence without pulling rank.

Maybe they are:

- Peers or higher-ups from your own company

- People from other companies (vendor, supplier or client companies)

- People that do report to you, but that are super-talented hotshots and prima donnas that simply do not respond well to orders.

Many projects are undertaken by temporary, cross-functional groups or "swat teams" that are put together solely for the purpose of the project, without affecting the company's organizational chart.

People forget that leadership is, first and foremost, a service. If you are not a person that fulfills a need for the people you lead, then you have no business being a leader, regardless of your rank in the company.

The service you provide might be providing information, representing people and projects to outside parties or higher-ups, engaging people to cooperate, imparting a sense of accomplishment and a sense of security. In short, your job is to help THEM be successful, even more than it is their job to help you succeed.

You must be known as a person who works hard on behalf of the group, knows his or her stuff, does his or her homework, plays fair, and honestly provides information and admits mistakes. Having these qualities won't instantly make you a leader, but NOT having these qualities will instantly take you out of the running.

If you have the above qualities, and can follow some of the following steps, you could be as (or even more) successful with a "volunteer fire department" than you could ever be with an organizationally dedicated staff.

Forget Positions

Whether the person you need to influence is the CEO or the janitor, don't look at that person as a function of a title or a number of digits before the decimal point on a paycheck. "Kissing up" to leadership or "talking down" to underlings will only get you suspected of dishonestly pushing your own agenda. Forget where that person sits on the organizational chart, and forget where you sit. Focus on your objective, your message, what you need that person to do, and why.

I was accountable for building and populating a proof of concept corporate intranet at a large financial institution years ago when I was a lowly consultant.

The people I needed information from were VPs, presidents of affiliated companies, and so forth. I had my doubts about whether or not they'd listen to me. They seemed to have their own culture and priorities that I was not a part of.

I knew my own project inside and out, of course. I studied about the departments they led, and talked to people who had experiences with them about their decision-making style and motivations. I made the appointments, bought some new clothes (probably not necessary but it was a good excuse and made me feel more confident) gritted my teeth and focused on the subject at hand; not the differences between us. I had remarkable cooperation and more assistance than I would have dreamed.

Many of these VPs told me later that my enthusiasm and knowledge of my objectives was the key to overriding their other priorities and getting me what I needed.

Don't Give Orders

Many management schools teach deadlines and accountabilities. Those things are very important, but trying to force a deadline or accountability usually does more harm than good.

It is very important to outline what you need. You must have a thorough understanding of the specific tasks that need to be done by specific dates to make the project work. However, you have much more success at getting deadlines and accountabilities that stick when people at least feel like they have some say in setting them for themselves. Outline what is needed, and ASK for that person's help and cooperation. Ask them how they could contribute. If they're in agreement with the objective, or at least see the value of it (in terms of company success, being seen as a "team player," or whatever incentives you can provide) they will generally accomplish things better than they could if assigned.

People have an innate need to be included and to be recognized as being good at what they do. If you show the connection between what you need, and having their own innate needs met, people will work very hard toward common goals.

This is probably best explained by example. You have a project to accomplish, and Frank is a person in the company who has a skill set you need. You have permission from Frank's boss to use some of his time only if it doesn't interfere with his regular duties.

Example 1—

Delivered by memo, e-mail, or by walking into Frank's cube: "Frank, I need you to do XYZ in two weeks."

Example 2—

Delivered over coffee: "Frank, I wanted to talk to you about this project because I understand that you have some experience with _____ and I'm told that you've done well with this sort of thing in the past. This project is very important because _____.
Let me tell you what I'm trying to accomplish in thirty days and maybe you can let me know how you could contribute."

Although Example 1 takes five minutes, and example 2 might take thirty minutes, and probably the cost of Frank's coffee, the results are remarkably different.

In Example 1, Frank is likely to put you off, refer you back to his boss (who suddenly has other priorities for him) or throw something superficial together to get you off his back. Example 2 will set up a respectful relationship where Frank will not only do XYZ, but may have other skills or insights into your project that you didn't know he had. He's also likely to do the task you "assigned" in a shorter time-frame (since he set his own) and meet his own deadline with higher-quality work.

As added benefit, Frank will also speak well of your project to his co-workers and may even intercede on your behalf to his own boss if need be.

Ask Questions

Many times you can lead without seeming to by asking the right questions in the right context, and letting someone else take the stage.

For example, you're in a meeting and making no progress. There is no real leader, or the leader is absent, and the group is muddling along.

Overtly trying to take charge of the meeting might work, or it might simply raise defenses and complicate the issue more—becoming a power struggle about who should be leading the meeting rather than having effort directed toward accomplishing anything.

The person who asks the right question will probably become the group's leader by default, and without opposition.

Examples of good leading questions:

- "What is our objective for this meeting?"

- "What is the next logical step from where we are?"

- "What is our real goal here?"

- "What do we each need to walk out of here with to feel that this meeting has been successful?

If the question is well-received, walk up the whiteboard, pick up a marker, and start capturing ideas.

Involve Everyone in Planning Sessions

If a project is large and complicated, and involves a number of people, involve the group in the planning process, rather than planning the project yourself and doling out tasks.

Start with a list of tasks you know need to be done. Ask everyone's input in adding to and refining the list. Then ask everyone to volunteer for the tasks that are the most interesting to him or her. There will always be some tasks left over that nobody wants—brainstorm ways to make these more interesting, less cumbersome, or to divide them fairly among the group. (It helps if you set a good example by being willing to roll up your sleeves and do a couple of the less desirable tasks yourself.)

Stroke Egos

There is nothing more flattering than being asked for an opinion or for help. If you need a person's help, assistance or support for a project, say so, and tell them why. Don't lie or exaggerate—insincerity is almost always obvious, as well as insulting. But if there's something positive to say, by all means, say it!

"I was told that you are very skilled with database conversions" or "I remember when you did something similar with ABC project and I'd heard it was very successful." Or "Jane told me that you were the best person to talk to about this subject." Or even "I'd really like your opinion on this project I'm working on."

Focus Forward, Not Behind

What do you do when someone who doesn't work for you does something wrong, or something that doesn't meet your expectations?

You can't call them on the carpet and chew them out, especially if they don't work for you. Threatening them with going to their "real" boss probably won't work, either, at least not more than once. Their "real" boss has other things to worry about besides your project, and won't like having their people criticized when they were good enough to lend them to you, to begin with.

Whether or not a person works for you, positive feedback works much better than negative. Again, be very personal, and as positive as possible.

Example 1:

Delivered via memo, e-mail, or in Fred's cube:

"Fred, XYZ was not done correctly, and now it's not working. It needs to be fixed today or the project will be behind."

Example 2:

Delivered in person, preferably on neutral territory (like another cup of coffee.)

"Fred, I've asked George to work on ABC, and he's having a little trouble understanding how to get XYZ to work. We're coming up on our deadline and under some pressure to make sure this works by Friday. I was wondering if you might have some time today to help him?"

The Asian principle of "face," or honor, works very well here. Always be willing to admit that perhaps the nature or details of the task were not communicated correctly. Focus forward on making progress on the project; rather than backward, analyzing mistakes and assigning blame.

Share Kudos

When you're congratulated on your phenomenally successful project, be sure to mention the people who helped you. Many people treat praise like a limited commodity—they feel it's worth more if you hoard it for yourself. We've noticed the opposite—credit, kudos and praise seem to multiply exponentially the more you spread them around.

- Congratulate people specifically (Fred did a wonderful job of XYZ, and did some wonderful 11th hour fine-tuning to be sure things worked well for us.)

- Congratulate people in writing (Memos, certificates of appreciation, letters, etc. that people can hang up in their cube or add to their portfolio of successes for their next evaluation.)

- Be public. Have a project wrap-up party or event, and invite everyone who had anything to do with the project, even tangentially.

- Include their bosses. "I appreciate you making Fred available to help me with this project. I understand it took some planning wizardry on your part to make this possible." Also, make sure their boss gets copies of the memos, letters, etc. praising their employees.

Sharing kudos not only feels good for you and them, but also ensures you have an easier time recruiting help in the future.

Include their bosses. "I appreciate you making Fred available to help me with this project. I understand it took some planning wizardry on your part to make this possible." Also, make sure their boss gets copies of the memos, letters, etc. praising their employees.

CONCLUSION

The trend in business, not only for special projects, but even for "business as usual" is away from hierarchical reporting relationships with command-and-control styles of management. Being able to master leadership techniques that work regardless of rank behooves everyone, from the CEO to the entry-level newcomer. Even if you occupy the top of the organizational chart, your projects and initiatives will be much more successful and your people will be happier, more accountable, creative, and productive if you follow these concepts rather than "pulling rank" to get things done.

14. Family Business—The Perils and Potentials of Doing Business with Family

THE OPPORTUNITY

Doing business with family members has NEVER been a neutral topic. Family businesses are a time-honored tradition. In contrast, many companies have formal policies against doing business with people you have outside ties with, just because of the (MANY) possible complications.

THE SOLUTION

What follows is a discussion of how to accentuate the positives, downplay the negatives, and make good decisions for YOUR situation when it comes to matters of family business.

Family Business in History—Tradition and Legacy

It has been a tradition since time immemorial for families to work together. Young people become apprentices to their older relatives and learn the inner workings of business. After "earning their stripes" and completing their education, these young people are often groomed for high positions in the companies. The connections, the early introduction to the key players and concepts, and the reputation they carry in their families' names provide their customers with the security of dealing with a "known entity," in what is now a very volatile marketplace.

There are many family dynasties that have spent many generations building reputations, building markets, and gaining experience that become their competitive advantage. The Gallo family in winemaking, the Eccles family in banking, and the Shane company in jewelry are examples of families that have (or had) several generations in building their businesses into vast empires.

There are even current tax breaks for employing your children. Some very smart families have their children work in the family business, and a portion of their salary goes into their education fund. This allows for additional tax advantages.

Working in a family business (as a non-family member) can present a unique set of benefits and problems. I worked for a small family-owned florist shop in college. It was extremely unwise to have a disagreement with a member of the "ruling family" because the rest of the family would hear about it almost instantly and your future with the company would be suspect. There was also much gossip among non-family members about the pointlessness of trying to be successful in a family business because no matter how hard you work, "you'd never have the right genes."

On the other hand, I worked at another family-owned publishing company whose approach was to treat all of their employees like family. We had a barbecue on the premises every other Friday, communication was extremely open, and it was a wonderfully warm and nurturing environment. My boss treated everyone like a son or daughter. They were happy to help out an employee whose home was damaged in a storm, (we were given half a day off on the condition we showed up at Dave's house in overalls with tools in hand) or to cover for a secretary who needed time off to care for a sick child. It was a surprisingly nurturing environment, unheard of in the modern, cold corporate culture.

Modern Corporate Culture—Keeping Things Simple

This is all very well and good if your family owns the company, but for the rest of us, working with family has some definite drawbacks, and even some formal obstacles. And for good reason!

Avoiding conflicts of interest, or the appearance of conflicts of interest, is central to the human resources policies of many companies. Most forbid direct reporting relationships between family members or even dating couples. There is the possibility that other employees will see a relationship as a factor in a raise or a promotion, or on the contrary, in a disciplinary action. A breakup, divorce or intergenerational family fight can make it very hard to maintain complete fairness and objectivity in the workplace. The HR department's job is to avoid any such turbulent possibilities by keeping things simple.

There is also the issue of confidentiality. Many people confide in their spouses and families about issues at work, which provides a much-needed outlet and is not likely to cause any harm if the spouse or family member's work is not related. But with interconnected projects and departments, there is always the possibility (or perception) that families that work together may have the advantage of inside or shared information that their co-workers don't have.

In his book *Office Romance*, Dennis M. Powers details what he calls Office Wolves, Office Hyenas, and Office Black Widows—people that can make life much more turbulent in an office where spouses or dating couples are working together. His "Wolves" are people who are so intent on dating a person in the office that they make life difficult for the object of their affection that doesn't reciprocate their feelings. "Hyenas" are people who enjoy being in the middle of whatever gossip they can dig up, and "Black Widows" are the injured parties from extracurricular office romances. All this can lead to a lot of, well, complexity, to say the least.

On the other hand, we spend at least forty hours a week at work, and pour out creative energy and inspiration and get to know people we work with. It's a fact of life that some of those people are likely to develop relationships. Powers reports that one third of all romances begin at work. Many people leave companies or start their own simply to spend more time with their families.

Many of the best qualities in the people we work with are also the best foundations for relationships—or the best qualities in the people we love and respect in our personal lives are the best reasons to work with them. Trust, understanding, shared values and mutual goals are all great reasons to work together.

With many companies merging, relocating, or becoming international, some companies are relaxing their policies about spouses and family members working together, especially at remote locations. An executive sent to Lisbon to open a new office agreed to go if his wife could also find employment there. The Human Resources department found an opening that fit his wife's qualifications, and made an exception to the HR policy since they would be working in the same department.

Love and Money—Working with Families

Here are some suggestions we've heard for maintaining familial bliss as well as sound business. Some of these guidelines also apply to doing business with friends, an equally tricky topic.

- It is important to be as courteous to your family as it is to strangers. We sometimes become too relaxed with family members just because we see them every day. We take for granted that they'll put up with our moods in ways other people wouldn't understand. This can lead to problems with family members, or with other employees who feel awkward seeing these interactions.

- Establish boundaries. Make sure you spend enough non-working time with your family members that you see them as individual people that you have a healthy relationship with outside of the company. Have separate family outings, holidays or weekend activities where you DON'T talk business.

- Be professional in public or at work. Expressions of affection could make other employees feel uncomfortable.

- If you want to be alone together or have a private conversation, go away from the company property for an intimate lunch or cup of coffee. But don't abuse the privilege and allow either person's duties to be neglected.

- If you are the employer, have very specific policies about reporting relationships and expectations of behavior to avoid conflicts of interest, sexual harassment, or the potential appearance of either. Working in separate departments, for example, might be an ideal solution where a couple can work at the same facility but avoid any potential problems.

- If you own a family business, be sure the lines of communication to non-family employees are good. Make sure that no one feels disadvantaged for being left out of conversations and decisions that take place around the supper table. Keep the appropriate people (based on their role in the company) involved in all decisions.

- Don't talk about your family members personal life with other members of your staff, except in terms that are absolutely non-controversial. (Don't tell your co-workers that you don't approve of who your daughter is dating, for example, if your daughter works in the next office!)

- Make sure each member of the corporate structure has the option to leave the company without impacting the company more than necessary. Don't assume that a person is a "lifer" just because he or she is a family member. Whether or not they take the "exit clause," just having one makes people feel less trapped and ensures that they are there by choice.

- Respect each others' decisions and authority. This may be particularly difficult for parents. Just because you're the Mom doesn't mean you can tell your son how to run his department. Keep your comments appropriate for your role in the company, rather than your role in the family.

- Appreciate the good things about each other. It becomes easy to focus on the negative when you spend a lot of personal AND professional time together. Remember (and point out) what you admire and love about one another.

CONCLUSION

Doing business with family and friends can be very rewarding. It can also be very complicated and difficult. It always involves an even more stringent standard of etiquette than usual, but if appropriate measures and safeguards are taken, it can make life, work and relationships a rich, rewarding tapestry that provides the best of both worlds.

15. The Power of Generosity—How Spoiling Your Customers is Worth the Money

The Opportunity

If you want something, give something.

—Deepak Chopra

Most companies are still in belt-tightening mode. You become painfully aware of this when you read the newspapers or deal with any company's understaffed and pinched customer service department. That will be a blinding contrast to any company who chooses to seize the opportunity to give the customer "a little something extra."

The Solution

Although the economy in the U.S. and elsewhere appears to be on the rebound, there continues to be a lot of focus on cost-cutting. We still hear of the occasional plant closure or round of layoffs. Every company has turned a microscope on their expenses. We fly economy class and stay in economy hotels. Companies like Tyson Foods and Honeywell have curtailed perks like on-site daycare. Customer service staffs have been cut to the bone, making hold times longer and service more cursory. Business lunches are held at cafeterias instead of bistros. Even postage stamps are now printed on cheaper paper (as those of you who may have recently tried to peel one out of the package to stick it to a letter have discovered!) According to consulting firm Towers Perrin,

60% of companies have reduced their merit pay increases by 3.5% below what they awarded last year. We're all tightening our belts in many ways we hadn't thought of five years ago.

There is a lot that is good about this introspection. There was a great deal of lavish spending in the 1990s that could not be sustained, and a lot of efficiencies that were overlooked because there was no need to be efficient when you have unlimited venture capital. Many businesses with implausible business plans or improbable chances of success were snapping up posh office space and hiring people at alarming rates. Streamlining some business practices was badly needed and is still a very smart thing to do.

While we're talking about efficiency—the most efficient way of improving your sales is to keep your current customers and get them to refer more. In How to Win Customers and Keep Them For Life, Michael Leboeuf demonstrates how, even in cold mathematical terms, it is much more efficient to concentrate on winning customers rather than winning sales. A satisfied customer is worth many sales in terms of repeat business and referrals.

New customers are much more expensive than established ones. Advertising is expensive and extremely inefficient. The market is saturated with advertising, and it's less noticed and less believable than an established relationship with a company, or a recommendation from a friend or neighbor. So the question becomes, how do you impress a current customer to the degree that they will come back for repeat sales and refer others?

Now is an excellent time to make your company stand out with some well-placed generosity. In comparison with your competitors, it might just pay to be lavish. The French in New Orleans have a custom called the "lagniappe" or the small gift. Cajun chefs often prepare a special small dish as an appetizer or dessert. The wait staff would deliver it with a flourish and announce "lagniappe from the chef!" There is a cost to the restaurant for following this custom, the ingredients and staff time to prepare and serve a lagniappe had to impact the budget of the restaurant, but the return on such a small investment is great. Preparing a lagniappe gives the chef an opportunity to practice his creativity on something he may not be ready to put on the regular menu yet. It makes the customer feel special and well cared-for. There may not be a way to measure this in the cold numbers of staff retention, and customer satisfaction. If one chef finds his job more satisfying and therefore performs better or refrains from moving to a different job; or if one customer, impressed with the level of service, returns and brings his family or clients for another visit; the store is well rewarded for a bushel of lagniappes.

Look for ways that your business might be able to employ this principle—empower your salespeople to offer a little something extra—announced only AFTER the sale is closed so that it doesn't seem like a bribe or incentive. Send a thank-you note after a sale. Throw in an extra small accessory, or offer a free follow-up service. Give all of your people more time and resources to treat customers in a way that is unexpected. Your people will love it, (it's only human to enjoy being generous, especially with the company's money!) and so will your customers.

CONCLUSION

While everyone else is cutting costs and making business a cheaper, colder place; now is a perfect time to stand out by demonstrating a little well-placed generosity.

16. Life in a Cubicle Zoo—The Psychology of Office Space

THE OPPORTUNITY

The cost of real estate, especially in certain locations (you know where they are) is so expensive that the goal of corporate facilities planners appears to be how to fit as many people into as little space as possible without violating fire ordinances or causing civil revolt among co-workers. What challenges are presented by causing your employees to live in a maze of cubicles? How can you promote an environment of trust, respect and professionalism while sitting practically on top of one another? How can you avoid damage to working relationships and productivity?

THE SOLUTION

There are two ways of dealing with facilities and space problems—one is by addressing the ideas, attitudes and use of the space you're stuck with. (This may be all you can do if you've been assigned space and don't have budget for changes!) The other option is to address the space itself and make some changes. Use ideas from both sections of this article for best results.

Changing Ideas and Attitudes

Changing your company's attitudes on time and space is not easy. You have to establish trust and accountability, make sure that your company's vision, culture, and lines of communication are intact. You have to measure staffers performance on objective criteria, not just the perception of "busyness" created by occupying a cubicle from nine to five every weekday. There are some lines of work that are more compatible with flexibility than others, but in many cases the solution to the cubicle zoo is to free the animals into a more natural habitat.

Time

Many employees request different schedules to meet their own needs—they're attending classes, taking care of children or parents, or accommodating a second job or hobby. But working "non-standard" office hours may have some benefits to the employer, as well. One employer sees flextime as an opportunity to resolve space issues.

Allowing employees who choose to work 10-hour days and have Fridays off causes a number of people to come in earlier, easing overcrowding in the company gym. (that used to be packed from 7:30 to 8:00 a.m. Now a smaller crowd shows up at the gym from 6:30-7:00 and 7:00-7:30.) This manager has part-time and temporary employees come in on Fridays to do administrative and filing work. They find they can catch up on the week's administrivia unencumbered by the office's usual inhabitants—nobody complains if you tie up the printer all day since there are few people there. Building maintenance and other items can be arranged to occur on Fridays, impacting the workflow less.

Geography

You may want to take a hard look at how many of your company's tasks could be performed remotely. Although it is still essential to get together for a really satisfying and stimulating collaborative exchange of ideas, how often are in-person meetings really necessary?

It may be possible for many staffers to work a percentage of time from home. Before offering this as an option (you'll probably have lots of takers) make sure you outline necessary equipment, determine who should pay for it (some companies require that employees provide their own home computers and phone lines, some foot the bill for these as well) and who will provide technical support when things go wrong (which they sometimes will.)

Changing the Space

Consider the use of space in your company. Does meeting your objectives require employees to spend a lot of time in isolated, concentrated thought? Does it require a lot of books, manuals, computers, peripherals and other items that take up space? Do people spend a lot of time on the phone? Do they talk with each other? Collaborate on a whiteboard? Handle physical items or models? You may find that the cubicle model (which assumes a great deal of isolated thought and a small amount of concentrated space) is not really suited for your line of work.

Have Minute Rooms, Hour Rooms and Day Rooms

One software development company has minute rooms, hour rooms and day rooms rather than cubicles. These rooms are designed for individual or collaborative work, and are designed to change as an employee moves through a day of different types of work and interactions.

Minute Rooms

"Minute rooms" are actual rooms (not cubicles) containing a small table, two or three chairs, and a phone. They have a partly-glass front (so you can see that they are occupied and by whom) but are mostly soundproof. They are designed for small conversations or concentrated work on a particular item. Minute rooms may be used for:

• Conversations between a small number of people

- Conflict resolutions that you don't necessarily want the whole company to overhear.

- Personal phone conversation without being overheard

- Working on a task that requires intense concentration without being disturbed.

Hour Rooms

Hour rooms are what are typically thought of as conference rooms for 8-10 people. They include a table, a whiteboard, a conference telephone, and other typical meeting accoutrements. Hour rooms are used for:

- Status meetings or team meetings

- Announcements and celebrations (Milestone parties, etc.).

Day Rooms or Project Rooms

Day Rooms or Project Rooms contain white boards, cork strips on the walls (for hanging project plans, posters, etc.) a conference table, and several workstations arranged into "conversational" groups. Everything is mobile.

Day Rooms or Project Rooms are "rented" for a day or group of days for a project team. During that time, the team "owns" the room and arranges the furniture however best fits the objectives and working styles of the project team. This type of team is used for.

- Large collaborative efforts

- Project work

Informal Space

Consider the informal spaces in your company—reception areas, places around the water cooler, break rooms, places where people tend to congregate and talk. In many companies, these spaces are after-thoughts—the employee "break room" is a converted supply closet, complete with awful lighting, chipping paint and the requisite legally-required posters. A fridge, microwave and a few folding chairs complete the "post-industrial era" look.

Consider instead an inviting reception area where staff and clients can mingle over coffee, with a few plants and well-placed upholstered chairs and sofas, or coffee tables and chairs.

CONCLUSION

It pays to rethink your working space. Rather than having your employees feeling like captives waiting for the opportunity to escape at the end of the day, you can provide people with the inviting spaces to work collaboratively or independently as they move through their day. They'll feel better, and you'll spend more of your time on vision and strategic direction and less time refereeing turf wars.

17. Effective Workforce Management—Gaining Competitive Advantage—A Personal Experience

THE OPPORTUNITY

We've all heard that any company is only as good as its people. The past year has companies run the gamut of workforce management techniques—one month they're aggressively recruiting and offering unprecedented signing bonuses and perks. The next month the same company finds itself laying off large numbers of people in response to market pressures. Then they find themselves shorthanded and unable to leverage new opportunities—so they go on a recruiting spree or hire back their old employees as consultants at greatly inflated rates. These companies are putting themselves at a competitive disadvantage—one cannot successfully compete in business without a dedicated workforce of committed people that are effectively engaged toward the company's objectives.

Acquiring, supporting and effectively managing a workforce can be a balancing act. I have accomplished this more successfully within each successive company I have worked with over the years. It definitely provides a competitive advantage if Human Resources (HR) refrains from focusing on financial compensation and benefits to the exclusion of other means of workforce management.

THE SOLUTION

A competitive advantage can result from effective employee acquisition, support and management if the following areas are properly addressed at the appropriate levels within the organization:

- Employment Security

- Selective Recruiting

- Motivators

- Participation

- Empowerment and Self Managed Teams

- Training and Skill Development

- Measurement.

Employment Security

This implies a commitment by the organization to its workforce. An employer that indicates through communications and actions that its employees are expendable will probably not attract nor acquire employees that have company loyalty, a sense of commitment, nor a willingness to spend extra time or effort for the organization's benefit.

The particular theme that is espoused is repeated and reinforced in everyday managerial practices. However, the general direction or vision comes from the highest sources in the organization, for it is repeated at subsequent levels down the organization. Whatever the message from Senior Management, it will be reiterated throughout the organization.

A positive workforce commitment by the organization at a minimum provides "one less thing" for employees to worry about. They can spend that extra amount of energy doing essential and positive things for the organization. If the commitment is displayed in more ways that words, the result can be quite amazing.

Experiences—Workforce Commitment vs No Workforce Commitment

Every organization has different directives or visions with respect to people. One had the attitude and vision that the company can operate without any particular person; that each and every person is dispensable. I did not perform enough research on this company before I hired on. I did not know this until shortly after starting. I thought that I could make a difference, possibly change attitudes through a grass roots movement. That was naïve. I was the fourteenth person in our department to leave during the twelve-month period before I acquired another job. The company could not acquire others to replace those that had left. I worked there long enough to find another job. Predictably, morale was low. It was difficult to get assistance with any project or effort. People were not trusted, nor were they valued for their knowledge or experience. Collaboration was almost nonexistent. People were afraid they would lose their jobs if they shared information. Nothing was provided to employees outside of a workspace and paycheck.

This firm is still in business today, but they haven't grown significantly since. That indicates to me that they haven't changed their policies or apparent philosophy with respect to people.

The antithesis of that organization is another that I have worked with. They always "manage for improvement." They are also a financial institution, but they not only espouse a commitment to the employees, but they live it!

Their financial compensation is better than any other in the area, although, it is not the best in the country. They have an interesting approach to job security. If my job was eliminated for any reason, I am automatically inserted into a "work pool" for a period of 1 year. I have that amount of time to interview within the company for any other job I may be interested in and qualified for. If I need education to become qualified for a job, the company will pay for that education. My pay stays the same during this time, with no increases. If the new job has a higher pay rate, my salary is increased appropriately. If the job has a pay rate that is less, but within my salary band, I keep my present salary. If it is less and I still desire to take the job, then an appropriate decrease will be negotiated.

This company provides a full range of sports, health and intellectual activities for its' employees. And because they have flextime, they can enjoy these activities on their own schedule. The company has several restaurants throughout their office buildings and they use only the latest technology in their offices throughout the world.

Selective Recruiting

If a firm is committed to maintaining, supporting and effectively managing its' workforce, it must also be very selective in the employee acquisition process. These people will be the client interface in some fashion or another. They must have the "right" attitude, personality, knowledge, technical and "people" skills—all of which are subjective and difficult to determine and measure through any acquisition process. But this is where it starts—probably the single most important detail to provide competitive advantage through the acquisition and management of balanced careerists.

A firm must find those people who can work best in the existing environment, can learn and develop with little supervision. The selection and acquisition process must be balanced and should be executed at a quick pace.

There are two schools of thought with respect to selection processes. There are those that extend the theory that applying a rigorous selection process invokes the feeling in the applicant that they are joining an elite organization. My experience indicates that the interview process is an extension of the nature of the company. If it takes a long time for the processes and decisions to be made and the process is confusing, one should not be surprised if many other processes and decisions are delayed and ambiguous.

Motivators

Financial compensation in all of its various forms is important. Some of these forms include high pay, incentive pay, bonuses, and various other options of which there are very many. (Including most of the factors listed in this paper—many employees these days expect participation, empowerment, training and skill development, and employment security, and selective recruiting as factors to a good or even "acceptable" working environment.

I am trading my most valuable asset—time, for financial compensation. I therefore expect to make the best deal that I can, and obtain the most compensation possible in return for my time. That said, financial compensation is not the only form of remuneration for time.

People are motivated by more than money, however, there are those that want to minimize the motivation capability of financial compensation. Financial motivation is a powerful factor that cannot be neglected, at least until we achieve some method of providing all things to every one.

Others as indicated above include health and intellectual activities, flextime, and many others limited only by the imagination. The downside is that these things require a company to be progressive. Thus far, I have encountered very few progressive corporations!

Participation, Empowerment and Self Managed Teams

Participation and empowerment are preconditions required for the implementation of a collaborative work environment that is necessary for self managed teams to evolve, survive and flourish. The preconditions necessary for participation and empowerment are several. Senior Management must provide the vision, support and resources for this venture to work. People have been ingrained with hierarchy in business. It takes a lot of understanding, patience, and most expensive of all, time; to begin to convert a hierarchical organization to one that is characterized by accountable, self managed teams.

Participation in decision-making processes increases satisfaction and employee productivity. Those organizations that provide participation and real empowerment as a mechanism to organizational development and allow employees to control their own work processes, have discovered that this is a very heady thing to invoke and watch.

Experience—Self Managed Team

I spent three years with an organization that started from a hierarchical structure and progressed toward the self-managed team environment. While in this organization, I was asked to lead a project to replace a mainframe computer that had failed. This type project typically requires approximately four to six months to complete if everything works "right."

Using the self managed team concept and appropriate project management tools, our team completed this project in ninety-six hours from the first meeting until a new computer in a new computer room was functioning in full production mode. Our team was a high performance team. To this day, we all would like to be involved in another project such as that one. The *esprit d corps*, or closeness generated from having a common goal along with the authorization to proceed as a self-managed team was absolutely amazing and beyond belief. There was absolutely nothing that would have prevented our team from making or beating the fast approaching deadline.

Note: No one worked more than a twelve-hour day during the project, except the project lead (me.) I insisted on it. It was sometimes real work to get people to leave and get rest for the next day!

There was, however, real fear from the middle aged and senior workers that an incentive particularly a badly administrated bonus pay out that came afterward, was just another ploy by management. To what end, I am not sure. But the distrust and in some cases, fear, is real. Hierarchical managers in many organizations have used or abused workers through inconsistent messages and sometimes downright untruthful communications in order to complete their own agendas.

In a true team oriented organization, team members tend to help each other during the pressure periods of team projects. Thus, when peer pressure is at its greatest, other folks on the team are willing to provide suggestions, or in some cases assist or coach a team member that is not able to perform up to expectations. The expectations that the team member is trying to live up to are typically of his own making.

Training and Skill Development

Many of the organizations that I have worked with—either as an employee or a consultant—have too little or the wrong emphasis on training and subsequent skill development. Organizational leaders must understand that given the premise that people are their greatest asset, then they must keep this asset polished, current and ready for production. This in its rawest form is done through training. But, the organization must follow through.

An excellent professional education system or program does not necessarily produce positive results. The follow through is providing a means for the freshly trained employees to use their new skills in some capacity that provides valid feedback and validation to the employee. This can be accomplished in a variety of ways. Career development—moving an employee from stage 2 to stage 3 as described by Brett Savage, *Novations*. In some cases, simply restructuring in a hierarchical environment, or a more progressive approach may be to move toward a collaborative or team environment as next step to self-managed teams.

And, let's not stop here. Something I experienced early in a "stage 2" portion of my career, cross-training. This has some interesting ramifications. One obvious implication is that doing more things makes the day more interesting and thus more challenging. One less obvious effect is keeping the work processes as simple as possible.

Experience—Cross Training and Skill Development

In 1975, I was promoted into a department that required managing twelve people in a fairly large organization. Half of these people were military, while the others were civilians. There was substantial discord, sniping, low productivity and obviously, low moral. My mission was to increase productivity. I could not offer promotions nor salary increases.

After several one on one meetings with each of the staff, we had an "all hands" meeting. The outcome was that each of the civilians would learn one of the military members' jobs. And, each of the military members would learn one of the civilians' jobs. Just before the close of the meeting, I provided some incentive. As soon as each member and I were satisfied that everyone knew each others' jobs, I would authorize in rotation a paid week off for each member of the staff, that would not count against their normal vacation. The caveat was that the member on "vacation" would be available by phone during normal work hours for the week. What that meant was that every person could look forward to a week off every sixth week.

Within the first two to four weeks, when people realized that this might actually work, our productivity started skyrocketing, along with the morale. I thought that was great, but it was nothing compared to what happened after folks started actually having time off! Unknown to us, our test was forthcoming in the veil of a no notice operational readiness inspection. We passed the inspection with the highest marks of any team up to that point.

Measurement

Measurement is vital to management processes.

It serves several functions. It provides the necessary feedback as to how well the organization is implementing change. Factors that are measured are likely to be noticed and acted upon, regardless of any consequence or judgement based on those measures. It seems that many people will try to succeed on measures even if there are no direct or immediate consequences. This was certainly true in the experiences that I have related.

Companies that are committed to achieving competitive advantage through people must make measurement a critical part of the process. If for no other reason, than things that are not measured, are not talked about and things that are measured are talked about. Whatever is talked about is considered critical and that forces first class attention to detail. Whatever is not measured, can and usually does become second rate if only in the minds of those involved, and this leads to poor quality.

CONCLUSION

Acquiring, supporting and effectively managing a workforce is a balancing act. It definitely provides a competitive advantage if Human Resources (HR) focuses on other effective means of workforce management such as Employment Security; Selective Recruiting; Motivators; Participation, Empowerment and Self Managed Teams; Training and Skill Development, and Measurement.

18. Successful Presentations—Sales Pitches and Pony Shows

THE OPPORTUNITY

After months of work, you have finally landed an appointment to make your pitch to that important client or financier.

How do you ensure that you make the best use of their time and yours, and more importantly, make sure that they do what you want them to? (Buy your product? Invest in your company or idea? Participate in a project?)

THE SOLUTION

Presentations are similar to documents. Rules of good "writing" (which is actually the organization and presentation of information) apply. Both are forms of communication, and they follow the same rules. The two cardinal rules of any communication are audience and purpose. Everything you are about to read, including physical arrangements, housekeeping, the content and structure of the presentation, the nature of interactions, the materials you distribute, and the closure techniques you use center around the audience and purpose.

Homework is the key to a successful presentation. Talent will only take you so far. Your audience may see any sign of unpreparedness as disrespect of the value of their time.

Audience

Be sure you know as much about your audience as possible. Research their names, backgrounds, and previous behavior individually and as a group. The more you know about their motivations and their means of getting what they want, the better you will be able to find a need and fill it.

Items to consider:

- Who do they report to?

- Who are their constituents?

- Whose opinions do they care about and why?

- What are their goals and objectives in their current or previous positions?

- What are their principles? What is important to them? Money? Power? The need to do good? Do they like to act anonymously or do they like recognition? Recognition from whom?

- How do they dress? (Superficial, but extremely important.)

- Is there anything about their national or ethnic backgrounds or customs that you should know?

- How well-informed are they on the topic you're presenting?

- Are they starting from square one?

- Do they have a good understanding of the underlying principles?

- Does the audience consist of people at different knowledge levels?

Purpose

What are you trying to accomplish with this meeting? What do you want them to do, know and feel at the end of the session? Is there a physical closure you're expecting (like the signing of a document or a vote on a proposal?)

Preparation

You probably want to do your main "sales pitch" during the presentation, but is there any information that would be useful for them to have beforehand so that they can review it and prepare questions? This can also level the playing field if different audience members are at different levels of awareness about the topic. If you're sending materials for review in advance, make sure they are professionally prepared, visually attractive, and make the instructions clear. Include a cover letter indicating that the enclosed materials may be helpful for them to review prior to the session.

These may be included with the agenda. Regardless of whether you send materials in advance, it is a very good idea to distribute an agenda to all participants to ensure they are invited and informed of the meeting and have some idea of what will be covered.

Before the presentation begins, it goes without saying that the speaker and/or people responsible for the presentation should arrive early, ensure everything is in order, and introduce themselves and make small talk with audience members as they file in.

Physical Arrangements

Most experts agree that a U-shape is the best possible environment for a presentation. This allows for the greatest degree of interaction between the audience and the speaker, and even allows for the audience to interact. They can see a person asking a question without turning too far or craning their necks.

This also allows the speaker to close the distance between him or herself and any member of the audience that seems to need extra attention (is talking to his neighbors, asking questions, falling asleep, etc.)

Housekeeping

After introducing oneself, it is a good idea to mention any practical considerations to ensure everyone understands what is expected and is comfortable with the way the presentation is to proceed.

If there are refreshments, ensure everyone has been served and has had a chance to finish so their attention will be on you, not the food. (When food and information compete for attention, it's been our experience that food will win every time!) Indicate the locations of restrooms and/or smoking facilities (if they are unfamiliar to your guests) and the planned schedule for breaks.

Also indicate whether questions and comments are welcome or whether you would prefer they be held during portions of the presentation.

The Presentation Itself

Structure

Your information can be structured in any number of ways—

- A screen presentation (slideshow, video or animation)

- A speech or lecture

- A group participation exercise

- A conversation or Q & A session

- Or elements of all of the above.

Interaction

Interacting with the speaker makes the audience invest energy in the topic of your presentation. People are much more inclined to support something they've invested in. We like to invite as much participation as possible, in terms of questions, discussion, and participation.

Ask the audience to help you out, and give them a specific task. (Writing a relevant concern on a piece of paper, or answering questions for you.) Show that you appreciate their unique perspective and expertise.

Even disagreement, as long as it is open and respectful, is better than no participation at all. Anyone who contends with you is doing you a favor by addressing something that other people in the audience are probably thinking. Answer questions head-on. If you don't know the answer, commit to find out and get back to that person (or the group) at a specific time, if possible.

Materials

As before, ensure all distributed materials are high-quality, visually appealing, and clear in purpose. Make sure you have extras. Depending on your strategy, you may wish to distribute materials before, during or after the conference.

- **Before**—If there are items you will be referring to—tables, charts, etc. that you would like your audience to study closely and take notes on.

- **During**—If you want to call attention to a particular item or point. Keep in mind that this disturbs the "flow" of the presentation by the very mechanics of distributing materials through the audience and ensuring everyone has one.

- **After (or at the end)**—These are effective for "souvenirs" to remind people of the conference and ensure they have contact information, etc. for later transactions or questions. This would include any closing documents, contracts, or "action items."

Closure

Wrap up the presentation by summarizing the content so that it will be easy for participants to remember and explain to others if necessary.

Make sure you've answered all outstanding questions, or have committed to deliver additional information at a specific time.

Make your request specifically and respectfully. Ask them to fill out a form, sign your proposal, vote "yes" on your proposal, or take a concrete, specific action. Even information sessions should end in a request for an evaluation of the session. Concrete requests leave no ambiguity of what you want of them.

CONCLUSION

It is more and more difficult to get people's attention away from the hectic needs of daily business. When you have the opportunity to make a presentation, make sure it is the best possible use of your time and everyone else's. Specifically outline your purpose, know your audience, and arrange the details to accomplish your objective.

19. The Library at Alexandria and Other Information Management Tragedies

THE OPPORTUNITY

The burning of the library at Alexandria has been referred to as a tragic loss of information and knowledge. Livy wrote that the library was destroyed when Julius Caesar torched the fleet of Cleopatra's brother and rival monarch. Another myth is that Hypatia, a fifth-century scholar and mathematician of Alexandria, was dragged from her chariot by an angry Pagan-hating mob of Christian monks. The Christians had her burned alive in the library in a fit of religious fervor.

Whatever the cause, there is no way of knowing what mathematical, philosophical, scientific, and other treasures may have been among the 40,000 volumes thought to have existed in the library.

Today, there are great treasures of knowledge lost every day in every corporation. These treasures are not the result of wars, political or religious uprisings, or anything so meaningful. They are lost by pure accident, negligence or equipment failure.

In the course of running our small business (Ravenwerks) for the past five years, we've had hard drive failures on two of our seven computers. Thanks to the obsessive attentions of our resident technical wizard, all of the data was backed up. In both cases, less than a day's work was lost.

Another thing we've run into at corporations large and small is the simple misplacement of information. Someone leaves the company, taking with them (sometimes inadvertently) the only knowledge of a cryptic or incomplete filing system. Or the power goes out while you're scorching through a brilliant proposal or presentation. Or you simply forgot where you filed a document (paper or electronic.)

THE SOLUTION

Here are some suggestions to prevent tragic loss of the products of intellectual labor:

Automate Backups

Backing things up is sometimes the last thing on people's minds when they're concentrating on tasks at hand and trying to get through a hectic day. Any system you can set to automatically back up is cheap insurance against loss.

Set up an automatic save while you're working on documents using office applications (like MS Word or WordPerfect.) The default is usually to save approximately every 10 minutes, but as fast as I work, 10 minutes would be an unacceptable loss to me. I've set mine to save every 2 minutes. The autosave works in the background and I never notice it. (If autosaves slow your machine down enough to bother you, try freeing up some disk space or upgrading to a faster processing speed.)

Set up nightly or weekly backups from your PCs or file servers. You can back up to a separate system, or to ZIP or JAZ discs or CDs. Keep one copy of everything at a different physical location. (On a computer or on your storage media.)

Review Your Filing System.

As your business evolves, it's worth the time and energy to review whether your filing system is actually working for you, or if you've outgrown its structure.

Get everyone to participate in the same filing system. If everyone keeps their own files on their own PCs, you won't have access in case a person is out sick or their equipment fails. Set up guidelines for even remote or work-at-home people to save their work to the network and make sure it gets backed up and others can understand how to get to it.

Look into Knowledge Management Products

Products such as search engines (for online material) or filing and indexing systems give you more options for finding specific documents or objects. Broadvision®, Documentum®, Verity®, and others supply different types of version-control and searching capability. (And different strata of financial impact when you install them!) If the loss of a document would impact you financially, these items can quickly pay for themselves.

CONCLUSION

It doesn't take a civilization-changing war, or a mob of angry Christians to cost you 40,000 volumes of precious information. Odds are, if you handle large amounts of information, some of it will disappear for one reason or another. But it's not something people typically think about unless it's happened to you. At least once.

20. Job Hunting—How Not to Become the "Prey"

THE OPPORTUNITY

If you're going through Hell, Keep going.

—*Winston Churchill*

Several folks have suggested the need for an article of this type.

The following will try to expose the hype, (while not providing any…) and make suggestions to enhance your possibilities of successful (and hopefully short!) job hunt.

I have changed jobs on average every two to two and half years. Quite a number of these changes required a relocation—typically paid for by the acquiring company. The lessons I have learned, experiences I have had are fairly typical. This from having compared "notes" with many of my coworkers, and others I have helped to find work.

In our present economy, jobs are more difficult to acquire. In part this is due to technology, in part, lack of integrity, lack of trust, and insecure managers. Also, it is due to the wrong people in the Human Resource department of most corporations (see HR as a Competitive Advantage, Rather than a Roadblock at **http://www.ravenwerks.com/leadership/hr.htm**.)

First, a brief word about the most sweeping change in the job hunting experience—technology. It helps because of email. You can get résumé, cover letters, etc. to the desk of the hiring manager—sometimes bypassing HR, or at least having made it through HR. But the downside of technology (read Internet) is that enterprising individuals have learned to "broadcast" that is transmit copies of résumé (for a fee) to a database of managers all over the US (and Europe.) Even the known websites such as Monster, Hotjobs, etc are fraught with problems they try very hard to overcome.

In this article, I cover three of the common pitfalls that face job hunters, and conclude with some suggestions on how to successfully get yourself employed.

THE SOLUTION

This article explores issues with, and suggestions for improving your chances with, three elements that loom large when trying to find a job in today's job market—resume broadcasting services, monstrous information overload (our pet term for popular Internet job boards) and employment counseling services. We will conclude with some advice about what actually DOES work, even in today's challenging employment climate.

Issues with Resume Broadcasting Services

There are a lot of less-than-reputable resume posting services on the Internet that sound like a dream come true to the beleaguered (and possibly desperate) job hunter. They use different wording, but the basic premise is that they provide your resume to hiring managers that are inaccessible to you without their help.

Oh, they will all say that these are current managers that are looking for your skills…but the truth is a little different. They have searched various free public databases that list corporate officers and senior managers complete with their email addresses, phone numbers, etc. The only "trimming" they do is to route IT résumé to IT managers, or accounting résumé to accounting managers, etc. For this service, you will pay as high as $100.00 or more, with an average of about $69.00

On the surface, this sounds like a very good thing—but at last count, several hundred "companies" that perform this function…for several thousand folks looking for jobs…that means that these "selected hiring managers" receive hundreds, if not thousands of résumé in their email boxes daily. If that were your problem, how would you resolve it? If you took the time to look through those, you would glance at the first few lines of the resume to see which one is the closest fit, or give up and hire a recruiting firm.

Dealing with Resume Broadcasting Services

Contract with these firms carefully, unless the amount of money is insignificant to your budget. These folks will typically lure clients with marketing hype such as "millions of jobs available…" on their web sites. But when you try to use them, they require subscription or a fee for broadcasting or other usage.

Stick with the known websites such as Hotjobs, Monster, etc. Most reputable companies that use the Web will use a well-known service.

Issues with Monstrous Information Overload

Monster, Hotjobs, and other well known websites of this caliber have a revolutionary approach, that is great in theory but fraught with problems they are trying diligently to fix. The most serious is that by the time a posting from a corporation is released on Monster, Hotjobs and others, the company has already filled it. I have spoken with the HR departments of several companies that use these job related websites about this problem. They apologize, but "things move slowly…" etc.

In actuality, companies are quick to post for jobs, but slower to remove old ads. Getting a person when you need one is a pressing "must do now" task for the HR department. Cleaning house and removing old ads gets relegated to a once-a-week (if that often!) piece of meaningless paperwork for HR professionals that they "get around to" when they can.

Dealing with Monstrous Information Overload

Respond to ads as quickly as possible. Also, do not use this as your only method of search. It is not as reliable as it once was.

Issues with Employment Counseling Services

This is one that I find particularly disgusting, because they are very expensive. These are companies that offer "placement counseling," invite you to motivational seminars, and they send you books—sometimes more than one—full of hype about building résumé, about how to market yourself with a resume, etc. But they tell you nothing of value in the books.

They will tell you there is a very lucrative part of the job market that most folks don't use. That is, they are in constant contact with hiring managers of the Fortune 100 firms or something just as ludicrous…they will help you modify your resume, and provide you with a database of managers names, addresses linked with corporations, etc.

The fees for this service start at about $5,000.00 and go up. The "qualify" an individual based on amount of salary they currently or last had, money invested, and so forth. Then they decide what to charge.

What they fail to tell you is that this is, at best, 1% of the market. A very small market percentage for such a large investment.

Dealing with Employment Counseling Services

Again, contract with these folks carefully, unless the amount of money is insignificant to your budget. These folks will typically lure clients with marketing hype such as "our last client signed with XXX Corporation for 76% more that he was making in his previous job. And the job was never advertised."

CONCLUSION

In spite of what all the spam and hype would lead the typical job-seeker to believe, there are two tools available to everyone that work better than anything else. A majority of the jobs in the world are filled by one or both of these methods.

Networking

The best (and quickest) method to find the job that you will enjoy the most is networking. No matter what you espouse, or think, or what your personal philosophy is concerning 'good ole boy networks,' most jobs are filled through personal contacts. It is still the best and sometimes only way to find a job, even and especially in today's economy.

Try to place yourself in the managers' place. You, the manager, have somehow managed to keep your job in the turmoil of today. You cannot afford to hire someone that you don't know. If you look at the various poles on the major resume web sites such as Monster or Hotjobs to name the popular ones, the majority of respondents indicated that they have "enhanced" their résumé in some manner. The reason given—everyone does it, and they do it to be competitive. Is this the type of person you would want to work for you?

If the manager finds someone through his or her network of friends and associates that may not be exactly what he needs, but the person is trusted by his network or is part of his network, he will choose this person over an unknown that he must try to find through résumé that are broadcast to everyone, and that probably have been "enhanced." And so would you or I.

If you have not done so, clean your desk, place a blank piece of paper and pen or pencil on the desk, and sit back and think about all of the people you know, and what they do. This is a beginning of the definition of your network. If you have stayed with one company for many years, include all of your peers, supervisors and others that you have worked with and for. Also, include those contacts that you may have made in the course of business that may be outside of your company. You never know which contact will be the one that helps the most.

If you've had several jobs, list all of your past supervisors, peers and others in each of those companies. Maybe you helped someone in another department when you were in between tasks or taking a break. These folks can be very helpful as well.

Try talking to different folks within the last company that you worked for. Just ask them for ideas or advice on where you should look, or whom you should talk with. As you continue to define your network, then begin to 'work' it, you will be surprised at where you will be lead by following suggestions, ideas and advice of those you contact.

Also, by using your network, you will be given a positive, upbeat introduction to whomever you will be interviewing for the prospective job.

No matter how you look at it, networking has more positives than negatives. It is also how the world works.

Another note—you can (and probably should) do this exercise even if you are currently employed. Get in touch with people you haven't heard from in awhile, find out what they're up to, where they're working, how things are going for them. Send them birthday and holiday cards. Have coffee or lunch with people to catch up on old times. If anyone needs a favor and you have the ability to help, by all means do it. Keep the karma stacked in your favor. This does more than improve your social life. Your network is more effective if you've had frequent and regular contact with people before you need their help!

Finally, the best time to look for a job is while you are employed and happy with the job that you have. You should always be looking. If offered another position, you can always turn it down politely. Or it may be the ultimate dream job you have always wanted! If so, take it, and exit your current company politely and with plenty of notice. Offer to help find a replacement, and become part of another network!

Persistence

The following experience illustrates how sometimes good old-fashioned persistence is a way in the door. I was the hiring manager in this particular scenario.

I had open requisitions for two folks, each with identical qualifications. Because of company policy and the need for corporate security, the HR department of this firm would let me review résumé for 1 hour only. I was provided with about 250 résumé. This particular firm refused to pay for outside recruiting assistance. That means that I had to look at about 4 résumé per minute, or I had about 15 seconds to review each resume for relevant experience.

The result of this was that I brought in 3 folks to interview, and ultimately hired 1. The day he started work, I received a call from another person that had also submitted his resume to our firm. This person had previously been a coworker of the person that I had just hired.

The caller wanted to know why I had selected his associate, and not him. Upon further questioning, I determined that each of these two folks had the same education, background and experience, and not only that, they worked side by side in the same department doing the same job for the same company!

My response was that I had not seen his resume.

I subsequently contacted HR and requested the caller's resume. When I reviewed his resume, I could clearly see why I had previously rejected it. (The format was not conducive to my 15-second search!) But, because of his persistence, and appropriate background, I interviewed and subsequently hired this person as well.

Resume format is a separate topic, and not covered here—but one that must be researched carefully. I related this story to point out that if I have an opening, and if the person is qualified, I am far more likely to hire an applicant who has the gumption to call me and persist in his pursuit of the position, than to continue reviewing résumé and conducting interviews.

21. Measuring Results—Are We There Yet?

THE OPPORTUNITY

How will you know when you're successful? How do you know if your company is performing optimally? The old saying "If you do what you've always done you'll get what you've always gotten," is not true in business these days. Even if you've always performed consistently well, you're likely to be outpaced if you're not constantly measuring results and raising the bar. But what do you measure?

If you count on your stock price or market share to tell you how your company is doing, you may be basing your assessment on external factors beyond your company's control. Many companies these days are "doing everything right" but their stock is still undervalued.

THE SOLUTION

You can stay up nights worrying about the stock market all you want, but you'd be better off getting some sleep and then focusing your energy WITHIN your circle of influence starting tomorrow morning.

Benchmarking—Where are we Starting from?

You may have a vague idea that your company is improving it's customer service, or a sinking feeling that sales might be cooling off. These "gut feels" are excellent indicators for where you want to start benchmarking, but you need to get some solid evidence before devoting your resources to improvement.

You can't balance a checkbook by feel (believe me, I've tried) or run a business by gut alone. The larger and more complicated the business, the bigger the need for benchmarking. Everyone sees the business from his or her own perspective and needs to be able to communicate clear, consistent health-and-status messages to the people and departments depending on them.

Benchmarks, of necessity, have numbers associated with them. Select the areas that are the most key to your company's bottom line, but that you have some direct control over. Market share or stock price, have a big impact on the bottom line and are definitely numbers, but they don't qualify as actionable benchmarking standards because those figures depend on a number of external factors. "Actionable" benchmarking standards may include the following:

- Percent of customers rating service as "excellent" (based on a survey)

- Number of add-on or suggestion sales of a particular item

- Number of repeat sales to existing customers

- Time from order to product delivery

- Number (or percentage) of your employees that have had product-based training (and achieved satisfactory scores on a test.)

- Number of customer complaints or requests resolved within 24 hours

- Number of minutes customers spend on "hold"

- Number of failed hits or broken links on a web site

- Number of new sales contacts per day (week, month)

- Ratio of new contacts to completed sales

- Number of miles on company vehicles compared to the number of sales/service calls completed.

Metrics—Do We Measure by Miles or Inches?

There are off-the-shelf tools for nearly every kind of benchmarking which you can customize for your own use. Or, you can always make your own—especially for those things that are different for your industry or customer base. Automating the measurement process does two things for you:

Measuring has to be easy. You can easily spend more time measuring than the measurements are worth unless you have a simple, process-based tracking mechanism in place that ALWAYS works.

An automated system has a built-in objectivity that helps promote fairness and efficiency. People may feel uncomfortable if they have the perception that they are being "judged" by their boss, but seldom object to having a process measured by a tool.

Examples of tools

Customer surveys (delivered at the time of sale, or a few days after) can be done by phone, by mail, or by website or e-mail.) Information you get from your customers based on your own questions is extremely valuable, and although not every customer will take the time to fill it out, most appreciate the fact that you care about their opinion. Having a contact after the sale can also fill a number of other purposes—ensuring all outstanding issues or questions have been addressed, for example.

You may need to use time and date entries on forms in your business processes to statistically track items though your internal processes.

There are automated phone systems that will keep track of time spent on hold, and issue reports.

Training employees is vitally important but expensive. If you do not test your employees, you lose half of the value of their newly acquired knowledge. FedEx tests their employees on product knowledge twice yearly. Employees who do not pass are required to attend additional training and retest. An employee failing three tests is encouraged to move to a non-customer service position. This can have added value by giving you an opportunity to recognize high scores or excellent "academic" performance. A simple multiple-choice quiz can be given at the end of a training session, or integrated into computer based training (CBT).

Many software applications can be used to track website activity and broken links.

You might revise the increments that would be useful to measure once you have a body of data to analyze and determine how useful the comparisons are.

Goals—Where Do We Want to Be and When?

Prioritize your measurements. What are the areas that are most in need of improvement—not necessarily in numbers, but that would bring the biggest results to the bottom line with the least expenditure to implement change? Boil that concept down into a single sentence that includes a number and a date.

Examples of goals from the "actionable" metrics listed above:

- Achieve a 90% "exceptional" rating on customer surveys within 6 months (from a benchmark of 50%.)

- Increase sales of a suggestion or add-on item by 50% within 30 days (from 10%.)

- 99% of all customer service employees will achieve passing scores in product knowledge by January 31 (from no product knowledge training, assuming it's October.)

- Order to delivery time on Product X will not exceed 3 business days (from a benchmark of 8 business days.)

- Number (or percentage) of your employees that have had product-based training (and achieved satisfactory scores on a test.)

- No caller will hold longer than 2 minutes (from a benchmark of 7 minutes.)

Goals should be a stretch, but achievable. You may make a goal incremental—by breaking it up into manageable chunks—give half credit for getting halfway there, for example. Make sure that the resources to achieve the goal are available—for example—you may need to spring for product training, additional phone lines, or express delivery service of materials. Collaborate with your people on what is necessary to get that goal. As one project manager puts it: "Don't tell me it can't be done. Tell me what you NEED to get it done."

SLAs—Everyone Pulling Their Weight

You can set up internal service level agreements between teams or departments to ensure that everyone is pulling their weight to deliver on the goal.

For example, the sales staff can't be expected to meet their numbers if product is held up in manufacturing and they can't guarantee a delivery time (or worse—have missed delivery time!) An agreement, preferably written, that a product will be available within 3 working days would ensure a reliable number for the sales folks, and would create a measurable, (and rewardable) standard for manufacturing.

After going through the process of negotiating and writing SLAs, the rank and file in many companies have a new awareness of how their jobs contribute to the overall picture. The experience of synergy and being part of a larger whole adds to the motivation and creativity they bring to their jobs every day.

Incentives—What's In It For Me?

Being able to quantify a team or department's contribution to the final product gives a basis for the company to evaluate compensation. Bonuses based on contribution—to meeting the numbers that management sets has obvious value by rewarding the producers.

Always make a lot of noise about incentives. Award bonuses in public (at high-attendance meetings, for example.) Announce them in newsletters or post them on posters. This does a couple of things—incentees get more than just money, they get the recognition of their peers. Also, it focuses attention in a very material way on the metrics and people start watching their numbers when they see "what's in it for them."

Capturing Lessons Learned—Best Practices

The only thing that's certain is that you're not going to do everything perfectly the first time around. After your time period has passed for your goal, get the people involved together and review, preferably in an open-forum type session—what was done well, and what could be done differently in hindsight.

Take this information into consideration, then set the bar higher for your next goal, or turn the focus to a new one.

CONCLUSION

By benchmarking, setting goals, measuring progress, providing incentives, and capturing lessons learned to go forward, you have begun an upward spiral of continuous improvement. By constantly improving and changing your business processes and involving your entire organization, you stay flexible to market changes and ahead of the competition.

22. Marketing Strategies—The Myth of the Mousetrap

THE OPPORTUNITY

You have the perfect product or service to offer. You can supply this product or service better, faster, and cheaper than the competition. However, the old metaphor about the world beating a path to your doorstep just because you've built a better mousetrap just doesn't seem to be going according to plan. You have a website that is generating no traffic. Or your website is generating lots of traffic but no buyers.

You've spent a fortune on direct mail that ends up lining birdcages. You produced radio and TV commercials that cause people to flip channels. You feel like your advertising money is going down a black hole. In a world full of marketing phenomena that turns flavored carbonated water into a multi-billion dollar industry, why are customers still ignoring your product or service?

THE SOLUTION

You are marketing a product or service. Unless you are lucky enough to be the sole source on the planet for this product or service, (and to some extent, even if you are) your success depends on your marketing plan. Your marketing plan must include the your strategy to target your most likely potential buyers, speak to them at the right time and place, and create an opportunity for them to buy that is irresistible.

Finding Your Buyers

- What demographic group is most likely to buy your product?

- What need does it fill?

- What income does a buyer need to make in order to afford it easily?

- What professions are your buyers most likely to be engaged in?

- What common problems or complaints might they have?

- What geographical areas do they live in?

- What pastimes and other activities do these groups also share?

- What alternatives does the consumer have? What are the advantages and disadvantages of competing items?

> *"As a CIO…I should be prepared to meet (customers) wherever they want (to do business), whether it's the Microsoft Network, the Web or a telephone with voice response."*
>
> —*Jeffrey Rayport, Harvard Business School*

If you're seeking financing for a business venture, you write this all out in a business plan or marketing plan. We advise that you do the same, even if you're financing your own venture. Getting it all out on paper allows you to think it through in a linear, straighforward way. It gives you a "conversation piece" to begin discussions with your team or with knowledgeable people in your field. It gives you a point of reference to in the future to ensure you're still "on track" or to thoroughly explore reasons for changes. It also gives you a starting point for discussion with professional advertising and marketing consultants, many of whom bill by the hour. The more efficiently and completely they understand your objectives, the better, and less expensively, they can help you.

Getting Their Attention—"Creating the Need"

The old advertising paradigm is that the more senses you can involve in the advertising experience, the more effective your advertising can be. Your graphics must be clear, high-quality, and attention-getting.

If your product or service is a new one, how is a customer going to "know that he needs it?" For example, there is no physiological need for soft drinks. Medical science has proven that carbonated, sweetened drinks are not the most effective way to quench thirst, improve sports performance, or any other "need." So why are Coke® and Pepsi® multimillion dollar industries? Because those companies are very, very good at "creating the need." Advertising from Coke and Pepsi has been so effective that anyone planning a party or event, or even has a few people over to watch the ball game, will serve soft drinks, or at least has the thought occur to them.

Of course, all this sensory experience must be in keeping with the image you want to keep. You will never see an advertisement for a high-income investment company sticking fluorescent orange flyers on the windshields of parked cars, even BMWs. You will, however, see them using a bull in a china shop on the TV ads to get your attention!

The line between catchy and cheesy is a line that advertising agencies spend their time detecting and walking meticulously. It's not easy! Spend a few minutes thinking about your favorite advertisements—what did you like about them, and why?

Establishing Credibility

Being in the right place at the right time is crucial. Getting the attention of potential buyers is crucial. The pivotal factor once you have their attention and have what they want is to establish your credibility in the eyes of the buyer. Especially where they have lots of providers of this product or service to choose from. In many cases people will buy from the "most reputable" source, even if they have to pay more to do so. They want to feel secure about a number of things:

- You will be there when they have a problem.

- You have a warrantee or return policy that is better than the competition.

- You represent yourself professionally and treat customers courteously and thoughtfully.

- Your written and electronic communication is high-quality—your graphics are good, your spelling and grammar are perfect, the paper of your brochures feels and looks expensive.

- Your web site functions perfectly—no broken links or outdated information.

- You use a secure connection at least for the consummation of any transaction where money or personal information is exchanged, and you have an link to an explanation of why it is secure and how it works if guests are interested in reading it.

- You make a "people connection." This is closely tied to credibility, but it also has to do with the human need to interact, be recognized, and be respected.

Whether the transaction takes place on the Web, with printed and mailed material, or in person—you should provide the customer with a means to connect with at least one person from your company. On the web, this can be accomplished with a "people" page that shows the members of your organization with a little biographical information and possibly a picture. This should reflect the professional theme of the rest of your material (high-quality pictures, perfect spelling and grammar, etc.) but should also show a "human side" by listing hobbies and interests, kids, and even pets.

Closing the Sale

It is amazing how many times companies follow the marketing cycle flawlessly to the point of purchase, and then fall flat.

As a customer in a store, I am often annoyed after I have invested the time to make selections, evaluate prices, and decide to purchase; only to be inconvenienced by the process of doing so. Wandering aimlessly through a clothing store looking for an attended cash register, clicking around a site only to receive error messages, or waiting in an office while a car dealer talks to his manager or fills out repetitious paperwork by hand will quickly thin the patience of the most determined buyer. Parting the buyer with his or her money is something that should be done as quickly, thoughtfully, and delicately as possible. Here are some thoughts: Ensure your "closing" process is as streamlined and automated as possible. All of the following suggestions boil down to ways to show respect for the customers' privacy, the value of his time, and appreciation for him doing business with you.

- Never ask the customer for the same information more than once. Internal people and processes should pass information from one part of your system to another.

- Make sure you have easy backups for every piece of the process that could break down.

- Test the process regularly.

- If you are collecting information for other marketing purposes, ASK the customer to participate by answering a few questions about their experience, rather than making it a condition of sale.

- Send them a questionnaire a few days after their purchase, or have comment cards available.

- Never sell or lend your mailing list to anyone without first obtaining your customers' permission. If you become known as a source of "spam" or unwanted solicitations, your reputation loses bigtime.

Ensuring Encores

Maintaining relationships with buyers that have conducted a transaction with you in the past is significantly less costly than marketing to new prospects. They know how to find you, you've already established credibility, they've survived your processes and are reasonably familiar and therefore comfortable with them. Hopefully, they've already associated your name with a positive experience. How can you best leverage all that work that's already been done?

Stay in Touch

You can stay in touch with customers in welcome ways by asking for their opinions and experiences. Send a survey a few days after purchase. If someone makes a particularly helpful suggestion, send them a thank-you letter letting them know how you implemented their suggestion.

Referrals

Consider incentives for word-of-mouth referrals. For example, have a phrase like—"You get 10% off your next order when your friend buys from us." printed on your statements, invoices of other correspondence with established customers. Make sure that this discount is part of your process (see closing process) above so that references or "commissions to customers" are quickly acknowledged and transacted.

Consumable/Repeatable Products or Services

If your product or service is one that customers buy over and over again (consumable products, for example) send advertisements at the time you estimate that your customer will need a refill or new product.

Durable Goods

If your product or service is something that people should only need to purchase once in several years, consider carrying accessories or parallel products that your buyers are likely to need. Or partner with a company who sells these items. For example, manufacturers of cellular phones often partner with airtime providers to sell packages that keep customers in touch and loyal.

CONCLUSION

Staying ahead of the changing economy is getting more and more difficult to do by working harder. Adapting to changes and working smarter requires specific focus. Focusing on the core competencies of your company is the means to develop that focus. More specifically, you need to determine what core competencies are needed to meet your company's specific goals and objectives. Once this "wish list" of core competencies is developed, you need to identify gaps and overlaps, and resolve the gaps by developing or augmenting your current staff. Continued effort is needed to make sure those competencies and skills are being leveraged by everyone in your company.

23. Mergers and Acquisitions—Change Without Damage

THE OPPORTUNITY

If you're not working for a company that's merging, you either have been or will be soon, it seems. These are just a few of the mergers or negotiations that have been in the news:

- WorldCom & Sprint

- British Airways & KLM Royal Dutch Airlines

- American & Delta Airlines

- AOL & Time Warner

- BP Amoco & Atlantic Richfield

- Wells Fargo & Norwest Financial

- First Security & Zions Bancorporation

- First Security & Wells Fargo

Although most of the mergers and acquisitions that make headlines are very large companies, very small companies merge even more often. Small dot-coms are bought by larger ones that want their products or don't want the competition. Mom & Pop retail outlets are purchased (or sometimes just displaced) by chain outlets.

It's nearly impossible to be in business these days without at least considering merging, acquiring or being acquired.

THE SOLUTION

Being able to merge or acquire (or be acquired) gracefully is an art that can greatly enhance your ability to survive, and thrive, in an environment of constant change. In order to accomplish a merger with as much positive impact and as little damage as possible, you need to get legal help, communicate, and synergize.

Get Legal Help

Know exactly what to do and what not to do until the deal closes. Be sure you know what requests, reports and other information needs to be filed with the appropriate government agencies, and special agencies and groups governing your particular profession.

Communicate

Some people do better than others with change. Almost nobody deals well with uncertainty. The more information is available, the less potential damage your risk from rumors and misinformation. Concentrate your communication efforts on these areas:

Between the companies merging

- To your employees

- To your customers

- To your shareholders

- To the public

Between Companies

This depends a great deal on where you stand with one another. Mergers of equals aren't always friendly, and takeovers of tiny companies by huge ones aren't always hostile. The level of respect and communication shown to each other, especially at the highest levels of leadership, tends to set the tone for the entire endeavor, so be very careful.

Be positive about all parties concerned, especially when you have an audience. Spend as much time as possible getting to know the positive sides of the other company.

Employees

The attitudes of your employees will filter to the public, to customers, and to shareholders. They are probably the most powerful force you have, to either bring you through the merger with flying colors or to bring the company to its knees.

Be as open as you legally can. Immediately set up "collection points" for employee questions and answer them as quickly, completely and honestly as you can. Even when the answers aren't what they want to hear, getting things out quickly will eliminate the fear of the unknown, (which is often worse than fears of known specifics.)

Layoffs or reductions in force (RIFs) can often be avoided with internal placement and retraining programs. Although this may seem expensive, it is much less so than negative publicity in the markets you do business in. It also helps you keep a loyal, dedicated staff that is committed to the success and growth of the new company, because they see the benefit of having other opportunities.

If you have RIFs, handle them as respectfully as possible. Do notifications individually, in private. Offer whatever assistance you can to help them find outside employment. Your ex-employees and their families (who many also be customers and shareholders, or influential in the community) will appreciate it.

Customers

Some of your customers will see this as a negative thing, no matter how many practical benefits you can show them.

Show them anyway. Spend the time exploring the merger from the customers' shoes. What benefits might they have had with the old entity that they might lose with the new? If any products or services are being lost, be able to demonstrate what they are being replaced with.

Arm your customer service staff with the answers to customers' questions, in the form of advertisements, brochures, scripts for the call centers, and personal meetings with your important clients. Be sure they understand the benefits of the merger, and be sure they know you're as committed to them as ever.

Shareholders

Hold shareholder meetings as scheduled until the merger closes, even if you're being acquired. (This is often a legal requirement, as well as being a good idea.) Communicate the reasons for the merger or acquisition as clearly as possible. It may be a good idea to get people from the acquiring or merging company to attend as guest speakers, or to have them available for questions.

Show that they still control as much of the company as legally possible, and explain changes as they happen.

The Public

Issue press releases on any important developments and status changes. The media will hear about it anyway, and you can control the "spin" if you get it out first (rather than making the media rely on the analysts to interpret things.)

Continue customary advertisements and public relations campaigns. Don't disappear in the middle of the merger—they can sometimes drag out for months and have people wondering whatever happened to you if you step out of the spotlight for too long. One of the things you bring as a strong partner in the relationship is your customer base. Don't do anything now to compromise that.

Stay Positive

It can be easy to slip into the habit of blaming the merger for every complication that happens. People end up telling customers that statements are late because of the merger, telling suppliers that payment is delayed because of the merger, and telling other departments that internal processes are fouled up because of the merger. After hearing this for a few months, even the optimists will start wearing down.

Be honest about the extra time and effort this requires, but keep the picture of the benefits of merging out there in front of people as well. Communicate the vision of updated computer systems, larger sales territories, more capital, or whatever benefits you expect to realize.

Synergize

Don't be possessive!

Department or unit managers tend to become territorial when threatened. Give them some incentive to be cooperative and open. Give whatever assurances you can of new opportunities for those who are open to them and helpful with the process.

Opportunity for Process Improvement

This is a great time to recognize and replace processes that "have always been done that way" but are outgrown or outdated. Since systems must be redesigned anyway to accommodate a new corporate structure, now is a good time to improve them at no (or little) additional cost. Assign task forces to investigate new technology and new ways of doing things while mapping out new workflows.

Collaboration/Synergy

When you run into a problem or new situation, ask the merger partner to collaborate with you. (Where legally permitted, of course.) Getting your programmers, sales managers or accountants get together and brainstorm solutions to a common problem is a good way to get the problem solved, and to cement relationships.

Economies of Scale

Maintaining two separate empires, like maintaining two separate households, is expensive. Take advantage of opportunities wherever possible. You don't need two HR departments, for example, and having two will create confusion and rivalry. Combine departments whenever possible (functionally, geographically or both) and redeploy the other resources on a new project or effort.

CONCLUSION

Change is frightening to people, and therefore to companies. Mergers and acquisitions are agents of change, and are looked upon with a certain amount of fear and dread. Fortunately, they are also a good way to breathe new life into organizations at a time when there is much life to be had. Technology has advanced to the point where replacing or redesigning old systems can be an excellent investment. Because of advances in communication, geography means less now than it ever has. Mergers and acquisitions can be done well, if you keep an open mind, stay flexible, and stay positive.

24. Leading Generation X—Getting In Touch with the Energy

THE OPPORTUNITY

With the rise of high-tech jobs, you're finding yourself in need of bright, talented people. What you're finding, however, is that today's job seekers are nothing like anything you've ever dealt with before. They're acquiring vast repertoires of technical skills at a very young age. They expect more from their jobs than people ever have. They may state rather shocking political or religious views around the coffee-maker in the morning, or with posters in their cubies. They listen to a very strange eclectic mix of industrial rock music and nature sounds.

How does one attract, lead, manage and retain such people?

THE SOLUTION

You can leverage this workforce, and build a culture of mutual benefit by understanding who they are, respecting their influence in the work-force, and understanding what turns them off and what motivates them. It is possible to leverage not only their technical savvy but also their energy and enthusiasm to your corporate cause.

If your company is seen as progressive and forward-thinking, this group is wonderfully loyal, adaptive and inventive in helping frame and achieve corporate success.

Who are They?

"Generation X" is a nebulous term assigned to the generation of twenty to thirty year olds in our society (specifically, the culture in the United States, although most of the world has felt the effects of "Generation X.) As a population, they are more technologically savvy than any group of people has ever been. A number of them come from single-parent households or mixed family groups. They feed billion-dollar industries in entertainment, apparel, and snack food, that cater exclusively to them.

Like all young people, they tend to be a bit more extreme than their older counterparts. A company lunch in a typical high Generation X-population office might include huge amounts of caffienated beverages and bottled water. You may see an equal amount of Meat-Lover's Super Cheese Extra-Cholesterol Pizza next to Vegan Macrobiotic Take-Out in square boxes eaten with chopsticks. They seem equally at home in pinstriped suits; or unshaven in cut-offs and flip-flop sandals worn to work.

Their speech varies from MBA vocabulary verbiage, to pigeon-Java laced with slang.

They have lived their entire lives in an unprecedented time of relative peace and economic prosperity. They have grown up with computers in their homes and schools. We are just now beginning to see the effects of these advantages on human development.

What Is Their Influence on the Workforce?

These are people who grew up in a school system saturated with technology. Apple, IBM, 3COM, Netscape, Microsoft and many others have made huge contributions to public and private schools. This was not merely an altruistic gesture, these companies saturated the young, emerging markets, and hoped that their young prodigies would take the technology home with them and influence family buying decisions in getting personal computers into homes and their parents' offices. They were overwhelmingly successful.

As a result, we have a population that refuses to waste time on manual tasks, or waste time waiting on machinery when they know that there are more efficient means of getting things done. Many of these people would not be caught dead reading a book with the word "Dummies" in the title. They know their skills are light-years ahead of where their older counterparts were at their age. But many of them also feel that they've missed something. Many of them grew up with less adult input. Many of them are very independent, or depended on their peers rather than their families to fulfill their social and emotional needs.

They form strong, family-like bonds with their friends and peers; and if these happen to be co-workers, they are willing to spend long hours and make sacrifices if they will be recognized for their contributions to group success. They expect to be consulted when management decisions are being made that touch on their areas of expertise, and they want to see how their work contributes to the bottom line of the company.

This is the generation that has spearheaded much of the teamwork-oriented organizational movements. They have also been the inspiration and impetus for profit-sharing and employee ownership compensation packages.

What Turns Them Off?

This is a population that few companies can afford to alienate—as a workforce and as a consumer market.

The best way to alienate them is to take an extreme approach to leadership and management—either by micromanaging or by caving in arbitrarily.

Micromanaging

If you don't have the technical skills they do, don't try to tell them how to do things. Give them very specific boundaries or functional requirements for the product or result that needs to be produced, but don't get into the detail of how to write Java code if you don't know an applet from a bean.

Caving In

Your role as a leader or manager is to ensure that deliverables get produced, and that clients are served professionally. Generation Xers understand that without deliverables and clients, their jobs are not secure. They expect you to do your job, even when they grumble about particulars. As long as you are reasonable and fair, you will get along fine on the whole. (Which is not to say there won't be occasional storms!)

Although they may seem to have the world by the tail, they are turned off by people who cave in to every request and violate their own principles and rules, even on their behalf.

Balanced Leadership

They expect reasonable limits. They will typically have more respect for a few simple but rigidly (and universally) enforced rules that are well-publicized and understood. Rules that are seen as arbitrarily enforced, superficial, or discriminatory will probably be ignored, or complied with grudgingly and only when someone is watching. They internalize rules that make sense to them—where they can see the value in complying or the harm in not complying. Respect your companies principles and rules, do not change them without due process, or keep them without recourse.

It is also important to make consequences relevant to the situation. For example—you have a programmer with excellent skills, but who routinely violates the dress code. Many companies ignore his behavior but keep him in a back-row cube where he's less likely to be seen; or deny him a performance bonus (although he's performing excellently.) A more specific approach would be to discuss with him the possibility of a more responsible position, but one that would require customer contact, and let him make the choice. Another would be to enforce a disciplinary process each time a violation occurs that is consistent with the company's policies.

Respect his right to dress that way, but not necessarily on company time, depending on the circumstances, existing standards, and needs of the business. Make sure you also respect your own rights to objectively apply standards. If it's time to revamp the dress code, by all means do so. But do it universally and then enforce it.

What Motivates Them?

Generally, what motivates Generation Xers are the same things that motivate the rest of us. There are a few items that seem more intense to this group, however. Being recognized for their contributions. Give them an opportunity to shine. Be sure the requirements are challenging, specific, real and realizable, and then shower them with public recognition when they meet those requirements.

Being fairly compensated for their contributions. While some companies may object to paying what they see as an exorbitant salary or bonus for a twenty-something year old; others use specific measures and offer incentives for meeting objectives regardless of age or position.

- Trust (being trusted, even with small things at first, by their managers, leaders and co-workers)

- Recognition (being consulted in their field of expertise, being visibly and publicly thanked for their contributions to group success, especially.)

- Artistic/Intellectual Freedom (being told the specifics of what needs to be produced, but not how to produce it.)

- Personal Freedom (being allowed to dress the way they like, listen to music they like, etc. within reasonable limits—ie. after 5 or while working weekends; or having "khaki Fridays" where business casual dress is acceptable. This will need to be evaluated depending on your industry, the amount of client contact, etc.)

- Food (This is actually a motivating factor for any demographic group. Notice the boost in attendance at any non-mandatory meetings where refreshments are served! Food is actually a fairly inexpensive way to provide social opportunities and show a kindness to your workforce, regardless of demographics.)

- A non-judgmental, listening ear (that doesn't agree with everything they say, but respects their right to their political, religious, and other views.)

CONCLUSION

Young people will amaze you with their energy, creativity, and innovation, given half a chance. If you don't provide that chance, your company risks high turnover, technological obsolescence, and losing touch with a very lucrative market. If you approach relationships respectfully—realizing the potential of each individual, and if you look for and cultivate the beginnings of working relationships; you have an abundance of opportunities to leverage their energy, technology, creativity, fresh ideas, enthusiasm and fascinating friendships.

25. Collaborating with Dragons—And Not Getting Barbecued!

THE OPPORTUNITY

You know who the "dragons" are. You may work for one. One might work for you. One might be your client. You might have several on your team. (Heaven forbid!)

Dragons are difficult people that you simply can't ignore.

The reason you can't ignore them is because they are powerful. That power may come from a number of sources: An exclusive or difficult to acquire skill set.

- Relationships with important clients or higher-ups.

- Knowledge of the business that would be difficult to do without.

- Position within the company

Whatever the reason for their power, the difficulty in dealing with them can be equally diverse: They are irritable or excitable.

- They react in unpredictable ways.

- Their communication skills or style is different from yours.

- They don't listen to you.

So, what do you do?

THE SOLUTION

People who are difficult to deal with are often the very same people who are best able to help or hinder your projects and ideas. If you refuse to deal with difficult people, and deal only with those who are friendly, cooperative, and share your philosophies and communication style, you may have a much more peaceful worklife, but unfortunately you will also give up a lot of opportunities to really shine—to collaborate with the best skill sets or get backing from the most insightful, powerful people.

Intensity can go both ways. The best collaborations are much more likely to come from your strongest opponent than from someone who is congenial but weak or apathetic.

Put It In Perspective

Chances are, you've been a dragon yourself at one time or another, and chances are this particular dragon isn't actually out to get you, no matter how things may seem at the moment. He's out to get what he wants, and whoever gets in the way is likely to get roasted. It's nothing personal.

Proceed With Caution

Although you need not take things personally, you should take things seriously. Dragons are to be handled with care. Reduce conversations to writing when appropriate. You can say—"I'm just going to summarize our conversation and send it to you as an e-mail so that I'm sure I understand the problem the same way you see it—please review it and let's discuss any misunderstandings."

This way, you have a written record that you can refer to later in explaining your position or your actions, or defending yourself legally if necessary.

You may want to inform the people you report to of the conflict so that they hear it from you. Always be complimentary of the person you're in conflict with, although you do need to explain the point of contention. The important thing is to make sure this DOESN'T sound like you're telling on the other person.

We gave that up in kindergarten.

Kill With Courtesy

Losing your temper, raising your voice, or especially, writing nasty memos will get you nowhere. Even people who would take your side will be embarrassed and tempted to distance themselves from your immature behavior.

If anything, be MORE courteous than normal when dealing with dragons. Make sure no one can fault you for your lack of manners.

Find the Motive

It might go against the grain to try to walk in a dragon's footsteps. The last thing you want to do is be like them, (ugh!) or see things from their point of view. Sun Tzu, in the Art of War, correctly said that knowing the enemy is one of the vital keys to victory.

If you can understand where they're coming from and what they're after, you will know when to fight and when to dodge.

Compare His Motive to Yours

It is very rare to be directly in conflict with someone else, especially when you work for the same company. Usually, you want the same thing on a larger scale, but have different perspectives of how to accomplish the same thing. You may want to improve the bottom line by reducing expenses, while he wants to improve the bottom line by launching an expensive advertising campaign.

Your motives don't diverge until it comes down to the means of accomplishing the same thing.

If you can't brainstorm with the dragon in the room (they can be very disconcerting!) do some brainstorming on your own. In the example listed, can you find a way to accomplish his motive without compromising yours? Can you reduce expenses in other ways? Can you achieve the same results as an expensive ad campaign with less money? Can you use internal creative talent and get the ad agency involved later? Can you pay them out of a different budget? Barter for services?

Propose Your Solution

When you do this, it is particularly important to speak the dragon's language. (This is another instance where knowing your opponent well comes in handy, since most of us don't speak fluent Dragon.) If he's a visual communicator, draw on a whiteboard or use an animated presentation. If he likes things printed in black and white, prepare a formal document. If he's informal, meet him for coffee and talk.

Don't expect an answer at the same sitting. There may be trust issues, conflict residue, and other barriers to agreement. Plan another meeting in a couple of days after the dragon's had the opportunity to think it over calmly and check out the details. And don't be insulted if he does check your math, research your sources, and so forth. He's just being diligent.

Be Flexible

If the dragon wants to alter your plan, let him, within reason. He may just need to feel like it's partly his idea.

Move On

No matter how this turns out, be a good sport about it. Don't gloat about your dragon—taming exploits. If the dragon gets wind of it, you're toast. At best, you'll ruin any chance of future collaborations if you make him feel like he's been manipulated.

CONCLUSION

It takes a lot of energy to get powerful and difficult people on your side and keep them there. There are times when the best you can do is to avoid direct confrontation and understand one another better, but there are also times when the alternative point of view forces you to work harder, think more creatively, and then find the best in yourself, your ideas and your projects. Dragons can be wonderful allies.

26. Etiquette for Recruiting New Employees

THE OPPORTUNITY

You have an opening in your company and you need to find the best possible candidate, and fast. Whether or not you have a Human Resources department, a lot of the work and decision-making is going to fall to you, the manager, to ensure that you accomplish that goal in the best possible way. After all, you're going to have to live with the results of your search!

THE SOLUTION

Following is an outline of the process with some discussion of how to do it well, including:

- Posting or Advertising

- Correspondence with Candidates

- Negotiating Terms

- Closing the Agreement

- Starting Out a New Employee

Although you may be short-handed and in a hurry to fill the position, it's worth the time to get it right.

Posting or Advertising

Even if you're going through a Human Resources department that has a file of procedures and templates for advertising or posting the position, there is usually quite a bit of leeway in how you go about doing this.

So many postings or advertisements for jobs really have very little to do with what the company is actually looking for! Many companies will overstate the requirements in hopes of getting the best possible candidate, but this may 1) limit the number of responses you receive and 2) discourage some candidates that would be ideally suited for the job but feel it ethically inappropriate to apply if they don't fulfill the letter of the requirements. Other companies use very generic job descriptions that are not very informative about the actual requirements or conditions of the job. This will cause you to receive a large number of applications from people who are nowhere near what you're looking for.

You will want to ensure that you have the best chance of getting the right candidate by being as specific and detailed as you can in the posting you generate, and placing it where it will be seen by the most appropriate candidates.

Also include specific instructions about how you want people to apply—decide whether you want applications only, or want them accompanied by résumés, salary histories, personal references, transcripts or other copies of credentials; and also indicate whether you want paper copies or want them submitted electronically.

Some companies do themselves an injustice with their electronic means of sorting résumés by using software to search for specific words or terms. Many qualified candidates may simply be using the wrong terms to describe their experience and qualifications. It is worth spending some time going through applications "by hand."

Correspondence with Candidates

Once someone has responded to your ad or posting, you have an ethical responsibility to respond to them in an appropriate manner.

In our current economy, most HR departments—and some senior managers receive résumés by the thousands each day. Some applications are solicited, while some are not.

Many companies have websites where prospective employees can post résumés, sometimes for specific jobs, other times in the event positions become available. In fact some progressive firms hire ONLY through the Internet.

These sites allow managers or HR representatives to do key word searches for specific skill levels. This is all well and good. However, a high percentage of these sites as well as HR departments and senior managers do not respond appropriately (if at all) to solicitations for résumé.

In the ever-changing world in which we live, one can never predict who is going to work for whom. (Or be a client of whom!) More and more people are willing to change jobs for increased responsibility, pay and just to be treated decently. In fact, more people are willing to uproot their families and relocate in order to find a job where there are decent people that are willing to appreciate a hard working person and say thanks for a job well done.

Companies develop reputations based on the initial presentation to prospective employees. This reputation can spread quite rapidly via the Internet chat rooms, email and personal networks. Through these three venues (and others), a reputation (both good and bad) can spread rapidly around the globe.

The initial representation of a firm to a prospective employee aside from whatever marketing information he or she is aware of, probably begins with the corporate web site. This is followed by the ease of providing a resume to a solicitation. The most telling and potentially most damaging to a firm is its response to a prospective employees resume submittal.

There are still many reputable firms that use the Internet for résumé solicitations, yet when a résumé has been submitted, fail to respond or respond in a miserable fashion. Who has not submitted a résumé to website of a firm and received NO response? It is as though the résumé has fallen into a 'black hole.' to use an astrophysics term. Questions then abound. Did it really get submitted? Did the connection fail? Do I need to resubmit? Do I have the requirements for this opportunity? Did the company already fill the position?

Following are some samples of responses to résumé submissions we have received from various subscribers (in no particular order):

- Thank you for your interest in (Company Name). Your résumé will be reviewed against our current open positions. If there is further interest we will contact you to schedule a phone or on-site interview.

- What response? (A large number of our participants though that their résumé had gone into a "black hole," as there was no acknowledgement or response at all.

- One subscriber actually received a letter in the mail! What a concept! It reads in part…(firm name) would like to thank you for submitting a résumé for the (position.) Although we found your résumé to be impressive we have found a candidate that best matches our needs at this time. We appreciate your interest in (position name) and offer you continued success in your job search.

- Thank you for applying for the position of (Position Description.) We have received your application and are currently reviewing your experience and qualifications.

- We're flattered! Thank you for submitting your résumé to (company website name.) If you are selected for an interview or if further information is needed, a recruiter will contact you. Otherwise, we will keep your résumé in our database and will contact you if an appropriate position becomes available.

- Thank you for your interest in (Company Name!) To apply for (position name) position, just stop by any one of our offices and complete an Application for Employment. We have an assessment screening that all applicants must take. The assessment screening takes about 1 hour to complete. The assessment can be done at the same time as the application, or you can make a return visit for this portion of the application process.

If you have additional questions, please feel free to contact me.

Hr Representative
Company name
Human Resources Recruiting
Street Address
Name of City, State, Zip code
Phone #
Fax #

These run the gamut from nothing to super sweet to providing contact information. Which would you prefer to receive?

Corporations should take a look at how the respond (or don't) to prospective employees. It doesn't take much to complete the picture and begin or continue to spread an outstanding reputation!

Negotiating Terms

You've found an ideal candidate, and want to go the next step.

Presumably, there is a set of terms on either side of this equation, including

From the company—

- Financial compensation, including
  - Salary
  - Bonuses
  - Retirement plan, etc.
  - Profit sharing or other plans
- Benefits, including
  - Health benefits
  - Vacation/time off
  - Any other benefits
- Office/equipment, etc.
  - Car/ car expenses
- Education plan
  - Academic
  - Professional
- Career path

- Etc.

From the candidate

- Expectations of performance

- Hours/Availability

Some of these will be non-negotiable, depending on your company's policies and capabilities. Others will be on the negotiating table. Although most people spend the most time (and energy!) negotiating the financial side of this equation, it is important to have clear communication about the other items on this list. Being flexible about some of these items may give you some opportunities to work with candidates that would otherwise be outside of the salary range. If a candidate's salary requirements are out of reach, for example, you may be able to offer some financial or non-financial remuneration that would make up the difference in that person's requirements. Being able to work at home, for example, or being able to accommodate an educational goal might make the difference.

The candidate may want to have some time to discuss with his family and/or other prospective employers.

It is reasonable to expect a certain amount of "playing one against the other" by the candidate—if he has another offer, he may bring that information into the conversation. This might be a legitimate negotiation on his part, or it might be a bluff. Either way, if you stick to your principles and the company's policies, the bluff will be to the candidate's detriment if it doesn't meet your requirements.

Have a detailed explanation of expected performance and objectives, and include an appropriate checkpoint about 90 days into the transition to ensure that the company and the employee are both meeting each other's expectations. Some companies call this a "trial" or "probation" period and include a legal clause indicating that the person could be terminated at this point if things are not working out. They may include a raise or bonus if things are going well.

Read *Getting to Yes* by Roger Fisher, William L. Ury, Bruce M. Patton for an excellent discussion on negotiations of all types.

Once this is all agreed to, be sure to reduce the conversation to writing and have it signed by both parties. Consult your legal counsel to get a form for this that is legal in your area.

Setting up a New Employee

There are many considerations to bring an employee "on board" in a way that is most likely to make him or her successful.

Many companies assign a "buddy" to help the employee through the transition. It's important to have someone to introduce him around, answer questions, and help acquire the appropriate equipment, office space, software, and so forth.

If an employee is relocating to your city, some companies even extend a service to help spouses and families locate housing, shopping, schools, and so forth. This can save a lot of time and frustration on the employee's part and build goodwill.

CONCLUSION

Recruiting and training a new employee is a considerable expense. Although it may seem time-consuming and expensive to follow these steps and it may be tempting to cut corners, making an error in the process makes it even more costly—since you could end up with the wrong person in the position, (and go through all of this again, and add the expense and trauma of a termination!)

The average employee takes at least four to six months before they transition from being an expense to being an asset. The better job the company does of "transitioning in" a new employee, the shorter that time period will be. And the more successful your company will be in meeting its objectives with the right people.

Afterword

Each of us is on a journey. It is up to each of us to make the best of this journey. This book provides a framework to help make the necessary choices while building corporate and business relationship with customers, clients, workers and co-workers with the focus on enjoying the "journey." After all, we spend at least half of our waking hours working. This daily journey joins with longer journeys accounting for assignments, projects, and jobs we've held, careers we've pursued and finally the very fabric of the lives we can look back on.

Life is too short to waste time and energy hating your job, resenting the time you spend at it, and struggling against the people you work with or the organization you work within. Hopefully, you've gained some insights on how to turn that time and energy toward aligning your mission and goals with those of your team and your company, and toward enjoying your job.

As an illustration, consider a vacation where you must travel by automobile from Los Angeles to San Francisco. Assume all highways are impassible except for the Coast Highway. No matter how much you "push" yourself and your car, the amount of time saved by speeding and cutting corners will be only minutes. But if you slow down, enjoy the sights and scenery, and stop at one or two of the fruit stands along the way, you will arrive at most an hour or two later, but much more refreshed. You will have enjoyed the journey as well as the destination.

There is a passage that always comes to my mind whenever I get into a car or airplane or on a motorcycle for a long journey. It speaks to the process of aligning yourself with the other forces in the world, working with them rather than against them, finding allies, and discovering outcomes that are more and better than you could have imagined:

> Until one is committed there is hesitancy,
> the chance to draw back, always ineffectiveness.
>
> Concerning all acts of initiative (and creation),
> there is one elementary truth,
> the ignorance of which kills countless ideas and splendid plans:
> that the moment one definitely commits oneself,
> then Providence moves too.
>
> All sorts of things occur to help one that would never otherwise have occurred.
>
> A whole stream of events issues from the decision,
> raising in one's favour all manner of unforeseen incidents and meetings and material assistance,
> which no man could have dreamt would have come his way.

I have learned a deep respect for one of Goethe's couplets:

"Whatever you can do, or dream you can, begin it.
Boldness has genius, power, and magic in it."

—W. H. Murray
From the Scottish Himalayan Expedition

Best wishes on all of your journeys!

About Ravenwerks

Ravenwerks is a company committed to your personal and organizational success. We provide tools, information, inspiration and assistance to help you find opportunities to succeed and make the most of them.

We believe in looking at ordinary business situations from an extraordinary point of view. We believe that nearly any problem can be resolved (or at least substantially improved) with the infusion of positive communication.

ABOUT THE ONLINE COMMUNITY

Our online community consists of a web site and newsletter that serves a wide range of businesspeople from all walks of life—from students to CEOs in large companies and small.

The online community is a means for this diverse, inclusive group of people to "get together" for mutual assistance and support.

The Web Site

The web site, **www.ravenwerks.com**, consists of articles organized into the topics of Global Business, Leadership, Teamwork, Best Practices, Marketing, Customer Service and Technology. The web site receives approximately 1000 visitors per day from over 100 countries. The web site is also the gateway to our other services, including the newsletter, information about our books, and contact information to reach us. The web site has won numerous Accolades & Awards from our readers.

The Newsletter

The newsletter is published monthly to subscribers who have requested to receive it. It is e-mailed free of charge, and contains a question and answer section (readers submit questions or business problems, and readers respond to them) an essay, and news and information about Ravenwerks recent activity, events, and new articles.

ABOUT THE SERVICES

We provide services such as speaking engagements on topics of leadership, teamwork, and motivation. We also offer facilitated workshops on teambuilding, project kickoffs and wrap-ups, conflict resolution, and other topics. Contact us with your specific needs and we'll collaborate on an appropriate session and agenda to meet your objectives.

ABOUT THE RAVEN

Many people have asked us "what does Ravenwerks mean?"

Well, we can only reply that this is not the Edgar Allen Poe "Nevermore" variety of Raven, in fact it's quite the opposite.

Hiking or mountain biking in Arches National Park in southern Utah, you'll see ravens as a stark contrast to the red rocks and blue sky and occasional puffy white cloud. The ravens are black, but iridescent—they display all colors, depending on how the sun hits them. They also soar high above the breathtaking scenery and take it all in. You know they're seeing the landscape from a very different point of view than we earthbound creatures.

Philosophically, we do the same—look at situations from a different angle to see all the colors and possibilities in the situation, and to view the business landscape from a very different perspective.

Other Books From Ravenwerks

- Taming the Dragons—50 Essays from the Business World published 2001

- Coming Soon—A Traveler's Guide to the Corporate World—Questions and Answers

ABOUT TAMING THE DRAGONS—50 ESSAYS FROM THE BUSINESS WORLD

How will YOU succeed in today's tough environment?

You're dealing with budget cuts, mergers and acquisitions. Your company (or the one down the street) has just announced layoffs. Those still employed are facing stiffer workloads and are filing weekly reports on their activities to prove their worth.

A good manager in the post-Internet boom corporate climate has to be shrewd, competitive, observant, and tough as nails. The paradox is that at the same time he or she is expected to be ultimately ethical, compassionate, likeable and respectable. How is that possible?

Taming the Dragons presents 50 exceptional solutions for all-too-common business situations, problems and opportunities you'll recognize from your workplace.

Taming the Dragons is an:

- Excellent addition to your business library

- Great source of information & inspiration

- Perfect gift for boss, co-worker or employee

- Great conversation-starter for discussions with partners & vendors

The strongest impression that I am left with is that the issues discussed and points made were connected with the "real world" or organizations and business. And that is an important achievement. Too many books and articles written these days seem to be talking about some non-existent world where there is no "nitty-gritty" or "hurly—burly." And in a very large measure, the nitty-gritty and hurly-burly is what the business world is made of. Not many rational, linear, orderly events or experiences.

Joseph C. Bentley

Professor of Management

University of Utah

Reviews from the Barnes & Noble web site:

Average Rating: 5 stars

A reviewer, Professional educator / mentor, 5 stars

A marvelously creative presentation on the lost art of 'people skills.'

Taming The Dragons—A long overdue publication reflecting information that should be at the very least taught in B-School. These essays reflect an underlying philosophy that should be ingrained from birth. It should not only be mandatory reading for all managers but should be taught at the three major levels of education in this country (US)—that is—college (undergrad and graduate levels) and as ongoing professional education in all walks of life. I agree with a previous review that most of these principles apply not only to business, but to our every day life. And with that thought, maybe these principles should be taught in high school as well...

A reviewer, Senior IT Executive, 5 stars

Having read all of the 'right stuff' here is what you NEED!

Taming The Dragons is a must read for all managers as well as any person that deals with other people throughout their lives. These principles apply not only to business, but to people interactions in every day life. I have already used several of these principles! They are easy to understand and implement. Its about time to read something without the 'fluff' that is actually usable! Taming the Dragons is on par with the One Minute Manager and Who Moved my Cheese.

A reviewer, an IT manager who reads a LOT, 5 stars

Great resource for managers

Unlike many other business books in which you wade through a lot of theory with little or no substance you can actually use, this book offers very practical ideas you can apply immediately. Enjoyable reading style.

About the Authors

Paula Gamonal and John Williams have worked on separate and collaborative projects to improve business environments. They have worked on developing project management strategies and systems, and communication strategies and systems. They both enjoy building and facilitating high-performance teams, and enjoy traveling (especially motorcycle touring) and photography. They are co-hosts of the Ravenwerks online community at **http://www.ravenwerks.com**

Paula has a B.A. in Mass Communications from the University of Utah and a black belt in the martial art of Tae Kwon Do.

John has a B.A. in Business from Golden Gate University and an M.B.A. from the University of Utah in International Business.

0-595-65465-7

CPSIA information can be obtained
at www.ICGtesting.com
Printed in the USA
LVOW12*2335171017

552830LV00005B/28/P

CONSULATE OF THE SEA
AND RELATED DOCUMENTS

CONSULATE
OF THE SEA
AND RELATED
DOCUMENTS

Stanley S. Jados

The University of Alabama Press
University, Alabama

PREFACE

Catalonia, birthplace of *The Consulate of the Sea*, has undergone many religious, governmental, racial, and geographic changes in its long and colorful history. It is a coastal territory in northeast Spain, stretching from the Pyrenees at the French border southward along the Mediterranean. In 801, it was conquered by Charlemagne (785-811) and established as the Spanish Mark.[1] The County of Barcelona was constituted in 817 under the Frankish crown, and the Counts of Barcelona became the chief lords of this region in the ninth century. In 1137, the County of Barcelona was united with the Kingdom of Aragon through the marriage of Count Raymond Berengar and Petronella of Aragon.

The Christian *Reconquista* of Spain gained strength in the eleventh century with the decline of the Caliphate of Cordova. Christian military campaigns aided by the Knights Templar and Hospitalers deprived the Muslims of much Iberian territory but the struggle continued until the end of the fifteenth century before the last Islamic state on the peninsula was conquered. The reconquered territories were added to Castile and Aragon to form the Christian kingdom of Spain.

In spite of their absorption by the Spanish kingdom, Catalonians retained their own system of law, their language, their legislative assembly, and especially, their regional pride and individualistic disposition. Catalonia had also experienced popish control due to the excommunication of Alfonso IX of Leon (1188-1230), who was determined to marry, within the prohibited degree of relationship, Berengaria of Castile. He was supported in this endeavor by King Sancho VII of Navarre (1150-1194). To regain the pope's good will, Alfonso and Sancho undertook a

---

1. Mark or March, a term of Germanic origin given to newly conquered territory governed by a margrave or marquis of extraordinary military power. Such colonies became the centers of colonization and Germanization under Charlemagne.

v

crusade against the Muslims that resulted in a great victory for the Christian forces at Navas de Tolosa in July 1212. Pedro II of Aragon (1194-1213) was crowned in Rome by Pope Innocent III (1198-1216).

After the union of the crowns of Castile and Aragon in 1475, Catalonian individualism asserted itself in many revolts against the Castilian kings. These revolts resulted from the harsh treatment suffered by the Catalans and infringements of their autonomy, but eventually they were totally assimilated politically, although never culturally, into the Spanish kingdom.

It was primarily Catalonian merchants and adventurers, such as the mercenary Roger de Flor, the infamous scourge of the Italians and Greeks, who were responsible for the expansion of the House of Aragon up to the fifteenth century. Catalonian coastal cities had been famous trading centers since the Phoenician era and in the Middle Ages presented serious commercial competition to Venice and Genoa.

In the Middle Ages Spanish culture, to a large degree, was conditioned by exterior influences. Her language, customs, architecture, social and political orientation are all indicative of foreign invasions and domination. Old French, one of the Romance tongues, was the language of the Catalonian intelligentsia, as evidenced by manuscripts, poetry, and songs that have survived to the present day. Provencal was the Romance language of southwest France, and the one that most influenced the development of Catalan, the earliest Spanish vernacular used in government documents in the reign of Ferdinand III, king of Leon and Castile (1217-1252). In time, Catalan was replaced by Castilian while the Provencal dialect gained the support of William IX, Duke of Aquitaine (1080-1127) as well as that of his descendants, Eleanor of Aquitaine, and her son, King Richard I (1189-1199) of England, all patrons of balladists and writers in that tongue.

The Albigensian Crusade (1209-1229)[2] and the introduction of the Inquisition drove many intellectuals from southern France into Italy and Spain, further entrenching this language. Thus, the Iberian peninsula up to the fifteenth century was the home of many languages and dialects. In each of these dialects the influence of Latin is immediately evident. Therefore it was proper that *The Consulate of the Sea* be published in a dialect that all literate persons could read and understand, bearing in mind that every educated person in the territories of Catalonia as well as elsewhere in Europe would have reference to this compilation. It made little difference

---

2. The Albigensian Crusade (Catharist) was a reaction of the lower classes against clerical corruption but was soon espoused by the nobility who saw a chance to appropriate Church lands.

whether one was privately tutored or attended Church-controlled schools (for there were no others) staffed by clergy. Latin was the required language, as it was the key that unlocked all the mysteries of any Romance dialect.

Commercial intercourse between many nationalities and races can be easily traced to Hamilcar Barca, the Carthaginian, who founded commercial colonies in Spain following the First Punic War (268-241 B.C.). His illustrious son, Hannibal, followed his father's policies in commerce. After the Second Punic War (218-202 B.C.), Spain became a Roman province. The struggle for control of Spain by the Visigoths, Vandals, and the Byzantine Emperor Justinian I (518-556) and the conquest of the peninsula by the Mohammedans in 711, are all part of that nation's colorful history. Each of these struggles resulted in drastic curtailment of trade. The inauguration of the Crusades in the eleventh century provided the necessary stimulus for a revival of trade in these regions.

Christian control of the Levantine ports (Syria, Egypt, Lebanon, Turkey, etc.) and the Mediterranean islands provided an unobstructed avenue of commerce to the East. Venice, Genoa, and Pisa began to reap fantastic profits from this trade. Even the northern pirates of Wisby, who had ravished shipping in the Baltic and North Seas, turned to legitimate trade because it proved more profitable and less hazardous. The Catalonians with much prestige in trading from the earliest period of history were quick to grasp the opportunity. It was not long before Barcelona once again became one of the richest trading centers in Europe.

By the early twelfth century trade had spread to southern France. Merchants from Spain crossed the Pyrenean passes into France and continued on to the Flemish coast and German territories. The meeting of merchants on the broad plains of Champagne to trade their merchandise became an annual affair eagerly awaited in all parts of the commercial world. On the seas the merchants were exposed to pirates and privateers, to shipwreck and death. Meager knowledge of navigation, lack of proper navigational instruments, the nonexistence of lighthouses and beacon lights, dependence upon favorable winds, and the inability of vessels to withstand severe storms often ended in aimless sailing until the depletion of water and food resulted in the death of all aboard. If shipwrecked on foreign shores, custom permitted the local inhabitants to keep all salvaged cargo including the vessel. If driven by storms toward an unfriendly or enemy territory, they were often enslaved or put to death, if it was inconvenient to collect ransom for their release. The development of a convoy system provided some degree of safety but increased the cost of transportation of merchandise, due to the necessity of hiring armed naval units.

Overland travel was equally hazardous. Trade routes were

usually controlled by brigands or mercenaries in the service
of some local lord who preyed on caravans. For better protection merchants generally traveled in large caravans accompanied by an armed escort. There were practically no improved
roads, hence almost all merchandise had to be carried by pack
animals. Bridges across the many rivers that had to be crossed
were either nonexistent or in a poor state of repair; nevertheless, heavy tolls were levied on the merchants by the local
rulers who owned these bridges. In fact, many of these bridges
were mere footpaths unable to support the heavy pack animals.
In such cases, caravans were ferried across at even greater
expense.

Rainy and cold seasons were unsuitable for travel. There
were no inns or way stations where the merchants, their retainers, and their animals could find shelter and food. Commercial fairs, which were first organized in the twelfth century,
were usually held in large commercial cities where the merchants found some protection from the petty provincial despots.
A round-trip journey required many months to complete, barring
accidents and delays. Many caravans never returned from a
trip, their cargo stolen, and their retainers killed, sold into slavery, or held for ransom. The introduction of the "peace
of the fair" by kings, bishops, and other nobles in territories under their control, provided complete protection for the
merchants while they were attending the fair and also protection while traveling to and from the fair. This protection
was accomplished by a pass issued by a powerful king or lord
who threatened reprisals on any people who would dare to molest
the merchants.

Each commercial city had its own laws and customs, its own
system of justice. Any merchant who was not a resident of the
city in which he carried on his trade was regarded as a foreigner. For protection the merchants needed a reliable code
of general laws and impartial courts. In time the various customs and statutes were written down for all to observe and
obey. Because the cities profited greatly from such commerce,
the local governments began to enforce these ordinances. A
court system presided over by the "lord of the fair" was established to cope with any trade or behavioral violations by
the merchants. It was a merchants' court with jurisdiction to
control prices, quality of goods, and provide protection for
the merchant and his property. Generally, these courts were
called *pied poudre* courts, named after the dusty footed merchants who frequented them. These informal courts met in session at any time of the day when the need arose to settle some
dispute. The laws or ordinances that these judicial bodies
enforced were not promulgated by kings or other rulers, but
were merely customary laws of the merchant class.

In time this body of merchant law gained recognition and

was being enforced in all the ports and trading centers of Europe. It remained largely unwritten but differed very little between countries. Commercial activity created many new coastal cities and reestablished old trading centers. Importation of many new types of merchandise created new markets and began to break down the manor economy of many areas. As more goods arrived, merchants no longer depended on seasonal trade but conducted business daily in permanent establishments. Soon the economy of many states became totally dependent upon foreign trade. Commercial intercourse between East and West brought goods from many distant lands, primarily luxury merchandise. These in turn helped to drain off gold from Europe, adding a new problem to the emerging national economies. The coastal cities of the Mediterranean and the Adriatic became ideal avenues of commercial exchange between Europe, Africa, and Asia.

Until almost the end of the fifteenth century, when new territorial discoveries made additional routes possible, trade from the East to Europe was carried on mainly over one of the three well-established paths of commerce. The first or most northerly stretched directly westward from China through the Gobi Desert, linking such great trading centers as Samarkand and Bokhara to the Caspian Sea region, from whence one branch led to the southwest through Asia Minor and Syria to the Black Sea and the Mediterranean; the second branch went north around the Caspian and reached the Black Sea; the third branch ran northward into Russia as far as Novgorod and beyond. The second route was the southernmost and mainly a water route. It started from the rich Malabar coast of India, crossed the Indian Ocean, and continued through the Red Sea to its northern end. There the goods were unloaded and carried by caravan to Cairo, Alexandria, and other smaller trade centers in that immediate area. The third route lay somewhat to the north. It also originated from Malabar, passed through the Persian Gulf from where the goods were carried overland to the Black Sea or to the Mediterranean. Marseilles on the Mediterranean and Bordeaux on the Atlantic were often distribution centers for goods bound to other port cities as well as all major inland cities in France, Germany, and even Slavic areas. Similarly, Barcelona, Venice, Pisa, Naples and other coastal cities served as distribution points for other areas. There were, of course, many other less well-established routes that served practically all parts of the known world.

There were of course many other sea and land routes that reached to practically all parts of the known world. Dangerous sea routes were protected by powerful royal navies making shipping relatively safe, especially after Arab sea power was broken.[3]

---

3. I refer to the Arab power prior to the Crusades. The emergence of Seljuk Turks in the 11th century and the Ottoman

Although most of the commercial activity was privately owned, it was generally supervised and partly controlled by the state because it contributed greatly to the national economy.

From China and India came perfumes, silks, dyes, spices, aromatics, drugs, and tapestries. From northern Europe came furs, horses, leather, hemp, tar, tallow, beeswax, amber, salt, fish, and slaves. Markets of the Near East and Arabia supplied fine woods, rugs, carpets, tapestries, exquisite cloth, jewelry, and metal products. Most of this luxury merchandise was reexported at a considerable profit, becoming the basis for new wealth. To properly handle the growing exchange of goods, which could no longer be expedited on a barter basis, coins of gold and silver were minted. One of the earliest of such coins was the bezant (byzant), which became a standard coin for the early Byzantine merchants and later for merchants of all nationalities. Soon other nations and commercial cities followed in minting their own coins. Many of the rich merchants began to act as brokers leaving the actual trading to those less prosperous.

Motivated by potential profits, merchants of every nationality ventured into overseas trade. Factoring stations and distribution centers were established by major commercial houses leading to the establishment of price controls and the development of monopolies. By the beginning of the thirteenth century in all large commercial cities there appeared a new class of people eager to share in the profits of trade. The concentration of money in commercial cities provided new opportunities for investment of surplus capital in new industries producing a variety of merchandise for new and expanding markets. New trade routes were opened, better merchandising methods were devised, and the first signs of modern capitalism appeared. The rise of nationalistic feeling became associated with commercialism. National pride was associated with the volume of commerce. Economic imperialism produced keen competition among nations for control of specific markets. The stronger states began to resort to the use of military power to establish economic spheres of influence, denying to weaker states the opportunity of competing for the richest markets.

The slave trade, which originally began with the sale of Christians by their Mohammedan captors and of Arabs by the

---

Turks in the 13th century ended the Arab dominance over commerce in the Mediterranean. The new rulers of former Arab territories greedy for money eagerly sold privileges and concessions guaranteeing noninterference with commercial shipping by European merchants. In addition, the establishment of powerful royal navies by European states further contributed to relatively safe shipping.

Christians, proved so profitable that it expanded into a specialty trade often chartered by local kings as an exclusive monopoly. It became nonrestrictive in that it included not only captured Christian or Arab prisoners but people of all nationalities and colors. This type of slavery continued and increased in volume well into the late seventeenth century.

Religious convictions appeared to have had no restraining influence on the merchant class. In the earlier period the papacy was occupied with other problems, such as territorial aggrandizement, heresies, crusades, internal disorder, and theological issues. When commerce developed to the level of controlling national economies, whatever position the Church might have taken on the moral and ethical aspects of commercialism was completely ignored by the merchant princes, and the papacy no longer had the military potential to enforce its dicta.

Perhaps a classic example of profit potential in this era of crass commercialism was the German House of Fugger. Johann Fugger, a weaver of Augsburg, entered into overseas trade about 1380 on a very modest scale. In less than one century his descendant, Jacob Fugger II (Jacob the Rich) (1459-1525), controlled vast real estate holdings, fleets of merchant ships, rich gold and copper mining interests, and the largest and richest banking business in Europe. He was able to lend huge sums of money to Emperor Maximilian I (1499-1519) in exchange for certain commercial favors. By using this money to bribe the Electors, Maximilian was able to assure for himself the election to the Imperial throne. In return, he ennobled the Fugger family. By establishing a novel system of communications and by having spies within the courts of European ruling families, he was, before anyone else, able to get any information he needed for his business transactions. A system of runners, mounted messengers, fast ships, signal lights on hills and mountains brought news of wars, victories and defeats, floods, shipwrecks, and other disasters or significant changes in the political and economic outlook allowing him to manipulate trade, corner the market on many commodities, furnish money to aid the favorable outcome of battles, and thus be in a position to amass wealth unmatched by any other commercial family in Europe.

Merchants of Pisa, Barcelona, Venice, Genoa, and other cities were able to get special concessions and preferential treatment in all foreign ports by payment of special fees and bribery of officials. Arabian merchants motivated by huge profits were often instrumental in helping European merchants obtain special concessions in Baghdad, Damascus, Alexandria, and other parts of the Islamic world. Special districts were set aside for the use of European merchants in most of these foreign ports and were vested with a degree of extraterritoriality. This practice led to the establishment of permanent trading posts that were free from all interference by local officials. Increase in commerce necessitated the establishment of regulatory agencies and the enactment of special legal codes. In order to achieve some degree of uniformity in the enforcement of mercantile law, it was necessary to codify these ordinances, publish and circulate them, in order that all engaged in such trade would be aware of their existence.

Probably the earliest known compilation of marine laws are the laws of Hammurabi, *The Babylonian Index,* of the eighteenth century B.C. The Phoenicians, a great seafaring people, promulgated other laws that governed sea commerce in the Mediterranean, about 2000 B.C. The Greeks, who followed in the Phoenicians' footsteps, adopted the Phoenician code adding some of their own ordinances. Greek court records of the fourth century indicate that these laws embraced litigations relating to marine loans, construction of vessels, buying and selling of vessels, lading charges, responsibility for the cargo shipped, and other contractual matters. The island of Rhodes, a commercial center, adopted many of these Phoenician statutes,later referred to erroneously as the Rhodian Laws. The Romans, who succeeded the Greeks as the Mediterranean world's commercial power, adopted, edited, and embellished these early statutes and saw to their enforcement within their empire. References to these early Phoenician laws can be found in the writings of Plautus, Cicero, Livy, Strabo, and other Roman publicists.

The rising Byzantine Empire found these Roman laws in general acceptance in most trading centers. It is claimed that the Byzantine emperor, Leo the Isaurian (714-741), issued a code of laws called in Greek, *Nomos Rodion Nautikos,* named after the Rhodian Laws. However, upon close examination, the Isaurian statutes have actually no relation to the earlier Rhodian Laws.

Thus, customs and traditions of the merchants, ordinances of commercial cities, proclamations and decrees of kings, pronouncements and papal bulls enacted over many centuries began to emerge in the medieval period as ordinances for all commercial activities, and in time gained universal acceptance and enforcement.

There existed as early as the eleventh century institutions of merchant and marine guilds that issued ordinances regulating maritime commerce. These guilds often served in an advisory capacity to the royally and locally appointed judges who had been invested with authority to arbitrate all disputes relating to marine trade. Due to the rapid expansion of commerce, additional functionaries were appointed to arbitrate the increasing number of disputes of this nature. The kings of Aragon, among others, often endowed commercial cities with special charters and privileges empowering them to create such offices with powers to regulate all commerce within their do-

main. By the end of the fourteenth century the office of the
Sea Consul was well entrenched in most Mediterranean trading
centers. Special tribunals called *Consulatus Maris*[4] were founded and authorized to arbitrate all commercial and noncommer-
cial maritime disputes.

The first such codification was published in 1010, entitled,
Customs of the City of Amalfitina, "written and proclaimed in
the year of Our Lord 1010." A second codification was published in 1063 in the city of Trani. In 1509, an edited copy
of the Ordinances of Trani of 1063 was incorporated into the
statutes of the city of Fermo. It is also known that in the
area of the Baltic and the North Seas, Schleswig, Riga, Wisby,
Hamburg, Lübeck, and other cities of the Hanseatic League
adopted some of these laws as early as the ninth century, and
that they were officially published in the thirteenth and fourteenth centuries under the auspices of the Hanseatic League,
under the title *Waterrecht,* following a conference of League
members in 1407. These compilations were usually referred to
as the Laws of Wisby. In the thirteenth century, the Laws of
Oléron were promulgated by Louis IX, (1226-1270) king of
France. The British *Black Book of The Admiralty* also dates
its beginning to the middle thirteenth century. All these
compilations contributed significantly to the later formation
of internationally acceptable maritime law. All of these attempts at codification are best exemplified by the codification, publication, and general acceptance in the fifteenth
century of the *Consulate of the Sea*. Azuni referred to the
Consulate, as a document "whose authority is above all others."[5] Perusal of modern international law will reveal its
roots are contained within provisions included in the *Consulate of the Sea*. These early ordinances relating to naval combat, marine insurance, safe passage, contraband goods, enemy
goods on neutral vessels, neutral goods on enemy vessels, and
many others are to this day part of the body of the law of the
sea.

Material contained in this manuscript consists of three
separate codifications of statutes, royal proclamations, and
ordinances of city councilmen, which regulated marine commerce
in the Mediterranean regions from the eleventh to the seventeenth centuries.

Part I, numbering forty-three articles, prescribes methods
of electing the Consuls of the Sea and Judges of Appeal, the
juridical competence of each, and procedural regulations regard-

---

4. Consular Court

5. D.A. Azuni, *Droit Maritime de l'Europe* (Paris, 1805),
   vol I, p. 392.

ing adjudication of cases brought before them. Article 43
prescribes the oath of office for attorneys of Majorca, decreed by King James I (1213-1276) of Aragon, and promulgated before the year 1275. It is not known when and by whom this
oath was imposed upon the attorneys of Barcelona and other
cities. Francis Celelles, the original codifier of these
documents, omitted Articles 44 and 45, probably because the
contents, relating to shipments bound for Alexandria, were
unintelligible.

Part II, Articles 46 through 334, contains the bylaws of
the year 1343, and refers to two main areas of marine law. The
first area, Articles 46 through 297, is concerned with the generally accepted customs of marine trade, while the second area,
Articles 298 through 334, relates to privateering, piracy,
armed naval expeditions, convoys, marine insurance, bills of
exchange and other sundry matters. In the original manuscript
at the Bibliotheque Nationale in Paris, the following inscrip-
tion appears at the end of Article 217: "The book ends
here. Glory be to Jesus Christ. Amen." Celelles changed this
sequence by noting at the end of Article 247, "Till now we
have discussed laws and ordinances relating to armed units."
At the end of Article 334, he added: "At this point ends the
book generally called the *Consulate*." There follows a series
of proclamations of these articles by several kings and city
councils dating from 1075 to 1270. Pardessus, probably the
most reliable of the many researchers who had engaged in ex-
haustive study of these documents, was of the opinion that all
of these proclamations were fabrications without any basis in
fact.[6] Part II ends with a statement that the original book
was "printed by Peter Posa, priest and printer,on July 14,
1494, at Barcelona."

Part III, lacking pagination, contains royal proclamations
of King Peter III (?) (1276-1285) of Aragon, and the Ordinances
of the City Council of Barcelona. It is actually an addendum
and does not appear to have been part of the original manuscript. It is evident that while editing the manuscript
Celelles added several ordinances and withheld many, including
the Ordinance of the Council of the City of Barcelona of 1484,
relating to marine insurance, which superseded the Ordinances
of 1435, 1436, 1458, and 1461. The 1494 edition of the *Consulate* does not contain the title page, and no explanation is
given in the body of the book for this omission. It is believed to have been lost.

The first printing of this compilation in the Catalan language, executed by Company and published at Barcelona has been

---

6. J.M. Pardessus, *Collection de lois maritimes antérieures au
   XVIII siècle* (Paris, 1828-1845), vol. V, p. 323.

lost. Many authorities in this field believe that some of the
material contained within the pages of the *Consulate* actually
existed before the year 1075, but that it had been codified
much later. Pardessus, in his manuscript *Dels bons stablimens
e costumes de la mar,* fixed the date of codification in manuscript form at 1340.[7] He may or may not have confused this with a
compilation published by an unknown publicist in 1370, in
Catalan, entitled *Consolat de Mar*. The title *Lo Libre de Consolat de Mar,* appeared for the first time in the Ordinances of
the Councilmen of Barcelona in 1435, and in printed form in
the 1494 edition. It appears to have served as a model for
the Catalan editions of 1502, 1517, 1523, and 1592. Fenwick,
in discussing the early development of maritime law wrote, "a
very important body of collections of maritime customs setting
forth the rights and duties of merchants and shipowners of
different countries in their dealings with one another...and
in particular the *Consolate del Mare* of the fourteenth century."[8] Pardessus and Azuni disagree as to the origin and
content of the famous *Consolate del Mare*.[9] Azuni ascribed it
to a compilation made at Pisa, which was formally blessed by
Pope Gregory VII (1073-1085) in 1075.[10] Pardessus, refuting
Azuni's contention, ascribed it to a collection made in Barcelona, written in a Romance dialect, under the title *Consulat
de la Mar,* and published in the fourteenth century.[11]

   In spite of the many shortcomings of the original manuscript,
Pardessus referred to it as: "...too well known and famous, not
to read the opinions of all these writers which wrote about
it..."[12] Casaregis judged it a "monumental contribution to
early private international law. ... The above was accepted as
a basis and norms for all marine contracts by all the people
of Europe engaged in commerce and deserved to be called, *Uni-
versalis Consulata*."[13] Bonnecase argued that "within these

---

7. J.M. Pardessus, *Dels bons stablimens e costumes de la mar*.
   (handwritten copy) (Paris, 1837), vol. II, p. 37 ff.

8. C.G. Fenwick *International Law* (New York, 1965), 4th ed.,
   p. 13n.

9. Pardessus, *Droit Maritime,* vol. II, p. 323.

10. Azuni, vol. I, pp. 413-439.

11. Pardessus, *Collection,* vol. V, p. 367.

12. Ibid., vol. II, p. 1

13. G. Casaregis *Consolato del Mare*. Bassano; 1788, p. 63.

articles, there are present...all contemporary marine institutions and at least [the] nucleus of these institutions."[14]
De Cussy believed that the *Consulate* was the basis for the
marine laws of France, Flanders, the Ordinances of the Hanseatic League, and the Laws of Wisby."[15] Arnold Vinnius,
often quoted by Azuni, stated that according to the foremost
Italian, French, and English writers "...the major share of
laws practiced by these nations in disputes in sea matters
has been incorporated from the Consulate."[16]

Meticulous care has been taken in translating the original
manuscript to preserve the thought, connotations, and meaning
of the language as used and understood at the time of publication of the manuscript. In the original manuscript the terms
patron, captain, master of vessel, commander, have been used
interchangeably to designate a person in command of the vessel. This often leads into confusion since a patron may have
been an able-bodied seaman who merely leased the vessel from
its owner in order to engage in trade, or he may have been
hired by the owner of the vessel to command it for a predetermined fee or a share in the profit the vessel would earn.

> Stanley S. Jados
> Des Plaines, Illinois
> August, 1974

---

14. Bonnecase, M. *Precis de Droit Maritime*. Paris: 1932,
    p. 37.

15. Cussy, de F. *Phases et causes Celebres du Droit Maritime
    des Nations*. Lipsk: 1856, vol. I, p. 10

16. Azuni, quoting Vinnius, vol. I, p. 397.

CONSULATE OF THE SEA AND RELATED DOCUMENTS

PREFACE OF CELELLES

To the glory and praise of Jesus Christ, the Most Holy Virgin Mary our Intercessor, the great saints of God, Saint Helena, Saint Michael, Saint Anthony, and Saint Clara, patrons and intercessors of sailors, and in praise of the whole Heavenly Hosts.

Because there are many ambiguities in the definitions as well as in the resolutions and decisions contained within the pages of the *Consulate Book*, I, Francis Celelles, in order to rectify these errors, and motivated solely by good intentions, having sought and profited by the advice of learned and experienced men as well as patrons of vessels, merchants, sailors, and others, have attempted after much labor and research in the original documents to make the necessary corrections as far as that was possible; and in order to achieve uniformity and sequence, I have determined to add several chapters, ordinances, and other documents related to the subject matter contained in this book.

Furthermore, because the articles contained in the book were misplaced, I prepared an index that is arranged in the following manner: First are listed all the entries relating to the election of Consuls, Judges of Appeal, Clerks, as well as the judicial procedures established for these courts. Next, information relating to the construction of vessels, outfitting and capacity of the same. Lastly, all the possible circumstances that may befall a vessel while moored or under sail. The initial entry in each category is given in large letters. It identified the topic that will be discussed, followed by citations of all the pages in the book that have reference to this topic. This procedure, which made it possible to collect all the information relative to any topic mentioned anywhere in the book, is followed by a page number and the number of the Article. This procedure makes it very easy to refer to any item within the book.

CONTENTS

PART I

PROCEDURES USED IN THE CONSULAR COURTS

PART II

THE BENEFICIAL CUSTOMS OF THE SEA

Part III

ORDINANCES RELATING TO ALL ARMED SHIPS ENGAGING IN
PRIVATEERING AND ARMED NAVAL EXPEDITIONS.

PART IV

RELATED DOCUMENTS

PART I

PROCEDURES USED IN THE CONSULATE COURTS

1-Procedure for the Annual Elections of Consuls and Judges of Appeals

Each year on the day before Christmas, elders of marine corpor- ations, senior members of the sea guilds,[1] patrons of vessels and sailors or a majority of them shall assemble at the church of Saint Thecla, and there by election and not by drawing of lots, shall elect by an unanimous or majority vote two members from among the membership of these associations, one from each association, but not from any other guild, organization, office, or profession, one Consul and one Judge of Appeals who will hear cases on appeal from the de- cision of the Consuls.

These elections shall be held by the authority vested in the Elders of the Sea Guild under the charter granted to them by His Majesty the King and his predecessors.

2-The Consular Oath of Office

On Christmas Day[2] the newly elected Consuls will be administered their oath of office in the Church of the Most Holy Virgin of the Can- dles by the Civil Judge of the City of Valencia,[3] provided that the Civil Judge had taken the oath of his office before His Majesty the King or the Governor-General, swearing that he would perform the duties of his office impartially and honestly and that he will mete out justice impartially to those of humble origin as well as those of rank and distinction, and that he will remain loyal and faithful to His Maj- esty the King.

3-Installation and the Administration of the Oath of Office to the Judge

---

1. Generally the term "senior members" is used. However, in a few instances the designation "senior sailors" appears to be preferable.
2. December 11-12 according to the Julian calendar. The holy day, Christmas, was used to emphasize the dignity of the office.
3. Assembly held in a large church to accommodate all members and to stress the solemnity of the occasion.

of Appeals.

On the day after Christmas the Consuls, accompanied by a few members of the Sea Guild, will present the newly elected judge to the Procurator of the Kingdom of Valencia or to his representative in whose presence the judge will take an oath that he will perform his duties impartially and conscientiously. Anyone who is presented to the Procurator in this manner as Judge of Appeals will be certified by the Procurator as a Judge.

Such is the custom. Although it had been stated that His Majesty the King or his Procurator would designate the person annually who would exercise the office of the judge, the Elders of the Sea Guild have exercised this privilege because His Majesty the King and his Procurator have never at any time since the inception of this privilege exercised their prerogative.[4] Therefore the procedure outlined should be followed.

4-How the Consuls Select a Clerk for Themselves and for the Judge of Appeals.

Consuls select persons who in their opinion appear to be best fitted for the performance of this office. However, if a Clerk who had served in the previous year appears to them to be satisfactory, they may retain him during their year in office. Other Consuls who will be elected later may follow this same procedure if they believe that the incumbent Clerk is fit to be continued in office.

The Judge of Appeals will adjudicate the issues with the help of the Consular Clerk after the Consular inquiry of the issues has been completed.

Consuls retain the authority to discharge the Clerk for cause and appoint another person to fill this office. The incumbent Clerk who was originally trusted with the duties of this office cannot contest the provision of this law.

5-Description of the Consular Seal

Consuls in their court will use a circular seal of office containing the Royal Coat of Arms on two sides of the shield, and on the third or bottom part of the shield there shall be a field of sea waves. Encir-

---

4. Reference here is made to the Royal Charter issued in 1284 by King Peter II of Aragon. The first Judge to hold this office was appointed in the manner prescribed. His successors were actually elected by the Sea Guild membership.

4

cling the seal there shall be a legend; *Sigillum consulatus Maris Valentiae pro domino rege.*[5]

This seal is used by the Judge for any purpose which calls for an official seal. This seal is to be kept and guarded by the Clerk of the Consular Court.

6-Qualifications and Disqualifications for Consuls and Judges

Those who are Consuls in a given year cannot succeed themselves into office until their immediate successors have vacated the office; similarly a new Judge will be appointed each year. However, the Consuls and the Judge may be reelected after an interval of one year, and one of the Consuls finishing his term of office may in the following year be elected Judge of Appeals. Similarly a judge finishing his tour of duty may be elected Consul for the following year.

7-Consuls May Designate Anyone They Wish to Finish Their Unexpired Term of Office

Both of the Consuls, or either of them, due to illness or business pressure or because of other necessity which will require that they leave the city of Valencia may appoint anyone they wish to fill their place as long as such a person is a member of the Sea Guild; the Judge of Appeals may do similarly.

8-Procedures Used by the Consuls in Pursuance of Their Official Duties and Primarily About Their Power to Issue a Subpoena

If there be deposited with the Consuls a written request that they arbitrate an issue, which lies within their jurisdiction in accordance with the customs of the sea, they will issue a written subpoena dispatched by a special messenger to the person so named. The party subpoenaed must reply to this order through the same messenger within the time limits set by the Consuls.[6]

In his reply the accused will present evidence in his favor if he is able to refute the charges; in addition he will list the counter charges if he intends to use them in the litigation brought against him.

The accused shall reply to the charges made against him and in his refutation he shall state the motives for his defense, if he has any.

---

5. "Seal of the Consul of the Sea in the dominion of the King of Valencia."
6. If delayed by the former, the messenger had to be paid an extra fee.

The accuser must repudiate these denials.

Each of the litigants will have three days to make and to deny these charges; however, a longer or shorter period of time may be decided upon by the Consuls. After the charges and the refutations have been made, and if the litigants demand, but not otherwise, although the litigation would not be illegal without this, the litigants will swear an oath[7] that they will not slander, that they will speak the truth and that they will in good faith answer the demands made and explain their motivations in the cross-examination made by one or the other of the litigants. If one of the litigants makes an objection to some issue and promises to submit evidence upon demand to substantiate his objection, he may ask for postponement. The first postponement, if granted, will be of ten days' duration. It will be possible to get four ten-day postponements provided that the party demanding them will take an oath that the fourth postponement is not demanded because of maliciousness or in order to prolong the litigation.

If it should happen that the litigants have witnesses who live far away, the trial will be delayed depending on the distance of the domicile of such witnesses as stated in the testimony of the litigants.

In each instance when a delay is granted the litigants will be ordered to be present when the trial is resumed while their witnesses testify, because these witnesses were summoned by the litigants, otherwise testimony under oath will be taken from these witnesses without the litigants' presence.

After all the postponements have been granted, the trial held, and all the witnesses examined, the Consuls as soon as possible will inform the litigants when the decision will be given. Upon the demand of the litigants a public examination of witnesses will be conducted. The litigants are not required to waive appeal at the time the decision is rendered. If an appeal is made, the sentence of the Consuls cannot be carried out.

Before or after the examination of the witnesses each litigant is allowed to present any documents or other creditable written data which can later be introduced and used as evidence.[8]

9–Creditability of Witnesses

---

7. *Sacramentum calumniae*. This oath consisted of a statement from the accuser that his accusations were bona fide and made in good faith and from the accused that his defense and counter charges were valid and made in good faith.

8. Written depositions under oath and in the presence of witnesses were acceptable by all responsible lay and ecclesiastical persons.

After the witnesses are questioned, neither of the litigants will be allowed to make any written or oral reservations and objections to the testimony given by the witnesses or to the witnesses themselves.

However, if one of the litigants should assert that the witnesses or some of them called by the other litigant are his relatives who were called by him to testify in his favor, or that they are enemies of the litigants against whom they testified, or are persons of ill repute, the Consuls and their advisors[9] ought to take these charges under consideration and judge the value of such evidence dependent upon the reputation and the rank of the witnesses.

10-Litigation Procedure When Litigants Are Summoned by a Written Subpoena.

The Consuls, after summoning the litigants to be present at the reading of the verdict, will repair together with the Clerk to the meeting of the city Merchants' Guild and there order the charges to be read and explain the course that the litigation had taken, and will ask the advice of the Elders of the Guild. Next, they will call the meeting of the Elders of the Sea Guild, order the charges read in their presence, explain the course that the litigation had taken and ask for their advice. If, however, the Consuls desire to ask the advice of the Elders of the Sea Guild first, they may do so.

If they receive the same advice from the Merchants' Guild and the Elders of the Sea Guild, they will announce their decision. If, however, the advice given to them by the Elders of the Sea Guild is in disagreement with that of the Elders of the Merchants' Guild, or if the Consuls cannot accept their reasoning in this issue, the Consuls will decide the case on the advice given them by the Elders of the Sea Guild, because disputes ought to be resolved in conformity with their opinion and not with that of the Elders of the Merchants' Guild; if this be the will of the Consuls, since they are not forced to seek advice, neither by the provisions of the charter of His Majesty the King, nor under any other provisions or circumstances. They had been merely following an ancient custom in such matters.

11- Concerning Appeals

Anyone who feels aggrieved by the verdict mentioned previously, may appeal within a ten-day period from the day the decision was

---

9. These advisors could not be called a jury within the present meaning of the word. Their prestige, however, dictated to a great degree what the verdict would be.

publicly announced. Such an appeal is presented to, and accepted by, the Judges of Appeal of the Consulate together with the transcript of the trial which had been heard by the Consuls instead and in place of the usual letter of request. In this appeal it is necessary to list all the objections relating to the trial which the appellee believes to have been illegal and improper. [10]

12-Procedures Followed When Appearing Before the Judge of Appeals

The appellant is required to present himself with the Clerk of the Consular Court before the Judge of Appeals to file an appeal and to sue for vacating of the verdict, reversal of the decision, or for the review of the consular decision; the Judge having received the transcript of the trial is obliged to set a date for the review of the case and to summon the appellee to present himself in his court on that date.

However, if the appellant does not petition for an appeal orally or in writing within the prescribed ten-day period, the decision of the Consular Court will stand and be put into effect.

13-In an Appeal Proceedings No New Evidence or Issues May Be Introduced

In an appeal neither of the litigants is permitted to introduce any new issues or attempt to prove any new charges, and the presiding judge in conformity with the well established customs, which were followed by the Consuls, related to the issues and the petition for appeal, should give a decision in such an appeal after receiving proper advice. Such are the provisions of the charter given to the Elders of the Sea by His Majesty the King.

14-Procedure and Time Limitation for Lodging an Appeal

The appellant should file an appeal immediately. If he allows thirty consecutive or non-consecutive days from the day he filed an appeal to pass without pressing the issue, he shows by this lack of interest that he has dropped the issue and that he accepts the decision of the Consuls. [11]

---

10. It was a well established custom that the judge of a lower court would submit his legal opinion and a progress report of the case to the Judge of Appeals. This was changed to include the entire transcript of the trial.
11. The non-consecutive period probably refers to the legal holidays and religious holy days which occurred within any given thirty day period.

15 Procedure for Issuing the Decision in an Appeal

The Judge of Appeals together with the Clerk will seek advice from the Elders of the Merchants' Guild as well as the Elders of the Sea Guild, as well as from others from whom advice was sought in the original hearing according to the procedure mentioned before. After receiving their advice, and if after determining that the Consular decision was impartially arrived at, he will approve it; but if he determines that it was erroneously arrived at, he will declare it null and void and will change it in conformity with the opinions received. There is no appeal from the decision of the Judge of Appeal, no matter what that may be, and no litigant can raise any objections. [12]

Such are the terms of the charter bestowed upon the aforementioned Elders by His Majesty the King.

16-Challenge of Jurisdiction

If in any issue the person subpoenaed should challenge the jurisdiction of the court, the Consuls will resolve this matter before they can undertake any other issue. If after receiving advice they decide that they do have the jurisdiction to adjudicate the case, they shall force the person subpoenaed to submit to their jurisdiction, and will proceed to resolve the issue in conformity with what has been stated before. If however, after receiving due advice they determine that they lack the jurisdictional power to resolve the matter they shall refer the matter to the proper jurisdictional authority for adjudication.

17-Concerning Judicial Decisions Issued in an Oral Summons

If some issue is brought before the Consuls orally, the Consuls will hear the accusations made by each of the litigants and the oral testimony of the witnesses; they will also become well versed with any documentary or other pertinent information, and after this is accomplished, they will proceed with the litigants to the Elders of the Merchants' Guild to seek counsel; and there each side will present its grievances; this procedure should be followed in order that the litigants would not claim that the Consuls failed to properly present to the Elders, whose advice they seek, all the accusations as they were presented to them.

The Consuls then shall give a résumé of the testimony of the witnesses and shall present documents and other data which had been given to them by the litigants. After this is done, the litigants are ex-

---

12. One could appeal directly to the King if one had well-connected friends at the Court.

cused and the Elders of the Merchants' Guild offer advice to the Consuls on the issue brought for their consideration.

Similarly, in the manner mentioned above, Consuls repair to the Elders of the Sea Guild in order to seek their advice; and after receiving it orally, they arrive at a verdict and issue their decision.

If either of the litigants demand that the decision be proclaimed in the ceremonial form and that the issue to which they were parties be reduced to a written document, this shall be done.[13]

In all cases where the accusations are made and the testimony is given orally, there are no time limits set to produce the evidence, nor are other juridical formalities followed.

18-Appeal from Oral Decisions

Anyone who feels wronged by the abovementioned oral decision may announce orally within ten days that the decision was unjust. In such instances the Judge will proceed to the Consulate and there in the presence of both litigants will ask the Consuls what motivated them and on what grounds they reached their decision. Furthermore, the Judge accompanied by both litigants will proceed to the Elders of the Merchants' Guild and the Elders of the Sea Guild in order to ask their advice in the matter under consideration. This does not mean that they seek advice from the same Elders who had given it before but from other Elders, and after receiving it they will announce their verdict which will have to be prepared in writing according to the form prescribed in the charter of His Majesty the King.

The appeal process mentioned above should be concluded within thirty days, otherwise the decision of the Consuls will become binding as mentioned before.

19-Court Costs of an Original Litigation

Consuls shall have no authority to impose any court costs upon the litigants in any case of original litigation.

20-Court Costs in an Appeal Litigation

If the Judge of Appeals upholds the decision of the Consuls, he will in his verdict order the appellant to pay the legal expenses suffered by the other litigant in such appeal process.

If he overrules the Consuls or finds that the appellant was justified

---

13. Posted on doors of public buildings after proper and repeated announcements were made by the town crier.

in filing the appeal, he will not impose any court costs against the appellant because the latter was justified in making such an appeal, nor will he impose any court costs against the appellee.

21-Proceedings Which Can Be Brought Before One Consul

If one of the two Consuls is absent or is engaged in other pursuits it is possible to bring cases or other juridical matters including investigations before a single Consul; however, all findings in any investigations made and all decisions reached must be announced jointly by both of the Consuls and not only by one of them.

22-Jurisdictional Competence of Consuls

Consuls shall have jurisdiction in all matters relating to lading charges, damages suffered by the cargo loaded aboard the vessels, wages of sailors, shareholders of vessels, sale of vessels, throwing of cargo overboard, command of vessels entrusted to patrons or sailors, indebtedness of shipowners who took out loans to equip the vessels, obligations of the merchants to shipowners, obligations of shipowners to the merchants, of all salvage found on the sea and the sea shore, outfitting of vessels, galleys, barques, and of all types of agreements which generally refer to the customs of the sea.

23-Execution of Sentence

Consuls oversee the execution of their sentences as well as those of the Judge of Appeals; all fines will be collected from the personal property, the vessels, and other possessions of the person found guilty. This shall be done in the following manner: upon the demand of the party who won the judgment the convicted party will be ordered, in a period of ten days from the date of conviction, to pay the amount awarded from the cargo and other possessions which are free of claims, or from the possessions of third parties which he designates, and whose possessions are not burdened by claims, and can be sold to satisfy the judgment; otherwise the claim will be paid from the possessions of the guilty party as designated by the party who was awarded the claim payment. [14]

24-Disposition of the Property of the Convicted Party

The City Summoner will within ten days make public all personal property of the convicted party as designated by him, his vessels, or

---

14. Inability to repay an obligation resulted in imprisonment.

any other property of whatever type listed by the convicted party. If the convicted party does not list such property, the aggrieved party will designate the possessions of the convicted party and they will be sold at a public auction to the highest bidder; and from the proceeds of the sale the damaged party will receive the sum awarded in addition to all expenses which he suffered in this litigation, after he gives a guarantee that he will return the amount awarded if another party should present an earlier and more justifiable demand to the above-mentioned award.

25-A Creditor Who Cannot Post a Guarantee Bond

If a creditor is a foreigner or if he is a citizen of the city and will testify under oath that he cannot find a bondsman or guarantor, the City Summoner will post an announcement, that the Consul will pay a specified amount for the property which belongs to a given person, to such a creditor, who under oath had testified that he could not find a guarantor; however, if anyone should claim that he has some right or claim to the auctioned property, or has money due to him for some of this property, he should report to the Consuls within thirty days, to prove the validity of his claim; otherwise the money will be paid to the creditor without further delay.

In the event that no one makes such a demand within the thirty-day period, the amount of the awarded claim will be paid by the Consuls without bond.

26-Disposition of the Real Property of the Convicted Party

In the event that the convicted person does not have any personal property, such as seagoing vessels or other watercraft, but he owns real property, the Consuls should write to the city court or to the court in whose jurisdiction such property is located, stating that they awarded a specific amount in damages to be paid from the estate of that person to another party, and that their decision was upheld by the Court of Appeals, if an appeal had been made, and because the convicted person does not have any personal property from which the Consuls could satisfy the claim awarded, they petition such court that it would in their stead and in their name carry out the judgment out of the real property of the convicted person, because the Consuls do not wish to attempt to sell the real property, this not being the customary procedure of their office.

Thus the aforementioned court acting in the capacity of an executor of the Consular decision will carry out the execution of the sentence according to the decree of the Consuls or the Judge of Appeals, and in accordance with the procedure established by the special provisions of the charter given to the city, or by following the custom of the locality where the real property is located.

27-Concerning a Patron Who Demands Payment of Lading Charges and a Merchant Who Refuses to Pay Such Charges Due to Loss or Damage of the Cargo Shipped

If a patron of an open vessel or other vessel demands from a merchant payment of lading charges for transporting his cargo, and the merchant claims he is not obligated to pay until the patron will furnish him with an itemized bill of lading which would account for the loss of certain cargo, which he claims on the basis of a list furnished him by his partner, or on the basis of any other claim that such cargo was loaded aboard the vessel, or if he claims that the cargo was damaged due to the carelessness of the patron while the patron claims that such charges are unfounded, the merchant will be forced to pay the patron of the vessel at once and without further delay lading charges for all the cargo delivered in good condition, as well as for the cargo that is waterlogged or damaged in other manner, provided that the patron will furnish to the Consuls a guarantor who will promise to completely satisfy the demands of the merchant concerning the cargo which he claims has been lost, waterlogged, or damaged by the negligence of the patron.

This type of demand for payment of lading charges need not be presented in writing under the condition that the amount of the lading charges will be attested to in a document or the merchant will admit the amount due in some other accepted manner.

28-Concerning Remuneration or Wages of Sailors

In a litigation over wages due to a sailor who is suing a patron of a vessel for his wages the charges need not be presented in writing. [15]

29-Prosecution of a Patron for the Recovery of a Loan

In a litigation over a loan based on a written promissory note given to a creditor by the patron of a vessel, the claim made need not be presented in writing, but the creditor must appear before the Con-

---

15. This was essential due to the illiteracy of the sailors. It would have been a great burden and expense to demand a written allegation from a poorly paid sailor who would have been forced to hire a notary or an attorney to prepare such a document.

sular Court and demand that he receive satisfaction on the basis of the promissory note. If the time limit on the note has expired, the Consuls will order the patron to pay the amount due to the creditor in three or four, but no longer than ten days, depending upon the amount of the loan, or to designate cargo free of liens of third parties, and paid for, which can be used to satisfy the amount of the promissory note. Otherwise the cargo designated by the creditor will be used to satisfy the lien.

After the completion of these arrangements, the creditor will be paid in the manner established above in order that the decision of the Consuls be carried out.

30-Posting of a Bond to Assure the Execution of a Verdict

If the summons demands that the defendant furnish a guarantee in the action brought against him; otherwise he must be restrained, summoned, and if he is a foreigner, he must furnish a guarantee bond at once, or it will be necessary to lock him in the city jail and keep him there for the duration of the trial. If he swears an oath that he has no means with which to pay the amount which will be assessed against him, he should be let out of the prison, unless he was imprisoned for other cause, according to the customs of the sea, pursuant to which he must be further restrained in chains until he satisfies the terms of the judgment against him.

However, if a citizen of the city is summoned, and if the Consuls are aware of the fact that he has the means which would suffice to pay the claim, they should designate the date by which he will furnish a guarantor. If the Consuls after receiving such a demand did not force the guilty party to produce a guarantor, and the person summoned fails to appear before the Consuls and cannot be found, and his possessions are not sufficient to satisfy the judgment against him, the Consuls will be forced to reimburse the aggrieved party from their own personal means to the amount adjudged.

31-Consular Jurisdiction

Marine Consuls have complete jurisdiction in all matters which must be arbitrated according to the basic laws and customs of the sea, which are described and explained in the customs of the sea. [16]

32-Regarding Priority of Claims of Creditors When a New Vessel Is

---

16. This refers to the laws and customs written within the pages of the Consulate.

Auctioned to Satisfy the Creditors

If upon the demand of a creditor, an open boat or any other type of newly constructed vessel is sold before launch and prior to its leaving the drydock or if it has undertaken any voyage, the suppliers of wood, tar, nails, pitch, sails, and other equipment which has been purchased to outfit the vessel, regardless of whether or not these suppliers have any written proof, will be entitled by law to be paid first before any other creditors who shared in building the vessel, from the sum realized from the sale of such a vessel, and they will be paid even before any of those who had extended credit to the vessel's builders and have written proof of this.

33-When the Amount Received from the Sale of a Vessel Is Insufficient to Satisfy Claims of All the Creditors

If the amount realized from the sale of the aforementioned vessel is not sufficient to pay the shipwrights and the suppliers of lumber, pitch, nails, caulking, and other supplies used in the construction of the vessel, the money should be divided among them according to the amounts due them, because creditors of this category have equal rights to the available assets and no preferential treatment can be asked for [by any of them] or given any consideration.

34-Which of the Creditors Has the Legal Priority to a Claim When a Vessel Is Sold After Completing Its First Voyage

If after completing a voyage, an open boat or any other type of vessel is sold upon the demand of the creditors, the first persons to be paid from the proceeds of this vessel's sale will be the sailors and servants aboard the vessel, because no one can have a prior and more just claim than the sailors and the service personnel to be paid from the money realized from selling such a vessel.

Next will come the creditors who had advanced money for the construction of the vessel according to the date of their loans, beginning with the earliest date.

Finally, the rest of the creditors beginning with the earliest dated loan; each creditor upon being paid will provide a guarantor who will guarantee that the sum will be returned if he is not entitled to it, or if he takes an oath that he cannot produce a guarantor, there will be a public announcement made of a thirty day payments moratorium, as has been stated previously.

In the event the vessel had already completed a voyage and there remain some obligations to be paid to the personnel and suppliers of lumber, pitch, nails, caulking, and other materials which were neces-

15

sary for the construction of the vessel, this category of creditors, if they lack written proof of the amount due them, will have no privileged claims and cannot have prior claims to those who have written proof of the amount due them.

If the equity of the patron of the vessel who had arranged these loans is insufficient to satisfy the claims of the creditors, the difference will be met by the guarantors if they had guaranteed that the patron would repay these loans; otherwise they will not be held responsible for the repayment of these loans, because the patron of the vessel was not authorized to use them as guarantors if he failed to receive from them the authority in writing that they would guarantee the loans.

35-When the Wife of a Patron Has a Prior and More Justifiable Claim

If the wife of the patron of a vessel has received a legal judgment to her share of her husband's wealth and the right to anticipate the increase of that wealth, and the husband has no other property sufficient to satisfy her economic rights, and this property has been submitted by her for liquidation, she will be able to place a claim on the proceeds from the sale of the vessel; if according to her marriage certificate it appears that she had prior claim to her husband's wealth than any creditor relative to the sale of such a vessel, then in such a case her right to share in the equity her husband had in the vessel will be judged prior and more justifiable than the claims of all her husband's other creditors. [17]

36-Procedures to be Followed by Consuls in Arbitrating Disputes

The Consuls are empowered by the charter of His Majesty the King to arbitrate all disputes brought before them immediately and in a summary manner without any publicity and without the formality of a regular judicial procedure, that is, based on the justice of the facts brought to their attention and in conformity with accepted procedures as dictated by customs and laws. [18]

37-Consular Fees are to be Paid by the Litigants

In all cases of litigation brought before them either orally or in writing, in which the Consuls will issue a decision, they will receive

---

17. She had the right to demand at least the amount she brought to her husband in the form of a dowry.
18. *Sola facti veritate attenta.*

a fee from each of the litigants amounting to one penny for each livre awarded in damages. This is to mean that if the litigation is for 100 livres in damages and the decision of the Consuls is to award 20 livres or nothing at all, they will still receive from each of the litigants one penny for every livre asked in the suit, and in that proportion for the amount awarded in any suit. [19]

38-Fees of the Judge of Appeals

The Judge of Appeals receives compensation based upon the sum awarded by the Consuls in the amount of three pennies per livre but only if the case has been brought before him in the process of appeal from the Consular decision and not under any other circumstances.

39-Suspicion of Partiality on the Part of the Consuls

If one or both of the Consuls are excluded from arbitrating an issue because they are suspected of partiality by one of the litigants party to a case before them, and these suspicions appear to have been well founded, they must select one Elder of the Sea Guild, if only one of the Consuls is excluded, but if both of the Consuls are excluded, they must select two Elders who are above reproach, from among the membership of the Sea Guild.

Together they adjudicate the issue and arrive at a decision, but do not receive a higher stipend than the aforementioned three pennies per livre awarded from each of the litigants, and they divide this fee amongst themselves.

40-Suspicion of Partiality on the Part of the Judge of Appeals

If in like manner the Judge is excluded from the case upon suspicion of partiality, he must select one member of the Sea Guild, who will be acceptable to both litigants, and with him he will adjudicate the issue under appeal and will share his stipend with him.

41-The Manner by Which Consuls and the Judge Arrive at Decisions in Accordance With the Customs of the Sea or After a Consultation With Other Parties

Consuls and the Judge of Appeals arrive at decisions by reference to the basic customs of the sea, which have been written and specifically provided for this purpose; however, in the event that these

_____

19. Livre, a French coin equal in value to a pound of silver.

written customs fail to resolve the issues, they arrive at their verdict with the advice and agreement of the Elders of the Merchants' Guild and the Sea Guild, given by a majority vote, taking into consideration the quality of persons who give counsel.

42-Demand of a Guarantee When Seizure of a Vessel Is Ordered

In all instances when the Consuls order seizure of a vessel and its cargo as a guarantee, according to the provisions of the law, if, however, the lading charges for the cargo aboard have not been paid, it will be exempted from seizure; in such cases a guarantee seizure is not generally demanded.[20]

43-Decree of King James Regarding the Oath of Office of Attorneys

We make it known, that we James,[21] by the Grace of God, King of Aragon, Majorca, and Valencia, Count of Barcelona and the City of Urgel, Proprietor of Montpelier, wish and ordain for the greater welfare of the City and Kingdom of Majorca, which we ordain for us and for our heirs forever, that all attorneys take the oath of office by repeating the following:

I, so and such, take this oath, that I shall faithfully perform the duties of an attorney-at-law, that I shall not accept any litigation which in accordance with my conscience I shall consider unjust, and that I shall not listen to, defend or encourage anyone to accept any evil undertaking or utter malicious accusations in any litigation under my direction; if, however, at the beginning, or at halfway, or at the end of any case in which I am acting as the defense attorney, the issue will appear to me to be unjust, I will inform the party whose defense I have undertaken, that I shall not use any means which are in conflict with my conscience, that I shall not enter into any agreement and that I shall proceed in such a way so as to aid my client in telling the truth.

With this statement we come to the end of the procedures used in the Consular courts.

---

20. Such an order did not exempt from seizure any cargo owned by the patron of a vessel.
21. King James (1213-1276) issued these ordinances for the Island of Majorca.

PART II

THE BENEFICIAL CUSTOMS OF THE SEA

At this point we begin with the beneficial customs of the sea.

46-Material Contained in Succeeding Articles

Herein are contained regulations and beneficial customs of marine intercourse, which the well-informed people, having journeyed throughout the world, imparted to our predecessors who wrote them down in learned volumes, all of them relating to the proper customs to be followed.[22]

In the material which follows one can learn in what way a patron of a vessel is obligated to the merchants, to sailors and passengers, and other persons aboard his vessel, and also what are the responsibilities of merchants, sailors, and passengers toward a patron of a large or a small vessel. We call a passenger any person aboard the vessel who is required to pay for his transportation in addition to any charges for his cargo.[23]

47-The Information That a Patron of a Vessel Should Make Available to His Partners When He Undertakes Construction of a Vessel

We begin. When a patron begins construction of a large or a small vessel and wishes to attract others to invest in this venture, he shall announce publicly how many shareholders he will accept, what will be

---

22. In the copy from which this was translated Articles 44 and 45 are missing. The actual text of the Consulate begins with Article 46. Between Articles 42 and 46 there is some data impossible to understand, improperly paginated, relating to shipment of cargo from Alexandria. In the original manuscript at the Bibliothèque Nationale, there are two sentences relating to this. They were numbered 44 and 45, probably by Celelles, but in the printed copy these pages are missing and have been lost.

23. A passenger was any person who had no cargo aboard. A merchant-passenger whose cargo was aboard the vessel paid no fare unless the amount of his cargo was insignificant.

the dimensions of the vessel, its capacity, its width, length, and draught.[24]

48–Concerning a Shareholder Who Refuses or Is Unable to Raise the Amount of His Subscription

If the patron of a vessel explained all these particulars to the prospective shareholders and they promised to raise the necessary amount of money, each shareholder is bound to subscribe in the amount that he had promised. If such a shareholder would not or could not fulfill his promise, the patron of such a vessel can force him to fulfill his obligation through legal means or he may borrow the amount which the latter had promised to invest in this venture.[25]

Let us assume that the latter shareholder was to invest one-sixteenth of the total price of the vessel and actually was able to invest only one-thirty-second of the whole cost of the vessel (we can also think in terms of one-tenth or one-fourth); thus if the shareholder was to raise the amount mentioned but failed to do this, the patron of the vessel may borrow the amount the former lacks in order to complete the total which he had agreed to invest.

This article has been written so that the party who undertakes to build such a vessel should not begin the project if at such time he knows that the shareholders are going to refuse to raise the promised quota.

49–When a Shareholder Dies After Making Only a Token Payment on the Amount He Promised to Invest in a Vessel

If anyone had promised another person that he would share in the cost of constructing a vessel, and after making such a promise should die before the vessel in which he promised to invest should be constructed and outfitted, neither his heirs nor any other person who has the possession of the property of the deceased person shall be obligated in any way to the patron of the vessel, to whom the deceased person had promised participation in this venture, unless the deceased had in his last will or by some other method placed this obligation upon them.

---

24. This information was generally posted on doors of various guilds.
25. The term patron is used to indicate the principal owner of the vessel, or some other person entrusted with the command of the vessel by its owner or owners. In either case it is used to designate a person who has supreme authority over the vessel in the port and on the high seas.

If, however, the deceased had made partial payments toward the amount he had promised to invest in the vessel and it should happen that this amount was sufficient to cover the whole amount of his promised participation, his share should be sold before the vessel is permitted to leave the locality in which it was constructed, regardless of the article which states that no vessel can be sold or placed on the auction block before it had completed a voyage.

This procedure is followed because a deceased person is not required to pay any attention, or follow any regulations, ordinances, or customs, unless before he died he had taken out a loan, accepted command of a vessel or had caused some injury. There is still another reason; specifically, on the day that a shareholder is dying all corporations in which he had interest are liquidated, it being known that such a shareholder will not be able to fulfill the promise by which he had pledged to invest a given sum of money.

50-When the Patron Changes the Dimensions of the Vessel Under Construction Without Consultation with the Shareholders

Let us now discuss a patron who after beginning construction of a small vessel orders that it be constructed larger in width, depth, and length and orders it built one-third or one-half larger than originally planned without any consultation with the shareholders. Let it be known that the shareholders are not obligated to anything more than was originally agreed to. Therefore, if the patron enlarges the vessel, the shareholders will have the same degree of claim to this vessel as if they had actually agreed to increase their investment for that purpose, with this exception, when the shipbuilder increases the dimensions of the vessel beyond the measurements given to him by the patron with the understanding of the shareholders.

If the patron wants to increase the size of the vessel, he should approach each of the shareholders and ask each of them to increase the amount of his investment and thus ascertain which of them agree and which disagree to the proposed changes in the size of the vessel.

Let us suppose that four of the shareholders disagree with six; since six are more than four, and nine more than eight, therefore this is done so that the disagreement of two, three, four, or five shareholders, if they constitute the minority, would not prevent the enlargement of a vessel. Thus the shareholders who would be opposed to the enlargement of the vessel in which they had promised the patron they would invest will be obliged to agree with the majority of the shareholders. All the shareholders thus must agree to this arrangement.

51-Degree of Obligation of the Shareholders When the Patron Wishes To Increase the Size of the Vessel

In conformity with what has been stated in the previous article, when the patron wishes to enlarge the vessel, he should notify all the shareholders of his decision; if they all agree he may enlarge the size of the vessel, in such cases there will be no difficulties. It was also stated that he may enlarge the vessel if the majority of shareholders agree, since a disagreement of four or five shareholders should not prevent the enlargement; it was not made known, however, what are the obligations of the shareholders who opposed this proposal and to what they are not obligated; thus disputes could arise due to this confusion.

Due to this and in order to avoid all disputes our ancestors proposed a solution which they adopted and formulated in the following manner: Even though the vessel can be enlarged without doubt by the agreement of the majority of shareholders, it is also necessary to include and consider the objection of the minority shareholders who expressed opposition, because there could be amongst them those who, finding themselves in a situation of being forced to subscribe a larger amount than they had estimated when the construction of the vessel began, would be forced to borrow money or to exchange or sell some of their property, which under many circumstances would not be profitable for them to do.

Such a procedure would be unjust, because very often a person buying a share does this on the basis of friendship with the person who is undertaking to build the vessel rather than from any expectation of profit; because of this it would be improper that such a person should suffer a loss. For the reasons stated above our ancestors who first traveled throughout the world decided and approved that such action would be inequitable.

Therefore, they stated and ordained that if a shareholder has opposed the enlargement of the vessel due to a lack of funds and had originally promised to invest one-eighth of the amount necessary to build the vessel, he will be obligated to invest only one-sixteenth of such an amount and the patron of the vessel cannot demand any more than that amount from him. This is allowed because the shareholder cannot fulfill this obligation due to the fault of the patron and not due to his own failure, since he was opposed to the enlargement of the vessel. Because of this the patron of the vessel cannot force him to increase his investment in the vessel.

In such circumstances the patron must find other shareholders who would be able to invest the amount which the original shareholders are incapable of doing. This solution is very beneficial to the patrons of the vessels because it does not completely release the aforementioned shareholders from all responsibility, and was adopted in order that it would not bankrupt the patrons of vessels; for there is no reason that someone should have more right to the wealth of his fellow being than the one to whom such wealth belongs, or to the amount of money he had pledged to invest.

Nevertheless, if the shareholders who lodged the protest constitute the minority, but are able to invest the full amount without suffering any damage, the patron of the vessel to whom they made the promise of investment will be able to force them to fulfill their promise according to the procedure established and foreseen in the previous article. It is, therefore, proper that in all circumstances the voice of the majority be decisive.

For the reasons enumerated each patron of a vessel should be very careful, when attempting to build a vessel, to proceed in such manner that no disputes will arise for any reason between him and those who agreed to purchase shares in the vessel.

The above explanation was included herein in order that this matter would be properly interpreted.

52-When the Shipwright Arbitrarily Enlarges the Vessel

If a shipwright proceeds to enlarge the size of the vessel contrary to the agreement reached with the patron, he must pay half of the cost of enlargement and will also forfeit the wages due him for the time he spent in enlarging the vessel.

In addition, the shipwright is required to furnish each of the shareholders with the specifications agreed upon with the patron of the vessel and also explain the steps in the construction of the vessel, whether the vessel is constructed poorly or soundly.

53-Mutual Obligations of a Shipwright or Contractor and the Patron

Every shipwright or contractor working for a patron in building a vessel shall work expertly and industriously and shall in no manner lower the quality of his labor. If the shipwrights and contractors are doing their work well and efficiently and are capable of building the vessel ordered, or even a larger and better vessel, the patron who engaged them and entrusted them with the work undertaken and begun by his direction cannot discharge them during the period of the construction of the vessel even if he had some misunderstanding with them. Since they are doing everything connected with the construction of the vessel well and properly, the patron cannot discharge them because of some dispute even if he could find others who would agree to construct the vessel at a lower price; while the builders cannot stop work, desert the patron, or abandon the project until they finish the job, as they are capable of completing the task and are even capable of completing a bigger and better vessel.

If the patron of the vessel would discharge them from the responsibility of finishing it, even though they are capable and proficient and have done all the work necessary in connection with the construction of the vessel conscientiously, no other contractor shall accept this job unless the patron of the vessel under construction had reached an agreement with the master shipwrights who began the construction of the vessel.

The new contractor should not accept the patron's account of this matter but receive the consent of the masters who began the construction of the vessel.

If the original contractors agree to such a proposal and relinquish the work, then and not earlier may the new masters undertake the construction and begin their work; if they should undertake the job before the original contractors quit it and give their consent for others to finish it, they would by such action indicate contempt and unfriendliness toward the shipwright who undertook the task originally and actually indicate that they are glad of the misfortune that had befallen the others. Everyone should avoid as much as possible causing any misfortune and evil, since there is enough of this as is.

In addition, the patron of a vessel should avoid at all costs being an instrument of misfortune to the masters whom he had selected himself and who by his direction will begin to work for him, and if they perform their work well and conscientiously, whatever that task may be, he should allow them to complete the undertaking.

If, however, the shipwright and his coworkers who undertook the task are not proficient and do not know how to proceed with their work, the patron of the vessel under construction may release them from their responsibility, and in their stead hire others capable of completing the undertaking. The newly engaged shipwrights capable of building the vessel will not be required to get the consent of those whom they replaced because the former were incapable of proceeding with the work and unable to complete the undertaking. Furthermore, those who claim to be shipwrights and contractors and undertake a job but are incapable of finishing it and in that manner defraud people will be forced to reimburse the party who entrusted them with the job for all the losses and damages which he suffered because of their irresponsibility.

Every shipwright and every contractor must carefully decide what kind of work he can undertake and which kind he cannot. If, as a result of a poorly completed work, the patron of the vessel would have to pay damages to the merchants or suffer other losses, the shipwrights who failed to complete the work satisfactorily will be forced to reimburse him for the damages he paid the merchants and other losses which he suffered due to their inferior workmanship.

If they are without any means to pay for such damages, they shall be imprisoned and delivered to the judicial authorities who will detain them until they refund to the patron of the vessel all the losses which he suffered due to their negligence, because their action was tantamount to an act of robbery or as if they had taken something surreptitiously from his home.

The patron of the vessel is required to give to every master shipwright working on the vessel, in addition to the wages agreed upon, one penny per day for bread and wine unless they freely agree to collect this sum every Saturday. This will depend on the disposition of the shipwrights because the patron cannot force them to accede or refuse to do this.

If a master shipwright undertakes some work for a patron without having reached an agreement as to the amount of his remuneration, the patron will have to pay him the minimum wage paid other shipwrights who are engaged in construction of vessels, depending on the time of the year and other conditions prevailing in a particular nation.

Similarly, every shipwright and contractor who is paid daily for his labor or will be paid an agreed sum for the completed work must take care to perform his work skillfully and conscientiously in order to avoid the penalties stated above.

This article was written to prevent shipwrights and other workers from doing inferior work if they knew that no penalty awaited them for this, but also to protect them from damages; this penalty was decided upon in order that each worker would make certain what kind of work he is capable of doing before undertaking it.

54-When Shipwright and His Coworkers Undertake a Job Under Contract

If a master shipwright or a contractor undertakes some work for an agreed sum of money, he shall be bound to pay all the coworkers working on the vessel which he had contracted to complete. If the shipwrights employed by him are unaware that he contracted to build this vessel for an agreed sum of money, he must inform them of the details for the following reason: having not been informed of these arrangements, they would be cheated, if their employer was a cheat or a squanderer, or had no money to pay them their wages.

If the patron of the vessel under construction did not inform the workers of these arrangements, that is, that the master shipwright had undertaken the construction at a stipulated price, and the latter refused to pay them or lacked the means of paying them their wages, the workers can force the construction of the vessel to be held up until they are paid their wages as well as all the damages, losses, and expenses which they suffered. If the patron had explained to them that the job was undertaken on a contractual basis, and they understood this, they will not be able to halt the work later on whether the contractor pays their wages or does not pay their wages, because the patron had informed them before they undertook to work that the construction was undertaken on a contractual basis.

Furthermore, if the patron had informed the masters who are about to undertake the work that he will pay them when they have completed the job, and they proceed with it upon his demand, believing what he told them, he will be required to pay them as he had promised; and if the masters fail to pay the other workers or are unable to pay them, regardless of the fact that these master craftsmen were paid the full amount they were promised or if they were not paid, the patron will have to pay those workers who have wages due them, even if he had some money coming to him in rebate from the general master shipwright who had undertaken this job. It is only proper that these workers be paid because they undertook to work upon the guarantee made to them by the patron of the vessel. If he had not made such promises to them, they would not have undertaken this work and would have looked somewhere else for a job. Let, therefore, every patron beware, whether he engages people on contractual basis or for a daily wage, because whether he wishes or not, he will be required to keep his promise.

If a master shipwright or his coworkers, who had accepted an undertaking on a contractual basis, and agreed with the patron that they will have completed the work on a certain day or in a specified time, and the two contracting parties insert a penalty clause in their contract, if the work is not completed at the agreed time, the patron has a right to demand that they pay the penalty agreed to without any opposition. If, however, they had not established any such penalty clause, the builders will nevertheless still be compelled to reimburse the patron for any losses which he suffered or will suffer due to their inability to complete the work on time, the amount of damage to be ascertained by him under oath, but only if this damage has resulted due to the carelessness and inability of the shipwrights. If the delay did not result from their carelessness and inefficiency, it would not be just that they pay any damages or even an agreed penalty since

28

they were not guilty of bad faith. Occasionally there occur interruptions in work due to the will of God or justice; for such delays no one can be held responsible and there is no reason why anyone should be punished.

If, on the other hand, the patron refuses to pay the master workmen the agreed amount and they suffer some damage or expenses because of this, the patron will become responsible to them in the same degree as they were to him. This is only just and in conformity with logic.

55-When a Shareholder of a Vessel Desires To Sell His Shares

It should also be made known that if any shareholder wishes to sell the shares which he has in a vessel, he must first notify the patron of the vessel of his intentions; the prospective purchaser of these shares must do likewise. If the patron refuses to agree to such a proposal, the new shareholder cannot take possession of these shares until the vessel has completed a voyage. This procedure is followed because the original shareholder, through maliciousness, could by this transaction cause the patron of the vessel to be removed from his position. For the same reason the shareholders cannot force a sale of the vessel, if this be contrary to the wishes of the patron of the vessel, until the vessel has completed the journey. After the journey has been completed, the vessel can be put up for sale upon the demand of the shareholders or the patron. The shareholder must under all circumstances leave the choice to the patron: whether to sell his share or buy the share of the former; this choice resides within the patron unless the vessel is placed on sale at a public auction.

This article was written because the patron devotes much labor and experience to the difficult task of undertaking construction of a vessel, which would have not come into being had he not undertaken the task.

56-Procedure Followed in Auctioning Off the Vessel When the Patron and the Shareholders Will Be the Only Bidders

It was stated and proclaimed in the last article that a vessel cannot be sold until it completes a journey. This pertains to a newly constructed vessel, as well as to a vessel bought in common with the knowledge and approval of all or the majority of the shareholders. It was also stated that every shareholder must allow the patron of the vessel priority bid in order that he be able to acquire the shareholders' interest in the vessel, or that the patron has the right to sell his share first if the vessel is not offered for sale at a public auction. Thus it should be understood that there is no logical or important reason that one or two shareholders through thoughtlessness or being blinded by their own wealth could force a public auction of a vessel, in which they have a share, if the patron is opposed to this. It is only proper that this should not be allowed to happen. Why? Because often a great majority of patrons of vessels are forced to raise a larger sum of money than they anticipated when the construction of the vessel was undertaken; in such circumstances it should be concluded that these patrons do not have any more money and do not even have a possibility of getting additional loans. There is still another reason, namely, the patron experienced much trouble, pain, and anxiety, and also much discomfort during the period of time that the vessel was under construction. It would not be just and there is no reason that due to malicious disposition of one or two shareholders or because of their misunderstanding with the patron, the shareholders could bring about a public auction of a vessel, and thus, as stated above, they could completely get rid of the patron of the vessel and cause great damage to him, so that he would be completely ruined, or at least lose the greater portion of his wealth while the shareholders would actually not increase their wealth through such course of action. Therefore it is just that neither one or two shareholders should be able to force a public auction of a vessel contrary to the wishes of the patron of the vessel, as has been reasoned above.

If, however, a vessel has completed a voyage, as was stated above and the majority or all of the shareholders wish to sell the vessel or offer it for sale, they will be within their rights to do this, and the patron of the vessel shall not oppose them unless there had been some other agreement made between them or some promise made to him. If there is no such agreement or promise, the vessel can and may be placed on sale. This means that the shareholders have the right to force the patron or demand that he be forced by the courts to a sale at public auction, since this is in agreement with law, logic, justice and custom. If, however, in any such issue there should be a difference of opinion, it should be decided by the will of the majority; for the will of the majority and not that of the minority ought to be followed. Therefore, if the majority or all of the shareholders wish to sell the vessel in opposition to the patron, the latter must agree to the sale on these conditions: that he whoever offers most will acquire the vessel.

If, however, the majority or all of the shareholders do not wish to attempt to sell the vessel, the patron of the vessel is not required to agree with the minority unless he would so choose. Above all, it should be remembered that if one, two, or three shareholders wish

30

to sell their shares to the patron, or force him to sell his shares to them, this shareholder or these shareholders should make the following declaration to the patron of the vessel: "Either you will give us such an amount for our shares or we shall give you such an amount for your shares."

The aforementioned shareholders can force the patron of a vessel to submit to this whether this agrees or disagrees with his sentiments. Actually the patron of a vessel has a right of choice, unless this has been circumvented by some prior agreements, protocols, or pledges.

Similarly, the patron of a vessel can force the shareholders to a sale of a vessel by the same means and methods as the shareholders can use to force the patron to sell the vessel.

If there is an agreement between the patron of the vessel and the shareholders to place the vessel on sale by auction, all of them are considered shareholders in common, unless there was a specific and explicit understanding between them that one of them would have a priority right to the purchase of the vessel.

Likewise, when there is an auction held, and the interested parties have reached an understanding that they will allow the bid to the one who makes it first, this priority will have to be honored. If there has been no such commitment made or a promise made that someone will be allowed a priority bid, no one will be bound to recognize a right to a prior bid by anyone else unless he wishes to do so.

This article was written for the reasons given above.

57–Selection of a Clerk, His Oath of Office, His Obligation To Faithfully Fulfill the Duties of His Office, and His Punishment for Malfeasance of His Office

The patron of a vessel may, with the approval of its shareholders, hire aboard the vessel a clerk, provided he is not related to him. [26] The patron will demand that the clerk take an oath of office in the presence of the sailors, merchants, and shareholders, if the latter are aboard the vessel, that he will be equally loyal and obedient to the merchants, patron of the vessel, sailors, passengers, as well as all other persons aboard; that he will keep the register;[27] that all the

---

26. This is the verbatim translation of the original text. Pardessus, however, translated it to mean: "The patron can hire a clerk who is related to him provided he has the approval of the shareholders to do this."

27. This cannot be referred to as the ship's log since the entries within it were limited to cargo, monetary matters, and agreements between merchants and others aboard the vessel.

entries he makes in the register will conform to truth; and that he will keep account of what is due each person under the law.

If such records are not kept by a clerk but by some other person, nothing contained within shall be accepted with any degree of authenticity. If the clerk should make any false entries in this register, his right hand shall be cut off; he will be branded on his forehead with a hot iron; and all his possessions shall be confiscated whether he or some other persons had made such false entries in the register.

58-Authority and Functions of the Clerk

The ship's clerk has the following authority: The patron of a vessel cannot without his knowledge and presence load aboard the vessel any cargo, and no sailor may unload, relocate, or release any cargo without his approval. If there should be anything lost or missing aboard the vessel, be it a chest, a bale, or other merchandise or for that matter any item whatsoever, which the clerk had entered into the register, or which had been taken aboard in his presence, he will have to pay for it. If the clerk does not have the means with which to reimburse the aggrieved party, this damage must be paid for by the owners of the vessel even if it were necessary to sell the vessel to repay the damages, setting aside, however, enough money from the proceeds of the sale to pay the wages due to the crew.

The clerk has the authority to buy and sell all sorts of items and especially chains, foodstuff, ropes, and all other marine supplies without the knowledge and approval of the patron of the vessel; however, when it is necessary to equip the vessels with sails, he must inform and get the approval of the patron of the vessel and the patron must inform and get the approval of the shareholders who are aboard the vessel, before this purchase can be made. If the shareholders should refuse his request, he may do it contrary to their will because sails are an essential part of the equipment of the vessel.

59-Security of the Ship's Register

In addition, the patron of the vessel will require that the clerk take an oath that he will not sleep ashore while the vessel is moored without taking the keys of the chest in which the register is kept; and that he will never keep the said chest unlocked, subject to the above described penalty.

60-Concerning the Rights of the Patron, the Clerk, the Shareholders, and of the Confidence That Should Be Credited to the Authenticity of Entries Made in the Register

The owners of the vessel shall reimburse the patron and the clerk for the money expended for the purchase of food and beverage aboard the vessel; in addition, they must reimburse the clerk for his footwear and for the ink, paper, and parchment which he will use. The patron of the vessel should receive at least as much as any other member of the crew who is capable of navigating the vessel. He has the right to free freight equal to the amount of his wages[28] as part of his remuneration, and the clerk will be compelled to allow him this privilege, and enter this cargo as well as the cargo carried by other members of the crew under free freight in the register. If a shareholder would also be a member of the crew, the patron shall demand a statement under oath from the helmsman regarding the wages that should be paid him and that the patron must pay him; however, if in the opinion of the patron the former should be paid more than the helmsman decided, he may pay him more.

If the wages of the clerk have not been predetermined before the voyage is undertaken, he should be paid the amount generally paid clerks and officers of the deck; if, however, the patron wishes to increase the amount, he may do so.[29]

The patron of the vessel can demand an accounting from the clerk of the vessel at any time, regardless of whether the clerk is related to him or not. The patron of a vessel cannot engage one of his relatives as a clerk without the express approval of the shareholders or merchants. If the clerk has disgraced himself by making false entries in the register or by stealing,a patron cannot engage such a clerk whether or not he is related to him.

In addition, the clerk shall make an accounting to the shareholders every time they demand it, whether he is leaving his position or is remaining in their service aboard the vessel. The clerk is required to give an accounting to each shareholder of everything which he took aboard from him as cargo under the bill of lading, and also of what he spent, sold, and bought.

The clerk may demand a deposit of money to be held in escrow equal to the amount due for lading and other expenses connected with the cargo carried for each merchant and shareholder, also for passengers and sailors, as well as all other persons required to pay freight for cargo belonging to them, for which he must be reim-

---

28. *Pakotilia:* merchandise carried by members of the crew, free of any lading charges, for speculation. The amount of free freight goods was usually equal to the amount paid in wages.
29. It is evident that this depended upon the type of vessel. See detailed data in Articles 306 and 308.

bursed.[30] All the sums expended for wages of the crew and other expenses must be entered in the ship's register. The register is more authentic than a privately kept account book because the entries in the register cannot be questioned, whereas those accounts which are privately maintained can be. Everything, however, which is entered into the register must be above reproach and shall be written in it with this provision, that when the entries are being made, the vessel is moored or that the clerk while making entries in it was on shore.[31]

61-Responsibility of the Patron of a Vessel Toward Merchants and Passengers

If you wish to learn of the responsibilities of the patron toward the merchants aboard his vessel, you will learn about them now. The patron of a vessel is required to protect and guard the merchants, passengers, and all other persons who are aboard, whether they be commoners or persons of title and rank; aid them to the best of his ability against all persons of evil intent; also protect them from pirates and privateers and all others who may want to injure them.

Furthermore, the patron of a vessel is obliged to protect and guard their cargo and their other possessions in the manner described above.

In addition, he exacts an oath from the helmsman, officers of the stern deck, shareholders, sailors, and others aboard—all those who receive any remuneration aboard the vessel—that they will act with unanimity with all their power to protect and guard the merchants and their property and all the rest who are aboard the vessel; that they will not carry malicious gossip; that they will not seek disputes and provocations; and that they will not steal from anyone among those mentioned. Finally, that they will not take anything off the vessel or bring anything aboard the vessel without the knowledge of the clerk or the helmsman, and that they will not take anything off or place anything aboard the vessel at night or during the day without the knowledge of the helmsman or the officer of the guard.

---

30. Contemporary customs demanded inclusion of charges for handling, storage, transfer, custom fees, etc., in addition to the charge for carrying the cargo.
31. Article 253 contains additional data. It points out that no agreement made aboard while the vessel was sailing was binding unless accompanied by and made with certain strictly observed provisions and circumstances.

62-An Oath Required of the Helmsman

The patron must administer an oath to the helmsman similar to the oath taken by the sailors; but, in addition, the oath will include a promise that he will truthfully answer all the questions asked by the merchants, and that he will not navigate to, arrive at, or depart from any port without their approval.

The helmsman is, however, authorized to do anything else, after a conference with the officers of the stern deck, such as cutting down of masts, furling or unfurling of sails, changing the course of the vessel, and doing everything else which will be to the benefit of the vessel, with these qualifications: that he is sufficiently well trained in his profession; that he knows when to set and when to furl the sails, rearrange the cargo, quickly clear the decks, and maneuver the vessel about in order to gain the advantage over an enemy vessel.

If he is not proficient in doing these things, and there is aboard the vessel an officer of the guard or an officer of the stern deck capable of doing these things, the helmsman should be removed from his position and replaced by such an officer.

If the helmsman, however, is proficient in his trade, all the provisions of the agreement made with him should be carried out. If the patron of a vessel should want to discharge the helmsman because of some prejudice on the part of the patron, he may do so provided the helmsman has received his wages. If he has not, the patron must pay him his wages before he can be discharged.

A helmsman who is incapable of performing the duties of the position which he has assumed, as has been stated herein, must assume all the expenses and damages which resulted to the vessel due to his ignorance or inability to perform his task properly. The helmsman, if he is in good health, should sleep fully clothed; he is required to help the crew to get the vessel ready to venture safely into the open sea and to get the vessel ready to sail without any delay. He must be loyal in the same degree to the merchants, the patron, sailors, passengers, as well as to all others with whom he has any relations.

63-Damage to Cargo Resulting from Improper Storage or Other Kind of Negligence

The patron and the helmsman should not store or order the cargo to be stored in a damp place, or store crates, chests, or bales of cargo in such a manner that damage would result to the cargo. It should not be stored near the masts, near the steering wheel, on the bottom of the vessel, in the prow of the vessel or in any other place where some damage would result. In addition, the patron of a vessel is responsible to the merchants for many other things. If their cargo aboard should become waterlogged due to improper storage, or through seepage in the deck around the openings for the masts, or from leaks in the bottom of the vessel, or through the openings around the steering wheel, or through the anchor chain openings in the prow of the vessel, or by storage of cargo in unprotected areas of the vessel, or, finally, due to the lack of proper pitch and tarring of the vessel, the patron, if he has sufficient means, must pay for all of the damage which the merchants may suffer due to water seepage, If the patron of the vessel is unable to pay the damages, the vessel must be sold to satisfy these claims, and neither the shareholders of the vessels nor any of the loan makers who advanced money for this voyage can make any priority claims. The only exceptions are the crew who cannot be deprived of their wages.

64-Waterlogged Cargo

The patron of the vessel is required to pay for the damage caused to the cargo aboard the vessel due to dampness caused by seepage through the deck, through the portholes, or due to lack of proper protection of the cargo from the elements.

If, however, the cargo was damaged because the decks were swamped by heavy seas and not because there was seepage through the deck which was properly tarred, the patron is not obliged to pay for the damages to the cargo.

65-Further Explanation of the Above Article

In the previous article it was stated, explained, and written that if a vessel was swamped by heavy seas and the cargo was waterlogged and damaged, the patron of the vessel was required to pay all the damages suffered by the merchants through this mishap.

This should be understood to mean the following: If a vessel is sailing through a storm so severe that it will swamp the vessel and the cargo aboard will become waterlogged and damaged, the patron of the vessel will not be held responsible for the damage to the merchants or to whomsoever the cargo may belong, because the damage did not result from any negligence on his part.

This article is written because no one can circumvent the will of God and the power of the sea and wind. For the same reasons, if bad weather causes damage to the steering gear, steering rods, sailing yard, sails or other equipment, and the cargo aboard the vessel is damaged due to the ravages of the storm, or due to waterlogging, the patron of the vessel cannot be held responsible for such damage, because none of this damage occurred due to his negligence.

66–Additional Data on Waterlogged or Damaged Cargo

In agreement with what has been stated above, the patron is released from all responsibility for the damages to the cargo which has been waterlogged or damaged by water if the vessel was swamped by high seas. Our predecessors wanted to explain the circumstances stated above, that if the deck of the vessel is swamped in spite of the fact that it was well tarred, the patron will not be held responsible for the resultant damages to the cargo if a vessel is swamped by high seas.

In order to avoid all disputes between the patron and the merchants over these matters, our ancestors, in order to explain what they meant by proper pitching and tarring of the vessel, stated the following: If the deck of the vessel was tarred up to the deck rail or above it, and also up to or above the openings for anchor chains, the patron of the vessel cannot be held responsible for the damage or waterlogging of the cargo, even if the water seeped through the deck.

Why is this so? Because when the merchants hired the vessel they should have assured themselves that the vessel was water tight; and also because if they had discovered that the vessel leaked through the upper deck, and did not say anything about this to the patron of the vessel, the patron cannot be held accountable for the consequences.

If, however, the merchants informed him about it and made sure that he understood them, he shall be held responsible for all the promises made and obligations undertaken relative to the safety of their cargo. Further: If the deck of the vessel was tarred to below the base of the deck rail and the vessel is swamped through the upper deck, the patron will be held responsible for all the damage due to waterlogging of the cargo from whatever causes, and this is due to the fact that if the base of the deck rail is intended to strengthen the vessel, it is also there to be tarred.

From the above reasoning our ancestors issued this embellishment and this explanation in order to prevent any disputes between the merchants and the responsible individuals who sail the seas and who are in command of vessels.

67–Cargo Damaged by Rats or Lost Through Other Causes

If any property or merchandise aboard the vessel is damaged by rats, and there is no cat kept aboard the vessel, the patron is held responsbile for the damages.

Any goods or possessions loaded aboard the vessel and entered in the ship's register, which are subsequently lost, will be the responsibility of the patron of the vessel and its owners must be compensated by him for their loss.[32]

68-Merchandise Damaged Aboard the Vessel Due to Lack of a Cat

If any merchandise or cargo is damaged by rats while aboard a vessel, and the patron had failed to provide a cat to protect it from rats, he shall pay the damage; however, it was not explained what will happen if there were cats aboard the vessel while it was being loaded, but during the journey these cats died and the rats damaged the cargo before the vessel reached a port where the patron of the vessel could purchase additional cats. If the patron of the vessel purchases and puts aboard cats at the first port of call where such cats can be purchased, he cannot be held responsible for the damages since this did not happen due to any negligence on his part.

69-When Cargo is Damaged Due to Storage in a Damp Place

Further, if the patron stores the cargo in a damp place without taking proper precaution, he should be required to pay all the resulting damages.

70-Proper Protection of Cargo

A patron of a vessel should not protect the cargo of one merchant from spoilage at the expense of the cargo of another merchant. If he should do this and the cargo used to protect another cargo stored underneath it should be damaged, he will be required to pay the damages.

71-Explanation of the Article Above

The patron of a vessel should not protect the cargo of one merchant at the sacrifice of another's cargo; if he does this and the cargo of the merchant used to protect the cargo of another was damaged by placing it on top of other cargo, the patron shall pay the damages for the damaged cargo.

It was not stated, explained, or illustrated, however, that the patron of the vessel should not use the cargo of one merchant to protect the cargo of another; if he does this and the cargo used for this purpose suffers damage, he will be responsible for all the damages. For

---

32. Sulphur, used for fumigation, was considered an essential item in supplies taken aboard a vessel.

this reason and in order to avoid all disputes between the merchants and the patrons of vessels, our ancestors, who first began to circumnavigate the world, wished to give the following explanation:

If all or part of the cargo which the merchant loaded aboard the vessel is heavy, and the patron of the vessel takes steps to protect the cargo of only one of the merchants and the cargo of the other merchants be damaged, he will be held responsible for all the damages.

However, if aboard the vessel there is heavy cargo belonging to one merchant (and the rest of the cargo belonging to the other merchants is packed in large crates) even though the heavy cargo was stored at lower levels and has been damaged, the patron cannot be held accountable for the damage, if the vessel was properly tarred and the water did not seep through the deck or the portholes to cause the damage. This is because it is proper and has been customary to store all heavy cargo at the lower deck of the vessel. Why is this so? In order to make the steering of the vessel easier, as it would be dangerous and harmful to the vessel to store the light cargo requiring large storage place at the lower level and the heavy cargo at the upper level, because this would make the vessel top-heavy and in danger of sinking, and it would be impossible to navigate the vessel properly.

However, if all or some of the merchants had heavy cargo aboard, the patron should store this cargo on the lower decks proportionally, keeping in mind the way to avoid suffering any losses, as has been stated above.

For the above reasons our ancestors brought about these changes and these explanations, in order to avoid disputes, dissatisfaction, cheating, and fraud between the patrons of vessels and the merchants who travel throughout the world.

72-Cargo Waterlogged While Being Loaded or Unloaded

You should know that when a bale or a chest becomes waterlogged while being loaded or unloaded, the patron of a vessel will not be held responsible.

In all instances where damages have to be paid, of which we have spoken or will speak about in the articles related to marine matters, the patron of the vessel is obliged to pay his share of the damages the vessel must bear, and every shareholder must likewise pay his share, as the vessel actually must pay the whole amount of the damage.

73-Loading and Unloading of Cargo

You should also know that the patron of a vessel is required to load and unload the cargo, if he agreed to do so with the merchants; if, however, he has not made such an agreement, the merchants must make arrangements with the sailors (it should be understood, that is, if they are located on an uninhabited seashore) as to the loading and unloading of their cargo.

74-Responsibility of the Sailors While Loading the Vessel

The crew is obliged to carry the cargo up to the gunwales but is not required to store the cargo, if the patron did not promise this to the merchants. However, if he had made them such a promise, he should also reach an understanding about this with the crew and as-certain whether the crew will agree to do this.

Nonetheless, if the patron finds himself on some uninhabited shore with his vessel, and the merchants cannot find any people who would perform this task, the sailors are required to load and unload the cargo, but must receive for this service additional remuneration commensurate with the wages which would have been paid to those who would have performed this task, the amount to be determined by the navigator of the vessel.

This article was written in order that neither the patron nor the merchants would undertake a voyage fruitlessly; however, if it is possible to find people who will unload the vessel, the sailors should not be required to do this work.

75-The Vessel's Cook and the Provisions a Merchant Takes Aboard

The patron is required to provide the merchants with personnel capable of properly storing their cargo, if necessary with the aid of winches, but the merchants must pay them for this work. In addition, the patron is required to take aboard their personal effects, sea chests, crates, and stores of provisions for each merchant. If a merchant or a person on his staff should wish to load on provisions or other merchandise which he intended to sell aboard to the crew, he is required to pay the customary lading charges on such merchandise.

76-Required Accommodations Which Must Be Provided for a Merchant Aboard the Vessel

The patron must assign proper quarters aboard the vessel to each merchant; the navigator will summon the merchants, and in the presence of the clerk he must assign the best accommodations to the merchant who is paying the highest amount of lading charges.

77-Accommodations for Merchant's Servants

The patron of the vessel is required to transport the sea chests and the bedding of the merchant, as well as a servant or companion, who is essential to his successful undertaking of the voyage, and must also provide sleeping accommodations for the servant. If the merchant is paying very low freight charges, that is to say, if he is going to Acra, Alexandria, or Armenia, or in that general location, and is paying less than twenty silver pieces in freight charges on his cargo,[33] the patron of the vessel is not required to transport his sea chest, nor his servant or companion, unless the merchant pay the proper charges for their transportation; and the merchant himself is not entitled to free accommodations.

78-Explanation of the Preceding Article

If the vessel is bound for the Barbary Coast or for Spain, or is returning from these locations, and the merchant is paying less than twenty-four gold pieces for the freight charges on his cargo, the same procedure should be followed as mentioned above.[34]

79-Stolen Provisions

The patron must pay full damages for any provisions stolen aboard the vessel by one of the sailors.

80-When a Merchant Delays the Sailing Date of a Vessel

The patron of a vessel should delay the sailing date to wait for a merchant who has been detained by certain obstacles. If a merchant after having paid lading charges on his cargo has it unloaded from the vessel because of some fear of danger or because of export restrictions, the patron of the vessel is not required to refund him the freight charges. However, if circumstances change and the situation is favorable for the shipment of these goods, the patron of the vessel should transport these goods within a period of two months to the originally agreed upon destination.

81-Merchant Who is Fearful to Undertake a Journey

---

33. Barcelle, most probably a Barcelonian silver coin of undetermined value.
34. Bezan or bezant, a gold coin probably of Byzantinian origin used commonly in Western Europe after the return of the Crusaders.

A merchant who had his merchandise loaded aboard the vessel but due to fear of the enemy, that is, fear of the enemy navy or pirates, wishes to have his cargo unloaded, may do so, if the rest of the merchants who have shipment aboard wish to do likewise, whether or not the probability of danger has been ascertained. If only one merchant entertains such fears, but the majority of merchants do not withhold their shipment, the merchant who refuses to ship his cargo must pay the lading charges due on his goods or must negotiate a new agreement to the satisfaction of the master of the vessel.

82-Unloading of Cargo of a Merchant Who Refuses to Ship It Due to Some Fear of Danger

If it is ascertained that a merchant is justified in fearing some enemy vessel, the patron of the vessel must unload his merchandise whether or not he has paid the lading charges. However, if the object of fear no longer exists, the merchant should reload his cargo aboard the vessel if the patron of the vessel demands it. If in the meantime the merchant has sold this cargo and will not ship it aboard the vessel as originally contracted, he must negotiate another agreement with the patron and pay the lading charges which he would have paid shipping other merchandise per hundred weight. This is proper because the patron of the vessel incurred expenses for feeding the sailors, paying their wages, and paying for other expenses.

83-Obligations of a Patron to the Merchant Who is Shipping Goods Per Hundred Weight

If a merchant engages a vessel to ship goods by hundred weight, this is to mean, that he has agreed to load aboard an agreed number of quintals of goods, the patron is obliged to accept a quarter more quintals of merchandise than originally contracted for; in this manner, if the merchant contracted for a shipment of three hundred quintals of goods, the patron must accept four hundred quintals provided that the merchant will reach an understanding as to the increased shipment in sufficient time.

If, after the time agreed upon to load the cargo has passed and the merchant who had engaged the vessel to ship his cargo has failed to load this cargo aboard, the patron of the vessel may take on cargo of other merchants in order to carry a full load. If a merchant after making arrangements to ship a given amount of cargo withdraws from such an agreement, and this agreement was made in writing or in the presence of witnesses, or it has been entered into the records of the ship's register by a clerk who had taken the oath of his office, the merchant must reimburse the patron of the vessel for all the expenses and costs connected with the proposed shipment of cargo, provided he withdraws from the contract before the cargoing of the vessel begins.

If such a merchant should attempt to withdraw from such an agreement after the cargoing of the vessel begins, he will be required to pay half of the agreed lading charges without any opposition, and the patron will have to pay half the wages due to the crew, provided that the sum equal to half the amount of the freight fees which the vessel would be paid if it carried full cargo had been paid to its master.

The master of the vessel shall equip it with the necessary sails and other equipment in accordance with the promise given to the merchants, and be ready to sail on the date agreed to with them.

The merchant must pay the agreed cargo charges without any delay or hesitation, and the master of every vessel has a right to withhold sufficient amount of the cargo from the merchant, equal in value to the amount due for the transportation of his cargo, if he fails to pay the lading charges due.

84-Breach of Contract by a Merchant

If a merchant who has agreed to ship a certain amount of cargo or a given number of quintals of merchandise, or who has agreed to supply all the cargo which the vessel is capable of carrying, refuses to deliver such a cargo to the vessel, whether it be a given number of quintals or quantity of bulk merchandise, but does this before such cargo is at the loading site, he is required to reimburse the patron of such a vessel only for the expenses connected with the proposed voyage.

If it should happen that the merchant delivered the cargo to the loading site or pier, whether all or most of the cargo, and then decided not to ship this cargo nor to undertake the voyage, he will be required to pay the patron of the vessel one-third of the estimated amount of the cargo fees he would have paid had he shipped the amount of cargo he had promised.

To continue: If the latter merchants have decided against making the journey after loading aboard part of their cargo, they shall pay the patron of the vessel one-half of the agreed lading fees; similarly, if they loaded aboard all their cargo, which they had intended to load aboard, and they decide to forego the journey before the vessel has unfurled its sails, they shall also be required to pay half of the agreed lading fees.

If, however, the vessel upon which they had loaded their cargo had already unfurled its sails, and then they demand to withdraw from the voyage, they shall pay the master of the vessel the full amount of the transportation fees agreed upon.

Furthermore, everything stated above must be carried out without any opposition.

Further, it should be borne in mind that there shall be no attempt to cheat or defraud anyone in the situation described above, by which the merchants would want to withdraw from an agreed voyage in which they had promised to participate by shipping a specified number of quintals of cargo, or capacity of vessel cargo on which the shipping charges had been paid. If a patron of a vessel can prove that trickery or deceit had been used by the merchants in withdrawing their shipment of cargo, the merchants shall be required to pay the full agreed sum or reach a new agreement with the patron, provided he consents to it.

It is proper indeed, that as the patron of the vessel be held responsible for his obligations to the merchants, they too must keep their promises to the patron, unless they could justify their actions by some well–established custom, as has been pointed out above.

85-Concerning a Merchant Who After Agreeing to Ship His Cargo
Sells It

If a merchant after engaging a vessel to ship specified quintals of cargo, whether or not it constitutes capacity shipment, withdraws from the shipment of such cargo by selling it, he shall be required to pay the patron the full amount of the cargo fees for which he had contracted.

What is the reason for this? Because it can be assumed that the merchants, who had agreed to ship the cargo, received by selling it not only the usual amount of profit but in addition the amount that would have been paid for transporting such cargo and that they had agreed to pay to the master of the vessel.

Further, it should be remembered that if the vessel engaged to carry the cargo was to have been loaded at the same location where the agreement was concluded, the matter should be entrusted to arbitration by two Elders of the Sea Guild, and whatever be their decision must be carried out, and neither the merchants nor the patron of the vessel may dispute their decision.

The crew of the vessel must abide by the terms of agreement reached between the merchants and the master of the vessel.

Further, if the vessel engaged for this purpose was to proceed to another location to pick up this cargo, and the merchants sell the cargo before the vessel arrives, and cannot provide other cargo to be loaded aboard the engaged vessel, they shall be required to pay the full shipment charges to the patron of the vessel whom they engaged to carry their cargo.

Why? Because it is necessary and proper that the merchants fulfill their responsibility to the patron in the same degree as the master of the vessel toward them; otherwise the patron would suffer great loss; it would likewise not be just and proper that merchants should reap profits while the patrons of vessels be ruined financially because they trusted the merchants.

If, however, the vessel engaged was to proceed to another location to pick up cargo, and before the vessel sailed, the merchants had told the patron that they intended to sell this cargo, and this happened before the vessel actually unfurled its sails, the matter should be submitted to arbitration by the Elders as has been mentioned above.

This article was written for the reasons stated above.

86-Shipment of Specified Amount of Cargo

The patron of a vessel shall be required to carry the full amount of cargo contracted for, while the merchant must pay the full lading charges as agreed to with the master of the vessel.

87-Loading of Cargo Aboard the Vessel Without the Knowledge of Its Patron

If a merchant, without informing the patron of a vessel, should load aboard his vessel more cargo than agreed upon, the master of the vessel shall be within his rights to charge him for carrying this cargo according to his own estimates.

88-Minimum and Maximum Shipping Charges

Let us assume that one merchant paid the master of a vessel the sum of one millares[35] per quintal of cargo and promised to ship a specified number of quintals of freight, while another merchant paid him a sum of one hundred besant per quintal; the master of the vessel is required to transport the cargo of the merchant who paid him one millares as well as of the one who paid him one hundred be-

---

35. Millares, a medium-sized silver coin, 4.55 grams in weight, introduced by Constantine. A coin generally used in commerce of the medieval period, originally minted in Montpellier.

sant, and store both shipments in equally safe space, for he must remember that he will be forced to pay the same proportional damages on goods which were shipped at one millares per quintal as those shipped at one hundred besant per quintal. He should not refuse to transport the cargo of the merchant paying him one millares per quintal in the quantity agreed, and should treat him in the same manner as he would treat a merchant paying him even two hundred besant per quintal.

When the agreement is made concerning the amount of cargo or the number of quintals of merchandise to be carried, any additional cargo carried may be transported at the cost decided by the patron unless he promised the merchant to transport any additional amount at the same price, and the merchant notified him of the additional cargo to be shipped within the period of time mutually agreed upon.

89-Failure to Take Aboard Cargo Consigned for Shipment

If a patron of a vessel or a clerk acting as his representative agreed to carry cargo of some merchant, and this agreement was made in writing or in the presence of witnesses, or by a handshake, or by an entry being made in the ship's register, he must fulfill this obligation. If the master of a vessel cannot take aboard such a cargo and leaves it behind, and the merchant informs him that if such cargo is left behind, the patron will be held responsible for it, this responsibility of abandoning such cargo will fall upon the shoulders of the patron, unless before setting sail he would reach a new agreement with the merchant. The patron will be forced to replace or pay for such abandoned cargo based on the amount such cargo would sell for at the port of destination where he was to deliver it.

If such cargo abandoned by the patron of a vessel should be lost or suffer partial or total spoilage, the damage will be assessed against the patron who had left the cargo under such conditions. If due to some misfortune, it should pass that the cargo aboard the vessel, that is to mean, all the goods and merchandise carried by the vessel, should be completely lost, while the cargo abandoned on shore should be safe, the latter will belong to the patron of the vessel and not to the merchants to whom it actually belongs.

It is justifiable that if the patron of the vessel is required to return to the merchants as much cargo as they had owned, or to pay them the amount the cargo would be worth at the place of destination, and thus he will suffer a serious loss, it is equally just that a merchant or merchants suffer the loss while the patron gain, when all the goods carried aboard the vessel are lost while the goods abandoned on the shore are saved. Why? Because it would be contrary to reason and justice that patrons of vessels should find themselves in a more disadvantageous situation than the merchants.

If it should happen that the cargo aboard the vessel is salvaged and the cargo abandoned on shore is lost, the patron, as stated above, must reimburse the merchants for it; if the cargo abandoned on shore was saved while the cargo aboard the vessel was lost, the patron of the vessel will not be required to pay any damages to the merchants and thus will benefit by this.

If, however, the cargo aboard the vessel is salvaged, the master of the vessel is required to reimburse the merchants, as has been stated above, with this reservation: that the merchants must deduct from the damage claims, which the patron must or should pay them, all expenses which they incurred or had to incur, had the patron taken aboard the rest of the cargo which had been left on shore. Excluded from this should be the cost of provisions from which the merchants cannot deduct anything, because they would have had to bear the cost of the provisions if the cargo had been taken aboard; therefore, it would be unjust to deduct anything in such a situation.

If only part of the cargo aboard is lost, the damage must be deducted and taken away proportionally to the amount and evaluation of the damage which the patron of the vessel is obliged to pay the merchants for merchandise left on shore. Furthermore, if it was necessary to dump the cargo overboard due to some misfortune, the value of the cargo thrown overboard must be subtracted proportionally from the value of the damages for the merchandise left on shore.

If it should happen that a patron of a vessel would take aboard only part of the cargo on which shipping charges had been paid and had left part of it on shore, the merchants will make a deposition, of which we have spoken above, and the patron will be held accountable in the manner prescribed above.

However, if the merchants, aware of the fact that part or all of their cargo has been left behind, had made no comment about this, and did not call to the attention of the patron the abandonment of their cargo or oppose this action in any other way, or if the patron of the vessel informed them himself of the situation, or if he had ordered that they be informed about this, that they will bear the responsibility for the cargo left behind, and these merchants would not say anything or oppose it, or warn him of his responsibility for the cargo, they will suffer the damages if the abandoned cargo is lost.

What is the reason for this? Because the merchants did not protest, did not disapprove of this, did not remind the patron of the vessel of the previously mentioned responsibility when they saw that part

47

or all their cargo was being left behind on shore that he, not they, would assume the damage for the cargo, should it be lost. In addition, if they had made proper depositions to the master of the vessel and had reminded him of his obligations, the patron, realizing that he, not they, will be held accountable for the damages of the cargo left behind, would have taken better care of it.

There is yet another reason. If a patron of the vessel had stated that the merchants themselves would be liable for the damages to the cargo left behind on the shore, and they did not disapprove of this and did not caution him of his responsibility, it appears that it would be proper to interpret that the merchants were not interested in their own cargo which was left behind on the shore, since they had shown no opposition to this state of affairs and did not warn him. Therefore, it is just that the merchants themselves, as stated above, should bear the sole responsibility for the cargo left behind on the shore, regardless of whether or not this cargo was lost.

If it should happen that the merchants ask the patron of the vessel engaged that he load the cargo remaining on shore on another vessel and he accedes to their wishes, and then this cargo should be lost in part or completely or is damaged or deteriorates, the patron of the vessel cannot be held responsible for this since he loaded such cargo aboard another vessel with the express permission and knowledge of the merchants.

If a patron of a vessel loaded the remaining cargo on another vessel without the knowledge of the merchants to whom it belongs, and this cargo is partly or totally damaged, destroyed, or lost, he will be required to pay all the damages, because, as stated above, he loaded their cargo on another barque or vessel without their express permission and approval; and this is proper. Why? Because no one should make a disposition of the property of another except to the degree that the owner of the property consents and gives his approval.

If it should happen that the merchants engage a vessel and show their cargo to the patron of this vessel, and inform him that they cannot remain aboard but must leave, and entrust the cargo to his care, and if he agrees to accept this responsibility, and the merchants trusting him will depart after reaching an agreement with him as stated above, he is required to carry the cargo which he accepted and took under his command and care, in the manner mentioned above, unless during the loading of the vessel some unfortunate accident should occur, in which case he cannot be held responsible for such cargo. Why? Because no one accepts responsibility which would result in personal loss.

If it should happen that he would abandon such cargo on shore, he will be required to return to the merchants in quality and quantity or in cash the value of the cargo he had agreed to carry, the value to be determined by the price of the cargo at the location where he was to proceed to unload such cargo. Thus the patron of a vessel is responsible and should be held accountable for the cargo he left behind, regardless of whether such cargo is safe or is lost, because, as has been said above, he had taken this cargo under his trust and command, except under the circumstances mentioned above, which could have taken place before or after loading the cargo aboard.

Further, if a merchant engages a vessel to ship some cargo and after paying for the lading charges leaves the vessel with or without the knowledge of the patron of the vessel, who did not accept such cargo under his command and care, as mentioned above, and at the moment the vessel is being cargoed, the patron or some other person identifies and locates the cargo, it should be loaded aboard the vessel.

If the patron or a member of his crew cannot identify and locate this cargo while the vessel is being loaded and due to this the cargo remains on shore, whether this cargo is lost or is safe, the patron of the vessel will not be responsible for its well-being and he will not be forced to pay any damages in case of spoilage or disappearance of this cargo, because the merchant left the site under the circumstances mentioned above. There is, however, one exception, and that is, if the merchant left some person with instructions to show the patron of the vessel or his representative (i.e., the clerk) the location of the cargo during the loading operations.

If the person left behind by the merchant to show the cargo to the patron of the vessel, shows it to him and releases to him the custody of it when the patron or a person designated by him is in charge of loading the vessel, and the patron or his substitute refuses to accept this cargo and refuses to load it aboard the vessel, and abandons it on shore, whether this cargo remains safe or is lost, the patron of the vessel will be held responsible for it to the same degree as if the above mentioned merchant was present personally, because he had left a person in charge who in his name attempted to release this cargo for shipment.

It is necessary, however, that the merchant or the person designated by him to release the cargo will be able to prove the truthfulness of their accusations against the patron. If, therefore, the merchant or the person he designated in his place to facilitate the transfer of the cargo, as mentioned above, can prove his claim, the patron of the vessel will be required to pay the merchant for all resulting damages, as enumerated above, following the procedure outlined above.

If, however, the merchant cannot prove what has been discussed above, or if the person who was acting in his stead did not designate and deliver the cargo to the patron of the vessel, and thus the cargo was left behind on the shore, the patron will not be responsible for the damages, whether the cargo left behind remained in good condition or was lost, because the merchant left the cargo without taking proper care of it. It is, therefore, proper that the merchant would suffer the damage, because he deserved this, failing to take proper care of his cargo; however, under all other circumstances which have been discussed above the patron shall reimburse the merchants for all their expenses and losses except for the cost of the provisions.

If it should happen that after the departure of the aforementioned merchant, the patron who accepted the former's cargo under his protection and command should load it aboard another vessel and subsequently this cargo is damaged in some manner or is partly or completely lost, or the vessel on which the cargo was loaded fails to arrive at the port of destination of the cargo even though the cargo under the personal command of the patron arrives there on time and, due to the late arrival of the above mentioned cargo, its value decreased, which would not have happened had the cargo been placed aboard the vessel personally commanded by the original patron, he will be required to pay the full damages because he loaded this cargo aboard another vessel, not his own, without the permission of the party to whom the cargo belonged.

Further, if the merchant had reached an agreement with the patron before the former's departure that if the patron cannot take his goods aboard his own vessel, he may load it aboard another vessel, and after conclusion of such an agreement the patron had it loaded on another vessel, the patron shall not be required to pay any damages, whether the cargo is lost or not, or whether it arrives on time or late, because there had been an agreement made before the departure of the merchant that the patron could load this cargo aboard another vessel if he could not have it loaded aboard his own, unless the patron has failed to fulfill his obligations, that is to say, that the patron left this cargo on shore while he loaded other cargo aboard his vessel.

If the patron reached the original agreement with the merchants to load their cargo on another vessel, and the master of the second vessel left it on shore (this means that the cargo will remain at the spot where lading was arranged for), the master of the second vessel will be required to pay the merchants all damages suffered in the same manner as the patron of the vessel who had originally made the agreement would have been forced to pay had he taken this cargo aboard his own vessel, excluding completely and without any reservations all agreements and protocols concluded between the patron and the merchants, for any reason whatsoever.

This article was written for the reasons stated above.

90-A Patron Who Abandons Cargo Upon Which Lading Charges Had Been Paid in Advance

A patron of a vessel who has contracted to transport cargo by a written agreement or orally in the presence of witnesses or by an entry into the ship's register or by a handclasp[36] shall be obliged to carry such cargo. If he refuses to carry this cargo or cannot load it aboard his vessel and abandons it on shore, he shall be required to repay the merchants with the same quality and quantity of cargo or its equivalent in cash, at the price this cargo would have brought at the port of its destination, unless the patron can make or had made a different agreement with the merchants before the vessel left the port where the original arrangements for the shipment of the cargo were made. However, if the merchandise left behind has been lost, and the patron of the vessel failed to arrive at some agreement relating to this, the loss of this cargo will be attributed to the patron, who will be forced to pay the merchants in the manner discussed above.

This article was written because many patrons of vessels preparing to undertake a journey demand very low lading fees, and when the journey is almost ready to begin find other merchants who are willing to pay high freight charges; if the above mentioned regulations were lacking, the cargo on which low shipping charges were paid would be left behind, and the cargo on which high lading charges were paid would be loaded aboard the vessels.

91-Damage of Cargo Bound for Specified Destination

If a patron of a vessel which is located in a specific locality agrees to transport cargo to another agreed location, he shall transport this cargo to the specified location in his own vessel.

If, however, a master of a vessel, without the knowledge and approval of the merchants, should load their cargo aboard another vessel (even though this vessel was larger and more seaworthy than his own vessel), and this cargo be lost or damaged, or the party to whom this cargo belongs should suffer some damage or bear some expense due to this, the patron of the vessel who was originally engaged to carry the cargo shall be required to pay for the lost cargo and all

---

36. A handshake to bind an agreement was considered as valid as a written instrument if witnessed by others.

other damages and expenses suffered by the owner of the cargo, and the claim made under oath by the owner of this cargo shall be accepted without question.

Further, if the patron informs the merchants that he does not intend to proceed to the place to which he had promised to deliver their cargo, and also informs them that he would like to load their cargo on another vessel, which he will name, he may do so if the merchants agree. However, if the merchants refuse to agree to such an arrangement, he cannot proceed to do this, but if he does load their cargo on such a vessel, he will be held responsible for their cargo, as stated before. In the event that the merchants agree to this arrangement, and the cargo is damaged or lost, the patron cannot be held responsible for any part of the damage claimed because he had proceeded in this matter with the knowledge and approval of the majority of the merchants concerned.

92-Regarding Proper Equipment, Sailors, Helmsman, and Cargoing of Merchandise

The patron must equip the vessel with proper sails, which he has shown the merchants or which he claimed he had aboard in making a written deposition, or had stated this orally in the presence of the helmsman and the crew. He cannot discharge the navigator or any of the sailors without the agreement of the merchants until the completion of the voyage, nor can he sell or give away any sails or other equipment which belong aboard the vessel. He is also required to supply members of his crew for the cargoing of the vessel.

93-Vessels Sailing in a Convoy

The patron of a vessel must sail in convoy with other vessels, be they large or small, if the merchants demand it. In addition, if the patron wishes to sail in convoy with another vessel, be it large or small, he may do so after seeking the counsel of and receiving the agreement of the navigator, officers of the stern deck, and the rest of the crew; likewise, when there appears to be danger from meeting a privateering or pirate vessel,[37] they cannot and should not oppose sailing in convoy, unless they judge that to do this would result in damages to them or to the vessel.

---

37. *Mals Lenys* actually would include units of official navy of unfriendly nation as well as privateers, pirates, and even private vessels owned by an unfriendly merchant or patron.

94-Obligation to Aid Another Vessel in Distress

If a vessel located in some specified place is ready to set sail for another place of destination, and some other vessel, larger, smaller, or of the same size, bound in the same direction, does not dare to sail alone due to fear of enemy vessels, and its master begs the master of the former vessel to attach a line so that the two vessels may sail together, and this is agreed to, the promise must be fulfilled unless stormy weather prevents it.

If these two vessels sail out from the location where such an agreement was made or the promise given, and the patron of the vessel who promised to attach the towing line to the other vessel does not intend, or fails, to keep his promise, and the patron who had been promised this aid sailed out feeling secure, should he suffer any damage from pirates or other unfriendly craft before reaching the port to which he was promised help by the former patron, the patron who had promised him a tow line and had failed to do this will be required to reimburse him for all the damages, without any dispute.

What is the reason for this? Because if the patron of the vessel which was to provide the tow line had not made such a promise, the patron of the first vessel would not have ventured to sail. He actually sailed feeling safe because of the terms of the agreement he had reached with the master of the vessel who had promised him assistance.

If, however, a vessel sailed without receiving promise of aid from another vessel, and if the former vessel is damaged, its owners and no one else will be liable for the damages.

If it should happen that the patron who had made an agreement or had given a promise to attach a line to another vessel fulfills his responsibility, but the line is cut by the pirates and the two vessels are separated, or the line is cut by another enemy vessel or stormy weather, and the patron, in spite of his effort to keep his promise of help, cannot give such aid, neither he personally nor his vessel will be held responsible for damages suffered by the other vessel, because he could not fulfill his promise due to the circumstances stated above.

Further, if a patron of a vessel who had promised to attach a hold line to another vessel has received or shall receive for this service a stipend, and the vessel which paid this stipend shall be lost or damaged, the patron who had received the stipend shall pay all the damages which the vessel from which he had received the stipend had suffered, as well as for the cargo aboard the vessel, to the degree of the damage suffered. An exception will be made in a situation when a patron who had received a stipend or an award had announced at the moment he had received this stipend from the patron who was fearful of sailing out alone, that should there be an incident brought on by fate, neither he personally, nor his vessel, nor the cargo aboard it will be subject to the damages that will have to be paid. It should be understood that an incident brought about by fate occurs when he may be forced to cast off the line due to stormy seas or because of a threat of pirate vessels, privateers or other craft. If, however, a patron who had received a stipend or award had made a reservation to the patron who had entertained such fears that neither he, personally, nor his vessel, nor anything aboard his vessel will be used as a guarantee to pay for the damage which may be suffered by the vessel which had asked for aid; this reservation also applies to the patron of the vessel who paid for such aid or will pay for it, if he makes it at the time the payment is made or after it has been made.

Further, any patron should be sure to be on guard when entering into such agreements, whether or not he receives a stipend for such service, that he will act impartially. Because, should he make such an agreement or give such a promise without the approval and knowledge of the merchants who are aboard the vessel or have their cargo aboard it, the merchants will not be obligated in any way should such an incident take place. On the other hand, should these merchants suffer any damage, loss, or diminution in the value of their cargo due to such an arrangement on the part of the patron who entered into it without their knowledge and approval, the patron will have to pay them full damages, even if the vessel and any other property which he owns has to be sold.

This article was written for reasons given above.

95–Disposing of Cargo Overboard

The patron cannot throw any cargo overboard or order any other person to do so until a merchant aboard his vessel first throws some of it overboard; only then can he order the cargo to be tossed overboard in the amount necessary to prevent danger to the vessel. On such occasion the clerk shall prepare an agreement, as if he were on shore, and the patron must share in the damage resulting from the necessity of dumping such cargo overboard to the extent of half the value of the vessel.

96–Cargo Thrown Overboard

The value of the cargo thrown overboard in stormy weather or due to pursuit by enemy vessels will be assessed proportionally to the value of all the cargo aboard, and the vessel must pay damages to half the value of the vessel.

97-Procedure of Evaluating the Cargo Thrown Overboard

When any cargo is tossed overboard, as has been discussed above, it should be evaluated in the following manner: If it was thrown overboard before the vessel covered half the distance to its destination, it should be valued at the price at the point of departure. If it was disposed of after half the distance was traversed, the cargo tossed overboard as well as the cargo saved should be evaluated according to its value at the port of destination.

98-Procedure for Reimbursement for Cargo Thrown Overboard

If the patron, in agreement with the merchants, loaded their cargo aboard his vessel with the purpose of delivering it at a specified port of destination, and during this voyage due to chance of fate he should encounter bad weather or enemy ships or some other danger which would necessitate tossing overboard a portion of his cargo, he should do the following as soon as his vessel and the rest of the cargo aboard reach the port of destination: Before releasing any of the remaining cargo to the merchants who were to receive it or to whom it belongs, he should retain an amount of the cargo equivalent to the value of the cargo thrown overboard, or even a greater portion, in order that neither he personally nor the merchants to whom the lost cargo belonged would suffer any loss, damage, or liability. This is done because each of them has already suffered serious damages, and also in order that the merchants who had already lost some of their cargo would not be forced to sue the patron of the vessel or the merchants to whom the salvaged cargo belongs.

The value of the cargo thrown overboard should be determined according to the actual value of the cargo lost, and the patron of the vessel will be required to share half the amount of the damage, that is to say, up to the amount which would be half of the value of his vessel. Furthermore, if the patron of the vessel demands that lading charges be paid on the cargo salvaged as well as on the cargo tossed overboard, he must be paid as if all of the cargo had been saved; however, under such conditions the patron will be required to share the damage in the amount that he received for carrying the cargo in the same degree as the cargo salvaged.

What is the reason? Because the patron received payment for the cargo which was thrown overboard as well as for the cargo which was saved. It is, therefore, just that in accepting lading charges for car-

55

go saved and lost, he should be obligated to share in the damages to the whole amount of these lading charges.

Further, if the patron of a vessel demands and receives payment for carrying only that part of the cargo which has been saved, he will not be required to share in the damages to the amount he had received for carrying such cargo, and the reason for this is that he has been damaged enough, because he has lost the amount he would have received for the cargo which was thrown overboard.

To continue: If a patron of the vessel demands payment of the lading charges and is paid the freight fees only for the cargo that was saved, he will not be expected to share in the damages to the amount of the lading fees received because he has been damaged enough, as he has lost the amount he would have received for carrying the cargo which has been thrown overboard.

99-Formalities That Must Be Observed in Relation to Throwing of Cargo Overboard

When a storm overtakes a vessel and its master is convinced that there is a possibility that the vessel may sink unless he disposes of some of the cargo aboard, he should explain this to the merchants and inform them in the presence of the navigator and all persons present on the deck in the following manner: "Sirs, merchants, if we do not lighten the load, we will find ourselves in danger and expose all on board, plus the cargo and other merchandise and possessions, to a total loss. If you, gentlemen merchants, consent that we reduce the load we have aboard, we will be able with the aid of God to save all the people aboard as well as most of the cargo. If, however, we do not throw some of the cargo overboard, we will find ourselves in danger of losing our lives and all our possessions."

If the majority or all of the merchants express approval, it will be possible to proceed to get rid of some of the cargo by throwing it overboard. At least one of the merchants aboard, if it is impossible for all of them to do so, will have to personally start dumping the cargo overboard, and only if one or more merchants start tossing the cargo overboard will the patron be able to do likewise and order others to do the same, until enough cargo has been disposed of and the danger averted.

Under such circumstances the clerk of the vessel will be able to set in writing all agreements as if the vessel were moored. If, for some reason, the clerk could not set this in writing, the sailors can attest to all the agreements made and promises entered into between the patron and the merchants, because the clerk was unable to enter them into the ship's register. This is done in order that all agreements and promises made between the merchants and the master of the vessel are entered into without any deceit or fraud.

If, however, it should happen that there are no merchants aboard the vessel, the patron under such circumstances will act in the name of the merchants, and whatever action he pursues he should do so only after he reaches an understanding with the navigator, shareholders and the members of his crew. After he has reached such an understanding with those mentioned above and proceeds to toss cargo overboard, his action will be as binding as if all the merchants were aboard or as if all the cargo belonged to him personally. In such a circumstance the patron will also have to share in the damages due to the necessity of disposing of the cargo to the amount equal to half the value of the vessel, and the merchants to whom the cargo belongs cannot question his decision for throwing the cargo overboard as long as this was carried out in the manner prescribed above. The damage resulting from this will have to be shared proportionally depending on the quantity and quality of the cargo thrown overboard.

This article was written in order that a patron of a vessel could be able to act in such an emergency when the merchants are not aboard the vessel. If the patron was unable to act in the name of the merchants under such circumstances, the result would frequently be loss of life, vessel, and all the cargo. That is why under such circumstances the patron can and must act in the name of the merchants, who are not aboard the vessel. It is obviously more sensible to get rid of some of the cargo than to sacrifice human life, the vessel, and all the cargo.

100-Obligation to Declare the Cargo to the Clerk of the Vessel

As soon as the vessel unfurls its sails, the merchants shall make a declaration to the clerk of the vessel of everything they had loaded aboard and which had not been entered into the register. If anything is found aboard which they have not declared, they will be required to pay the highest lading charges permitted for every quintal of merchandise, because they brought aboard this merchandise secretly. If it should happen that they had not declared these goods by the time the vessel had set sail, and later these goods are lost, waterlogged, or thrown overboard, they will not be entitled to any reimbursement, because they had made no declaration of such merchandise.

101-Arrival at Port

A patron of a vessel cannot enter any port without the express permission of the merchants; if he should do this and the merchants suffer any damages through some incident, the vessel will be held accountable for all the damages they suffered. The clerk must verify this matter by making an entry in the ship's register, regardless of whether or not the vessel is moored. However, if the master of the vessel needs something essential in order to continue the journey, he must inform the merchants that he cannot continue the voyage without procuring the equipment, or that he must make repairs, or that the vessel must be tarred or caulked or outfitted with sails. Under such circumstances the merchants must agree to his entry into such a port, provided that the navigator and the sailors certify under oath that they are acquainted with this port. Nevertheless, if there should be a privateer moored in that port and the merchants fear him, the patron cannot enter such a port unless the merchants agree to it. If the merchants refuse to allow him to venture into such port, even if there appears to be no danger there, and one of the merchants announces, "I do not wish to enter this port," he will have to pay all the damages which may result due to this.

102-Concerning the Promises Made by the Merchants to the Patron

Here we will speak of the responsibility to keep promises made by the merchants to the master of a vessel. The merchants will be required to keep all the agreements made with the patron, and which have been entered into the ship's register. To continue, if a merchant took upon himself some special obligation, and made this promise in writing or had it entered in the vessel's register, he will be obligated to fulfill it in every detail.

Therefore, if a merchant made an agreement with the master of a vessel to ship a specified amount of cargo, it makes no difference whether or not he was aboard the vessel when he made this agreement with the patron. If later he cannot provide the amount of the cargo agreed upon or lacks the means to purchase the agreed amount of cargo for shipment, he will be required to pay the lading charges on the amount contracted for, whether or not it is loaded aboard the vessel.

103-When a Merchant Wishes to Unload His Cargo[38]

If the majority of the merchants decide to unload their cargo, every

38. This actually refers to unloading of cargo before the voyage begins, due to fear of danger to the vessel and the cargo. Further explanation is given in Article 130.

merchant can unload his own cargo, without paying any lading fees, and the master of the vessel, who had not been paid the lading charges, cannot demand any.

Further, the patron of a vessel shall wait with his vessel until the date agreed to take aboard their cargo and carry it. This means the cargo and the personal effects of the merchants as had been agreed.

104-Concerning Merchants Who Wish to Unload Part of Their Cargo

When a vessel has set sail and it should happen that the majority of the merchants, or the merchants to whom the greater portion of the cargo belongs, wish to stop at some port to unload the cargo, they are privileged to do this regardless of the distance of this port from the location where the voyage began. But the patron of the vessel under such circumstances can also force the rest of the merchants, that is those whose cargo constitutes the minor portion of the load, who do not wish to unload their cargo at this port, to unload it, and to demand payment of all the lading charges. If the master of the vessel allowed a rebate of shipping charges to the merchants who unload the greater portion of the cargo, he shall be obliged to allow a rebate to the merchants who are shipping the lesser portion of the cargo aboard; thus, all the remaining merchants should be treated in the same manner as the merchants who had shipped the major portion of cargo aboard this vessel. The wages of the crew shall be lowered in proportion to the amount received in lading charges.

105-When a Patron Is Delayed by a Merchant

When the merchant did not pay the lading charges on the cargo he was to ship, and the patron of the vessel waited for the agreed period of time to take this cargo aboard, the merchant shall be required to load this cargo aboard. If he should refuse to do this, he will be required to pay the patron of the vessel the full amount of the shipping charges.

106-In Case of Necessity, a Merchant Should Make a Loan to the Master of the Vessel

In addition, in his relations with the patron of the vessel, the merchant is obligated in the following manner: If a patron declares, while the vessel is moored in some port, that he must buy new sails or other equipment which is essential to the safe operation of the vessel, and the merchant aboard the vessel has the means, he will be forced to make a loan to the master of the vessel in the amount determined by the navigator of the vessel to be sufficient to meet this emergency. For this reason, all shareholders and loan makers aboard the vessel are obliged to assume this responsibility also, in the presence of the merchant mentioned above. If, however, the patron of the vessel, or its shareholders, or the former loan makers find some other person who will be willing to make such a loan, the merchant aboard the vessel will not be required to make the loan.

107-In Case a Need Arises a Merchant Must Loan Money to the Master of a Vessel to Make It Seaworthy

In addition, if the master of the vessel needs money and cannot obtain it in the manner discussed above, and finds himself in an uninhabited location, but must have the money to put the vessel in seaworthy condition, and the merchants mentioned before do not have the money to make him a loan, they will be required to sell part of their cargo in order to buy the equipment necessary to make the vessel seaworthy. [39] No shareholder or any person who had made a loan to the patron prior to the departure of the vessel may oppose this, and the merchants who had sold part of their cargo shall be repaid first, provided that the sailors have received their wages. Further, it must be stressed that the patron of the vessel must be absolutely certain that money borrowed will be used to purchase the necessary equipment to make the vessel seaworthy.

108-A Merchant Should Supply the Vessel With Food

In addition, if there should be a lack of provisions aboard the vessel for the crew and other persons, and a merchant has such provisions, he must make them available for a communal use, and the patron of the vessel will divide this food equally among all the persons aboard. The merchant is not allowed to retain more food than the share received by any other person aboard. If the vessel reaches a territory where food may be purchased, the merchant may demand the return of these provisions in the amount which had been requisitioned, and the patron will be required to replace such provisions.

---

39. The manuscript evidently refers to a location where no one is able or willing to make such a loan and not to an uninhabited territory.

In addition, if the master of the vessel wishes to drop anchor near the shore, in port or at any other place where there is a chance that it will be lost, he should do this with the knowledge and approval of the merchants. [40] If the merchants demand that he drop the anchor, and he refuses to do it, and if the anchor or the anchor chain should be lost, the patron and the crew will have to pay full damages, because they refused to do this.

Further, if the vessel lost its anchor in some bay, gulf, or in some other waters where it had stopped upon the demand of the merchants, the cost of the replacement of the anchor will be assessed equally on all the cargo aboard the vessel, and the owners of the vessel will not be required to share in this expense. If, however, the vessel dropped its anchor due to fear of an enemy vessel, the price of replacement will be borne equally by the owners of the cargo and the owners of the vessel in the amount equal to but not more than half of the value of the vessel.

If the master of the vessel abandons a lifeboat with its crew upon the demand of the merchants, the cargo of these merchants must bear the expense of the purchase of a new lifeboat and the expenses of the crew up to the time the crew returns to the place where the vessel is moored. The vessel will not be required to share in the cost of such an incident.

110-Abandonment of a Boat Being Towed

If a vessel towing a boat which has been swamped with water, finds it necessary to tow it in that condition, and if the merchants insist that the tow line be severed and it should be done, and the boat abandoned, the resulting damage will be assessed against all the cargo aboard, but the owners of the vessels will not be required to share in this damage. If, however, the tow line breaks, and is not severed to please the merchants, the latter will not be required to share in the damages.

111-Throwing of Cargo Overboard in the Absence of the Merchants

If, when the master of the vessel cargoed it at some location and remained anchored at that place, or in some other location, and all the merchants without exception are ashore, leaving only the master and the crew aboard the vessel, there should appear armed enemy

---

40. Necessity for dropping of anchor was mentioned in Art. 101.

vessels or a sudden unexpected storm should develop so that the patron cannot take the merchants aboard, and if, due to the above mentioned circumstances the patron was forced to pull in the anchor and leave the merchants on the shore and also, fearing the approaching enemy vessels, judged it necessary to throw some cargo overboard or had thrown the cargo overboard in order that he be able to escape them or to be able to defend his vessel more effectively, or because of the impending storm—under such circumstances, tossing of the cargo overboard has the same validity as if all of the merchants were aboard the vessel. In such cases it is necessary that the master of the vessel act with the approval and advice of the crew of the vessel, and that the clerk not neglect to enter into the ship's register all the resolutions which had been made aboard the vessel in the presence of the whole crew.

If the clerk could not make these entries in the ship's register due to the circumstances mentioned, he should do so as soon as the ship is moored and before he disembarks from the vessel. If it should happen that the clerk has been ashore during such a situation, but aboard the vessel there are servants of the merchants, the patron shall assemble the crew and these servants and ask their advice; he shall then repeat or order someone to repeat the decisions they have reached as many times as it will be necessary in order that everyone aboard the vessel shall remember them. This is done so that when the patron meets the merchants who had been left ashore, there would arise no possibility of a misunderstanding, and so that no one from among those who had taken part in these deliberations could claim that he did not hear what had been decided and that no one had consulted him about the actions that had been taken.

If the patron follows the procedure outlined above, everything that he does will have the same validity as if the majority of the merchants were present when these decisions were made. If it should happen that, due to the proximity of enemy vessels or storm, the vessel was steered unto shoals, and the patron acted according to the procedure described above, in concensus with all those enumerated previously, and with their express knowledge and agreement, none of the merchants or any other person can invalidate any agreement or any decision they had reached. Any person who challenges his action will be forced to pay for all the damages and losses, costs, and injuries, which the patron who had this unfortunate incident suffered due to such a challenge.

Everything which has been stated must, however, have taken place without any deceit or fraud. If anyone from among those enumerated above is able to prove, without the shadow of a doubt such deceit or fraud, the guilty party will have to pay to the damaged party and to those who prove such deceit and fraud all the damages they suffered.

Further, investigation of such fraud charges should be made by persons of wide experience, free from all suspicion, and, in particular, by parties who know the profession of sailing and are familiar with the issue which they are called upon to judge. Why is this so? Because it would not be fitting that the testimony of porters or persons of low estate be accepted as evidence in such matters, as they are easily bribed; and also if the captain's version of the situation was accepted based on the testimony of such low persons, he could very easily ruin the merchants, because the testimony given by persons of low birth, who can be bribed, does not and cannot have any value whatsoever in any issue.

112-Apportionment of Salvage Expenses

The merchants shall proportionally pay all the expenses connected with the handling of the cargo except that of cargoing the vessel. If, therefore, it is necessary to weigh anchor because of bad weather or other reasons, in order to find refuge in a port or straits in some other location where the cargo or the vessel can be saved, the cargo will be subject to assessment in proportion to its value and quantity. If the merchants aboard the vessel did not have identical quality of cargo—if for instance there is a party of five merchants and another party of two or three merchants, and these two merchants have the same or even a larger cargo than the group of five merchants—the amount of damages that the party of two merchants agreed to pay as part of the salvage costs will also have to be paid by the merchants having the lesser amount of the cargo aboard.

Further, all these transactions must be carried out honestly without deceit and without forcing of one's personal opinion, and the merchants must state under oath that they will proceed honestly in this matter. This article is intended above all to guarantee to the vessel any damages that it may suffer in the event that such guarantees were made to the vessel. The vessel, however, enjoys this privilege, that when the merchants promise in a given situation to pay the salvage costs, they will fulfill this responsibility, whether or not such a promise has been executed in writing under the conditions that the clerk of the vessel was present in person and personally heard these promises made. The clerk should enter these matters into the ship's register without delay as soon as the vessel is moored, since the vessel and he were on the high seas when these agreements were concluded.

113-Who Is Classified As a Passenger

Now we will discuss the responsibilities of the patron of a vessel toward the passengers aboard his vessel and the obligations of the passengers toward the patron of a vessel. The same situation will obtain whether the reference is made to a large vessel or a barque. A passenger is a person who pays the patron for his own transportation as well as for the transportation of his effects which are not part of the cargo. Therefore, every person whose cargo amounts to less than five quintals shall be required to pay passage fee for his own person; and no one can be properly called a merchant who is paying less than twenty besants in lading charges. The master of the vessel is not obligated to carry the chest, nor a servant, nor anything else if the passenger is shipping less than ten quintals of cargo unless they had reached another agreement. If such a passenger loaded anything aboard the vessel without the knowledge of the master of the vessel or the clerk or some person whom the patron and the clerk appointed to represent them to oversee the cargoing and lading charges, and if the passenger has not shown his cargo to one of these persons, the patron of the vessel may demand that such a passenger pay the highest lading fees which are paid for any cargo aboard the vessel, in proportion to the weight of his cargo and other possessions. Similarly, any person who comes aboard the vessel without the approval of the master or clerk of such a vessel may be charged any amount the patron decides for his accommodations aboard the vessel.

114-Cargo Loaded Aboard the Vessel Without the Knowledge of Its Master or the Clerk

If there is loaded aboard the vessel so much cargo as to endanger it and for this reason the patron does not want to carry all of it, the clerk shall order that the excess cargo be unloaded on the shore, and the master of the vessel shall not be held responsible for payment of any compensation for the damage that may result to the cargo unloaded, unless it had already been entered on the ship's register. It should be understood that when the vessel has unfurled its sails and has sailed out of the port, merchants, sailors, passengers, and all others aboard the vessel who had brought aboard any effects or merchandise shall come to the clerk and declare everything that they had brought aboard. If any of them fail to do this, neither the patron nor the clerk will be responsible for any damage to any such cargo or effects.

115-Undeclared Personal Possessions and Effects

If, due to some misfortune or other circumstance, it becomes necessary to dump some cargo overboard, and if in the presence of witnesses the effects of a merchant, passenger, sailor, or other person aboard were thrown overboard, but this property had not been entered into the ship's register or was not declared to the patron, clerk, or their representative who had been empowered to oversee the cargoing of the vessel, the patron of the vessel will not be required to pay any damages if such effects are lost, damaged, or waterlogged, even if there were witnesses who had observed that such effects had been loaded aboard. If, however, undeclared goods are found upon unloading the vessel, the patron may arbitrarily determine the amount of lading charges due on such goods, and the merchant will be forced to pay these charges without any resistance.

However, if the clerk had entered such goods into the register before or after the vessel had sailed, the patron will be required to pay damages if such goods are lost.

116-Responsibility of a Patron Toward Passengers

Further, the master of a vessel shall provide proper accommodations and water for the passengers and carry them to the destination agreed upon. If a patron has received a deposit on the fare the passenger will pay, he must carry out the promise he had made to the passenger; on the third day after the deposit was paid the passenger should approach the patron to find out the sailing date. If the patron should mislead the passenger by giving him a later date and due to this the passenger fails to be aboard when the vessel sails, the master of the vessel shall return to the passenger the full fare which would have been paid plus all the losses suffered by the passenger due to the patron's negligence. If, however, the passenger has removed himself from the vicinity of the vessel without finding out the actual date of sailing and fails to return at the time the vessel unfurls its sails, even if he had paid the full fare or had given the master of the vessel one thousands marks, the patron of the vessel is not required to return anything to him. [41]

---

41. A silver mark; its value differed according to time and country. The Venetian mark weighed 233.856 grams, Spanish mark 230.348 grams, the Portuguese mark 229.500 grams.

117-Passenger Accommodations, Death of Passenger Aboard the Vessel

The master of the vessel or his representative, namely, the navigator, will assign the passenger his accommodations, and the passenger must accept the accommodations provided for him. If the passenger dies, the navigator may assign his accommodations to any person he chooses; the deceased person's best suit of clothes rightfully belongs to the navigator, and any money which the deceased had on his person will be taken by the master of the vessel, if the deceased did not have a relative aboard the vessel the master will keep it safely until they reach a port where the heirs can demand that he surrender it to them at any time within a three-year period. If after three years have elapsed and no one claims this estate, the money will be used, with the approval of the local bishop, for the repose of the soul of the deceased.

In order that a proper accounting of the estate be made with the bishop or a local court, the clerk of the vessel will prepare a list of the money and all other possessions of the deceased in triplicate, retaining one copy for himself, give one copy to the merchants, and give the third copy to the master of the vessel. After returning to the country of origin of the deceased, the clerk shall show a copy of the inventory of the possessions of the deceased party to the local bishop or his secretary, or to the local pastor, who shall transcribe the inventory into the parish register.

If the patron of the vessel is not considered reliable enough to hold such money because he is a poor manager or a wasteful person, he must post a bond.

If he is unable to post such a bond, he shall deposit the money in a safe depository in order that if anyone should claim this money within the three=year period, he will be able to get it. If the master of the vessel should die, the money should be placed in a safe and secure place.

118-Right of the Patron to the Effects of a Person Who Died Aboard His Vessel

In the situation described above, the master of the vessel shall receive as part of his compensation or wages the bed and one suit of clothing of the deceased person, that is, after the navigator has received one suit of clothing. If the person who died aboard the vessel did not leave many possessions, the master of the vessel should not even receive that much. If the property of the deceased party amounts to less than one hundred besant, the patron should take only the clothing and turn all other effects of the deceased into cash by selling it.

119-Exceptions to the Preceding Article

If, however, a person who died aboard the vessel had undertaken the voyage as an ordinary passenger, [42] neither the master of the vessel, nor the navigator, nor any other person aboard will receive anything from the effects left by the deceased. Nevertheless, if this passenger had undertaken a voyage beyond the sea or some other long distance, the patron as well as the navigator should receive what has been mentioned above. There are often many persons who undertake a long journey with a small amount of merchandise, or who are sailing to settle in some distant country and are referred to as passengers. If any of such people die aboard the vessel, the patron should not receive anything from among their effects. Under such circumstances, if there is no consul aboard the vessel, [43] the patron is required to store all the possessions of the deceased, if the latter did not leave a last will, did not leave an executor of his will, and did not leave a beneficiary. If there are no relatives of the deceased aboard the vessel, the patron should store all the possessions and keep them until he is able to return them to the deceased's relatives, his wife, or his sons, or to those to whom the property should be returned.

The clerk should make a detailed inventory of all these belongings, retain one copy for himself, give a copy to the patron, and proceed in the manner which has been established and discussed above.

120-Share of the Jolly-Boatman and the Guard of the Vessel in the Effects of a Deceased Passenger

The jolly-boatman shall receive the boots, knife, and the belt of the deceased passenger, while the guard of the vessel, his trousers but both of them must see to the burial of the dead passenger, either some place on land or in the sea.

---

42. This is to distinguish between an ordinary passenger and a merchant who is accompanying his cargo and is not considered a passenger in the pure sense of the word.
43. Reference is made to a consul who would be aboard a naval unit and not an ordinary cargo vessel. The position of a consul aboard vessels is discussed in more detail in Articles 327 and 333.

121-Food Left Aboard the Vessel by the Deceased Passenger

Further, any provisions left by a passenger or any other person dying aboard the vessel will be taken over by the patron of the vessel.

This article pertains to passengers or other persons traveling from one place to another, as has been stated before.

122-Failure of a Passenger to Sail Aboard the Vessel After Making Payment for His Accommodations and His Cargo

If any of the previously mentioned persons has paid the patron for his fare but wishes to remain ashore, the master of the vessel shall not be required to refund the fare.

Further, if a passenger, or some other person, or a merchant has made an agreement with the master of the vessel regarding a shipment of cargo, and wishes to sell this cargo while ashore at the location where the contract was made or at some other place, and the amount he would receive for this cargo is insufficient to pay the lading fees agreed upon, it should be designated for payment of these fees even if it is sufficient to pay for these shipping charges. Should the merchant have other possessions more valuable than his cargo, it cannot be assessed to pay for the lading fees due on the cargo of lesser value, and in that manner pay the patron the fees due.

This article was writen to prevent the merchants from misleading each other and also, that they do not take out loans on cargo which is of little value, but on cargoes of substantial value.

123-Obligations of a Passenger

The following are the obligations of a passenger and every other person toward the patron aboard the vessel: He shall be required to help, to protect, and to watch over the vessel, and not to disembark until the journey is completed, unless the patron agrees to some other arrangement.

This article was written because many patrons often take mechanics and soldiers aboard as passengers and charge them a lower fare, which they would not do if they knew that these persons would not participate in the defense of the vessel, and many merchants travel aboard such vessels because they feel safe with soldiers aboard.

In addition, all the passengers and others traveling aboard are required to take part in the deliberations and to conduct themselves according to the customs and traditions which have been established, and which must be followed by all aboard the vessel.[44]

124-Patron's Obligations to His Sailors

Let us assume momentarily that a patron engages a sailor for service aboard his vessel. Whether such sailor is good or evil, knowledgeable or ignorant of his trade, he must pay him the agreed wages, with this reservation, that if this sailor was engaged as a carpenter, a shipwright, or a helmsman, and he is not capable of fulfilling the task he was hired for, and the patron believing that he was able to perform the task had not hired another in his place, the patron of the vessel shall pay only as much as the helmsman and the clerk decide under oath that he shall receive.

125-Dismissal of a Member of the Crew

Let it be known that a patron of a vessel may discharge a sailor from his service before the journey is completed for the three fol-lowing reasons only: Firstly, for stealing; secondly, for fighting; thirdly, for failure to carry out an order given by the helmsman. The helmsman, however, cannot order a sailor to do something which he has no right to order; and the sailor cannot be discharged for the first violation but only after the fifth.

If, for the sixth time, he fails to carry out an order of the helms-man, the patron, or some other person acting in his place, he should be discharged from service. It is, however, mandatory that the person who gave an order to a sailor is capable of carrying out such a command himself.

To continue: There is still another reason why a sailor should be discharged and that is, if he violates his oath, because if he was allowed to do this the merchants could not have any confidence in him.

126-A Sailor Cannot Be Discharged in Order That Another Person Could Be Hired at a Lower Wage

Further, if the sailor contracted with the master of the vessel to serve aboard the vessel for a specified wage, and the patron should find another sailor willing to serve for lower wages, he will not be

---

44. In case of danger to ship and cargo from stormy seas or enemy vessels.

able to discharge the former if the agreement was sealed with a hand-shake. Such an agreement must be fulfilled as if it has been entered in writing in the ship's register.

127-A Master of a Vessel Cannot Discharge a Sailor in Order to Hire a Relative in His Stead

Further, if a sailor has contracted with the master of a vessel to serve as a member of his crew, the patron cannot hire a relative or any other person in his stead, if the enlistment was accompanied by a handshake or entered into the register, and is binding whether or not the sailor was aboard the vessel when the contract was entered into. If the master wishes to discharge him he will have to pay his wages, as if the sailor had served during the entire trip. Moreover, if the sailor fell ill after working aboard the vessel for three days, the patron will be required to pay him one-half of his wages, even if the sailor had to be left behind on shore. Should the vessel be moored while in another country and the crew should decide that the sailor is too ill to undertake a voyage, the master shall pay him one-half of the wages due him for the trip; should he not have the means to pay him, he shall borrow the necessary amount because a sailor must receive his wages. Should the master of the vessel die, the executor of his estate shall fulfill this obligation.

128-Death of a Sailor Aboard the Vessel

Should a sailor become ill and die aboard the vessel, his effects, as well as his full pay, will be given to a relative if there is one aboard the vessel, who, in turn, will deliver these possessions to the deceased sailor's children or to his wife if she was living with him while he was alive. This will be done whether or not the deceased had made such stipulation before he died. If his wife, however, has been unfaithful to him, or had not been living with him at the time he left the country, or if she fled from their domicile after he left on the journey, the master of the vessel with the agreement of the clerk and the approval of the local court shall surrender these effects to the nearest relative of the deceased.

129-Death of a Sailor Before Sailing and After the Vessel Sails

If a sailor dies after his enlistment for a specified voyage, and be-fore the vessel sailed, by the will of God, one-fourth of his wages due will be paid and delivered to his beneficiaries. If this sailor had been paid his full wages before he died, all this money belongs and must be given to his beneficiaries, and the master of the vessel cannot challenge the validity of such a payment or demand any refund.

130-Sailors Paid on Monthly Basis

If a sailor agreed to serve aboard a vessel for a fixed monthly wage and then should die, his beneficiaries must be paid all the wages due him and given a financial accounting for his whole period of service.

131-Obligation of a Patron in Regard to a Sailor's Right of Free Freight

The master of a vessel is also required to pay the sailor his wages at the location where lading charges are being paid. If the sailor pays for his own food while aboard the vessel, he should inform the master if he intends to serve aboard on the return voyage. In addition, the patron of a vessel is required to allow the sailor to store his free freight merchandise aboard the vessel if he is carrying any such goods, if the sailor had not already stored such goods aboard. It should be understood that such merchandise will not be assessed for any damages resulting from the necessity of dumping cargo overboard.

Further, the value of such free freight merchandise that a sailor brings aboard should not be higher than his wages and cannot amount to more than fifty besants. Should the sailor have such merchandise valued at one hundred besant, he will be required to pay the lading charges on only fifty besants worth of his goods. If his merchandise is valued at forty, thirty or twenty besants and this value approximates his wages, he will not be liable for assessment on the basis of his merchandise for any damages due to dumping of cargo overboard.

A sailor can store his free freight wherever he pleases aboard the vessel, but the patron shall not be responsible if it becomes damaged or waterlogged. A sailor bringing aboard free freight should notify the clerk and have this merchandise entered into the ship's register. Should he fail to do this, his merchandise shall be confiscated. Moreover, he must make a deposition consistent with truth concerning this merchandise, and should he lie about this matter, he shall be deprived of all of this merchandise if it is proved that he uttered a falsehood, and the local court will confiscate all of his merchandise, giving the patron of a vessel one-third of it.

132-Explanation of the Preceding Article

In conformity with what has been stated before, free freight merchandise belonging to a sailor is not assessed for damages resulting from cargo being thrown overboard in case of necessity. It was not, however, made plain and conclusive how this statement should be interpreted. For these reasons, well-informed and learned people who had first circumnavigated the earth wanted to make this clear by stating the following: If the sailor had purchased this free freight merchandise with his own money, that is, before he received his wages for service aboard this vessel, aboard which he had stored this free freight merchandise, in the manner mentioned above, and due to some unfortunate accident, it is necessary to dump some cargo overboard, such a sailor will be required to share in the damages resulting in proportion to the value of his free freight merchandise and the value of the cargo dumped overboard.

If, however, the master of the vessel due to his good will and friendly disposition, pays the crew their wages before the journey begins or has made loans to them, such sailors shall be obligated to share in the damages resulting from cargo being tossed overboard to the amount of half of their wages.

If the value of their free freight merchandise amounted to more than one-half of their wages, they shall be forced to share in the damages due to the necessity of dumping of the cargo overboard in the amount which is above the amount of one-half of the wages they had been paid.

If it should happen that the master of the vessel does not wish to extend them loans or pay their wages for the whole voyage before it is undertaken, they shall be required to share in the damages resulting from the necessity of dumping cargo overboard to the degree mentioned above.

Further, when a patron has paid the wages of these sailors, regardless of where and when this has taken place, they shall be required to share in the damages which will be assessed against their free freight merchandise only in the amount equal to one-half of their wages.

This article was written for the reasons mentioned above.

133-Free Freight Merchandise of the Crew

The patron of a vessel is obliged to take aboard and transport the amount of free freight merchandise of the crew as he had promised, while the sailor is obliged to load it aboard the vessel before it is fully cargoed. If the vessel has been cargoed to capacity and the sailor wants to bring his free freight merchandise aboard, the master of the vessel is not obligated to take it aboard. If, however, a sailor wanted to load his merchandise aboard before the vessel is fully cargoed, and the master of the vessel resisted this, he shall pay the sailor the amount of the lading charges he received for the cargo equal in amount to the free freight merchandise of the sailor, but under such circumstances the sailor cannot load anything else aboard.

134-Lading Charges Paid on Cargo Which Has Replaced Free Freight Merchandise

A sailor should not and cannot give up his right to carry free freight merchandise to a merchant or to another sailor who enjoys similar privileges. If, however, he should consent to this, the master of the vessel can demand that the sailor surrender the gratuity which he was paid for this privilege.

135-Labeling of Cargo Aboard the Vessel

Neither a sailor nor a merchant or anyone else shall label any cargo after it has been loaded aboard the vessel. If anyone should proceed to do this,the master of the vessel may confiscate it. The former ought to lose all the cargo labeled in this manner.

136-Roster of Duties Aboard the Vessel

In addition, if the master of the vessel is required to pay the sailors for storing the cargo aboard the vessel, he shall pay them the full amount due them. If the vessel is small he should pay them half as much as if the vessel were large. He shall also allow them six days to make purchases of any goods which they intend to take with them.

One-third of the crew shall man the vessel one day, one-third the next day, while the last third of the crew shall perform all other duties essential to the well-being of the vessel.

137-Loading Aboard of Merchandise Belonging to the Crew

The master of the vessel shall allow a sailor to load and unload his free freight merchandise with the use of the ship's boat. The other members of the crew shall help him to do this.

138-Source of Wages for the Crew

Further, the master will pay the wages of the crew from the lading fees received for carrying the cargo. If this is insufficient to meet the payroll,he shall borrow money to pay them. Should he fail to secure a loan, he shall sell the vessel in order to get sufficient funds for this purpose, for the crew must be paid before creditors or shareholders get their share. A sailor must be paid even if the only thing remaining with which he can be paid is one nail, [45] unless the vessel had left on another journey.

If the master of a vessel during a voyage borrowed money from the crew with their consent in order to increase their wages through speculation for profit, and then in a subsequent voyage suffered a catastrophe, the crew must be paid for the first voyage without increment even if the remains of the vessel had to be sold. Even if the only thing that remained of the vessel was a single nail, it must be used to pay the crew. No loan maker or any other person can oppose payment of the crew, no matter what remained from the vessel, because it had been so decreed.

139-When, in What Manner, and from What Sources Should the Crew Be Paid

The patron of every vessel shall pay his crew at the place where he has received payment of lading charges in conformity with what has been stated in the preceding article. This refers only to a situation where there has been no agreement made between the crew and the master, under which the master of the vessel is required to pay the crew after returning to the location from which they began the journey. If such an agreement has been made, the sailors shall not and cannot demand payment of their wages until after the return to the location where they had made such an agreement with the master, unless the master is willing to make some concession out of his good will. The patron shall, however, be required to pay their wages immediately upon return from the voyage to the place of its origin without any conditions or opposition.

If any of the sailors should suffer any loss or damage or expense relative to the payment of the wages due them, the patron shall be held accountable for all the losses and damages they suffered due to his failure to pay them their wages.

If there has been no agreement concluded between the patron and the crew, and there has been no conditional provision imposed, the patron shall pay them their wages in the amount agreed without any delay, after he receives payment of the lading charges, and in the same species of money as he had received from the merchants. [46]

45. Nails were hand made and so valuable they were often used in lieu of coins.
46. It was essential that the crew be paid with the species of predetermined value at the port of cargoing the vessel. Since there were many types of coins in circulation having different value

If it should happen that the merchants are deceivers, or that their cargo which he is carrying shall be worthless, then the lading fees charged on it which they were to pay the patron, and in lieu of this payment they leave the cargo with the master of the vessel, regardless of whether their cargo is sufficient in value or insufficient to pay the lading fees, the crew must be paid, even if the vessel has to be sold for a price insufficient to pay their wages.

No loan maker or any other person can be opposed to this and under no circumstances shall he make an issue of this matter. It is essential, therefore, that the crew shall be paid at the place where payment was promised them, unless the crew out of its own free will is willing to wait for the wages due.

This article was written in order that every patron of a vessel be on guard as to whose and what kind of cargo he will accept for shipment, because it is immaterial whether he receives or does not receive the lading charges due. He will still be required to pay the wages due the crew under all circumstances.

140-Wages Paid Sailors from the Proceeds of a Sale of the Vessel

Above all the responsibilities of the master of a vessel are the following: If his vessel is taken over by the judicial authority or any other party, and the merchants in conspiracy with the patron sell the vessel secretly, so that the judicial authority would not be informed about it or for some other reason, and then the patron repurchases the vessel through some intermediary, a sailor should not be deprived of his wages, because the vessel and the potential lading charges are still in the master's jurisdiction and he will again be able to ship cargo aboard it. Therefore a patron cannot discharge a sailor without paying him his wages.

Further, a sailor shall share proportionately, as will the merchants, to the extent of one-third of his wages as well as in the profits he made from his wages in any damages and losses which will occur. [47]

Further, if the master of a vessel should wish to lay over during the winter months, the merchants cannot pose any opposition. However, should the master of the vessel wish to lay over during the winter although he could have undertaken the return journey and in the interim the situation should develop requiring the sale of the vessel,

in different locations, this practice was essential to guarantee the crew a just wage.

47. Refers to the wages used by the sailor in buying merchandise for speculation.

as has been stated above, he shall be required to pay the crew its full wages, and the crew shall not be obligated to share any part of its wages in any damages which may have resulted.

This article is being written because a sailor has to obey the orders of the master of a vessel, and such a sailor would be spending an entire winter season without getting any increase in wages, using his energy and his clothing without any self-benefits, while the patron delayed the voyage in the hope of reaping profits. Therefore full wages must be paid the sailor without any opposition and without any deductions for any losses.

However, there is an exception to this: If a patron after a mutual understanding has been reached announces an agreement providing for the increase in the wages of the crew and for paying the crew for the time wasted. If there should be such an understanding to which the sailors agreed freely, the obligations of the master to his crew will also include the same obligations toward the shareholders;[48] the vessel and wages of the crew actually constitute a single element in all matters related to them. If there actually has been no agreement reached, all payments shall be made as stated above.

Further, a patron is required to pay a fee for a sailor in every locality where such fees are levied whether it be a penny or a larger amount. This should be paid to the community where they are located, and the payment must be borne by him because he is obligated to do this.[49]

141-A Patron Shall Post a Surety Bond for His Sailors

In addition, the patron shall be required to post a surety bond for the sailor to the amount of the wages due the sailor if such a sailor has not as yet received his wages, as well as a surety bond for the merchandise which the sailor has aboard the vessel, its value to be determined by the patron. He shall also help the sailor in every manner that he can, provided he does not interfere in any quarrels in which the sailor is involved, or expose himself and respectable people aboard his vessel to danger and ruin.

---

48.   This refers to Article 247 which provides for hiring of sailors for a share of the profits which shall be made.

49.   Reference here is made to a community of mariners and not a political division. Probably similar to the modern practice of a member of a labor union paying token dues to a local of which he is not a member, being employed for a time in a location controlled by that local union.

142-Deposit of His Savings by a Sailor

The patron of a vessel is obligated to invest a sailor's money profitably after paying him his wages, in a manner considered most expedient by the patron, with the provision that he himself will not suffer any loss. If a patron is staying in a nearby or a distant city, and a sailor wishes to proceed there in order to invest his money, the patron should provide food for the sailor aboard his vessel for two days, but no longer if he does not wish to.

143-Filing of Charges Against the Patron by the Sailors

Furthermore, every patron of a vessel must provide food for his sailors during a voyage, even if they have lodged charges against him.

144-Explanation of the Preceding Article

In conformity with the resolutions made in the previous article, the patron should furnish food for his sailors during the time they have lodged charges against him. It was not stated, however, why, and in what manner he shall do this.

Due to the lack of proper explanation of this matter in the previous article, patrons of vessels could suffer great damages. Therefore, well-informed people, who had written and proclaimed these customs and ordinances, fearful that such great damages may result, have introduced modifications and clarifications of some of these ambiguous articles, in order to prevent the occurrence of any disputes or damages.

In relation to the previous article, they state and affirm that patrons of vessels must provide food for sailors who have brought charges against them, but only in specified cases. First instance would be under the following circumstances: If the master of the vessel would not provide sufficient nourishment for the sailors, as has been customary and stated, explained and certified in one of the former articles. [50] Second circumstance: If he should fail to fulfill the terms of the agreement reached with the sailors on the date of enlistment. Third circumstance: If during the journey he charted a different course and failed to inform the crew about it or had not mentioned this when they were concluding the agreement. Fourth circumstance: If he wishes to change the purpose of the voyage without their knowledge and approval; in addition, in each justifiable instance when he fails to adhere to all the promises he made to the

_____

50. Actually reference is made to Article 145.

77

crew when they were concluding the agreement. In all the above enumerated instances the patron of a vessel must provide sufficient food for the crew even though they have brought charges against him.

Further, the phrase, "changing of the purpose of a journey," should be understood in the following way: When a master of a vessel, finding himself in some locality where he can hire a new crew, would try to force the crew aboard his vessel to continue against their opposition. If he should change the purpose of the voyage because of the circumstances enumerated or due to the interference of the judicial authority, fearful of sailing to the destination where he had promised the merchants to deliver their cargo, the crew should continue to serve under him. In case he should be able to get higher lading fees due to this change of the course, he should likewise proportionately increase the wages of the crew.

For these reasons our forefathers, who first circumnavigated the world, inserted these amendments. Why? Because it would constitute great evil and cause great damage, if without regard to restrictions, date, or place which the vessel will reach, as well as without regard to the reason, the crew could without just cause, initiate actions against the patron of a vessel aboard which it serves; because there are sailors sometimes who, moved by fanciful desires and following their own impulses, do not care whether the patron will lose his vessel; they would even gloat over this misfortune. Because there are in the world many evil people who worry and despair when they see that another person makes profit and attains a degree of success, and because they themselves are unfortunate and worthy of pity, they would want to see all others in the same predicament; such is the objective of the people of such disposition. Also, because people of no account refuse to admit and recognize the fact that there would be in the whole world better people than they.

For this reason our ancestors wanted to delineate the circumstances and causes under which a patron of a vessel should be required to provide food for the sailors who have initiated charges against him, in order that in the future a person of no account could not deprive another person of his possessions.

It is for the reasons mentioned above that this article was written. If, however, a sailor should file charges against a patron of a vessel without well-founded reason and cause, he will be required to reimburse the patron, under whose command he enlisted to serve, and against whom he had brought action, for all the costs, losses, and damages which the patron suffered or will suffer because he unjustly forced him into litigation and loss of his property. If such a sailor should be without means to repay the patron, he should be seized,

taken before the judicial authority and turned over to them, and imprisoned and held in prison until he repays the patron under whom he
served all the damages suffered due to his malicious behavior, for he
should not have engaged him in such litigation and caused him such
injury. As a matter of fact, every person should beware of causing
without just reason any harm to another person, if he does not want
the harm which he had wanted to cause to another to be inflicted upon
himself; it would be therefore just that harm should come to a person of such caliber.

145-Food Which Must Be Provided for the Sailors by the Patron

To continue: Every patron of a vessel or a boat which has a deck
must provide the following food for the whole crew: Meat three times
per week. This means on Sunday, Tuesday, and on Thursday. On
the other days of the week he shall provide soup for them, [51] in addition to the bread given the crew each evening. Also three times per
week, in the morning and in the evening he shall provide them with
wine. To supplement the bread ration they should be given cheese or
onions or sardines or other kind of fish.

In addition, the master of a vessel is required to issue rations of
wine, if it will not cost him more than three and one-half besants. If
he procures raisins or even figs, he should make wine; if he should
not be able to get either figs or raisins or if they cost more than
thirty milliares per thousand rolls, the master will not be required to
issue wine rations.

Furthermore, the patron shall double the rations of the crew on all
official holy days. Finally, he shall employ proper personnel to prepare the food for the crew.

146-A Patron Shall Not Be Required to Furnish Meals for a Sailor
Who Does Not Sleep Aboard the Vessel

The master of a vessel is not required to provide food for the
sailors when they do not sleep aboard the vessel. [52]

147-A Sailor is Not Required to Serve Aboard a Vessel Bound for a
Dangerous Location

---

51.   In modern terminology this soup would most probably be a form
of stew, made out of mixed vegetables, meat, and flour, and
eaten with a ration of bread.
52.   Refers to vessels moored in port or offshore, and not to vessels
on the high seas.

Further, a master of a vessel shall not send a sailor to some dangerous locality. If the sailor refuses to proceed there, the patron cannot force him to do this.

148-Loaning a Sailor for Service Aboard Another Vessel

To continue, a patron cannot loan a sailor to serve on another vessel without his consent, except in a situation when a master of another vessel needs a master sailor or a sailor who is able to perform some duty which is indispensable to the other vessel, which cannot be performed by any person aboard his own vessel. Under such circumstances the sailor should agree to serve aboard the other vessel, but not to go ashore in this capacity, unless he should go ashore in the pursuit of the business of the vessel on which he had agreed to serve and with the provision that he will not be required to carry any heavy cargo or do anything else which he was not obligated to do.

149-Fees Paid by the Merchants to the Patron for Unloading a Vessel

A master of a vessel is obligated to pay the crew for unloading a vessel as much as he himself had received from the merchant for unloading the cargo at a specified location; thus, under this arrangement, whatever he receives from the merchants he gives to the crew.

150-Upon Completion of a Journey the Sailor Is Released from Service

If a master of a vessel undertakes another voyage from the location which was the destination of the vessel, and a sailor is unwilling to proceed on this voyage, he cannot be forced to serve him, provided that they are in a location where other sailors may be found willing to serve aboard this vessel. Should the master be unable to find such sailors, the former sailor should be given an increase in wages in the amount decided by the master, the clerk,and the helmsman to proceed on this voyage and depending on the value of his services in the new voyage as compared to the value of his services in the preceding voyage. The patron, however, cannot reduce the wages of any member of his crew.

If any member of the crew deserves a higher wage than he was given at the beginning of the journey, the patron shall give him an increase. There are many capable men, who wish to leave a country with which they have become well acquainted, and in order to do this will enlist for ridiculously low wages.

151–When a Vessel Is Sold in a Christian Nation

When a master of a vessel or some other person authorized to do this should sell the vessel to a stranger and not a shareholder in the vessel, he must pay the crew their wages, and they are released from his service. If these sailors should find themselves in a location where they do not wish to work, the patron or the person who sold the vessel will be obligated to care for their needs until they return to the locality from which they had departed.

152-When a Vessel Is Sold in the Territories of the Saracens

If the vessel is sold in the territories of the Saracens, the master of the vessel is required to provide them [the crew] with transportation and the necessities of life until they reach a Christian nation where they will feel secure.

153-Fear of Sailing to Specific Destination Expressed by the Sailor at the Time of Enlistment

If it should happen that a sailor enlisted by being entered upon the rolls in the ship's register, and if agreeing to serve aboard the vessel he made certain stipulations, which the patron entered into the register at the express wishes of the sailor, to the effect that this sailor would not feel safe if they were to sail to certain territories or waters, the sailor may refuse to sail there, and the patron of the vessel shall pay him half the wages due him for the journey and provide him with the necessities of life until he shall reach the territory where he shall feel safe.

However, if the sailor enlisted aboard a vessel without making such a stipulation, he will be required to sail wherever the patron of the vessel is required to sail with the merchants.

154-Obligations of a Sailor upon Enlistment

A sailor, from the moment he reaches an agreement with the patron of a vessel by a handshake, is obligated to sail with him to any destination in the same manner as if this had been accomplished by a notorial act. Beginning from the date of the enlistment he shall not absent himself from the vessel without the approval of the patron. If the sailor should have some matters to attend to away from the city in which they are located, he must get the permission of the patron; if the vessel should be moored in a foreign nation and the sailor wants to venture beyond the city, he shall leave all his belongings aboard the vessel for three days.

In addition, the sailor must pledge an oath to the master of the vessel that he will remain loyal and trustworthy, as was written in the article, in which we discussed what the merchants demand from a patron.

155-The Burden of Responsibilities of a Sailor

Further, a sailor is required not to leave the patron or the vessel under any circumstances except three: when he is about to become a master of his own vessel, or he is to be given a position of navigator, or by a special agreement.

If the patron or the person who hired the sailor should die, his effects left aboard the vessel should be designated to pay the sailor for the period of his enlistment.

To continue: The sailor is obligated to do all sorts of work—whatever is related to the vessel, to go into the forest to cut and process lumber, to help in the rendering of oil and to fire the stove, to accompany the crew of a whaleboat, to store and reload the cargo, and in each case when the navigator orders him, to go to fetch water, to load aboard everything that belongs to the merchants, to load on ballast, to carry aboard all kinds of equipment, to bring in wood, to help in the repair of the vessel in order to make it seaworthy, and to perform all sorts of other tasks which are necessary aboard the vessel, as long as he remains aboard such vessel.

156-Circumstances under Which a Sailor May Terminate His Enlistment.

A sailor hired to serve aboard a vessel may, after his name has been entered on the roster roll, [53] or after he has agreed to serve by a handshake with the patron or the clerk, free himself from the obligation of undertaking the journey for one of the following reasons: in order to be married, in order to undertake a pilgrimage to a holy place which he had vowed he would take before he enlisted, or, if he is a hand on the prow deck, in order to take a job as a hand on the stern deck, or to become a navigator, or if he will become a master of a vessel, provided he does this without any deceit or fraud.

157-Desertion of a Sailor

If a sailor, after enlisting and after taking an oath relating to his service, should desert, the master of a vessel may hire another in

---

53. It appears that in addition to the register which was maintained aboard there was also a log or a roster roll which was kept into which all matters pertaining to the crew were written.

his stead. If the replacement he hired should have to be paid a higher wage, the deserter must reimburse the master of the vessel for
this increase, under the condition that he was a sailor well versed in
the art of sailing.

158-Amendment of the Preceding Article

In the preceding article it was stated that a sailor who deserted after enlisting will be required, if the patron had to hire another to replace him and pay him a higher wage, to reimburse the patron for the
total difference in the wages paid to his replacement. This is to mean
that this shall apply if the situation developed at the place where the
enlistment was made. Nothing was mentioned about the obligation of
the sailor who, having enlisted, deserts after the vessel had sailed
away from the port where the whole crew was hired and had reached
a foreign port.

In order to make the above article clear, our ancestors who first
traveled throughout the world wished to embellish it and to make the
following correction, in order that the contents of the article would
not constitute cause for disputes and grievance. They stated that any
sailor who deserts while in a foreign country, when apprehended subsequently anywhere, will be required to pay for all the costs and
damages as well as all the expenses borne by the master of a vessel
in connection with his desertion.

Patron's deposition in this matter will be accepted and taken for
granted.

If such a sailor will be without means to pay for these damages,
he shall be seized and turned over to the judicial authorities, where
he will be detained until he is able to pay for all the damages and
losses which the patron had suffered as he had stated in his deposition.

The above corrections were incorporated within this article in
order to provide proper explanation of this matter.

159-A Vessel in Tow

Further, a sailor shall assist in the towing operation of a vessel if
ordered to do so by the helmsman in order that this vessel can be
towed into a port, unless such a vessel be an enemy craft.

160-Salvage of Cargo on the High Seas. Sailor Paid on Mileage Basis

To continue: Should a sailor find any object during the period of his enlistment, the vessel shall be entitled to three parts and he to one part of the salvage, regardless of the amount of the salvage, be it large or small. If the crew while sailing should discover some floating objects, they shall attempt to recover these objects which may consist of cargo, and when ordered by the master of the vessel shall attempt to recover these floating objects even if it is not cargo, provided that the crew receive its share, as has been stated above. The patron of a vessel is entitled to such a large part of the salvage because he feeds and pays the wages of the crew. If the patron leases his vessel to another party, the new patron shall be entitled to his share of the salvage because of the expenses he has undertaken in connection with the vessel. If he should die aboard this vessel before the expiration of the time for which he had leased the vessel, the value of salvage shall be added to his estate.

Further, if a sailor enlisted on a mileage basis, he shall be obligated to sail aboard this vessel even to the ends of the world.[54] If it should happen that the vessel returns to the port from which it had undertaken the voyage but not with the same cargo because it had been unloaded elsewhere, the contractual obligations of the sailor end. However, if the vessel had not unloaded its original cargo, the sailor is required to continue to serve aboard it on the mileage basis.

This article has been written because there are many merchants burdened by debts who do not wish to return to their native country, because of the poor reception they would receive there, and because of the fear that upon return their vessel would be sold at auction; thus by this means they would retain the services of the crew without end.

161-Patron's Obligations to the Merchants

A sailor serving aboard a vessel is required to remain in service only so long as the vessel is proceeding to the destination indicated by the patron at the beginning of the voyage. If the patron should sell his vessel, he shall find accommodations for the sailor aboard another vessel in order that such a sailor would be able to return to his place of domicile and to take care of his affairs.

If a master of a vessel upon completion of a voyage and after unloading the cargo and throwing out the ballast shall undertake another journey and happens to be in a locality where he can recruit sailors, he cannot force his original crew to continue service aboard for an-

---

54. There is no further explanation made of this type of enlistment. It is not mentioned under what conditions such enlistments were made or how the distances traveled were measured.

other voyage. However, if the vessel was located in an area where it was impossible to hire a new crew, the original crew should continue to sail with him provided that the patron is willing to pay them a higher wage considering all the circumstances in this situation.

This article is written in order that a vessel would not be forced to forego a chance of making another journey, because this should not be allowed to happen due to the unwillingness of the crew to continue to serve. If the patron appointed someone else to command the vessel, the agreement reached between the patron and the sailors will no longer be obligatory, because the patron gave up his command of the vessel.

162-Limitation on the Obedience to Carry Out Orders of Patron and the Navigator of a Vessel

A sailor is required to obey all the orders of the patron and the navigator of a vessel with this exception: that they will not require him to serve aboard another vessel. He is, however, bound to carry out all their orders relating to his service aboard their vessel.

163-Provocation of Argument by a Sailor with His Patron

To continue: A sailor who provokes an argument with his patron shall lose one-half of his wages and his right to free freight of any merchandise which he may have aboard the vessel, and shall be removed from the vessel. Should he use a weapon against the master of the vessel, he shall be seized by the crew, bound, put in the brig and brought before a court of justice. Members of the crew who refused to aid in disarming him shall be deprived of their right of free freight and of the wages which they received or should receive for the voyage.

164-When a Sailor Strikes His Patron in a Fit of Anger

Further, a sailor who strikes his patron in a fit of anger shall be adjudged a traitor and a perfidious person; he should be imprisoned and deprived of all that he possesses.

165-Proper Behavior of a Sailor Toward His Master

A sailor is required to suffer an affront from his patron. If the patron should attempt to assault him, he should flee to the prow of the vessel past the anchor chain. If the patron pursues him there, he shall flee to the other side. If, however, the patron should pursue him there, the sailor has a right to defend himself, providing there are witnesses who will testify that the patron pursued him beyond the anchor chain, which he is not allowed to do.

166-When a Sailor Disembarks to Go Ashore

Further, a sailor is not allowed to leave the vessel in order to go ashore without the approval of the navigator or the clerk, unless he is allowed to do so by the patron of the vessel because there is no work to be done aboard the vessel.

167-Theft Committted by a Sailor

To continue: A sailor who should steal cargo, equipment, or any other thing from the vessel shall forfeit his wages and his right to free freight if he has any merchandise aboard the vessel. The master of the vessel may put him in the brig, put him in shackles, and keep him in the brig for the entire journey, and upon completion of the journey he may turn him over to the judicial authority.

168-When a Sailor Maliciously Throws Food Overboard

A sailor who maliciously throws food or wine overboard shall be deprived of his wages and his right to free freight of any merchandise he may have aboard the vessel, and will be left to the mercy of the patron.

169-Punishment Awaiting a Sailor Who Leaves the Vessel Without Permission

In one of the previous articles it was stated that it is not allowed a sailor to disembark from his vessel without the express permission of the patron, the clerk, the navigator, or a person who was left in command of the vessel. That article does not explain or specify the consequences to the sailor who went ashore without permission. In order that there will not arise any disputes between the sailors who left the vessel without permission and its master, our ancestors explained in the following manner the article which relates to the situation when a sailor leaves the vessel without permission of the patron or the person who in his person is in command of the vessel:

If a sailor violates this rule and the vessel which he left to go ashore was damaged in some way due to his absence, as stated above, he will have to pay all the damages which resulted to the vessel due to his absence, since he was negligent when he left the vessel in this manner.

If the mentioned sailors are unable to pay the damages to him to whom the vessel belongs for the losses which resulted from their negligence, they shall be seized, turned over to the judicial authorities, and cast into prison, where they shall remain until they reimburse the person to whom the vessel belongs for all the damages he suffered or are able to make an agreement to that effect with him.

If the sailors go ashore at the port where their vessel has arrived, and where their patron has ventured in order to collect the lading charges due him or to arrange for a new shipment of cargo, or where the patron has gone ashore for any other reason, and as the result of their absence from the vessel without the permission of the patron or of a person commanding in his stead, the patron of the vessel loses some cargo or suffers other damages, the sailors guilty of this breach of discipline shall pay him for all the damages and losess which resulted from their negligence. If they are unable to repay him for the damages and losses suffered,they should be dealt with as has been stated above.

This article is being written because many sailors have such an exaggerated opinion of their value that they imagine that the patron of the vessel, the navigator,or any other person aboard the vessel does not even approximate their own stature; it appears to them that whatever they may do could not possibly result in damage. Therefore, every sailor must be very careful not to leave the vessel at will in order that he does not place himself in the position where he would be subject to the punishment mentioned above.

170-Violation of Dress Regulations

A sailor shall not undress for the night unless the vessel is moored in the port for a winter layover. Should he violate this rule, he should be punished for each transgression by being tied and dunked in the ocean three times while held by a rope. If he should violate this rule three times,he shall lose his wages and all the possessions he has aboard the vessel.

171-A Sailor Cannot Leave the Vicinity of a Vessel After the Cargoing Operation Begins

To continue: A sailor is not allowed to leave the vicinity of his vessel when the cargoing of a vessel begins in a dangerous locality, unless the patron or the navigator agrees to his absence. Should he remove himself without permission,he will be required to pay for the damages suffered by the vessel due to his negligence.

172-Sailor Is Forbidden to Sell His Personal Weapons

To continue: A sailor cannot sell his personal weapons until the voyage is completed. Should he do this, he will be left to the mercy of the patron.

173—Sailor May Not Remove Anything from the Vessel Without Permission

To continue: A sailor is not allowed to take anything off the vessel without notifying the clerk, the navigator, or the guard of the vessel. Should he do this, he shall be treated as a thief.

174—Sailor Should Not Sleep Ashore

To continue: A sailor should not attempt to sleep ashore without the permission of the patron of the vessel. Should he do this, he will be adjudged perfidious.

175—Sailor Shall Unfurl the Sails and Get the Vessel Ready to Sail

To continue: A sailor shall trim the sails and get the vessel ready to sail, whether or not the navigator is aboard. He is not allowed, however, to unloosen the hawsers or to pull up the anchor if he has not received an order to do so.

176—Proper Use of the Jolly-Boat

A sailor who is assigned to steer a jolly-boat shall carry all the people into it and for this reason must remove his boots. He shall also carry people out of the boat unto the shore. Should he refuse to do this and be unwilling to do this, he shall pay all the damages resulting from his refusal to perform this task.

177—A Sailor Shall Go to the Mill if Ordered

If the patron or the clerk of the vessel order that a sailor proceed to the mill, he must obey this order; he must also carry out all the other duties connected with the maintenance of the vessel. [55]

178—Personal Arms of a Sailor

To continue: A sailor must equip himself with proper weapons as provided for in the agreement he made with the patron. If he should fail to do this, the patron shall buy the necessary weapons for him and charge them to his account, without his consent but in the presence of

---

55. To procure flour for the vessel.

the clerk.

179-A Sailor Should Not Abandon His Vessel

A sailor is prohibited from deserting the vessel during a voyage; his wages shall be increased in the same proportion as the increase of the lading charges earned by the vessel.

180-The Crew Shall Load the Ballast and the Cargo

Sailors are required to unload the ballast at the point where the vessel begins the journey; they shall store and load the cargo and other merchandise carried aboard the vessel with the help of the boats belonging to the vessel; in addition, they are required to unload the personal belongings of the merchants, their chests and weapons, as well as to load and unload the ballast, as well as to load aboard and store all the cargo regardless of its kind, especially when the vessel reaches some unscheduled area due to some danger.

181-Sailors Shall Pull the Vessel Ashore

Further, a sailor is required upon a command given by a patron to pull the vessel on the beach or up to the pier and he cannot leave the vessel until this is done. If the patron did not order that the vessel be beached or pulled to a pier, the sailor shall help in making the vessel ready for a voyage; if he should fail to do this, he will be required to pay for all the damaged due to his negligence.

182-When a Sailor Dispatched on an Errand by the Patron is Kidnapped

If the master of a vessel dispatched a sailor to some locality on an errand, the sailor must proceed as ordered. Should he be captured by someone or suffer some damage, the patron will be held accountable; and should he be kidnapped, the master shall ransom him.

To continue: A sailor shall not be ordered to go farther than half a mile from the vessel, and he shall not be ordered to do so in a dangerous locale. Should he be captured by the pirates or forcibly restrained on land, he shall be paid his full wages as if he had served aboard the vessel during the entire journey.

Further, if he is not dispatched on some errand, he shall obey all the orders issued to him by a person whom the patron left in the command of the vessel while the patron was away.

183-Responsibility of the Crew Serving Aboard a Chartered Vessel

A proprietor of a vessel who has concluded an agreement to lease his vessel for a fee shall furnish everything that was included in such an agreement between himself and the lessee. If the lessee should act dishonestly and should refuse to pay the sailors who had agreed to serve under his command, the owner of the vessel will be held accountable for their wages for he should have been very careful to whom he leased his vessel.

If the owner of the vessel leased it to a merchant for a fee and will not be accountable for any expenses which the merchant will assume, a sailor is obligated to deport himself in the same manner as he would if the lessee was a patron of the vessel. The lessee will be actually considered a patron since he will pay the wages of the crew, pay the rental fee on the vessel, and assume other expenses. If the sailor had concluded an agreement to complete another round trip with the patron of the vessel, he shall not be required to fulfill it.

This article was written because often many persons being merchants and people of high character enlist as sailors, and would not wish to serve aboard a vessel rented by some rich but rude person; and due to the fact that the patron of a vessel severed his relations with a sailor, similarly a sailor can sever his relations with the patron, since the patron leased his vessel for a fee. When a vessel is leased for a fee, all the members of the crew who had agreed to serve under the patron must now serve under the party who leased the vessel. [56]

Should some object belonging to the vessel be lost during a storm and it cannot be recovered, the lessee of the vessel will be required to replace it, and must as far as it is possible, use whatever other equipment is available aboard the vessel. Should he buy food or any essential equipment needed aboard the vessel, he will be able to deduct that amount expended from the charter fee paid. The owner of the vessel is required to supply only what he had promised.

184-A Patron Who Promises to Carry More Cargo Than His Vessel Can Accommodate

A patron who promised the merchants to carry aboard a specified amount of cargo or a certain number of quintals of merchandise, and actually cannot fulfill such a promise, will have to provide the merchants with another vessel of the same or bigger capacity than his own vessel in order that they may be able to ship their cargo. If the

---

56. This pertains to a single voyage. The crew need not continue to serve under his command after the port of destination has been reached.

other vessel charges higher lading fees, he will have to reimburse the merchants for the difference. However, it will depend on the disposition of the merchants whether or not they will accept the other vessel, and in such a case the patron who had originally promised to carry their cargo shall reach some other understanding with them.

This article has been written because very often many patrons of vessels advertise that their vessel has a greater capacity than it actually has, exaggerating the size by a third or a fourth.

185-More of the Same

If during the negotiations over the transportation of cargo a patron of a vessel promised the merchants to carry more cargo, the merchants shall deduct from the amount agreed upon as lading charges for the entire cargo the lading charges for the cargo he cannot carry.

This article was written for the reasons detailed above.

186-Cargo Damages Aboard the Vessel

If a patron leased a vessel to the merchants for a fee or accepted cargo for shipment, charging them a specific amount per quintal of cargo, and shall store and transport this cargo on the deck of his vessel without the consent and approval of these merchants, and the cargo stored in this manner is lost or damaged, other merchants who are also shipping cargo aboard this vessel will not be required to pay for the damages suffered by the merchants to whom the lost or damaged cargo belonged, even if such a cargo had been entered in the ship's register. However, the patron of the vessel shall be required to reimburse the merchants who had suffered damage of their cargo or had lost it, to the full amount of its value.

If the patron is unable to do this, his vessel shall be sold to satisfy these claims, and neither the shareholders of the vessel nor loan makers nor anyone else shall lodge any opposition to this with the exception of the sailors who have the right to demand that their wages be paid first. If the proceeds from the sale of the vessel are insufficient to cover the claims, and the patron has other property, such part of this property shall be sold as will be sufficient to pay the damages of the merchants. The shareholders in the vessel are responsible to the degree of their investment in the vessel.

To continue: If a merchant to whom the cargo belongs told the patron and reached an agreement with him that the patron can store his cargo aboard wherever he wishes, just so he takes it aboard, and this was entered into the register or will be attested to by witnesses, but these witnesses should not have any financial interest in the vessel, or be receiving any gain from this vessel (however, the ship's register will always constitute sufficient evidence),the patron who had taken the cargo aboard under these conditions is not responsible for such cargo and if this cargo is damaged or lost, the damages will have to be assumed by the owner of such cargo. Neither the patron nor the other merchants aboard the vessel will be required to pay any damages whatsoever to the merchant who had loaded his cargo aboard the vessel under such conditions. In addition, the merchant will be required to pay the patron the lading charges agreed upon and reimburse him for all his expenses connected with this cargo.

This article was written in order to make certain that the patron should not store any cargo on the deck, with the exception of the equipment and tools needed for the proper care and maintenance of the vessel.

187–Merchandise Loaded Aboard Secretly and What Should Be Done With It If Necessity Requires That It Should Be Thrown Overboard

If a merchant or several merchants concluded an agreement with a patron either in writing or in the presence of witnesses or by making an entry into the ship's register to ship a certain amount of cargo— for example, a thousand quintals in weight, for we can consider this matter in hundred as well as thousand quintals, or even more or less —the patron of the vessel will be required to take aboard the amount mentioned in the agreement. If he cannot take aboard the amount agreed to, he shall be held accountable by the merchants with whom he concluded the agreement, in the manner discussed and established in one of the preceding articles. [57]

If, however, merchants or a single merchant who had engaged the vessel to ship a thousand quintals of cargo shall load aboard the vessel one thousand five hundred or one thousand two hundred quintals, or more or less, without informing the patron about this and without making a change in their agreement or without entering this matter into the register, and the witnesses had only heard one thousand quintals of cargo mentioned, and the vessel meets with some misfortune, or it is necessary to throw some of the cargo overboard, and the patron of the vessel is able to show and prove that the merchants loaded aboard the vessel more cargo than was contracted for and entered in the register, and that the vessel was forced to throw the cargo overboard or that it experienced other damage due to the sneaky and fraudulent loading of the cargo, such merchant or mer-

---

57. Articles 184 and 185.

chants shall be required to reimburse other merchants whose cargo was thrown overboard for the actual value of such cargo as well as other damages which the patron of the vessel suffered on their account.

If the cargo of the merchants who acted in such a bad manner as has been mentioned above is insufficient to compensate the owners of the cargo which had been thrown overboard and the damages suffered by the patron, if these merchants have other property, it shall be sold to compensate the former merchants whose cargo was thrown overboard, as well as the patron who suffered damages due to their deceit. Upon a deposition made by the merchants who suffered losses at the hands of those of whom we spoke above, as well as upon the deposition made by the patron of the vessel, a case of litigation shall be brought against them, as well as against the persons who cunningly and under pretense of friendship exposed some other person to the danger of losing his life.

If it should happen that there will be no need to throw the cargo overboard and the patron will also not suffer any damages, and at the time of unloading the vessel the patron discovered that the amount of cargo loaded aboard was in excess of the amount mentioned in the agreement, the patron shall determine whether such attempt at deceit should be turned over to the local court. If he decides to take this course of action, the cargo shall be divided in the following manner: The patron will take one-third of the cargo, and out of this share the shareholders in the vessel will get their share according to the amount of their investment in the vessel; one-third of the cargo will be taken by the court, and one-third of the cargo shall be set aside to be used for ransoming enslaved people, as an expression of the love of God.

If the patron of the vessel wishes to forgive the merchants to whom the cargo belonged, and does not surrender their cargo to the local court, it is within the power of the patron to demand from these merchants payment of the lading fees in the amount determined by him arbitrarily, as has been stated in one of the previous articles.[58]

Therefore, every merchant should be very careful not to load aboard a vessel more cargo than he has contracted to ship, and thus avoid in this manner the risk of being exposed to the treatment discussed above.

188-Necessary Equipment and Repairs Aboard a Vessel Leased for a Fee

---

58. Article 87

A vessel leased by merchants for a fee should undertake the voyage as specified in the terms of the agreement. If it should happen that the vessel undertakes such a long voyage that there will have to be repairs made aboard or the equipment has to be replaced, because it is partly or completely worn out, the owner of the vessel will not be required to undertake the repairs or replace the equipment, because he had equipped the vessel properly and had it in a good state of repair when he leased it. He will, therefore, not be forced to do anything during the voyage of the vessel because he did not violate any of the promises made to the merchants who had leased the vessel.

If due to the lack of proper equipment or tools needed aboard the vessel the merchants want to purchase these necessities, they may do so, and after the conclusion of the voyage they shall be allowed to take the equipment bought by them and the patron cannot prevent them from doing this.

189-Failure to Return the Vessel Leased for a Fee on the Date Specified in the Agreement

If the merchants retain the vessel beyond the time they had agreed at the time they leased it for a fee, they shall be required to pay an additional amount for its rental. If they should want to undertake another journey,they shall again negotiate a new agreement with the patron of the vessel.

190-Lack of Proper Equipment Aboard the Vessel Contracted to Carry Cargo Per Hundred Weight

If a vessel was engaged to carry cargo on which charges were paid per hundred weight and it lacks proper equipment, such as mast or anchor or rudder, the patron of the vessel shall purchase the necessary items when he reaches a port where such equipment can be purchased at an average price, that is, that the patron is authorized to pay up to twice the price such equipment would cost in the country from which the journey was undertaken. If, however, he could not purchase these items at that price, that is, at twice the amount he would pay for it in his own country, he is not required to purchase these items. Should he buy such equipment and the price he paid is above the double value price in his own country, the merchants will be obligated to pay for the additional amount expended in proportion to the amount and value of their cargo aboard.

In a situation when, before the above mentioned purchases have been made, it is necessary to cut the sailing-yard to make a rudder or rudder posts or some other necessary items out of wood due to the lack of this equipment aboard the vessel, the merchants will be required to pay for the sailing-yard, and the patron must buy a new one to replace it.

191-When a Vessel Cannot Undertake a Contracted Voyage Due to the Prohibition of Governmental Authorities

If in certain circumstances a vessel does not dare attempt a voyage due to the prohibition issued by the authorities of the location to which the vessel is bound, and the patron and the merchants learn they can enter a port in another territory, the sailors shall continue to serve aboard without getting an increase in wages, even if the distance to the new destination is over one hundred and fifty miles away from the port into which the vessel was denied entry. If, however, the vessel is paid an increase in the lading charges for this distance,the sailors shall receive an increase in their wages in the same proportion as the shipping charges were increased; if the charges were not increased,the sailors will not receive any increase in wages.

Further, if due to the mentioned prohibition the vessel is forced to put into some port and unload its cargo at some unexpected place, the wages of the crew will be increased in the same proportion as the increase of the shipping charges.

192-When a Vessel Due to the Restrictions Imposed by the Authorities Cannot Complete Cargoing and Is Forced to Sail to Another Location

When the merchants, after arranging with a vessel to pick up their cargo at some designated location, arrive there to pick up the cargo and there are met with some obstacles imposed by the local authorities which have forbidden shipment of certain goods out of the country, and if the merchants and the patron find another location where they may load such cargo, the patron, after reaching an understanding with the merchants, may proceed there, and no sailor can voice any opposition in this matter, as has been stated in the previous article. If the merchants do not raise the amount of the lading charges, the patron will not be required to raise the wages of the crew.

If, however, after reaching the location where they believed they could load on such cargo, they meet similar obstacles before the merchants complete their transactions and before the vessel can be partly or fully loaded, and due to these restrictions the merchants are not able to export the cargo which they had purchased, or any other merchandise which they would like to buy, and the patron insists that they get their cargo in order to get the vessel under way, and also demands, although he knows that they cannot get the cargo aboard because of the mentioned obstacles, even though they had paid the shipping charges and paid other expenses, and if due to this insistence on the part of the patron the merchants consented to sail, the merchants shall not be obliged to pay him either part or all of the shipping charges, because it was not due to their fault, but to the obstacles issued by the authorities that this delay occurred; and no one can oppose or act contrary to the will of God and governmental authority.

If the crew demanded payment of their wages the patron will not be required to pay them since he himself was not paid for carrying the cargo; if it actually be true that the crew would suffer a great loss because of this, it is also true that the patron of the vessel suffers even a greater loss, because he used his vessel, his time, and has undergone many expenses. The merchants shall, however, refund to the patron half of the expenses incurred by him in the amount declared by him in a deposition under oath; the merchants shall pay half of this amount without any opposition whatsoever but they are not obligated to pay another cent above this amount mentioned above, unless they wish to give him a little more for all the troubles he has undergone.

To continue: If at the time the merchants engaged the vessel they were aware of the governmental restrictions mentioned above, but in spite of this and in the hope that they would be able to get permission to load on such cargo, if they made certain financial arrangements with these authorities,[59] they undertook this voyage, and after reaching their port of destination to take on such cargo they were not able to get the permission of the local authorities to export such cargo, the merchants will not be required to reimburse the master of the vessel for his expenses, nor to pay for his losses and damages, because the patron of the vessel as well as the merchants knew of the impediments which existed.

For this reason the merchants are not required to pay the patron any lading fees nor any losses and damages he has suffered. If, however, the merchants knew about these impediments before

59. Generally refers to bribes which were often extorted from merchants by a variety of officials.

96

they engaged the vessel and the master of the vessel did not know about them, and he is able to show and prove that the merchants knew about these restrictions at the time they engaged his vessel, they will be forced to pay the full agreed lading charges and all the expenses; the patron on the other hand will pay the crew its wages in the amount they would have been paid had they successfully completed the whole journey, because he had been paid the full lading fees as if he had carried a full cargo.

Further, regardless of the type of agreement the patron should reach with the merchants, it must be taken for granted that the crew will be fully considered in its terms.

Further, if, on the other hand, the patron of the vessel knew of existing impediments, previously mentioned, while the merchants did not know that any such impediments existed, and they can prove this, the patron will be required to repay them all their expenses and losses including the amount they would have made in selling such cargo, because he was well aware of these restrictions but failed to inform them of their existence.

In such a case the patron shall also pay the full wages of the crew, if the members of the crew did not know of these impediments before they made an agreement with the patron to serve aboard his vessel. If, however, the crew was aware of these restrictions, the patron shall not be required to pay their wages.

Everything that has been written above must be carried out without attempting any deceit or fraud.

193-Patron's Responsibilities Toward His Crew Aboard a Vessel Leased for a Fee

The owner of a vessel who leases his vessel to another party for a specific fee must be very discriminating with whom he concludes such an agreement, because if the lessee should become insolvent,the crew would lose its wages. A mountebank or a cheat can more easily reach an agreement with a person of his own kind than with an honest person; therefore, a patron leasing his vessel to a person of such caliber would mislead the crew. Thus the crew after serving a short or a long time under such a master would have wasted their time, because he might disappear, and they would have served under a master who had become indebted to the owner of the vessel. If such a master should die or flee, the owner of the vessel shall be responsible for the wages of the crew and shall pay the crew for the entire period of service, unless he discovers some assets of the party who leased the vessel, or who died, or who had gone into hiding.

If it should happen that the patron of the vessel in order to mislead the crew introduced some person as a guarantor of a loan, regardless of whether he is indebted to him or not, and if the patron should die, the loan guarantor or the person who shall be in the command of the vessel shall be required to pay the crew its wages, for no member of the crew can be deprived of his wages whether the patron of the vessel has died,or because of some subterfuge, or because the patron has deserted, or because the creditor demands his money.

194-With Certain Exceptions, the Patron Must Undertake a Planned Voyage

A master of a vessel who has agreed to carry cargo for a merchant or some other person cannot refuse to undertake such a journey personally if he failed to make such a reservation with the merchant. Should he refuse to proceed on a journey in spite of the insistence of the merchants, he shall be liable for all the damages suffered by the merchants, because the damages resulted due to his negligence. If the patron refrained from making the journey with the approval of the merchants, he shall not be held liable for any damages. Under such circumstances he shall designate a person who will in his stead carry out all the obligations he agreed to with the merchants; the navigator shall under oath inform the merchants that the person designated by the patron to take the command is actually qualified to replace the master of the vessel, and should such a person not be qualified, the patron must provide another qualified person to take his place.

To continue: A patron may refuse to undertake such a voyage on four accounts, namely: due to illness, in order to marry, in order to undertake a holy pilgrimage if he had taken an oath to undertake such a pilgrimage before he had contracted to carry such cargo, and because of a prohibition imposed by the authorities. Each of the above mentioned reasons must be authentic and not an attempt at deception, and none of these reasons relieve the patron of the responsibility to provide some other person to take his place as commander of the vessel, as has been stated before.

This article has been written because many merchants entrust their cargo to a patron of a vessel due to mutual friendship or because of the fame he enjoys as a capable master of the vessel. If a merchant had known that a patron would refrain from undertaking the journey, he would not have engaged the vessel and loaded his cargo aboard it, even if he had anticipated a greater profit than the cost of shipping the cargo.

195-Foundering of a Vessel on Shoals Due to a Storm or Other Causes

If due to a storm or any other causes whatsoever, a vessel cannot avoid foundering on shoals or projecting rocks, the patron of the vessel in the presence of the clerk, the navigator, and the crew should immediately inform those aboard:

"Gentlemen, we cannot avoid shipwreck, and my conviction is that the owners of the vessel shall be held liable for the cargo and the owners of the cargo shall be held liable for the vessel."

If the majority or all of the merchants express the acceptance of this responsibility, and the vessel founders on the shoals, is wrecked, or suffers some other damage, it should be evaluated at the value it had before the accident took place, and the evaluation should be made by the patron and the merchants who have their cargo aboard if they and the patron can reach an agreement as to its value. If they cannot agree on the evaluation of the vessel and a dispute arises among them as to the value of such a vessel, the matter should be turned over for adjudication to two learned persons well versed in the matters related to the art of sailing. Whatever they decide and declare shall be carried out.

If the vessel has been destroyed, the salvaged cargo shall be used to pay the patron the full value of the vessel as had been declared by the two learned persons who had been entrusted with the adjudication of the issue.

However, all the equipment and other effects of the vessel that were salvaged from the vessel that had met with such a misfortune, shall be evaluated, and this sum should be subtracted from the sum at which the vessel had been valued, this is to mean, from the value of the vessel determined by the merchants to whom the salvaged cargo belonged as well as the evaluation which had been made by the patron or the two persons well versed in these matters, as mentioned before. This amount the patron shall deduct from the amount he is to receive for his vessel. If the master of the vessel would not agree to such an arrangement, the salvaged equipment and tools shall be sold at an auction to the highest bidder, for the patron under all circumstances shall receive the amount at which the vessel was evaluated.

If the vessel was not wrecked but its hull had been pierced or it was damaged in some other way, the patron of the vessel shall be required to share, together with the salvaged cargo, in the cost of the repairs that will be necessary, in proportion to the amount at which the vessel will be valued.

Further, if the patron announced that the salvaged cargo would be assessed for the damages suffered by the vessel and the merchants agree to this, and the patron did not accept any responsibility on the part of the vessel to share in the damage of the cargo, all the damages that resulted when the vessel foundered in the shoals or struck a rock shall be paid for by the salvaged cargo. The patron of the vessel shall not be obligated to share in the resulting damages because he had not committed his vessel to share with the salvaged cargo in the payment of the damages, and the merchants had agreed to this.

There is no need to discuss an accident when a vessel is completely wrecked and to repeat what has already been stated above. Nevertheless, if the merchants had informed the patron that the salvaged cargo shall be used to pay the damages for the cargo lost, and the patron together with the majority or all the merchants agree to this proposal, the value of the cargo salvaged shall be apportioned proportionally for the cargo that had been lost. The patron of the vessel shall be bound to share in the damages in the amount he will have received for his vessel.

If it should happen that there are no merchants aboard the vessel, the patron may and should act in their name; whatever action he takes should be taken in full understanding with the clerk, the navigator, and the crew. Thus whatever the master of the vessel does under such circumstances will be as valid as if all the merchants had been aboard the vessel or as if all the cargo had belonged to him.

196 - Shipwreck of a Cargoed Vessel

If a patron cargoed his vessel in order to carry it and unload it at some port designated in the agreement with the merchants to whom the cargo belonged, and during the journey a misfortune overtook the vessel and it foundered on the shoals, or was wrecked or damaged in some other manner, the patron shall be compensated in conformity with what had been agreed to between himself and the merchants before the misfortune occurred.

If the patron demands payment of the lading charges, he should receive them, provided a sufficient amount of cargo has been salvaged; if, however, no cargo is salvaged from the wreck, no one will be obliged to pay any of the shipping charges, since all the cargo has been lost. If part of the cargo is salvaged and the master of the vessel demands payment of the lading fees for the cargo salvaged as well as for the cargo that has been lost, he should be paid the full amount, but in such an event he shall be required to share the damages for the cargo lost to the amount he had received in payment of the lading charges and in proportion to the value of the cargo that has been lost.

If the patron of a vessel demands and is paid the lading charges for the cargo that has been salvaged only, he shall not be required to share in the damages resulting from the loss of the cargo because he has not been paid any lading charges for that part of the cargo.

If, however, there had been no agreement or an understanding reached between the patron and the merchants at the time the vessel foundered, was wrecked, or was damaged, the merchants will not be held responsible for any of the damages, unless they freely wish to compensate him for the damage to the vessel, because there had been no agreement made between them. They will, however, be required to pay the master the lading charges for the cargo salvaged, depending on the distance he had carried their cargo.

If there has been an agreement or an understanding reached between the patron and the merchants, the merchants are obliged to pay the damages to the patron of the vessel in conformity with what has been stated above, and the patron may retain a sufficient amount of the cargo as security until he is paid, and even a larger amount of the cargo in order that he will not be forced to pursue them and plead with them to collect the money coming to him.

No one can deny him this prerogative or demand that he accept some guarantor in lieu of the cargo or that he take some other cargo as a guarantee for his fees, and no court of law or anyone else should or can coerce him to do anything contrary to his decision in this matter.

197-Partial Unloading of a Vessel During a Storm and During Fair Weather

A vessel may reach the port where the cargo is to be unloaded during a storm or during fair weather. If it reaches the port on a day when fair weather prevails and unloads part of its cargo at a very low cost, and during the night or the next day a storm may develop and the unloading of the remaining cargo may cost one-half or two-thirds more than on the previous day when the discharging of the cargo began, the merchants whose cargo had been unloaded at a low price will not be required to reimburse the merchants whose cargo was unloaded at a higher cost, unless there had been an agreement reached among themselves that they shall aid one another in the cost of unloading all their cargo, if the cost of unloading one part of the cargo was higher than the cost of unloading another part of the cargo, because this happened purely due to a mere circumstance that some of these merchants had their cargo unloaded at low cost and others at a much higher cost.

To continue: If a vessel has unloaded part of the cargo and a violent storm develops resulting in the loss of all the remaining cargo aboard, the cargo that had been unloaded prior to the storm cannot be held liable for the damages due to the loss of the cargo that had remained aboard the vessel, unless the merchants had agreed that all the cargo carried aboard will share in damages to any part of the cargo. If there are no merchants aboard the vessel and the patron has decided that all the cargo be held liable for damage to any part of the cargo, his decision will be as binding as if all the merchants had been aboard and made such an agreement, or if all of the cargo belonged to the master of the vessel. The cargo is actually considered to be his, as it is under his care.

Should the vessel be wrecked or damaged, and the patron together with the merchants had agreed to make the cargo and the vessel mutually responsible for any damages to either, the salvaged cargo shall be required to share in the damages suffered by the vessel, as they had agreed. If there has been no such understanding or agreement reached, the party who has been damaged must assume such damage alone.

If there were no merchants aboard the vessel, and the patron together with the crew decided that the vessel and the cargo shall share mutually in any damages, this will be as valid as if all the merchants had been aboard the vessel or if all the cargo belonged to him; the cargo is actually his since it is in his care. If the master of the vessel made such a decision without the advice and consent of the majority or all of the crew, such a decision will not be valid. Therefore, all masters of vessels should beware that whatever they decide be accepted as binding.

198-Cargo Waterlogged Due to Negligence of Boatmen

Those who transfer the cargo by boat in the process of loading or unloading it, as well as those who work in transferring cargo on land, should perform their task well and with care so that the cargo will not be damaged by water, spoiled, or be lost due to their carelessness. Should the cargo be lost, damaged, or spoiled but not as a result of their neglect, they shall not be required to pay any damages to the merchants whose cargo was spoiled, damaged, or lost, because it did not happen due to any fault of theirs.

To continue: If during the loading operations the bindings or ropes of unloaded or empty chests, bales, or crates slip off, and they can prove this, they will not be required to pay any damages to the owners of these chests, bales, or crates or for any other waterlogged, damaged, or lost cargo, because it was improperly bound.

However, if such cargo during loading or unloading operation should become waterlogged, damaged or lost due to their negligence, they shall be forced to pay the damages to the merchants to whom the cargo belongs. Should they be incapable of paying, the burden will fall upon the party who was in charge of transferring the cargo by boat, if he has the means to pay such damages; if he does not have the means he shall be seized and detained in prison until he is able to re-imburse the merchants whose cargo was waterlogged, damaged, or lost due to his negligence or the negligence of the people employed by him aboard his boat, or working with him, because he will profit from this operation to the same extent as those working for him or even to a higher degree. It is therefore proper that he who will share in the profits, should also share in the damages.

Therefore, all those in charge of boats should be very careful whom they hire. If these people perform their task well, he shall realize his share of the profit. If they do it improperly or carelessly, the whole responsibility will fall upon him who is the owner of a boat, be-cause the merchants will not make demands upon those workers whom they do not know, but upon the one who is the owner of the boat.

For that reason, everyone who is in charge of a boat should be careful what type of workers he hires to load and unload cargo off the vessel into his boat, in order that he does not suffer any damaging consequences.

199-Loading or Unloading of a Vessel for a Flat Fee

He who is in charge of a ferrying boat, as well as the men working at moving of cargo to shore, when they have agreed to cargo or unload a vessel for a fixed fee or a specified amount of money, are required to accomplish this quickly, properly, and conscientiously. If they complete this task properly and conscientiously as stated above, the merchants or the patron of the vessel acting in their stead shall pay them the amount agreed to immediately and in full upon the completion of the task, without any disputations. If, on the other hand, the mer-chants delay and dispute this payment, and due to this the boatmen or the men who worked on shore transferring such a cargo should suffer some loss or expense, such merchants or the patron of the vessel who had acted in their stead shall pay all the losses and expenses due to their refusal to pay the agreed sum of money on time.

Thus in this manner the merchants or the patron shall proceed without causing any trouble, if the boatmen have completed their task as stated above.

To continue: If the merchants or the patron of the vessel suffered any damages or were forced to undergo some expense due to the neg-ligence of those ferrying the cargo by boat of working on the shore in handling the cargo, and they should fail to complete the cargoing or unloading of the vessel according to the provisions of the agreement, the boatmen or those handling the cargo on shore shall be liable for all the costs, expenses, and damages that the merchants or the patron of the vessel who had acted in their name had suffered due to their negligence, and they shall reimburse the merchants or the patron without any dispute.

If, however, they are unable to reimburse them for their losses, they should be seized and turned over to the proper authorities, and they shall be kept in prison until such time that they repay the merchants or the patron who acted in the name of the merchants all the losses that they had suffered or until they reach some agreement satisfactory to the merchants or the patron who had acted in their stead.

200-Vessels Lying at Anchor in the Order of Their Arrival in the Port

If behind the vessel that first dropped anchor in a port, at a sand bar, shore, or pier another vessel drops anchor, it should be moored in such a way that it will cause no damage to the vessel that first dropped its anchor at that point. If in mooring it some damage should result to the first vessel, the owners of the second vessel shall pay for the damage without any dispute.

However, if the second vessel arrived during a storm and could not be moored without causing damage to the first vessel moored, damages will not be paid for the damage caused since it did not result due to any negligence. In case of damage committed under such circumstances the issue shall be submitted for arbitration to learned people well versed in the art of sailing.

201-More of the Same

A vessel that reaches a port, a pier, or a shore and drops anchor and causes some damage to a vessel that arrives or moors later, will not be held responsible for repairing of the damage, if such a vessel was short of mooring ropes, or if it had used up all the mooring lines it had aboard and did everything else possible to avoid an accident, or if the vessel was moored at a place where it could not under any condition borrow or rent any mooring lines, and if the storm buffeted it so violently that the vessel could not be anchored properly. If under such circumstances it has caused some damage to another vessel, it will not be obligated to make repairs aboard the damaged vessel.

On the other hand, if this vessel had lines that were borrowed or rented, or if it was located in the area where the patron can procure such lines, or, finally, if those aboard the vessel that reached the anchorage later, warned those aboard the vessel that had arrived earlier that they should moor their vessel more solidly in order that it would not cause damage because the weather was inclement and there was danger of a storm, and the crew of the vessel moored earlier replied that they would not add any more anchor lines to make

104

the vessel more secure, and there came up a storm of which the crew of the second vessel to reach the port had warned the crew of the first vessel that had dropped anchor in the port, and the second vessel was damaged, the first vessel should pay for all the damages caused by it, because the crew of the second vessel that dropped anchor had cautioned and warned the crew of the first vessel of the impending danger.

Nonetheless, if the first vessel to have cast anchor used up all its mooring lines and undertook all possible means to safeguard itself, regardless of the fact that it was moored at a location where it could procure additional mooring lines, it would not be responsible for any damages that it would cause. No one can indeed suppose that the patron of the vessel, who had an opportunity to rent, buy, or borrow additional mooring lines would not have done so had he thought it was necessary, and would rather lose all that he possesses just to cause damage knowingly to another vessel. No one should suspect nor believe this.

This article was written for the reasons listed above.

202-Explanation of the Preceding Article

If some vessel is the first to drop anchor at some specified place, a vessel that reaches this place later must drop anchor in such a way that it will not cause any damage. If, however, it should cause some damage, it shall be held accountable for it in conformity with what has been stated, explained, and specified above.

To continue: The above shall be interpreted in the following manner: that the first vessel to drop anchor will not move its anchor or its mooring lines inward or outward of the shore after the newly arrived vessel has been moored. If the first vessel moored should move its anchor or its mooring lines after the arrival and anchoring of the second vessel, and suffer some damage, the vessel that was moored later shall not be liable for all but for only part of this damage, because it was the first vessel that moved its anchor or its lines either inward or outward of the shore.

Whatever damage was caused by the later moored vessel to the earlier moored vessel shall be given to arbitration of learned persons well versed in the art of sailing. They together with the advice that will be given to them by the Elders of the Sea Corporation and with the examination of their conscience, will be capable of deciding justly and properly the extent of the damages, in order to prevent greater damages and more serious misunderstandings from arising between the patrons of the vessels and other interested parties in this dispute.

On the other hand, if the earlier arrived vessel did not more or change its anchor and mooring lines either inward or outward of the shore, the later arrived vessel will be responsible for the repair of all damages caused, as was stated and decided above.

To continue: If after the later arriving vessel has been moored, it moves its anchor or its mooring lines, and as the result of this change in its anchorage, the vessel that arrived earlier suffers some damage, the responsibility for the repair of all the damage must be borne by the second vessel moored because it moved its mooring lines and anchors.

If, however, the first arriving vessel moved its lines and anchors more inward or more outward and the vessel that was moored later did not move its lines and anchors nor change its position in any way, the latter vessel shall not be held responsible for any damages, beyond the damages established and declared in the above statements.

Further, if, however, the earlier arriving vessel suffers any damage but not due to the negligence of the later arriving vessel, the latter will not be responsible for the payment of any damages suffered by the first vessel, as it was not due to the negligence of the vessel which arrived and was anchored later.

This article was written in order that all take care how they anchor their vessels so that they do not expose themselves, due to their conduct, to the above mentioned penalties. Let, therefore, all beware and be watchful, that whatever they do, they should do well and sensibly, so that they and others shall avoid the possibility of precipitating disputes due to such negligence.

203-Anchorage of Vessels

If one, two, or more vessels enter the port simultaneously, or anchor at a pier, shore, or some other spot, each of the vessels must drop anchor at such distance from the other vessel that under no circumstances could they cause damage to one another.

Further, if it should happen that a storm develops, each vessel must be anchored and moored securely and staunchly, and each vessel must take all possible steps in order to prevent damage to any of the vessels moored. If it should happen that during a storm one of the vessels lacking enough proper equipment collides with another vessel and causes damage, but the vessel that lacked some essential equipment had made every possible effort to be safely moored, and the equipment it had on board was of good quality and sufficient to take care of the needs of such a vessel or even a larger vessel, such a vessel cannot be called upon to pay the damage to the party that suffered it, as the damage did not result from the negligence of the vessel that lacked some equipment for the simple reason that the damage did not result due to the negligence of the vessel that lacked some equipment, and also because the party to whom the vessel belongs did everything in his power to moor the vessel securely, and even though there was lack of some equipment, the equipment that was available on board was sufficient and of good quality, and capable of mooring the vessel of that size and even a larger vessel.

Therefore, for reasons listed above, such a vessel will not be required to repair the damage it had caused to another vessel. However, if the patron of the vessel aboard which there was lack of equipment did not moor the vessel strongly enough as he should have, or if the mooring lines aboard it were not sufficient to anchor a vessel of that size or even a smaller vessel, and because of this the vessel had caused some damage to another vessel, the master of such a vessel will be required to pay for all such damages suffered by any vessel due to the poor quality or weakness of the mooring lines that the former vessel had aboard.

For those reasons every patron of a vessel should be careful and make sure that his vessel is moored properly, and should not keep aboard his vessel equipment that is insufficient in order that he avoid the penalties mentioned above.

204-Rental of Barrels

When a patron of a vessel has rented a number of barrels to use in a particular voyage or for a specified period of time, and the lessor stipulates that the patron cannot take possession of them or order some other person to take possession of the barrels until the rental has been paid as had been agreed, and that the patron must be personally responsible and accountable for them, and when the patron in spite of the imposed conditions, takes possession of such barrels and they are lost during the voyage or during the period of time they were rented for, the patron will be required to replace such barrels or pay their owner their value in addition to the full rental fee, not only for the period they were rented for or duration of the voyage, but also for all the time until he has satisfied the owner of the barrels.

Further, should the patron of the vessel who rented such barrels lose them through gambling, sell them, or lose them by his negligence, the procedure outlined above should be followed.

Further, if at the time of the rental of these barrels, their owner did not make any such stipulations to the patron of the vessel who rented the barrels, and subsequently they are lost, the owner of the barrels will have to suffer the loss, whether the patron of the vessel paid or did not pay any rental fee on such barrels, provided that the loss of these barrels did not result due to the causes mentioned above, that is, due to the fault of the master of the vessel and that the owner had not made such stipulations. The rental fee for the barrels shall not be included in that loss, for whether the barrels are lost or not the rental fee shall be paid to their owner. If the barrels have been lost due to the causes mentioned before, the patron of the vessel shall pay full damages to their owner.

If the owner of the barrels and the patron of the vessel could not reach a satisfactory agreement, the matter should be referred to two Elders of the Coopers Guild, who have seen these barrels and are experts in the cooperage trade, and whatever they determine under oath to be the amount due to the owner of the barrels from the patron who rented them will be decisive with this stipulation, that the rental on the barrels shall be paid in the full amount agreed.

205-A Shipment of Wine

A patron of a vessel who agreed to carry a cargo of wine for the merchants and promised to supply them sufficient number of barrels to accommodate the cargo, shall proceed in the following manner: He shall above all see to it that the barrels are made clean, then he shall order the crew or some other persons to fill them with water before they are loaded aboard the vessel; when they are filled with water he should show these barrels to the merchants or to persons acting in their stead for examination, asking them whether in their opinion these barrels are of proper variety and sufficiently leakproof, and if they desire that these barrels be loaded aboard the vessel.

If the merchants or persons acting as their representatives signify that they believe these barrels are leakproof and that they may be loaded aboard the vessel, and after they are loaded aboard and filled with the wine, then these barrels should leak and lose a certain amount of the contents, the patron of the vessel shall not be obligated to pay any damages whatsoever, because there is no negligence on his part, and because he had shown the merchants the barrels filled with water, and, finally, because he had loaded them aboard the vessel with their approval or the approval of their representatives who had stated that they considered the barrels sufficiently leakproof.

In such a situation the merchants are required to pay the full amount of the lading fees as agreed, for the wine that had been salvaged as well as for the wine that had leaked out, for the wine did not leak out due to any negligence on the part of the patron.

To continue: If the patron of the vessel had agreed to supply the merchants with the barrels, as stated above, but neither he nor his representatives showed these barrels to the merchants in order that they might ascertain if these barrels were watertight, and had loaded them aboard the vessel without the inspection by the merchants, and then the merchants suffered some damages due to leakage of the wine, the patron of the vessel will be forced to pay them damages, while the merchants will not be required to pay the lading charges for the wine lost, because they had not been given the opportunity to ascertain if the barrels were watertight.

If, however, the patron of the vessel had not agreed to supply the merchants with the barrels in which to ship their cargo as had been contracted for, because these merchants had their own barrels or had procured such barrels somewhere else, whether such barrels will or will not be watertight, and if some or all of the wine leaks out of these barrels, the merchants will be required to pay the full shipping costs as had been agreed when the cargo of wine had been loaded aboard the vessel, and this they must do without any argument or opposition.

This article was written for the reasons discussed above.

206-Rental of Equipment

A patron of a vessel who leased some equipment in order to undertake a voyage will not be required to pay the owner of such equipment any damages for the loss of such equipment, if the loss does not occur due to his negligence. He will, however, be obligated to pay the rental fee on the equipment.

To continue: If the loss of the equipment resulted due to the negligence of the patron, he will have to compensate the owner of the equipment for the full value of such equipment as it was evaluated at the time he leased it, or he shall replace such equipment with equipment of the same quality and in the same condition as the equipment he borrowed.

To continue: If such equipment was damaged or destroyed due to the negligence of the patron, he will be required to pay the damages in the manner stated above. If, however, the damage or breakage occurred not due to any fault on his part, he will be required to pay only the rental fee, as was stated before.

Nevertheless, if the owner of such equipment, who rented it, set a value on the equipment or made some other stipulation, and the patron of the vessel accepted such equipment with these stipulations, he will be required to pay the owner the value that had been stipulated or replace it with equipment of the same value. It will be left to the discretion of the owner of such equipment whether he will accept repayment or replacement for such equipment.

To continue: If the patron of the vessel took this equipment aboard his vessel on a journey other than stipulated at the time the equipment was rented, and during such a voyage the equipment was lost, the master of the vessel shall replace such equipment or pay the value it was worth at the time it was rented, no matter under what circumstances it was lost or damaged.

The rental on such equipment used on an unscheduled voyage should be paid on the same basis specified for the original voyage, and no matter what happens to such rented equipment, the rental fee must be paid in full.

207-Responsibility for Rented Equipment

The patron of a vessel who rented marine equipment, if such equipment is lost or damaged, will be required to replace such equipment with equipment of the same quality, or pay for it according to its value at the time of the rental. The owner of the equipment may decide whether he will accept replacement or cash payment.

Further, it is immaterial how the equipment was lost or damaged; it must be returned to the owner, and the patron who rented such equipment cannot enter any objections to this.

This article was written because many patrons of vessels rent equipment, and in the event that it is lost or damaged make all sorts of objections when the owner of such equipment demands its return. For the reasons mentioned above, a patron of a vessel should not and cannot enter into any controversy over this matter with the party who rented him this equipment.

208-In Cases of Emergency Any Equipment Left on the Shore May Be Taken by a Patron of a Vessel

Any master of a vessel may take equipment that he finds left on the shore, if he needs it to moor his vessel, fearing an approaching storm, or if he finds himself in a dangerous territory, provided that this equipment will not be needed by the party to whom it belongs, who would need it to moor his own vessel. If the owner of such equipment left on the shore is on hand, he should be asked for permission to use it. If the owner is not on hand, the patron may take such equipment, provided that he immediately notify the owner if he can find him or his representative authorized to act in his stead. If the latter demands a rental fee, he shall be paid such a fee because the equipment was taken without his knowledge, but not for any other reason.

Further, the patron who took such equipment must put it back where he found it as soon as the storm passes.

If the party to whom such equipment belonged suffered any damages or loss because of this, the patron of the vessel who had borrowed it shall pay all the damages and losses.

Further, if the equipment was lost or damaged in any way, the patron who borrowed it must make the replacement to the owner to whom it belonged with equipment of the same quality and value it had at the time it was borrowed, and he should do that without any hesitation or dispute. If the owner of the borrowed equipment refuses to accept replacement in kind and demands that he be paid in cash for such equipment, the two interested parties should attempt to reach an agreement on this matter. If they cannot, the issue should be referred to two Elders of the Sea Guild, who have seen this equipment, and whatever they decide will have to be carried out, and neither of the parties to the dispute can register any objections.

This article has been written, in order that a patron of a vessel will be able to borrow the necessary equipment to moor his vessel securely without the knowledge of the party to whom such equipment belongs. If it was necessary that the patron find the owner before he could use such equipment, he would probably, due to the severe storm that had overcome his vessel, lose his vessel and everything aboard it before he could find him.

For the reasons explained above, the patron of a vessel can use any equipment that is left unattended on the shore without the knowledge of its owner, if he needs it in the circumstances explained previously.

209-Rented or Borrowed Equipment

If a patron who borrowed or took equipment left on the shore in order to anchor his vessel, and took it along on one or more voyages without the knowledge and approval of the owner, and the latter due to this should suffer some damage or be forced to rent other equipment for his own use because his equipment had been taken by someone else, the patron who borrowed the equipment left on shore shall pay all the cost, expenses, and damages suffered by the owner of such equipment.

Further, he shall also pay the rental fee to the owner of such equipment, and the latter would be completely within his rights to demand a rental fee of whatever amount he chooses to set, and it must be paid without any opposition.

Further, whether or not the party who took such equipment without the permission of its owner should be turned over to the authorities as a common thief is completely dependent upon the party to whom the equipment belonged.

If the equipment was lost or damaged, the party who took it shall be required to reimburse the owner in the amount determined by the owner personally, provided that he makes the estimate of its value under oath.

This article was written because many patrons of vessels would take equipment owned by others, if the above mentioned customs were not adhered to, and which are being used to arbitrate all differences arising in these matters.

210-Command of the Vessel During a Specified Voyage

Any merchant or sailor or any other person who accepts command of a vessel for a specific voyage or to a specific place of destination, and during such a voyage or at the place of destination the cargo that he had accepted under his command is lost but not due to his negligence, shall not be required to replace such cargo or pay for the damages thereof.

Further, if the party who accepted the cargo under his command should proceed with such cargo to another place or port other than specified in the agreement and the cargo should be lost, he will be required to repay the entire loss to the party who entrusted such cargo under his command because he had taken the cargo to a different location or port of destination than had been agreed.

Further, if the party to whom the cargo was entrusted took it to another location or port than that specified in the contract and sold it at a profit, he shall turn over all of the profit made to the owner of the cargo, and cannot retain any part of it beyond what had been agreed at the moment he accepted the cargo under his command. Should he retain more than had been agreed to, he shall be treated in the same manner as if he had taken the money from the safety box of the owner of the cargo.

Should the cargo or the profit made on it be lost at the location where the party who had been given such cargo under his command was to make an accounting of the transaction to the owner of the cargo, the former shall be held accountable for all of the profit as well as the cargo entrusted under his command.

211-Restrictions Imposed Upon a Commander of a Vessel

If a party accepts command of a vessel for a specific journey to a designated port of destination, and having sailed away from the location where the agreement was concluded, arrives at the port of destination, and there is faced with pursuit by privateers or some other obstacles imposed by the local authorities, or threat of action on the part of unfriendly naval units, and due to these circumstances the cargo entrusted under his command is lost, he shall not be held accountable in any degree to the party who entrusted the cargo to his command.

However, if during the voyage and before reaching the place of destination, he had learned about the existence of the probable dangerous situation there, but in spite of this knowledge proceeded there, thus inadvertently allowing the cargo to be lost, he shall be required to pay full damages to the party who entrusted him with the cargo under his command.

If, however, the party who accepted command of the vessel had learned during the journey and before he arrived at the port of destination of the probable existence of danger there, and was able to contact the owner of the cargo and make an arrangement with him to take the cargo to another location where there was no probability of meeting with similar dangers, such an arrangement shall be valid even though the new place of destination was not mentioned in the original agreement, for this reason, that those who take command of a vessel assume the position of merchants toward a patron of a vessel; thus for the three above mentioned reasons, anyone accepting command of a vessel, may proceed with the cargo to another destination than had been originally agreed upon, provided that he will do this in order to protect the cargo and nor for any other reason and that he will do this without any deceit or fraud.

However, immediately after reaching the destination that had been agreed to with the patron of a vessel during the voyage, the one who had accepted the command of the vessel should sell or exchange all of the cargo entrusted to him and return to make an accounting of the transaction to the party who entrusted the command to him.

If the above established procedures were followed but the cargo was lost, even though such a port had not been specified in the agreement with the owner of the cargo, the party who had accepted command of the vessel shall not be required to pay any damages.

On the other hand, if after returning to the port of origin, as we discussed above, but before giving an accounting of the transaction to the owner of the cargo, the party who had been entrusted with the cargo took it to another location, and the cargo was lost, the one in charge of the cargo shall be held responsible for all of the damage.

If, as we stated in the previous article, the party in charge of the cargo had made a profit on it, he shall pay the owner of the cargo both the profit and the price he had received for such cargo.

212-Explanation of the Preceding Article

In conformity with what has been stated, explained, and decreed in the previous article, any person taking command of a vessel for a specific journey or to a predetermined destination, if he has learned that at such a port there exists a probability of dangers mentioned previously, and for this reason fears to sail there, may after reaching an understanding with the owner of the vessel proceed to another destination where danger will not threaten; in spite of the fact that in the agreement concluded with the owner of the vessel this location had not been previously mentioned.

However, in that article it was not stated or explained that the patron of a vessel who carries his own cargo in addition to the cargo entrusted under his command may act in the same manner as others who do not carry any personal cargo but only that which has been entrusted under their command, and whether such a party would be at a greater disadvantage. Thus, our ancestors had reached a conclusion and had decided that a master of a vessel who carries his own cargo in addition to the cargo entrusted to his command, or even one who does not have aboard any personal cargo but only cargo entrusted under his command, should not be at a greater disadvantage than any other person who had accepted command.

What are the reasons for this? Because many of those who accept command of the vessel do not have aboard any personal cargo but only that given under their command while they travel throughout the world. Further, if they were not entrusted with command of a vessel, they would amount to nothing. In addition, if the cargo is lost, they lose nothing because there was nothing in the cargo that belonged to them. On the other hand, regardless of what he transports, whether he carries any cargo of his own or not, the value of his vessel is greater than the cargo it carries that he had taken under his command; it would be, therefore, unjust that a patron of a vessel should be in a more advantageous position than any other party who had taken cargo under his command.

Further, it is an accepted fact that if there are aboard the vessel several other persons who had taken cargo under their command, the master of the vessel should consult with them concerning any dangers that may be imminent or may exist at the port to which they are bound; whatever they mutually agree upon and adjudge as proper shall be carried out and no one can oppose this.

Further, if aboard the vessel there was cargo that belonged to merchants who did not entrust this cargo under the command of the patron or any other person aboard but had only given the patron orders to release such cargo to a specified party at the port where it was to be unloaded, and if the patron of the vessel due to fear of dangers mentioned above refused to approach the shores of such territory, he should not carry the cargo to another destination because he was not commissioned to sell the cargo, but rather, he should return the cargo to the merchants who had placed it in his care. A patron who would take such cargo to a nonauthorized location shall pay all the damages if the cargo is lost.

Further, if the patron took the cargo to another location and sold it there at profit, he shall be required to return to the place of the origin of the journey and pay the merchants to whom the cargo belonged the price he received for the cargo plus all the profit. The merchants shall be required to pay at least for all his expenses and losses that he had borne but not for any more unless they wish to do so willingly.

114

Further, if the patron has aboard his vessel personal cargo in addition to the cargo entrusted to him to sell or if he does not have any personal cargo, but he was ordered to sell at his discretion all the cargo that he took aboard his vessel, and if this patron is fearful of approaching the shore where he was commissioned to sell the cargo, fearing the dangers that have been mentioned before, he may change the course of his vessel and proceed to another location where no dangers threaten; in such situations, however, the patron should act with the approval of the majority or all of the members of the crew.

If the majority or all of the members of the crew agree to his proposal without any degree of reluctance, that they are willing to sail to the place indicated by the patron, he may change his course and proceed there. If, however, the majority or all the members of the crew agree that the vessel should return to the port of departure instead, rather than to change its course and proceed to some other destination, the patron of the vessel should accommodate the crew. If he refuses to return to the port of origin but instead by the force of his authority changes the course of the vessel, and due to this all or part of the cargo is lost, the patron shall be obligated to pay the owners who entrusted the cargo to his care all the profit they declare the cargo and profit would have brought them, had the patron returned to the port of origin as the majority or all the crew members had advised him to do.

Further, if the patron of the vessel would act upon the advice of the majority or all of the crew members, he should not be required to pay any damages to the owners of the cargo if part or all of it was lost because he had proceeded with the approval of the crew; it is, therefore, only proper that the patron of a vessel should be able to alter the course of the vessel because he had been authorized by the merchants to use his discretion in respect to the cargo he had aboard, and if necessary he may with the approval of the crew throw such cargo overboard into the sea.

Due to the circumstances enumerated above, our ancestors provided these changes in order to prevent disputes that could arise in such matters. Everything that was stated above shall be carried out without fraud or deceit; if any subterfuge can be proved against the party who attempted it, he shall pay all the damages to the party aggrieved, without any delay and maliciousness.

213-Right of the Master of a Vessel to Dispose of Cargo Under His Command

If a person who accepts command of a vessel for a specified journey or designated port of destination is given the authority by the owners of the cargo to dispose of it as he sees fit, as if such cargo was his own property, and after returning from such a trip leaves this cargo at some location because he is unable to sell it, and if he states under oath that he handled this cargo as if it had been his own, the owners of the cargo who entrusted it to the master cannot demand any more than the master had accomplished in the transaction with their cargo; they must also reimburse the master for any expense connected with their cargo as had been provided in the agreement they had concluded.[60]

However, those who had taken command of the cargo, if they left it anywhere, must make every effort to recover such cargo in order to return it to those who had entrusted them with it. All this must be done without any deceit or subterfuge, and the cargo must be returned to its rightful owners as soon as possible.

214-Additional Data Concerning a Commander of a Vessel

If a merchant or any other party had entrusted a person with the command of a vessel under the condition that the master shall take such cargo to all the ports where his vessel shall sail in hopes of selling it, and the cargo is lost, the owner of the vessel and cargo shall assume the liability for any damages that may result.

If, however, the master of the vessel who took the cargo under his command should lose it in gambling or squander it away with loose women, or lose it due to debauchery or due to negligence on his part, or entrust the cargo to another party and it should be lost, he shall be liable for all the damages resulting to the party who entrusted such cargo to his care, and must pay such damages without any opposition.

215-A Promise to Give Command of a Vessel Must Be Fulfilled

A merchant or any other person who made a promise to give command of a vessel to someone and made this promise in writing or in the presence of witnesses, cannot withdraw such an offer from the party to whom he made it originally. If he should want to withdraw it, and the party who had been promised such a command had incurred some expenses in connection with the promised offer or had leased a vessel in conjunction with such a promise, he should be fully reimbursed for any expenses and damages.

This article is written because a party who had been given a

---

60. If the price set by the merchants for their merchandise was too high, the patron would return with it unsold.

promise of getting command of a vessel would not have engaged so large a vessel had not he depended on the promise made to him, but would have limited himself to engaging a smaller vessel, sufficiently large to expedite his own interests in getting ready to ship his own cargo on the journey that had been planned.

216-Additional Information on Commanders of Vessels

If a party is given command of a vessel, and having his own resources, he invested them at the place where the command was given him in addition to investing the money given him by others, and after arrival at the destination designated in the agreement, makes profit on the cargo in which his money had been invested, but makes no profit on the cargo of others who had entrusted him with the command, he shall be required to share the profit he made with the others who had made an investment in that journey.

If, however, he should lose only his personal investment in such a transaction, he will have to absorb the loss if the party who entrusted him with the command and gave him money to invest specified that the money was to be used only for a specific purpose.

If there had been no such stipulation made and he had lost both his own money and the money entrusted to him for investment by others, whatever profits or losses there were shall be divided proportionally to the amount of money invested by each party.

217-Money Entrusted to a Person

If someone entrusts a sum of money to a person with specific instructions to purchase a certain type of cargo, and the latter cannot find any such cargo for sale, he should find reliable witnesses who shall testify that he was unable to find such cargo, and therefore could not use the money given him to buy the specified cargo, in order to clear himself of any charges or accusations if other merchants had been able to buy the cargo he had been commissioned to purchase at the same place and the same time.

If perchance he was unable to prove that he was unable to find the type of cargo he was commissioned to buy and given money for, he shall be required to pay the party who entrusted him with such a mission the profit that would have been made if such cargo had been purchased in proportion to the amount of money the other merchants made in purchasing such cargo.

If he should use the money entrusted to him for other purposes in spite of the orders given to him by the party who ordered him to buy a certain kind of cargo, but he earns a profit on such a transaction, he

117

shall turn over all of the profit to the party who had entrusted him with the money. If on the other hand he had bought cargo other than ordered by the party who entrusted the money to his care, and should lose some or all the money in such a purchase, he shall be required to reimburse the owner of the money in the full amount because he had acted contrary to the orders he had received, for no one can have more right to dispose of the wealth of another person than he is given by that person.

If a person given money to make certain purchases was unable to make them and found himself in position to return this money to the party from whom he received it, but failed to do this, taking the money with him, and due to some unfortunate accident lost all this money, he shall be accountable for the full extent of the damage.

However, if he had not been able to return the money to the party who entrusted it under his care, and due to some unfortunate accident he should lose part or all of this money, the loss will be assumed by the party who entrusted him with this money because the loss was accidental and did not happen due to any negligence of the party who was entrusted with the money.

Everything that has been stated about money entrusted in the care of another person is similarly applicable to the care given to someone over cargo or other property, if such property is entrusted to another person accompanied by specific instructions.

This article has been written for the reasons enumerated above.

218-Command of a Vessel

If an owner of a vessel gives it over to command of another party in order that the latter may make a specific voyage, and if during such a voyage, while the vessel is sailing to or from the port of destination, or while anchored in the port of destination, the vessel is wrecked or damaged, the party who had accepted command of the vessel shall not be liable for any of the damages to the owner of the vessel, who entrusted it under his command.

However, if the party in command of the vessel changed the course of the vessel or undertook some other journey not included in the agreement that had been made between them, and if the vessel was wrecked or damaged, the commander of the vessel shall repay the owner of such a vessel the full value of the vessel plus all other damages that the owner had suffered. Should he be unable to pay such damages, he shall be imprisoned until he is able to satisfy the owner who had entrusted the vessel under his command; whether he is able to repay the owner of the vessel for the damages or not, the owner of the vessel is required to repay the shareholders their share in the

118

vessel as well as a share of the profit they are entitled to according to the amount of their investment in the vessel.

If, however, the command of the vessel was entrusted to a party with the full knowledge and agreement of the majority or all of the shareholders and the vessel was subsequently wrecked under the circumstances mentioned, the principal owner will not be required to pay the shareholders any damages, for the reason that every principal shareholder in a vessel should reach an understanding with other shareholders when he intends to turn over the vessel under someone else's command, provided this is to take place in the location where the majority or all of the shareholders reside. If, however, this was to take place where none of the shareholders of the vessel are present, he should not give the command of a vessel to any person except under the conditions explained above, namely, unless he becomes ill, or if he has contracted to carry a load of cargo to a destination where he personally fears some action by the governmental authorities will be taken against him, or if he has become engaged before he contracted to carry a shipment of cargo, and his friends are forcing him to marry before he undertakes the journey, or if he is about to undertake a pilgrimage to a holy shrine, which he had taken a vow to make before he contracted to carry the cargo; all of this shall be done without any attempt in subterfuge or deceit.

219-Command of a Vessel Given Without the Knowledge of Its Shareholders

If the principal owner of a vessel entrusts it under the command of another party without the knowledge of its shareholders, and the latter after completing the voyage returns and gives an account of the transactions during the voyage to the party who gave him the vessel to command; and if the latter in turn pays each of the shareholders his share of the profit due him on the basis of his shares in the vessel; and if the shareholders accept their shares of the profit due to them on the basis of the amount of their investment in the vessel, and then some or all of them inform the party whom they had made the patron of the vessel that they do not wish him to give command of this vessel to anyone without their approval; and if contrary to this stipulation the patron of the vessel proceeds to do so, he shall be responsible for all the damages, losses, and expenses suffered by the vessel.

If, in the circumstances mentioned above, the shareholders after informing the person whom they elected the patron of the vessel in which they had invested their money, would give command of this vessel to another party without their approval, or at least the approval of the majority of them, he shall divide among them, proportionally to the amount of their investment, all the profits made by the party to whom he had entrusted the command of the vessel.

If it should happen that the party who had been given command of the vessel under the circumstances described above should wreck it or damage it, the patron shall repay the shareholders all the damages they had suffered proportionally to the amount of their investment in the vessel, without any opposition whatsoever.

Further, if the shareholders knew and could see that the party they elected patron did not sail the vessel personally, but give the command of it to another person, and in spite of this agreed to accept their share of the profit earned by the party who commanded the vessel, and had not made any reservations about this matter to the patron, and if under such circumstances the vessel was lost or damaged, the patron of the vessel shall not be held accountable for the damages because the shareholders knew that he himself was not commanding the vessel, but gave the command of it to someone else, and mainly so because the shareholders had shared in the profits made by the vessel after completion of each journey due to them as part owners of the vessel.

It is therefore just and proper that if they took their share of the profits, although they knew that the person elected by them as the patron did not command the vessel personally, but entrusted the command to another party and if they did not reproach the patron about this, but with great satisfaction accepted the profits that the patron shared with them, therefore in the same spirit that they accepted the profits that the patron shared with them, they should accept the losses, damages, and diminution of income that the Almighty God had visited upon them.

This article was written for the reasons listed above. The contents should be interpreted, however, in the following manner: that the patron of the vessel resides in the place where all or the majority of the shareholders are domiciled, otherwise he cannot and should not entrust the command of the vessel to another person, except under the conditions explained and decided upon in one of the former articles.

220-Acceptance of Responsibility Individually or Collectively

If a patron of a vessel had accepted cargo belonging to a trading association in addition to accepting merchandise or money entrusted to his care by an individual merchant, and at the moment of acceptance of such cargo or money failed to inform the merchant that his cargo or money will be added to the cargo or money entrusted to him by the association, or did not make a written deposition that the money and cargo of such an individual must be considered as part and parcel of the cargo owned by the association that he had taken aboard his vessel, he shall be held individually responsible for the cargo or the money entrusted to his care by the individual merchant.

If he has been given cargo to sell, he shall pay the merchants the full amount he received for such cargo. In addition, he shall have discretion in purchasing cargo for money that has been entrusted to his care for this purpose, unless he was specifically ordered that the money received from the sale of the cargo not be used for any other purpose or that he only buy specific cargo for that money, as had been mutually agreed.

If he has been given money to buy certain cargo, he shall make a full accounting of what he had bought for the money he received from selling the cargo he carried, as well of what disposition he made of the money he had received. He shall make such an accounting after returning from the voyage and will return to the merchants all their money invested and profit made in such transactions, after deducting the compensation due him as had been mutually agreed.

It is actually immaterial to the patron of a vessel, who entrusted its command to another party, whether the association makes any profit or suffers a loss in such an arrangement; the person accepting the care of such cargo is merely required to make account of it. If in pursuance of his command of the vessel, he makes profit or suffers a loss, he merely makes an accounting to the patron who entrusted him with the command of the vessel of profits and losses, since he is not obligated to the association, as he had accepted command of the vessel not from the association but from another party, unless he had informed the association that he shall be responsible mutually to the association as well as to the patron who gave him command of the vessel.

The party accepting command of a vessel is not obligated to the association in any way whatsoever, regardless whether they make profit or suffer losses, and the members of the association are not obligated in any way toward the party who accepted command of the vessel. Whatever losses or profits he incurred concern him personally only.

If, however, it should happen that he accepts the responsibility for the cargo belonging to the association as well as accepting command of the vessel, and should mix the cargo belonging to the association with the cargo belonging to the party who entrusted the command of the vessel to him without informing the party who gave him command of the vessel about this, and due to this shall not be able to make proper accounting, the party who entrusted him with the command of the vessel can demand payment for his cargo at the highest prices that such cargo commanded at the place where it was sold as well as the highest possible lading charges for the cargo carried aboard and the highest potential profits that could have been made selling the cargo. However, the party who accepted command of the vessel must give full satisfaction to the patron who entrusted him with the command, because he had mixed his cargo with the cargo of the association without the knowledge of the patron. The party who commanded the vessel must make this adjustment without any argument or opposition.

221-Loss of Cargo and Bankruptcy of the Party Who Accepted Responsibility for Such Cargo

Any person who accepts responsibility for any property, and such merchandise is lost due to the circumstances mentioned in preceding articles, [61] shall not be responsible to repay such damages. If, however, the cargo taken under his care was lost due to other reasons than those mentioned above, he shall be required to pay the damages plus all the probable profit that would have been made on the cargo, unless he can show an acceptable reason for the loss of the cargo.

If he cannot demonstrate and prove an acceptable reason why such cargo was lost, and cannot replace such a cargo similar to the cargo given in his care because he is penniless and has become bankrupt, and he can be apprehended, he should be bound in chains, jailed, and kept in prison until he can reach some agreement with the party who entrusted such cargo to his care.

This article has been written because there are many persons who upon accepting responsibility for a cargo would steal it, if they knew that as a result they would not be faced with a penalty, loss, or diminution of their wealth; that is why the above resolutions were adopted.

222-A Patron Who Neglects the Vessel in Order to Attend to His Personal Affairs

If a patron of a vessel transports his own cargo in addition to other cargo entrusted to his care and cannot remain at the port where the vessel docked in order to sell his cargo, and if the vessel is ready to depart from that port but is delayed waiting for him to give the order to unfurl the sails, and if due to such a delay the owners of the vessel will have been put to some expense, the master of the vessel shall reimburse them from his own cash box. If he should remain at the port where the vessel was cargoed in order to sell his personal cargo without the knowledge of the shareholders of the vessel, and in the meantime the vessel had sailed, he shall be held accountable to the shareholders for any damages that may have been suffered by the

---

61. These circumstances were detailed in Articles 211 and 212.

vessel. If, however, he had reached an understanding with the majority or all of the shareholders that he could remain behind while the vessel sailed, and the vessel should suffer some damage, the patron of the vessel shall not be required to pay any of the damages suffered by the vessel to its shareholders.

Further, if the patron of the vessel had remained behind to collect on the lading charges due and not for any other reason, and due to this necessity of remaining behind, he had dispatched the vessel in order to avoid some expenditures, and the vessel so dispatched should suffer damages, the patron will not be obligated to pay these damages to the shareholders because he had remained behind in the interest of the vessel and not for any other reason. He shall act without any attempt at deception or fraud.

223–Summoning of the Members of the Crew to Act as Witnesses in Arbitration of a Dispute Between the Patron of the Vessel and the Merchants

If a patron of a vessel is involved in a dispute with the merchants, the crew aboard the vessel when this dispute took place shall not be called as witness by either side of such dispute to the benefit or detriment of either party. The ship's register shall constitute the basis for the testimony offered by both parties involved in the litigation. If the vessel has completed the voyage and the sailors have been discharged and are no longer in the service of the patron of the vessel, they can offer testimony for the patron or the merchants provided they are the disinterested parties in the dispute in which they are to offer evidence, and provided that they shall not profit or suffer any damages out of this dispute. If they could benefit or suffer damages as the result of the final settlement of such a dispute, their testimony shall have no validity, and they themselves shall be adjudged as perjurers.

224–Summoning of Merchants As Witnesses in Disputes Between the Patron of the Vessel and His Crew.

If the crew becomes involved in a dispute with the master of a vessel over matters that have not been entered into the ship's register, the merchants aboard the vessel present during such a dispute may be called as witnesses both during the voyage as well as after the voyage has been completed. They may offer testimony in favor of the master of the vessel or the crew, provided that they are disinterested parties to this dispute and that they will not gain or lose anything because of the evidence they give in testimony.

If, on the other hand, the crew of the vessel would be involved with the merchants aboard the vessel, the patron of the vessel may be called upon to give testimony in this matter after the completion of the journey, provided he is a disinterested party to this dispute.

Further, one sailor can be called to be a witness for another sailor after the completion of a voyage, provided that he is a disinterested party in this dispute in which he is called upon to give testimony and that he shall in no way benefit or suffer after offering such evidence.

Further, the crew may testify in any issue during the voyage, either in behalf of the patron of the vessel or the merchants in the following circumstances only: it can testify in case it had been necessary to dump cargo overboard, or if because of a storm the vessel had been wrecked or foundered on shoals, because in such situations it would have been impossible for the clerk of the vessel to enter these matters into the register of the vessel, which under normal circumstances would have provided the necessary evidence of any decisions or agreements that had been made aboard the vessel regarding these matters. [62]

This article was written in order that the crew would be able to attest to the happenings under such circumstances, even though the clerk had no opportunity to make any entries in the ship's register concerning these matters, because otherwise the patron of the vessel could deny all the agreements that had been made on such occasions which would be disadvantageous to him, and would only testify to matters that were beneficial to him, and the merchants would act similarly in their relations with the patron of the vessel.

For this reason the crew can be called as witnesses to testify to incidents that had happened during the journey, in order that there could arise no attempt at deceit. Under no other circumstances can the crew be called to give testimony in anything that happened aboard the vessel during the voyage, whether it would be on behalf of the patron of the vessel of the merchants, regardless of the nature of the dispute.

225-Testimony given by the Crew

If the merchants aboard the vessel engaged in any kind of dispute amongst themselves and called upon the crew to witness the difference of opinion, the crew may during the voyage as well as after the voyage has been completed be called upon to testify to what they had been

---

62. These matters were discussed in detail in Articles 60, 95, 99, and will be reiterated in Article 253.

called to witness, provided that the crew has no personal interest in the matter, and that the crew acts impartially in regard to both of the litigants, and has not received and accepted any honorarium or gifts from either of the parties to the dispute. If the crew had attempted to benefit one of the disputants through its testimony or if the crew had accepted an honorarium to do this, and this can be proved, the crew shall pay all the costs and damages suffered by the party against whom they have perjured themselves.

In addition, the aggrieved party can ruin their reputation and prosecute them in the courts of law, and even more importantly, no credence would ever again be given to any testimony they would give; if any person called them perjurers, no court of law could punish such a person for libel, no matter how many witnesses the former would present to establish their action for libel, but rather those who gave such testimony would be punished doubly by the courts for giving such testimony.

This article was written because very often merchants find themselves in circumstances when only the members of the crew are present during a dispute or when they conclude agreements or carry on a discussion. Thus, if it should happen that one of the merchants wishes to recant on an agreement he made, and the other merchant with whom he made the agreement demands that the former carry out the terms of their agreement, the merchant who refused and denied the existence of such an agreement could cause the other merchant to suffer serious damages. Thus, in such instances the crew of the vessel should offer testimony in disputes among the merchants in order to prevent any opportunity for fraud and deceit among the merchants.

226-Wages Paid the Navigator and Other Members of the Crew

A patron of a vessel who, for a specific voyage, engages the services of a navigator, whose wages will be determined at a later date, shall pay him at least as much as he pays his best officer of the foredeck or another member of the crew and even much more dependent upon the fitness and ability of the navigator.

If it should happen that some other members of the crew were engaged on the same basis, the patron of the vessel shall pay them wages based on how they perform or will perform and on the degree of their usefulness. The exact amount of their wages shall be determined by the navigator and the clerk under an oath administered by the patron, that they will determine the amount of the wages to be paid the crew members who had been hired under such conditions, justly and honestly according to their worth. The navigator and the clerk cannot act in this matter arbitrarily or be motivated by hate or a promise of some gain made to them, or in order to harm some member of the crew serving aboard the vessel for undetermined wages; they shall under the threat of punishment for perjury give the patron of the vessel an honest estimate of the amount of wages he should pay such members of the crew. The patron is required to pay the wages determined by the clerk and the navigator under oath and cannot raise any objections in this matter.

227-Damage Caused to a Vessel Due to Lack of Proper Equipment Aboard

If the patron had anchored his vessel near the shore, in port, or some other place, and the merchants aboard warn and caution him that he should provide a stout hawser to anchor the vessel, and the patron moored the vessel with a weak and unsatisfactory hawser, or if he did not have the proper equipment aboard the vessel to do this, although he had claimed that he did, and due to this the merchants suffer some damage, the patron of the vessel shall be required to reimburse them for their losses.

If the patron was without the means to pay for these damages, the vessel shall be sold. If the amount realized from the sale of the vessel was insufficient to pay these damages, and the patron has other property, it shall be sold to satisfy the merchants, with this reservation, that the crew will not lose any wages due them. The shareholders of the vessel shall not be required to share in the payment of these damages beyond the amount they had invested in the vessel.

This article was written because many patrons of vessels skimp on the equipment and do not equip their vessel properly, thus the vessel itself and the cargo aboard that belonged to the merchants will perish.

228-A Vessel Lost in the Territory of the Saracens

If a patron sailed into the territory of the Saracens and due to misfortune, storm, or action of armed enemy ships the vessel perished, he will not be required to pay the crew any wages, unless the vessel was lost at the same location where he had been paid the lading fees. If he had received such fees, he shall pay the crew full wages due them. If he had reduced the lading fees for the merchants, the crew shall accept a reduction in wages in proportion to the reduction of the lading fees received. If the patron owed the crew wages for another voyage, he shall pay them, as had been stated in one of the previous articles.[63]

---

63. Reference here is made to Article 138.

The patron who lost his vessel under the circumstances mentioned above shall not be required to furnish either transportation or subsistence for the crew until such time as they reach a Christian territory, because he had lost everything he possessed, and often even more than he possessed.

This article was written because a patron who lost his vessel is not required to furnish transportation or subsistence until they reach a Christian nation, because he does not even have the means to provide these necessities for himself.

229-Circumstances Under Which the Patron of the Vessel Shall Secure the Approval of the Shareholders of the Vessel Before He Accepts Cargo for Shipment

A patron who contracts to carry cargo destined for the territory of the Saracens or other dangerous places, should, if there are any shareholders present at the site where the vessel is being cargoed, receive their approval before he takes such cargo aboard. If he received their approval, he may proceed to load such cargo aboard, and none of the shareholders shall voice any opposition. If he should cargo the vessel without their approval, the shareholders may protest and sell the vessel at auction because the patron did not ask their permission. If, however, he had asked their permission, the shareholders cannot sell the vessel before he returns from the journey.

If the shareholders force the auction of the vessel that the patron had cargoed without their permission, and due to the sale of the vessel or for any other reason the patron is relieved from the command of the vessel, and the shareholders regain control of the vessel, the vessel shall make the journey as had been agreed with the merchant who had leased the vessel or had arranged to ship cargo aboard it with the party who had been the master of the vessel when the agreement was made. Let all who buy shares in a vessel remember that all the agreements made by the patron of a vessel shall be carried out.

However, if a patron of a vessel finds himself in the territory where none of the shareholders are present, he may use his judgment in accepting any cargo for shipment to any destination. If the vessel was damaged, none of the shareholders shall make any claims. On the other hand, if the patron of the vessel gambled away, squandered, or lost the vessel in any other way due to his negligence, the shareholders will be able to press their claims against him.

Further, a patron who accepts cargo for shipment to a Christian territory shall not be required to ask the permission of the shareholders to undertake such a journey, if he does not wish to ask their per-

mission, and no shareholder shall attempt to bring about the sale of
the vessel that had been engaged to carry cargo, until after the completion of the journey and return of the vessel. If the patron, upon
the demand of the shareholders, must provide them with a guarantor
that he will not change the course of the vessel during the voyage until he returns the vessel for their dispostion, the guarantor shall be
liable only to the degree decreed by the customs and the laws of the
sea.

If it should happen that the patron contracts to carry cargo to the
location mentioned above, and the shareholders are conveniently at
hand, and regardless of whether they know about this trip or are ignorant of it or whether the patron informed them about it, and they do
not oppose such a voyage, they will not be able to lodge any demands
for damages later. If the vessel should have been lost or damaged on
such a voyage, the patron of the vessel shall not be held liable for any
consequences that had occurred.

230-Ransom Paid or Other Arrangements Made With Armed Enemy
Vessels

A patron who encounters armed enemy vessels in the port, the
open sea, or any other place may negotiate and conclude an agreement with the officers and the admiral of such naval units as to the
amount of ransom he shall be required to pay them, in order that they
would not harm him or anything aboard the vessel, and the majority
or all the merchants who are aboard his vessel should be informed of
the agreement he was forced to make or will make with the officers
of the above armed units. With the advice and approval of these merchants he shall pay the amount agreed as ransom. The merchants
are required to repay him the sum paid out in proportion to the value
of the cargo they have aboard the vessel.

The ransom shall be paid by an assessment levied on all the cargo
aboard the vessel in proportion to the amount and the value of the cargo, and the patron of the vessel shall share in this payment to the extent of half the value of his vessel.

If there are no merchants aboard the vessel, the patron shall consult with the officers of the stern, the navigator, and officers of the
prow. He shall pay the ransom with the approval of all those mentioned above. The merchants whose cargo is aboard the vessel shall
not and cannot protest such payment of ransom, provided that the patron share in the payment of ransom in the amount equal to half the
value of his vessel.

To continue: If the patron should come upon armed naval units in
the places mentioned above, but these were units of a friendly power,

and he would wish to present a gift to the commander of such units or entertain him aboard his vessel, and the merchants are aboard his vessel, he is required to get their approval to proceed in this manner, or to act in accordance with the expressed desire of the crew as stated before. If he proceeds in the manner outlined above, he shall be reimbursed for his expenditures.

Further, if, however, the patron did not conduct himself in accordance with the wishes of the merchants aboard his vessel, or in their absence with the wishes of the persons mentioned before, but acted in this matter arbitrarily and gave such gifts without the knowledge of the merchants or without the consultation of the individuals mentioned previously, he shall pay out these expenditures from his personal cash box, and the merchants will not be required to reimburse him for the expenditure of money used to buy such gifts that he presented to the officers of these armed vessels.

231-Payment of Ransom to or Concluding of Agreements With Armed Enemy Vessels

If at the moment the vessel is fully or partly cargoed, it is located in an enemy territory or other dangerous locality, and is threatened by the arrival in the vicinity of unfriendly armed vessels, and if the patron of the vessel in order to avoid damage to the cargo aboard the vessel attempted to approach the enemy craft with some proposition that would guarantee safety to his vessel and the cargo, and the majority or all of the merchants are aboard the vessel, he shall be obliged to inform them of the terms he offered or intends to offer to the enemy officers of these vessels. With the approval and consent of the merchants he shall pay the amount of ransom agreed upon, and the merchants shall share in the amount paid in proportion to the value of their cargo aboard the vessel.

If it should happen that there would not be a single merchant aboard the vessel, but the vessel is anchored in waters adjacent to where the merchants are domiciled and can be reached by the patron in order to apprise them of the situation and of the agreement he had concluded or will conclude with the armed vessels in order to save his life and all the cargo aboard, he is required to inform them of this turn of events. If there was not sufficient time to notify the merchants of this happening, he shall proceed in such manner after obtaining the support of all the members of the crew. If he had acted according to these instructions, the merchants shall be required to share in the damages, as if they had been present, and shall not and could not raise any objections to the action he had taken in this matter.

Further, if the patron of the vessel had concluded an agreement although the majority or all of them were aboard the vessel or within an easy reach, such an agreement, concluded or that will be concluded without the consultation and approval of the merchants who were aboard the vessel or nearby where they could have been notified of this matter, is not binding upon the merchants whether all or only part of their cargo was aboard the vessel, because the patron failed to consult them in this matter. If, however, the merchants were in a locality where communication with them was an impossibility, and the patron concluded an agreement after consultation of the other persons mentioned previously, the merchants shall be required to reimburse him for the expenditures described above.

If by chance he should have concluded such an agreement without the knowledge of the merchants and without a consultation with the parties mentioned before, solely upon his own responsibility, he shall pay for all the expenses from his own personal cash box, and no one else will be required to share in these expenditures, because the patron had acted without the knowledge of the parties mentioned.

Further, if the vessel is anchored in one of the locations enumerated above after unloading its cargo, and if the merchants had agreed with the patron that he shall wait for them and that they will provide him with a new shipment of cargo, and in the interim armed vessels approach his vessel, and the patron in order to avoid any damage concludes some agreement with the command of such vessels, or if some unfortunate accident occurs that will result in the loss of his vessel, the merchants shall not be required to share in the damage or in the expenditures he incurred while waiting for them, because they had unloaded their cargo. They may, however, if they wish, reimburse him for these losses of their own free will.

If it should happen that the merchants did not cargo and dispatch the vessel in the agreed period of time, and in the meantime armed vessels arrive in the vicinity and the patron shall be forced either to reach a protective covenant with them or to lose his vessel, the merchants shall be required to pay the amount of the ransom agreed upon between the patron and the armed vessels or to reimburse him for any expense that he had incurred due to their negligence, because they had failed to dispatch the vessel on the date agreed to mutually.

232–Stolen Cargo

If a patron of a vessel took aboard at some designated location cargo of several merchants, or if such cargo belonged exclusively to one merchant, with the purpose of delivering it to another location, as had been agreed with the merchants or one merchant, and it should happen that the vessel while sailing should encounter armed or unarmed enemy vessels, and the evil people sailing such ships forcibly steal one-third, one-half, or three-fourths of his cargo, more or less, and the patron after arriving at the port of destination of his cargo refused to unload the remaining cargo and release it to the merchants or merchant to whom it belonged because they had not as yet paid the lading fees for the cargo that had been stolen by the enemies, such behavior is not and cannot be justified.

Why? Because the merchant is required to pay lading fees only on the cargo that a patron in the circumstances mentioned above delivered for him.

However, the incident discussed above should be interpreted in the following manner: If the merchants who cargoed the vessel, as had been stated above, should be in a state of war with the parties who had stolen their cargo, the vessel that carried their cargo, if it is saved, shall be required to share in the damages that had occurred proportionally with the cargo lost and salvaged. The patron on the other hand shall be paid the lading charges due him, and the merchants or merchant are not obligated in any other way.

Further, if there had been an agreement reached as to the mutual responsibility for all the damages, the cargo salvaged would not be assessed for the cargo that had been stolen, and the merchants to whom such cargo belonged shall not be required to pay the patron any lading fees for the cargo that had been lost, nor shall the patron be required to pay any damages, unless the merchants can show and prove that the cargo that had been stolen was lost due to his negligence or with his knowledge and approval. If the merchants can prove and substantiate this charge, the patron shall pay all their damages and satisfy them to the full extent of their demands without any opposition.

If the merchants cannot prove such a charge, the patron shall be relieved of all responsibility. On the other hand, the merchant or merchants to whom the salvaged cargo belongs shall pay the patron all lading fees due on the salvaged cargo but nothing more.

Further, if these merchants were in a state of war with these evil people who had stolen their cargo, but the patron of the vessel was not in a state of war with them, his vessel shall not be required to share proportionally with the salvaged cargo in payment of damages for the cargo stolen, unless, in conformity with what has been stated above, there had been an agreement concluded that in case of a disaster the cargo and the vessel shall mutually share the damages. As has been stated, in such a situation the merchants are required to pay the lading fees only for the cargo salvaged. [64]

64. This is the initial mention of the principle of enemy goods on neutral vessel, as part of the law of the sea.

Further, if on the other hand, the patron of the vessel was at war with these evil people but the merchants were not, the vessel shall be required to share proportionally in all damages that will occur. The shipping charges shall also be taken into account in sharing of the damages, just as the vessel and the cargo lost as well as that which was salvaged, if as it had been stated above, there was a proper agreement reached in these matters. If no such agreement was concluded, the cargo of one merchant shall not be assessed to pay the damages for the cargo of another merchant. The merchant who lost his cargo shall bear such a loss personally, but the patron of the vessel can demand payment of lading fees only for the cargo salvaged.

The patron who had hired sailors for such a voyage and agreed to pay them a specified amount for the completion of the voyage shall be required to pay them proportionally to the amount he had received in lading fees. If the crew is paid monthly wages, the patron shall pay their wages proportionally to the amount he received in lading fees.

Why? Because no one can prevent an attack by people of ill will. Nevertheless, if the sailors had made an agreement with the patron of the vessel to be paid monthly, that he shall pay them their wages each month on the day they enlisted, he shall be forced to pay them for as many months as they had served aboard his vessel, if their enlistment ended before the robbery had been committed, whether he had received his lading fees or not. What is the reason for this? Because such were the terms of their agreement.

If it should happen that the civil authorities or evil people should imprison the patron in some locality, but the location of his imprisonment does not prevent him from an opportunity of discharging his crew, he should discharge the sailors, regardless of whether such sailors were hired to work for monthly wages or a flat sum for completion of the journey. Under such circumstances he shall not be required to pay them any wages for the whole period of his imprisonment, as it is not his fault that he is not able to earn any money, for the impediment is not of his own choosing. In addition, the patron of the vessel is losing enough already, for he is deprived of making a living, and his vessel is wasting away.

However, if the patron of a vessel should be imprisoned by the civil authorities or some evil people in a place where he has ample opportunity to discharge his crew, but fails to do this, and retains their services, he shall pay them for the time they remain under his command.

Why? Because had he wanted to discharge them, he had ample opportunity to do so. As he did not want to do this, but retained them in his service, it is proper that he pay their wages for the whole time they remained in his service, unless there had been some reserva-

132

tions made relative to this matter at the time they enlisted aboard his vessel.

This article was written for the reasons stated above.

233-Screw-Jacks, Winches and Other Equipment Rented or Taken Surreptitiously

A patron of a vessel who rents or takes any winches, screw-jacks, or other equipment surreptitiously in order to launch his vessel or to pull it ashore shall not be required to pay any damages for the use of such equipment if he rented it at a higher rental fee agreed on with the person who rented him such equipment.

Further, if he had taken such equipment without the knowledge of its owner, he shall be required to pay for all the damage to such equipment, if he had used it, without any objections or opposition.

Regardless of whether or not such rented equipment shall be damaged, the amount of rental agreed to between the parties must be paid in toto without any delay or opposition.

234-A Promise Made to the Merchants by the Patron to Wait for Them for a Specified Period of Time Must Be Kept

A patron who in promising the merchants to carry their cargo stated that he will wait for them for a certain period of time before departing is required to delay sailing until that date, as he had agreed with them.

Should he sail before the date agreed upon with the merchants, and the merchants had suffered some damage due to this, he shall reimburse them for all the damages suffered due to his negligence.

If, however, on the other hand, the merchants failed to deliver their cargo by the date agreed and thus delayed the sailing of the vessel, and the patron had suffered some damage, the merchants shall reimburse him for all the expenses and damage due to their negligence.

If the patron due to fear of threat from local civil authorities, or approach of armed enemy vessels, or due to an impending storm, and only for these reasons, should set sail before the date agreed with the merchants, he shall not be held responsible for any damages the merchants had suffered due to his hasty departure, because this did not happen of his own will. For the same reasons the merchants shall not be held accountable to the patron for any damages he might have suffered.

235-Setting Sail on Date Specified in an Agreement

If the merchants who have engaged a vessel to ship cargo and agreed to dispatch the vessel by a certain date shall fail to do so by the day specified, the patron can, if he so desires, regardless of whether the agreement was made in writing or in the presence of witnesses and entered into the register of the vessel, or entered into by a hand clasp of the merchants and the patron, the latter may demand the payment of the amount provided in the penalty clause, if such a penalty clause had been one of the provisions of the agreement.

If there had been no agreement made between the patron of a vessel and the merchants relative to a penalty clause, the patron can demand that the merchants reimburse him for all the expenses incurred by him due to their negligence, with this reservation, that the delay was not occasioned by them, and was not an act of God or the turbulence of the sea. Under such circumstances the merchants shall not be required to pay the patron the penalty agreed to between them nor any expense he had incurred due to the circumstances mentioned above.

If, on the other hand, during the period of time agreed to by the merchants and the patron there should arise obstacles imposed by the civil authorities, the nature of which would make the merchants fearful of cargoing the vessel there and sailing elsewhere, or to export anything out of the country, they shall not be required to pay the patron of the vessel any damages since these were not caused by them. If, however, these obstacles had taken place after the period of time set by the patron and the merchants, and the latter had not dispatched the vessel due to their negligence, they shall pay the patron the penalty that had been decided and agreed to.

If, on the other hand, there had been no agreement made concerning a penalty clause, the merchants shall nevertheless be required to reimburse the patron for all the expenses that he incurred or will incur. All these damages and expenses shall be ascertained and estimated by two Elders [of the Sea Guild] well versed and experienced in the art of sailing.

The two Elders shall estimate and ascertain the damages and expenses that the patron of the vessel suffered due to the negligence of the merchants in a manner that will not be disadvantageous to one or the other side and that will make possible for both parties to remain friendly and on the best of terms. If the patron had been paid part of the lading charges, he shall pay the sailors their wages in the proportion to the amount of the shipping charges paid him.

Further, regardless of what arrangements are made by the patron of the vessel with the merchants, the sailors shall be bound by the terms of the agreement.

In the same manner, as has been stated previously, the patron shall be held accountable to the merchants, to whom he had promised to sail forth on a specific date but had failed to do so due to his own negligence.

If the members of the crew were hired for a specified amount of money to undertake the voyage, the patron shall not be obliged to pay them as he had not agreed with them as to the specific date of sailing. If, however, the sailors were hired on monthly wages, he shall pay them the full amount due them, as had been agreed at the moment they entered his service.

Our ancestors, who first began to sail throughout the world, had perceived and determined that matters related to damages, which could be suffered by the merchants as well as the masters of vessels, should be submitted to the Elders of the Sea Guild for evaluation and arbitration, because no one knows and can know whether some misfortune may bring him benefit or cause him some injury thus, it is best that such matters be entrusted to the prudence of the Elders for arbitration.

For this reason the article above has been written. If, therefore, there were no merchants, there would be no one for whom to build vessels. If there were no vessels, there would not be so many fine merchants as there actually are. Therefore the merchants must endure all sorts of abuses and indignities from the masters of the vessels, while the latter must endure even more from the merchants for many reasons not worth mentioning here or of repeating, for all of us are well aware and well versed in the issues under discussion here, and since all can see and know of all these matters, we shall not repeat them here. If there should be anyone who is ignorant of these matters because of his disinterest, let him turn to those who in his opinion should be much better informed than he is.

236-Vessel Cargoed With a Load of Clay Vases or Jars

If the vessel is to be cargoed with clay vases, the merchants shall provide experienced stevedores who will know how to load these vases and store them safely aboard the vessel, provided the merchants are in a locality where such stevedores can be hired for money. If they are in a locality where it is impossible to hire such skilled men for money, the merchants shall make arrangements with the sailors, who shall be required to load such cargo aboard. The merchants shall pay the sailors for this work according to the amount determined by the navigator, and the navigator shall proceed in a manner so that the sailors shall be well paid for their work and the merchants will not feel cheated. This should be left to the discretion of the navigator, as he acts in this matter as a scale of justice, which will weigh all and determine what is just and equitable for the merchants, the patron of the vessel, the crew, as well as every other person aboard the vessel or sailing on the vessel. He should not lean in his decision either toward one or the other side. If he should act arbitrarily in either direction, he shall be adjudged perfidious, and if this is proved against him, his oath given under any circumstances shall never again be accepted or given any credence.

Further, if the patron had promised and assured the merchants that he shall cargo the vessel, the merchants shall not be required to hire porters to do this, but the patron should reach an understanding with the crew that will perform this task. If the crew had agreed to do this work, he shall pay them in the manner described above. If the sailors agree to do this work for the patron of the vessel, he shall pay them in the amount determined by the navigator, in order that they be satisfied.[65]

237-Breakage of Crockery Aboard the Vessel

If a patron leased his vessel to the merchants, who cargoed it with a load of vases employing their own porters, and if one or more of these vases are broken, chipped, or cracked, the patron will not be liable for any such damage, regardless of whether the porters did their work well or poorly, because this did not result due to any negligence due to the patron.

The merchants to whom these vases belong shall pay the patron the full lading charges that they had agreed to pay for every vase loaded aboard. The latter should be, however, understood in the following manner: that the patron shall be required to show and return to the merchants all of the remnants or parts of these broken vases without any sort of opposition.

Further, if, on the other hand, the patron of the vessel is in charge of loading such vases aboard, and the porters chosen by him to do this work perform the task well and without any errors, and in spite of their care one or more of these vases shall be broken, the patron shall not be required to pay the merchants to whom these vases belong any damages; he should not, however, be paid lading charges on the vases that had been broken.

Why should the patron not pay for this damage suffered by the merchants? For the simple reason that no one should believe or judge that any patron would be happy if some merchant would suffer some damage while aboard his vessel due to his negligence or due to some

---

65. Earthenware actually included all sorts of pitchers, jars, crocks, vases, jugs, storing vats, although the term vases is most often used in the original manuscript.

circumstances that he could have prevented from happening. However, if the merchants could prove that the vases were broken due to the negligence of the patron or of the porters selected by him, the patron will be required to pay the damages to the merchants to whom the vases belong.

For these reasons the patron should not attempt to load the vessel with vases or order others to load them if the merchant or his representative would not be present while the vessel is being cargoed with the vases, in order to avoid responsibility for the damage.

Further, if at the time the vessel was being loaded, the merchants or their representative were present, and one or more of these vases were broken, the patron of the vessel would not be responsible for such damage, and the merchants should not and could not under any pretense refuse to pay the patron the lading charges due, because they themselves or their representative were present at the time the vessel was cargoed.

Further, if any vase has been broken during the loading or storing of such cargo, the merchants shall not be required to pay the shipping charges on the broken vases; but if such vases are broken at the time they are being unloaded, the lading charges shall be paid on such broken vases.

This article was written for the reasons given above.

238-A Vessel Commandeered by the Crew

A patron who leased a vessel with the stipulation that he would sail it to a predetermined destination should unload it as soon as he reached the port of destination. After unloading the cargo he had aboard, he should attempt to find other cargo for his vessel in order that he be able to increase his own earnings as well as the profit for the shareholders of the vessel. The crew should wait until he is able to get another shipment and not urge him to hurry, provided he pay them from the moment they had undertaken the journey.

If the sailors, ill-disposed toward the master of their vessel, took the vessel and sailed away from the place where the cargo had been unloaded without the permission and knowledge of the patron who was at the time on shore, they shall lose by such an act all rights to their persons, their property, and everything else they may possess. The patron of the vessel may have them bound in chains, surrender them to the civil authority, and bring legal action against them in the same manner as against those who would mutiny and deprive him of his authority. The above conditions prevail only when the vessel is anchored or hovering in friendly ports or waters and free from any imminent danger.

In addition, the sailors who would dare to commit such an act or agree to its commission shall be required to make payment of all damages, losses, and diminution of profit that the master experiences due to their behavior. Credence shall be given to the patron in these matters on the basis of an ordinary deposition made by him.

Sailors who have committed such an act, or have agreed to it, shall be jailed until such time as they are able to reach a satisfactory agreement with the patron or pay him the damages as he will see fit.

This article was written in order to prevent sailors from commandeering a vessel, even if the patron of the vessel had wronged them. Instead, they should repair to the local court and there charge him with his evil acts, which in their opinion he committed against them. It would not be proper if the sailors, at any given moment when they believed that the patron of a vessel had harmed them in some way or if he detained them in some locality contrary to their wishes, would be able to commandeer his vessel, aboard which they served.

For these reasons the penalties stated above were mentioned.

239-Purchase of Essential Provisions and Equipment for the Vessel

A patron who has leased his vessel profitably for a journey to a specific port of destination shall be required to purchase under the direction of the clerk all essential provisions and equipment for his vessel. In addition, if there is need for some equipment aboard the vessel, the patron should purchase it with the understanding and knowledge of the clerk. After making all the purchases of food and other necessities, he shall also purchase essential tools. If, however, the patron of the vessel is anchored at the locality where the shareholders in the vessel are present, he must ask their approval before he makes these purchases.

If the shareholders refuse to permit the purchase of these essentials, and the patron is convinced that the items lacking are essential to the welfare of the vessel, he shall not be deterred by the refusal of the shareholders but shall buy these essentials; and this is due to the fact that the shareholders will probably remain safe on shore and are indifferent to the dangers that others will face on the high seas, just as long as they are making profit. For these reasons the shareholders should not oppose the purchase of essential equipment, because the patron had determined that such equipment was vital to the safety of the vessel, and if it was lacking, the vessel would be threatened by great danger, and the patron himself would later be subject to accusations made by the merchants. For these reasons, therefore, the shareholders shall not be opposed to the acquisition of such equipment.

If the patron had any funds that belong to him and the shareholders

138

mutually, he should pay the crew and procure the necessary equipment. If he did not have any mutual funds on hand, he should together with the clerk make an account of all the wages due to the crew as well as all the purchases that were made by the clerk, as well as all the equipment that the patron will purchase, and arrive at the total amount of the expenditures. When the patron and the clerk have made an estimate of the amount of all the expenses, the clerk must personally approach each of the shareholders and inform him that he shall pay a specified amount, dependent upon the amount of his investment in the vessel. If the shareholders wanted to examine the account book, the clerk must show it to them. After the shareholders are informed and made acquainted with the account book as prepared by the clerk, each of them is required to pay the clerk the full amount, that is his share, proportionally to the amount of the investment in the vessel.

If there should be found among the shareholders one who refuses to pay his just share that is due from him based on the amount of his investment in the vessel, the patron may take out a loan, because the shareholder refused to pay his share, and his share in the vessel shall be used as a collateral for the loan as well as the payment of the interest on the loan, which the patron promised to pay the loan maker even if the whole amount invested in the vessel by the shareholder had to be used for this purpose, because it was due to his refusal to pay his just share of expenses that the loan had to be made. If it should happen that the vessel was lost before the loan was paid off, the former shareholder shall be held responsible for this indebtedness and shall pay it out of his other holdings, because the loan was negotiated with his full knowledge and due to his obstinacy.

Further, if the patron found himself in a locality where none of the shareholders were present, and if he did not have personal funds or mutual funds with him and was forced to arrange for a loan under such circumstances, all the investors in the vessel shall be responsible for the repayment of such a loan, and none of the shareholders shall oppose this.

If the vessel was lost before the loan was paid off, none of the shareholders shall be obliged to pay the loan maker anything, because the vessel was wrecked and lost. Let the loan makers beware when they make any loans, for the shareholders lose enough when the vessel is lost as they lose all their investment in such a vessel. For the reasons given above, the loan maker cannot demand anything from the shareholders in a vessel; he should be careful, therefore, when he loans out his money and remember that if a vessel is wrecked, its shareholders will not be obliged to pay for anything due from such a vessel.[66]

Further, if a vessel is located in a place where the loan maker shall demand repayment of the loan, and if the patron has in his possession his personal money or the money belonging mutually to all the shareholders in the vessel, he is required to pay off the loan at once and return the vessel to its shareholders, and with them to go over the account in order to determine the amount of profit made or the losses incurred. If he has made profit, he shall pay each of the shareholders his due, dependent upon the extent of his investment in the vessel, and in this manner divide among all the shareholders all of the profit. If no profit had been made, but rather a loss incurred, every shareholder is bound to reimburse the patron the amount due from him, dependent upon the amount of his investment in the vessel. It is only proper that he who wants to share in the profits should also share in the losses incurred.

If the patron does not have any personal money or money belonging to other persons, or earned by the vessel, or any mutual funds, and the loan maker forces the sale of the vessel in order to recover his loan, the patron is required, if there was any money left from the sale of the vessel, to proceed to the location where the shareholders are present and give each of them the amount due to him from the amount left over from the sale of the vessel.

If the master of the vessel was forced to sell it for the reasons listed above, the shareholders in the vessel cannot hold him accountable, unless they can prove that the loan he took out on account of which the vessel was sold, having been unable to repay it, had been taken to pay for his gambling or debauchery. Should the shareholders be able to prove such a charge against him, the patron shall be forced to return and to pay the shareholders their full investment in the vessel of the actual amount of money they had originally invested. Should the patron be without means to pay this obligation, he shall be seized, bound in irons, and imprisoned until he is able to satisfy the shareholders or pay the damages they had undergone.

If the patron of the vessel that had been sold under the circumstances mentioned before should fail to return with the amount left after the indebtedness had been paid off in order to go over the accounts with the shareholders and pay them their just shares, but instead proceeds somewhere else, and due to this loses the amount that he had with him to repay the shareholders, he shall be forced to pay the shareholders in the manner prescribed above or take the consequences as discussed above. If, however, he should proceed to some

---

66. Loan not covered by any collateral.

other locality with the money that had remained from the sale of the vessel and makes profit with it, he shall be required to share this profit with the shareholders in proportion to the amount each had invested in the vessel, and all this shall be done without any deceit or opposition.

240-Obligation of a Master of a Vessel to Render Account of Transactions to the Shareholders After Completion of Each Voyage

Every patron of a vessel should give an account of the transactions after completion of a voyage. If he should fail to render such an account after each voyage, and the vessel was lost or suffered damage, he shall be required to return and to pay the shareholders all of the profit made. The loss of a vessel cannot and should not free the patron from the obligation to return to the shareholders and pay them the profit that he had been able to make with the vessel.

If the patron could not do this because he was without means, and it is possible to apprehend him, he may be seized, detained, placed in fetters, and treated as had been mentioned in the previous article.

This article was written because there are many patrons who undertake new voyages before they have rendered an account of the previous voyage to the shareholders, and if it should happen that they lose the vessel, they claim they had lost also everything that they possessed. Whether the vessel was lost or not, patrons of vessels are in every instant required to render an accounting to the shareholders, as had been stated above.

In addition, the patron of every vessel must and should give an account to the shareholders of every journey that he undertook, both in regard to the profit as well as the loss, in order to avoid that the penalties mentioned above would not be invoked against him.

In addition, every patron is required, if he had made any profit on the money entrusted to him by the shareholders, to pay them their share of such profit. If it should happen that he lost the profit made on the use of their money, none of the shareholders shall suffer any loss, because the patron had retained these mutual funds contrary to the wishes of these shareholders.

241-Patron's Obligation to Submit an Accounting of His Activities, and, Death of a Patron Before an Account Is Rendered

If a master of a vessel completed one or more voyages and if while engaged in these voyages he returned once or several times to the locality where the majority or all of the shareholders reside, he should give them an account of each journey upon his return. If he should fail to do this, he shall be held accountable in the manner stated in the last article.

Further, if the patron kept on sailing, as had been mentioned above, without making an accounting of these trips to the shareholders and without paying them their share of the profit, they should demand that he render an account to them. If he should fail to do this, but without any malice or evil intention, they may take proper steps to force him to make such a report to them.

On the other hand, regardless of whether the shareholders summoned the patron or not, but did not resort to force in order to have him give such a report after he refused to do it, and in the meantime the master of the vessel had died, and only after his death the shareholders make demands for such an accounting from his beneficiaries or others who have received his wealth, demanding that they pay the shareholders their due share of profit, neither the beneficiaries nor others who may have gained control and possession of the patron's wealth can be required to give such an accounting or to pay them any part of the profit made by the deceased, if the shareholders cannot prove that there had been profit made, or if the deceased had not made such a stipulation in his will. [67]

If it should happen that the deceased patron had not left a will or a testament, the beneficiaries or those who have gained control of his wealth, are obligated to the shareholders only to the extent or the amount written in the will of the deceased or in the register of the vessel that the patron had kept. If there is an entry in the ship's register indicating that profit was made by the patron, his beneficiaries or those who have gained control of his wealth shall pay the shareholders, each one of them, his proper share of the amount entered in the register, even if it became necessary to sell all the remaining possessions of the deceased.

If it should happen that there is no entry in the register indicating that any profit had been made, but on the other hand there are entries of losses and expenses that the owners of the vessel ought to repay to the beneficiaries or to the persons who have the estate of the deceased patron in their control, or that the patron borrowed from others for the necessities of the vessel, the shareholders will be required to pay these obligations proportionally to the amount due from each. This resolution shall be interpreted in the following manner: that these monetary obligations were not incurred by the party who had been in command of the vessel while alive because of some negligence on his part that called for the expenditures of these sums.

---

67. Probate courts did not exist. Wills, oral or written, were left
    with relatives or church authorities.

If the shareholders could prove that these expenditures were made because of some negligence of the person who commanded the vessel while he was alive, they shall not be obligated to pay them, because it had been established by them that the money was paid out due to the negligence of the deceased. Otherwise, the shareholders shall pay these obligations proportionally to their investment in the vessel; it is only just and proper that they share in the losses as they would have willingly shared in the profit if there had been any profit. There is still another reason why such action is justifiable. When the deceased was alive, was patron of their vessel, and was in contact with them while traveling and sailing for them, they had not called him to square all the accounts with them and to pay them their share in the profit made.

If it should happen that the deceased had not left any last will or any other document and did not maintain a ship's register, the shareholders can make no demands upon the beneficiaries, and the beneficiaries or those who have the property of the deceased in their control cannot demand any reimbursement from the shareholders for the expenses made relating to the vessel, regardless of the number of witnesses regarding this matter, because no entries were made in the ship's register concerning such expenditures. Let, therefore, everyone be very careful in conducting his affairs, in order that he may not suffer any damage or be wronged.

This article was written for the reasons listed above, with, however, exception of any kind of agreements or promises made by the patron to the shareholders or by the shareholders to the patron.

There is still another situation that would constitute an exception to this rule: when a patron after squaring the accounts with the majority or all of the shareholders owed them part of the money that was due them as profit. If it should happen that the shareholders set a certain date by which he was to pay them this money, and before the date of expiration and before he was able to pay them the remaining amount he should die, the shareholders shall be paid from the estate of the deceased, even if it became necessary to sell all of his possessions.

242-Explanation of the Preceding Article

In conformity with what had been explained and ascertained in the preceding article, the patron of every vessel is required to give accounting to the shareholders upon completion of each journey. Should he fail to do this, he shall bear the full responsibility in the manner emphasized in that article. This obligation should be understood in the following manner: that the patron after completion of a journey or several journeys will reach the locality where the majority or all of the shareholders reside. If he should arrive at a port located in a territory where none of the shareholders reside and sail out of this port to journey and sail to various parts of the world, and at none of the ports where he anchored his vessel should he be able to find any of the shareholders, and a misfortune should overtake him, and he should lose part or all of the profits he had made with the vessel but not by any fault of his, he should not be required to repay the shareholders for the loss they suffered because the loss had not occurred because of his negligence.

Further, if at the time of sailing, the shareholders had agreed with the patron that he will be required while journeying and stopping at some port to send them their share of the profit he made on each journey, he shall be required to fulfill their wishes.

Further, if he failed to do that and kept their portion of the profit and subsequently lost it, regardless of how this misfortune happened, he will be obligated to repay the shareholders the full amount due to them. Should he be unable to do this, he shall be held accountable in the manner described in the previous article.

Further, if the shareholders had not made any such reservations when he was setting sail, he shall not be required to forward any money to them. Should he, however, send this money or it is lost, he shall be held accountable for it, because he sent it without being ordered to do so.

Further, the patron shall fulfill all the agreements and promises he had concluded with the shareholders at the time he was to sail. If it should happen that he failed to keep them arbitrarily he shall be held responsible for all the damages suffered and that will be borne by the shareholders.

If, however, he failed to keep the promises he made to the shareholders at the time of sailing, but this was not the result of his neglect but rather the expression of the will of God, the sea, civil authorities, or evil people, he shall not be answerable to the shareholders for failing to live up to his promises and agreements, because no one can circumvent or prevent the obstacles that God, the sea, or evil people place in one's path.

Further, everything that has been stated above shall be accomplished without any deceit or fraud. If such conduct shall be proved against a party, the latter shall pay all the damages to the party aggrieved, and this must be done without any hesitation and delay.

This article was written for the reasons listed above.

243-When a Patron Attempts to Increase the Size of His Vessel

A patron who would want to enlarge his vessel and this happens within the environments where the majority or all of the shareholders are resident, he must ask their permission to undertake this task. If the majority or all of them agree to his proposal for enlarging the vessel, he may proceed, and all the shareholders shall raise the necessary funds, each in proportion to the amount originally invested in the vessel. If one of the shareholders objected to this, it will be of no avail, because the enlargement of the vessel is to take place with the knowledge and approval of the majority, and should the patron of the vessel be required to take out a loan for this purpose, the objecting shareholder shall be held accountable for its repayment in the manner discussed in the previous article. [68]

If the shareholders will not wish to agree to the enlargement of the vessel, the patron cannot force them to support this project. He can, however, force them to do what we had discussed in the previous article. In addition, if the patron had the vessel enlarged without the approval and permission of the shareholders, they shall not be obligated to the patron in any manner whatsoever, except in the degree discussed in the previous article.

Further, if the patron happened to be in an area where none of the shareholders are present and wanted to enlarge his vessel, he may do so provided he proceeds in the manner as explained in the previous article, [69] and the shareholders may attempt to prevent him from undertaking this in the manner stated in that article. The patron will be obligated toward the shareholders according to the terms of the agreements and promises that had been mentioned in the article relating to the repair of vessels, for the simple reason that the enlargement of a vessel falls into the category of marine repairs.

244-Further Explanation of the Preceding Article

In the last article we had stated and explained that if a patron wished to enlarge the vessel and was in the locality where the majority or all of the shareholders are resident, he must ask their approval to proceed on his own volition. He can force them to do what had been said in that article, that is, to sell the vessel at an auction; the share-

---

68. The statement does not refer to Article 242 but to Article 48.

69. Reference made here is not to the preceding Article but rather to Article 245 and also to Articles 50 and 51.

holders also have the right to force the master of their vessel to sell it at auction. This is the correct procedure and has been the customary procedure that has been followed, but the auctioning off of the vessel shall actually take place.

It was stated and explained further that if the patron was located in the area where neither the majority nor all of the shareholders were domiciled, and wanted to enlarge the vessel, he may do so, and none of the shareholders can raise any opposition in this matter, with the exceptions made in the preceding article; this is all true. However, this proposal shall be understood as follows: that the patron may order the enlargement of the vessel under two conditions, namely, in order to be able to earn more profit by being able to carry more cargo, or in order to undertake a longer voyage, if he has the opportunity to make such a long voyage or has been given a chance to earn greater profits, when he knows and can perceive the opportunity to make more money for himself and the shareholders in the vessel by taking on passengers aboard the vessel or when there is a dire need for larger vessels sought by merchants for shipping their cargo.

If the patron undertook the enlargement of the vessel for one of the two reasons mentioned, the shareholders shall be required to share in all the expenses and costs that the patron undertook in relation with the enlargement of the vessel, unless these shareholders can prove that he undertook this task motivated by other reasons.

If the shareholders cannot prove these charges against the patron, they shall be required to accept his account of all the financial transactions related to this matter whether he earned any profit or suffered losses in this venture. Should the patron make any profit, the shareholders shall accept their share of the profit proportionally to the amount of their investment in the vessel. If on the other hand he incurred losses, each of them is bound to reimburse him in the amount proportional to their investment in the vessel.

It is equitable, therefore, that in the same manner that each of them would have shared in the profits, if the patron had earned profit, equally in the same manner each shall have to share in the deficits, if deficits had occurred, because the master of the vessel proceeded to enlarge the vessel in good faith and for the reasons given above, and because it cannot be proved that he was motivated by some other considerations.

Further, if the shareholders would be able to prove that their patron was motivated not by the reasons listed above when he undertook the enlargement of the vessel, but was motivated by vanity in order that people would look up to him as a commander of a large vessel, or had proceeded with this plan for some other improper reasons the shareholders shall not be required to share the cost of such an undertaking, if they do not choose to do so. In such a case the following steps shall be taken: all the expenditures of such a venture shall be submitted to two well-informed persons, who will examine, evaluate, and determine the validity of such expenditures, and whatever these two persons shall decide will be binding upon the shareholders and the patron, and neither side in this dispute shall enter any objections concerning the evaluation and determination made by these two well-informed persons.

In addition, in the event that the shareholders do not force the sale of the vessel, and the master of the vessel retains his command under the same conditions he had formerly, having the same shareholders in the vessel, the latter shall be liable for all the expenditures mentioned above but only from the profits they had received, which had been earned by the master of their vessel, in spite of the fact that the learned persons mentioned above had evaluated and determined the amount of such expenditures. The shareholders had already given the patron the benefit of the doubt by retaining him in command of the vessel, and in not refusing to accept and acknowledge the expenditures he incurred without proper and customary procedures. Such procedures should be followed in all kinds of disputes because it is necessary that such matters be settled justly and in conformity with decision given by learned arbitrators.

Further, if the shareholders had auctioned off the vessel in order to get rid of the patron and in this manner he no longer commands the vessel, they shall be obliged to reimburse him for all his expenses as had been evaluated, judged, and determined by the well-informed people, immediately after the vessel is auctioned off and the patron had been deprived of his position. If, however, the former patron of the vessel had taken out a loan to pay for the work of enlarging the vessel, as had been said before, without proper reasons, and had to pay or paid interest on the loan, the shareholders shall not be required to repay him the amount expended on the payment of interest, unless they would voluntarily wish to do so.

If after the patron had completed the rebuilding or the remodeling of the vessel and then took out a loan to pay for the work and cost of remodeling or enlarging the vessel, and had to pay a rate of interest on such a loan, the shareholders shall be obligated to pay such interest, each of them in the amount proportionally to the amount of his investment in the vessel, and this shall be done without any opposition whatsoever.

Even though it had been stated and explained in the previous article that the enlargement of a vessel shall be classified as repairs, which is actually a matter of truth, it is nevertheless much easier to refrain from enlarging the vessel than from making necessary repairs aboard it, if such repairs are needed. For this reason patrons of vessels should be most careful, if they wish to undertake some repairs or to enlarge a vessel when they are anchored in a foreign territory, to proceed with such work according to the well-founded customs in order to avoid being subjected to the above mentioned restrictions and losses, which may result in such cases. All special agreements and arrangements concluded between the shareholders and patrons of vessels relating to these matters are excluded from the above enumerated restrictions and penalties.

This article was written for the reasons mentioned within.

245-Repair of a Vessel

When a patron of a vessel in need of repair puts into a port where the majority or all of the shareholders are resident, he shall show them and explain to them the need of such repairs. If the latter agree, he should proceed and have the necessary repairs made, and the shareholders shall pay for such repairs, each in proportion to his investment in the vessel.

If any of the shareholders refused to pay their proper share due for the repair of the vessel, the patron should negotiate a loan, and the shareholders who had refused to pay his share of the cost of repair shall be held accountable for the repayment of such loan.[70]

If, however, the shareholders would not agree to the repairs of the vessel because such repairs would cost more than the value of the vessel, and that if after having made such repairs they would wish to sell their vessel, they could not even regain the amount expended in repairing the vessel, the patron should not proceed with the repairs without the approval of the shareholders, if he is located with his vessel in the same area where they reside, nor can he force them to agree to such repairs. On the other hand, he can force the shareholders to auction off the vessel since they will not agree to having it repaired. Similarly, the shareholders can force the patron to bring about the sale of the vessel, for neither party has any primary claim on the vessel, all of them are and shall be considered as mutual owners of the vessel, unless some special agreement was concluded between them, providing for special privileges for one of them when such a situation arises.[71]

If the patron had made repairs on the vessel without the approval

---

70. Reference here should be properly made to Article 48 and not to the previous Article.

71. Refer to Articles 55 and 56, and 49 for further explanation.

of the shareholders, none of them shall be held liable for the cost of such repairs in any degree since this was done without their authorization. However, the patron may deduct the cost of repairs from the profits he made with the use of the vessel, and none of the shareholders can enter any protest against his action. If the vessel should be wrecked before the patron had been able to deduct these expenditures from the profits, none of the shareholders will be required to pay him any damages. However, if some of the equipment was salvaged from the vessel, the patron shall have the right to take it, and no shareholder shall oppose this. If after paying for all the costs of repair there is some money left, the patron shall divide it among the shareholders proportionally to the amount of their investment in the vessel.

If any of the shareholders wished to sell his share in the vessel that had been repaired, he is bound to recognize the patron's priority claim to buy such shares, because of all the worry and care borne by the patron in repairing the vessel. If such a shareholder could not reach an agreement with the patron relative to the sale of his shares, the matter should be submitted to two Elders of the Sea Guild for arbitration, who shall evaluate the cost of the repairs in order to prevent any disputes between the patron and the shareholder, if such a shareholder should sell his shares in the vessel to another party. Everything that the above mentioned Elders decide and order shall be carried out, and neither the patron nor the shareholder who had initiated the dispute shall lodge any protests, and everything that the Elders had decided and announced shall be carried out according to the advice given by these persons who are well versed in the matters of marine trade.

Further, if the patron had arrived at a locality where none of the shareholders reside, and the vessel will be in such a need of repair that, without it, it would be impossible to continue to sail, he should proceed in the manner that would be beneficial to himself and the shareholders, since they are not available and since they had made him the guardian of their possessions. Therefore, he should be very careful not to harm himself or subject himself to suspicion by those who had given him their confidence. If the patron knows and is convinced in his mind and conscience that the repairs that are badly needed will be much more beneficial than damaging to the shareholders, he should proceed according to what in his judgment is indicated as necessary.

Whatever course of action he should take, whether to repair or to sell the vessel, it must be approved by the shareholders, because he had proceeded in good faith. The shareholders cannot doubt that the action he took was for the benefit of all, for everyone should consider with whom he enters into a partnership, with the exception of a situation in which it had been determined between the patron and the shareholders that the patron shall not be authorized to repair or to sell the vessel without authorization from the majority or all of the shareholders.

If the shareholders had not made such an agreement, they shall have to accept whatever action the patron had taken in such matters, with the exception of a situation in which the patron had gambled and lost their vessel, lost it due to debauchery, or lost it because of some other negligence on his part. Under such circumstances the patron shall be required to pay them damages as outlined in the previous article.

This article was written in order that everyone be very cautious with whom he enters into a partnership or to whom he entrusts his property and in order that the terms of all agreements be carried out.

246-Commandeering of Anchors

A master of a vessel who appropriated or ordered his crew to commandeer floats, buoys, or anchor buoys belonging to a vessel moored near by, will be required to pay the patron of the vessel to whom such anchors belonged the full value as estimated by the latter under oath, and in addition he must compensate him for all the damages that resulted from such rash action.

Further, the patron of a vessel whose anchors and other equipment were commandeered may initiate criminal action against the patron who had committed such an offense and charge him with theft.

Further, if any sailor should take an anchor belonging to the vessel on which he is a member of the crew without the knowledge and approval of the patron, that is to say, if he took such equipment without an order by his own desire, he shall be liable to the same penalty that would be imposed upon the patron of a vessel who ordered him to steal such equipment.

Further, if a sailor who had committed such a theft is unable to reimburse the master of the vessel from which such equipment was stolen for the loss of the equipment and the damages resulting thereof, such a sailor or sailors shall be seized, cast into prison, and kept there until they are able to reach an agreement with the patron and pay him all the damages and costs that had resulted from their action in the amount that will be given under oath by the master of the vessel from which such equipment was stolen, unless the patron of such a vessel would show them mercy, allowing them a period of time in which to repay him for the damage or allowing them to work out the amount due him for the damages he had suffered by their behavior. It will be up to the disposition of the master who had suffered such damages which of the above mentioned methods he will accept for the repayment of the damage, whether he will decide to have them kept in jail or have them work out the amount due him by taking them into his employ.

This article was written because if there should be no set punishment for such violations, many injuries and misfortunes would result. In addition, because any vessel that shall be anchored may in order to prevent collision or in order to prevent its foundering in the mud or scraping its hull on the rocks, may anchor these buoys about, and anyone removing such safety equipment should be punished as had been stated above.

247-Crew Hired Aboard a Vessel for a Percentage of the Profits

A patron who is sailing with a crew hired on the basis of a percentage of the profit shall make all these agreements and promises in writing with all the members of the crew who had agreed to sail with him for a percentage of the profit the vessel will make. In addition, he shall cause these written agreements to be made in the presence of the majority or all of the crew, and shall state what part of the profit will accrue to the vessel, what part to the crew, who shall get a larger portion, and specify the amount. All this shall be done in order to prevent a chance of any dispute between the patron and the crew at the time the profit is divided.

Further, the patron shall show all or the majority of the sailors collectively, if all of them cannot be assembled at the same moment, all the equipment aboard the vessel in order that should the crew together with the patron agree and decide that the equipment needed repair or reinforcement, the patron shall authorize the clerk to expedite this, so that later on there shall not be a possibility of a dispute between the patron and the crew over this matter, and above all so that the crew could not make any accusations, if part of the equipment should have been lost, that they had not seen any such equipment aboard the vessel, which they are asked to share in the cost of purchasing.

If the master of the vessel proceeds in the manner outlined above, the crew shall sail with him and perform all the tasks as if it was being paid a set sum of money. Furthermore, the crew cannot make any kind of reservations or objections except those that had been discussed in the previous articles. Thus, the patron of a vessel shall honestly and fairly divide any profits that he had made due to the goodness of God, giving each sailor his share as had been agreed between them and entered into the ship's register.

151

The navigator under the penalty of perjury shall estimate and ascertain the exact amount due to the crew in order that the members of the crew be paid fully and honestly whatever the patron of the vessel promised each one of them at the time of the enlistment. The clerk under the threat of the same penalty as had been prescribed for the navigator shall declare the amount due to the vessel and shall not do anything that would be more beneficial to the vessel than to the crew, but be very vigilant in order that the vessel as well as the crew receive and be given its just and honest share of the profit.

In addition, the clerk and the navigator should receive the amount that had been agreed upon when the enlistment of the crew was made. If there had been no agreement made concerning these matters, the clerk and the navigator shall receive one share each as a token of the trouble and care they had given to the welfare of the crew. However, these two shares shall be taken from the whole amount of the profit earned by the vessel.

Let us now discuss the various situations that may arise. If a vessel while sailing loses a mast, sailing-yard, or any of its sails, the crew shall not be required to pay for any of these damages, if the patron or the navigator had not issued an order to furl the sails before the mast, the sailing-yard, or sails were damaged or lost. If, however, the patron had given an order to furl the sails and the sailors failed to obey his order and as a result the equipment mentioned was lost, the crew shall be held responsible for this damage, which means that the whole crew shall share the payment for these damages.

If the patron of a vessel had given an order to drop the anchor at the spot where the vessel was located, and the crew informed him or the navigator that the anchor chains that he had ordered them to lower were not sufficiently strong to hold the anchors and due to this the anchors were lost, and the patron as well as the navigator although informed about the condition of the anchor chains had not ordered that anchor chains be replaced, the sailors should not be held responsible for the damages that resulted, because they had informed the patron and the navigator about this matter. If, however, the crew had not apprised the captain nor the navigator about the poor condition of the anchor chains and subsequently the anchors were lost, they shall be held responsible for the damage, because they had dropped the anchors without informing those in authority that the anchor chains were too weak and worthless.

Further, if due to a misfortune the vessel shall be wrecked or founder on the shoals, and the profit made by the vessel shall be sufficient to pay for the repairs of whatever damage had been caused, the patron may use the money for this purpose. Should the patron be unwilling to undertake the repairs, it should be evaluated and submitted to an auction between the patron and the crew members, and the minimum bid shall be the amount the vessel is estimated to be worth after it had been wrecked. If the master and the crew could not agree on the value of the vessel, the dispute should be turned over for adjudication to two Elders who are well versed in all the phases of the art of sailing,and whatever they declare shall be carried out.

If some of the equipment had been salvaged, it and all other salvage shall be evaluated and given to the patron. After the patron's claim had been satisfied, and there should remain some of the mutually earned profit, it shall be divided among all others in accordance with the predetermined arrangements.

If it should happen that the mutually made profit will not be sufficient to pay for the damage to the vessel, which had been partly or totally wrecked, the crew shall not be required to pay any of the damage whatsoever, since they themselves had lost enough, namely their time and their labor. Nevertheless, the crew is required to aid the master fully and loyally in salvage operations and return to him everything that had been salvaged.

Further, if it should happen that the vessel had earned no profit, the crew shall be obliged to pay the patron for their food rations the full amount he expended for t is purpose from the day of their enlistment until the day they leave the service of the vessel. They shall repay him this expense without any delay and opposition, for he has lost enough of his personal wealth using his vessel and his time. The patron can bring charges against the sailor who would refuse to pay him for these rations in the same manner that he would do if he had entrusted some money to the sailor and had written proof of it, and such a sailor should be imprisoned as long as he will not satisfy the patron and will not pay him the full amount owed to him, or until he makes some other agreement with the patron.

Further, if the patron can see and knows that the sailor who is refusing to pay for his rations is not doing this moved by hate or malice but only due to the fact that he has no means with which to pay the patron, the latter shall be willing to wait and give the sailor sufficient amount of time to make it possible for him to pay what he owes, provided that the sailor makes this obligation valid in writing or procures a guarantor, in order that the patron and his beneficiaries shall be safeguarded.

Further, if a member of the crew should lose some object while serving aboard the vessel and the vessel had earned a profit, the sailor shall be compensated for the lost article provided he can prove his claim. If he cannot prove his loss, no compensation shall be paid him. If it should happen that the vessel had earned no profit, no one will be required to pay for any lost articles, regardless of how many witnesses can testify to the validity of the claim, for everyone aboard had already lost enough, namely, his time and the labor he had performed aboard the vessel.

This article was written because there are many patrons who command old and decayed vessels, well aware of the fact that the crew shares in the damages to a vessel, would take steps so that they would at the slightest opportunity see to it that the vessel would be wrecked and in this manner recover more in damages than the worth of two such vessels.

For this reason, therefore, sailors hired on share basis in the profit the vessel will earn are responsible in case the vessel is wrecked for the damage only to the amount of the profit the vessel had earned, as had been stated and explained in the preceding article.[72]

248-Marine Equipment Commandeered by Armed Vessels

If a vessel sailing with a crew hired on share in the profit basis is unfortunate to meet armed ships and these ships take their sail or sails, lines or a line, anchor or anchors, or any other equipment, the whole crew shall share in the payment for this loss, meaning that every member of the crew shall share in paying for them. It should also be understood that if the vessel had earned any profit, it shall be used to pay for the equipment taken by the armed vessel.

If it should happen that the earnings made by the vessel are insufficient to pay for the cost of the lost equipment, the crew hired to serve aboard the vessel on percentage of profit basis are not required to participate in the payment for the lost equipment, because neither these sailors nor anyone else who leaves his home in order to earn money by sailing with someone does this with a conviction that if a vessel on which he agreed to serve should meet with a misfortune, his property left at home should be used to help to pay for the damage that the vessel on which he serves may suffer. If he were obliged to do so, it would have been better for him if he had remained at home. In addition, there is still another reason, and that is that such a sailor had lost enough already, namely, his time, the labor he put in aboard the vessel, and the clothing he has worn out.

Further, if the profit made by the vessel is sufficient to pay for the equipment taken off the vessel, the patron who shall be paid for the damage should take an oath in the presence of the entire crew that he shall do everything in his power and as soon as possible to make up

---

72. Reference is made to the next and not to the preceding Article.

these losses. If he is able to make up the loss, he shall repay the sailors the amount he had received in damages for the equipment taken forcibly by the armed vessels, and he shall do this without any opposition.

If it should happen that some of the sailors would assert that the loss of the equipment commandeered by the armed vessels should not be replaced at the expense of the money earned by their vessel, since the loss occurred due to fate, such a proposition cannot and should not be accepted. If these sailors or others by act of God or stroke of good luck found a chest filled with money or other very valuable items or a chest of equal value or other such items from which they could derive great benefit, there would be not one who would not like to take a share of such a find and would be eager to take even a larger share than would be due them, if this was possible.

Under such circumstances it is proper that in a situation where everyone wants to share without hesitation in the profit, similarly all should also share mutually in the damage that has occurred due to ill fate.

This article was written for the reasons stated above.

249-Waterlogged Cargo Carried in an Open Boat

If the merchants engaged an open vessel to ship their cargo[73] and after the cargo had been loaded aboard, it had become waterlogged or spoiled due to sea water that had seeped into the vessel or rain, the patron shall not be held accountable to the merchants in any degree, because this had not happened by his negligence; both he and the merchants knew very well that the vessel that they had cargoed was a vessel without any decks.[74]

If a patron of an open boat was located in a place where he could procure and place a canopy over the cargo, and the weather did not prevent him from accomplishing this, but he failed to take this precaution, the merchants can demand that he pay them damages for the spoiled cargo if they can prove his negligence for not protecting their cargo with a canopy.

Further, if the patron was located in an area where the volume of the sea waves and the power of the wind prevented him from spreading a canopy over the cargo or it rained so hard that the canopy could not hold the accumulation of the rain water, he shall not be obliged to pay for the damages to the cargo, which had become waterlogged or spoiled under the circumstances discussed above.

---

73. More detail given in Article 186.

74. Whaleboat, skiff, sloop, rowboat, etc.

Further, if, however, the vessel was swamped by sea water that poured over the gunwales and the cargo was damaged, the master of the vessel shall pay the damages suffered by the merchants to whom the cargo belonged. If, however, the cargo is damaged by water that seeped in below the gunwales even though the vessel was well tarred, the patron shall not be required to pay damage to the merchants to whom the cargo belonged, because his vessel was properly and well tarred.

Further, if a patron had promised some merchant that he would store his cargo well protected by a good canopy, but he did not protect it with such a canopy, and in spite of the promises given stored the cargo in some other location and the cargo became waterlogged or spoiled, the patron shall pay the merchant to whom the cargo belonged damages, because he did not store the cargo under a canvas as he had agreed with the merchant.

If the patron had stored the cargo as he had promised, but the cargo became waterlogged or spoiled in spite of all the precautions, he shall not be obliged to pay for the damage, because he had proceeded as he had promised the merchant that he would, and the merchant had agreed to provide the cargo under these conditions. Therefore, if the cargo should become waterlogged or spoiled when it is stored under a canopy, the patron will not be required to pay any damages because he had not been negligent.

Let, therefore, every patron be most careful in the promises he makes to the merchants, because he shall be bound to keep these promises.

This article was written for the above named reasons.

250-Employment of a Pilot

A patron who had leased a vessel for the purpose of sailing into waters unknown to him or any other person aboard the vessel should hire an experienced pilot; the pilot shall inform and satisfy the patron that the waters into which they shall sail are well known to him.

If the patron had been informed by the pilot that the latter knows every part of the waters to which the patron intends to sail in order to deliver the cargo he was engaged to carry, and if the pilot fulfills faithfully and diligently all the promises he had made to the patron, the patron shall pay him the full amount he had promised him without any hesitation, and should even pay him more than he had promised him, depending on the degree of knowledge he had of those waters and the type of service he had given, for the pilot had kept all the promises he had made to the patron.

Further, all the agreements that the patron had concluded with the

156

pilot should be according to the custom entered in the register of the vessel, in order that no disputes would be likely to issue between the patron and the pilot.

If it should happen that the pilot would not know the waters in the locality that he had claimed he knew well and will not be able to perform the services that he had agreed to perform, he should be immediately decapitated, and no mercy or leniency should be given him. The patron of the vessel may order that his head be cut off without taking this matter before any tribunal of justice if he does not wish to do this, because the pilot lied to him and exposed him, all those who are in his company aboard the vessel, as well as the vessel and everything aboard it.

It shall not, however, be within the exclusive determination of the master of the vessel whether the pilot is decapitated. Such a decision shall be reached after consultation and examination of the issue by the navigator, the merchants, and the rest of the crew. If the majority or all of those mentioned above have determined that the pilot shall be decapitated, the sentence shall be carried out; if they should decide otherwise, he will not be executed. Their verdict and no other punishment shall be inflicted upon the pilot, for if the pilots were left entirely to the disposition of the patrons, it could happen that the pilots would be decapitated merely to satisfy the hate that the patrons bore toward them, or in order to pocket the wages that were due to the pilots. Among the patrons as well as among other people there are those who lack all proper judgment, and there are also many patrons of vessels who do not know how to sail the vessel forward or backwards, and do not even have a conception of what the sea is. It would, therefore, be a great injustice that a person should lose his life due to some perversion or willfulness of a patron.

Let, therefore, all who enlist aboard a vessel as a pilot beware before they agree to such service that they are able to perform the service they had agreed to in order that the punishment prescribed above or some other punishment would not be inflicted upon them.

251-Security Personnel Aboard a Vessel

Every master of a vessel shall immediately, after unfurling the sails and departing from the port where the voyage began, appoint proper security personnel to watch over the vessel while it is under sail as well as when it is anchored in a port, near a shore, or in a canal, both in friendly as well as unfriendly territory.

If the vessel security guard should fall asleep while the vessel is under sail, he shall be deprived of wine rations for a single day as his punishment. If the guards fall asleep while on duty and the vessel is moored near the shore, in a port, or in a canal, they shall be deprived of their wine rations and meat, fish, or cheese rations that they get with their bread rations for one day. If it should happen that the guard falls asleep while on duty in an enemy territory, and the guard who fell asleep was guarding the prow portion of the vessel, in addition to being deprived of the rations mentioned above, he shall be whipped by the whole crew, or dunked in the sea three times while tied to a line; it will depend upon the patron and the navigator which of the two punishments will be inflicted upon him. If the offending guard fell asleep while guarding the stern of the vessel, he shall be deprived of his rations and drenched from head to foot with a bucket of sea water.

If one of the guards mentioned above had fallen asleep more than three times while on duty, he should be deprived of his wages for the entire voyage. If he had already been paid, he shall return his wages or be dunked in the sea, depending on the choice of punishment decided upon by the patron and the crew, because he had endangered his own life as well as the lives of all aboard the vessel.

For this reason the above article was written.

252–Salvaged Cargo

If some cargo is salvaged in the shallows, in port, or on the shore, regardless of whether it has been floating on the water or has been washed ashore, anyone who salvages such a cargo in the shallows, in port, or on the shore, if the waves had washed it ashore, shall be allowed to keep half of such cargo, provided he has notified the local civil authority about it. The governmental authorities shall place such cargo on public display for a year and a day. If the salvaged cargo would be of a variety that might spoil, it shall be sold and the money received for it shall be kept for the above mentioned period.

If after this period of time the owner of the cargo or the money received for it is not discovered, the local authorities shall present the finder of such cargo half of it. The remainder shall be divided into two equal parts. One part shall be retained by the local civil authority, and the other part shall be offered for the glory of God to an institution that shall be in need and where they will pray for the soul of the original owner of the cargo.

If the cargo that had been salvaged had been washed ashore, the finder shall be allowed to keep it, as will be decided by the Elders of the locality where the cargo was found. The same procedure shall be followed as had been explained above, and the share retained by the civil authorities shall also be divided in the same manner.

Further, should such cargo be found in the bay or on the open seas, it should be divided in the manner prescribed in one of the preceding articles, and there is no need to repeat or explain this at the present moment.[75] If it should happen that the cargo should be found at the bottom of the sea because it is too heavy to float on top of the water, it should not be sold or disposed of in any other manner, because cargo salvaged from the bottom of the sea shall be kept until claimed by its owner. The party who salvaged such cargo shall be amply rewarded according to the determination made by the local civil authority and two members of the Sea Guild who are trustworthy and who will be capable of arbitrating the issue judiciously. The civil authority shall place the cargo on public display and retain the money realized from the sale of such cargo, if such cargo was in danger of spoilage, as had been stated above.

If after the time set by the local authority or established by custom the rightful owner does not appear to claim such cargo, and no other person presents a claim against such a cargo, the town crier shall be ordered to make a daily announcement of this matter for thirty days. If the owner of this cargo appears to claim it within this thirty-day period, the cargo shall be given to him. Otherwise the cargo shall be divided in the manner prescribed in the article dealing with salvage of floating cargo; this should be done because the time set by the authorities for claiming of such a cargo by its rightful owner had passed.

Further, the above should be understood as follows: that the finder or finders of such a cargo had made acknowledgement of this to the local authorities within three days after finding such a cargo, provided that they shall be in a locality where such civil authority exists.[76]

If the finders of such cargo failed to report this matter within three days, they shall do it within a period of six days; if they are unable to make this report in six days, they shall be required and must do it within a period of ten days in order to avoid damages, losses, and deceit. If they should fail to report this matter to the proper authority within ten days, they shall be compelled to surrender the salvaged cargo under the circumstances mentioned before and treated as thieves in order to prevent them from disposing of the cargo in an arbitrary manner. They shall also lose all the rights they formerly had to the cargo that they had salvaged.

---

75. Reference is made here to Article 160.

76. Cargo found on uninhabited shores and islands was property of the finder unless a special agreement had been made aboard the vessel regarding such cargo.

Further, if the finder or finders of the goods did not report the matter to the proper authority within the ten-day period, but they can establish justifiable reasons why they failed to do this within the period prescribed by law, they shall be adjudged innocent of any attempt to deceive the local authority. They shall, however, be required to prove the circumstances that prevented them from fulfilling this obligation; otherwise action shall be taken against them by the authorities as had been mentioned above.

Further, if the cargo had been found and salvaged after an interval of one year and a day from the date it had been lost, its owner cannot make any claim upon it, and it should be adjudged the property of the party or parties who found it. This is just and proper, for with the exception of iron, steel, and other metals, any cargo that had been lost and remained underneath the sea, floating on the sea, or near the edge of the sea for a period of one year could hardly be identified by any markings or signs by which the owner could pretend or claim that this cargo belonged to him, unless he should be able to do this with the help of opportunistic people. Therefore, cargo found under such circumstances shall belong to the party who found it.

Further, if a party claims that such cargo had belonged to him and makes a deposition under oath that such cargo is his and had belonged to him, it shall be given to him provided that the party who found and salvaged the cargo is willing to return it to him and is given an award the amount of which shall be decided by the finder. If the finder refuses to return the cargo to the party who claims he is the rightful owner, he cannot be forced to do this by the authorities, unless the claimant would be able to prove with the aid of trustworthy witnesses that the cargo had belonged to him.

If, as had been stated above, he shall be able to prove that the cargo had belonged to him and is anxious to recover all of the salvaged cargo, he shall pay the finder all the expenses and costs incurred in recovering this cargo, and the amount shall be determined by the local authorities and arbitrated by two trustworthy Elders.

If the finder or finders of such cargo used it as a collateral for some transaction and made a profit, but in spite of this demanded that they be allowed to retain the salvaged cargo, they shall be rewarded as the custom directs. Any profit they made by the use of the cargo as a collateral or in some other manner shall be subtracted from the amount of their award.

This article has been written for the reasons mentioned above.

253-Agreements Concluded in a Bay or on the Open Sea

If an agreement is made or a promise given or an obligation assumed while the vessel is in a bay or on the open sea or any other part of the sea, it shall not be binding, regardless of the reason why such an agreement or promise was made, unless at the time such an agreement or promise was made the vessel was moored to the shore by a mooring line or some other line. This is due to the fact that very often there are aboard a vessel that is under sail merchants and other people of stature who are affected by the sea and become seasick. Such persons in order to reach land where they could be relieved and return to normal health, would, if they had one thousand silver marks, pay them to anyone who would demand them in return for landing them ashore. For this reason any such promise shall have no validity.

In addition, in case of a meeting with armed vessels, in order to protect themselves from the consequences and to avoid any potential danger, they would be willing to make agreements and give promises even beyond their ability to keep; therefore, all agreements made and promises given due to fear or force do not have and cannot have any validity.

If, however, the vessel was moored to the shore by a hawser or some other line, all the agreements entered into by both parties, regardless of how they were concluded, do have and shall have validity.

Further, if the vessel is in the bay, on the open sea, or on any other body of water, regardless of whether it will be moored to the shore by a hawser or not, and if aboard this vessel there are persons reaching agreements and making promises, such agreements or promises will be valid under four circumstances, namely: when the cargo must be thrown overboard, when the vessel is wrecked by the storm or some other unfortunate accident, when the merchants agree to pay damages suffered by the vessel due to some specified reason, or in case the course if altered, provided that the clerk will be present when such agreements are concluded and provided that as soon as the vessel is moored, he will not forget to make an entry into the ship's register of these matters.

For the reasons mentioned above, no agreement concluded in the bay, on the high seas, or in any other part of the sea shall be considered valid except under the four conditions mentioned and attested to in the previous paragraph.

If the vessel is anchored in the middle of the mouth of a river or in territorial waters, all the agreements concluded by the parties aboard the vessel shall be binding, whether or not the vessel was held ashore by a hawser because it is in a similar situation as if it were on shore, for the storm cannot drive it away or damage it in any way.

254-Agreements Concluded Between the Master of the Vessel, Merchants, and the Crew

The patron shall carry out all the agreements he had concluded with the merchants, the crew, or any other parties who are or will be interested in the vessel in any manner, and this shall be done without any reluctance or delay. If it should happen that a patron of a vessel would refuse to carry out any agreements or commitments he entered into, he will be required to pay all the damages suffered by the injured parties or that they may suffer in the future, and he shall do this without any opposition, even if it was necessary to sell the vessel in order to repay the damages, with the exception of a situation when the patron was unable due to well established practices or obstacles to carry out the agreements he had concluded with the persons mentioned above.

Similarly, the merchants, crew, as well as all other persons connected with the vessel are required to fulfill all the agreements that they had concluded with the master of the vessel without any delay. If they should refuse to carry out these agreements and promises, and they have any property, it shall be sold to pay the damages that had resulted by their refusal to carry out such agreements without any delay. If their wealth is not sufficient to pay these damages, it is proper, if it is possible, to arrest them, turn them over to the proper authorities, and imprison them for so long as they will be unable to pay the patron for the damages he had suffered or until the patron agrees to reach another agreement with them. The only exception would be if fate had prevented them from fulfilling the promises they had made the patron, since this did not take place as result of any negligence on their part.

This article was written for the reasons given above.

255-Responsibility for Cargo Entrusted to a Party According to the Customs of the Sea

If any person entrusts another in full confidence with his property (and by property we should understand it to be cargo) whether the agreement was made in writing or not, and without any other conditions than that the one who accepts care of such cargo accepts it according to the recognized customs of the sea, and with the restrictions that he shall not be held accountable for it if due to stormy seas or acts of pirates he had lost such cargo, the party who accepted such cargo shall sell it at the port of destination as designated at the moment he had accepted care of such cargo and shall try to dispose of it to the best advantage of the person who entrusted such cargo to his care.

However, if at the time they mutually agreed to this arrangement there was no mention made of the amount of money the one who accepted the care of the cargo would be given for the performance of this task, the latter should not deduct anything for his trouble, for he was not allowed to do this, but should immediately after the return from the journey for which he had undertaken the care of the cargo, report to its owner and give him the full amount he had received for the cargo. The owner of the cargo shall pay the party who had taken care of his cargo for his trouble and care proportionally to the amount he had received for the cargo. The amount shall be determined by the owner of the cargo, and the party who had been commissioned to care for and sell the cargo cannot force him to any additional obligation.

Therefore, let every person who accepts care of another's cargo be most careful when he takes this obligation that he shall not be left to the disposition of the person who entrusted him with the care of such cargo and be dependent for his wages upon the whim of the former.

The same principles shall apply to persons who accept care of money entrusted to them by another party, as apply in case of a cargo entrusted to their care.

256-Vessel Sold by the Patron Without the Knowledge of Its Shareholders

A patron who shall sell the vessel that he commands without the approval and knowledge of the shareholders is required immediately after the sale has been completed to return to the locality where the shareholders reside and make an account of the transaction and pay each of the shareholders the full amount due him in proportion to his investment in the vessel, if the shareholders wish to accept this. If, on the other hand, the shareholders refused to accept the money, the patron must return and surrender the vessel to them because he had sold it without their knowledge and authority.

If he could not return their own vessel to them, he shall return one of the same value, and in addition, the profit that he had made with that vessel, unless he can reach an agreement with the merchants more advantageous to him. If they cannot agree mutually to any settlement on this issue, it should be submitted to two trustworthy Elders who shall arbitrate the dispute; whatever they decide and order shall be carried out.

Further, if the patron had sold the vessel in the manner discussed above, and this sale is satisfactory to the majority of the shareholders, he shall only be obligated to pay each of them the amount due, because the majority had agreed that what he did was proper.

If it should happen that the patron after the sale of the vessel failed to return, in order to report on the matter to the shareholders and pay each of them the amount due [to each] from the sale of the vessel, but proceeds to another country, he shall be forced if he is apprehended to return and pay the shareholders the money due them plus the profits that the vessel could have had made, as estimated in their deposition made under oath. If he would be unable to pay them and end this matter to their satisfaction, he shall be held, turned over to the judicial authorities, and be imprisoned until he is able to repay the shareholders or reach a satisfactory agreement with them.

If the patron who sold the vessel cannot be located, but the shareholders locate the vessel that he had sold, they may seize it and institute legal proceedings. The court shall hear the case and award them judgment, provided that they can prove by submitting documentary evidence or witnesses who will testify that the vessel belongs to them, and if the purchaser cannot prove that the seller had the authorization from these shareholders to sell the vessel as he saw fit. Let, therefore, everyone be most careful that in purchasing a vessel he shall not suffer a loss.

Further, if the patron sold the vessel because it was over age or if the loan makers had it sold in order to collect their money that they had advanced the patron to purchase some essential equipment for the vessel, the patron shall be held accountable by the shareholders only in the manner and degree that has been described and explained in the article that discussed repairs of a vessel. [77]

257-Cargo Loaded Secretly Aboard the Vessel

If a merchant or several merchants conclude an agreement with the master of a vessel to ship bales or chests or other containers filled with cargo and, without informing the patron, attempt to secrete in these bales, crates, or other containers gold, silver, money, or other valuables without showing them to the master of the vessel or informing him, the navigator, or the clerk about this, and do not tell them specifically what they had hidden in these crates and other containers, and if due to some unfortunate accident it shall be necessary to throw cargo overboard, or the vessel will be wrecked or will founder in the shoals, the above mentioned crates, bales, chests, and other containers in which the valuables had been secreted shall be evaluated for damages only in the amount they were valued at the time

---

77. Reference made to Article 245.

of shipment, even if these merchants were able to produce witnesses who would testify that they had seen the merchants secrete these valuables within these containers, and this shall be done because the merchants failed to inform the patron, navigator, clerk, or the officer of the guard about this matter, and also because they had not insisted that this would be entered into the ship's register. If the vessel foundered in the shoals and such cargo was lost, they should be compensated only for the cargo that had been declared when the contract to ship such cargo was made.

If it should happen that the bales and crates into which valuables had been secretly placed, as had been discussed above, are not lost or thrown overboard, but it shall be discovered that other items were hidden in them, such bales and crates with all their contents, declared and undeclared, shall be assessed for the loss of the cargo thrown overboard or lost due to shipwreck.

Further, if the above mentioned items or cargo were lost by the negligence of the patron of the vessel or the clerk, they shall be liable for the damage in the amount the cargo had been evaluated at the time it was loaded aboard the vessel. This is done because there are some merchants who, if one believed everything they say when they suffer loss under circumstances mentioned above, of any crate or bale of cargo, would claim that its contents exceeded a thousand marks of gold or silver. For this reason no one shall be obligated to pay them any damage above the amount they declared that the cargo was worth at the time its value was declared when arrangements to ship it were made.

Let, therefore, every merchant be most careful that he declare everything when he is making arrangements to ship his cargo. Otherwise he may suffer a loss, as had been stated above.

258-When a Patron of a Vessel Authorized a Representative to Negotiate Shipment of Cargo

If a patron of a vessel authorized his representative to conclude shipment contracts for his vessel, whether this would amount to a portion of the cargo the vessel will carry or a capacity load, if the representative had concluded such a contract within the period of time he was given to accomplish this task, all the agreements he concluded shall be as valid and binding as if the patron himself concluded these contracts, for the representative acted in the person of the patron who had empowered him to conclude such agreements. Thus, an agreement concluded by a person who was authorized by the patron and given a specific time to accomplish this must be carried out, regardless of the fact whether such a contract shall prove to be profitable for the vessel.

If the patron after giving authority to his representative to contract for cargo within a given period of time would also himself contract for other cargo and as a result would have contracted for so much cargo that he would be unable to take aboard the cargo contracted for by the party whom he authorized to do this, he shall be required to carry the cargo contracted for by his deputy within the time limit that had been set, and will have to leave behind the cargo he personally had contracted for, or will be required to reach another agreement with the merchants who had made shipment agreements with his deputy. It is necessary that the party whom he authorized to procure shipment of cargo shall not be exposed to damages, even if the vessel had to be sold to prevent this.

Further, if the patron authorized another person to arrange for shipment of cargo without setting the date by which this should be accomplished, and before he had been advised by his representative that he did contract to ship cargo, the patron himself had also made agreements with others to take their cargo aboard, the patron shall be obliged to proceed in the manner described above.

Further, if the patron had ordered that his representative should be informed not to contract for any cargo, and the latter had been informed of this before he actually had made any contracts, he shall follow these instructions and not negotiate any such agreements. However, should he disobey the patron and proceed to contract for cargo, the patron shall not be held liable for any damages and shall not be liable to the merchants who had signed a contract with the representative, because the latter had been ordered not to negotiate any such contracts, for no person has more claim upon the wealth of another than that which the rightful owner will allow. If, however, such a representative had made shipment agreements before he had been notified by the patron, all such agreements will be binding, as had been stated above.

In addition, a patron who had authorized another person to contract for cargo should not personally conclude binding contracts until he is aware of the action that had been taken by his representative, in order that the damages mentioned above would not result.

259-When a Patron Attempts to Attach a Towing Line to a Raft Contrary to the Wishes of Merchants Aboard His Vessel

If a master of a vessel took on cargo at some point of his voyage and while sailing to the port of destination would come upon a raft, masts, sails, or other wooden objects floating in the sea, and would attempt to attach a line or would order that a line be attached to the flotsam in order to tow it as salvage, the merchants aboard his vessel are within their rights to demand that he abandon such salvage operations. If he should refuse to bow to their demands, and if these merchants announce and inform him that if he does not abandon the salvage, he shall be wholly responsible for any damage to their cargo aboard his vessel, and the patron in spite of the warning by the merchants pays no heed to their demands, such a patron shall be held liable for all the damage that may result to their cargo due to his negligence.

Should he be unable to reimburse them for the damage, the vessel shall be sold, and no one can oppose this action with the exception of the crew, which shall be paid its wages. If the amount of money realized from the sale of the vessel should be insufficient to pay for the damages, and the patron possesses any other wealth, it shall be sold and the merchants shall be paid the amount due them, for the damages occurred by his negligence. If his property is insufficient to pay these damages, and if he can be apprehended, he should be imprisoned and kept in prison until he has paid the claims of the merchants or has reached another agreement with them.

If it should happen that the patron would wish to take a few bales off the floating raft, he may do so if the merchants agree. Should he, however, attempt to take some cargo off the raft against their wishes, he shall be liable for all the damages as if he had taken the raft in line, as had been stated above.

If it should happen that there are no merchants aboard when the patron comes upon a floating raft and attaches a hauling line to it or if he takes several bales of cargo off the raft, and the merchants can prove that due to this they had suffered some damage, the patron shall be liable for all the damages in the same manner as prescribed above.

Patrons therefore should act in a manner that would not result in any damages.

260-When a Vessel Is Engaged to Deliver Cargo to a Specified Destination

If one or several merchants journeyed into a foreign country and had contracted with a patron of a vessel to come to that country in order to pick their cargo and deliver it to a specified location, and he should fail to arrive there on the date or within the period of time agreed to to pick up such cargo, the patron shall be liable for all the damages, expenses, and losses that they had suffered by his negligence.

If it should happen that the merchants had engaged another vessel because the vessel that had been contracted for first to pick up their cargo at a specified time had failed to arrive, and they should be forced to pay higher lading fees than agreed upon with the patron of the first vessel and thus suffered a loss, the latter should be forced to reimburse them for the amount in excess of the amount they had agreed upon originally, because the patron of the first vessel engaged failed to arrive to pick up their cargo as had been agreed.

If it should happen that the vessel originally engaged should arrive to pick up their cargo after the expiration of the date agreed upon, the merchants shall not be held liable to the patron of the first vessel if in the meantime they had engaged another vessel, because the patron of the first vessel had failed to arrive at the agreed time to pick up their cargo.

Further, if, however, the first vessel should arrive before these merchants had engaged another vessel, even though it was past the date they had agreed upon, the merchants are required to furnish the cargo to the first vessel as had been agreed. This resolution should be understood in this manner: that the patron of such a vessel shall be liable for all the damages, expenses, and losses they had incurred while waiting for him, if the merchants desire this. Their deposition under oath as to the amount of such damages shall be accepted as valid.

This should also be understood in this manner: that if the patron of the vessel with whom the merchants had originally agreed to ship their cargo was unable to arrive on the date they had agreed, not due to his fault but to some obstacles that were visited upon him by God, heavy winds, turbulent seas, or civil authorities, he shall not be liable for any damages, expenses, or losses incurred by these merchants because this had not been by his negligence. Should the merchants engage another vessel in the meantime, they are obliged to provide the cargo to the patron with whom they had originally concluded an agreement as well as cargo his vessel and dispatch him on the date agreed in the original contract.

If these merchants will be unable to provide him with cargo, they shall be liable for the lading charges that had been agreed upon between them, unless they suggest some other compromise to him and he is agreeable; should he refuse such a proposal, no one can force him to proceed against his will. In addition, if the patron had expended any money or had suffered some damage by the action of the merchants who did not dispatch him or refused to dispatch him on the agreed date, the merchants shall be liable for all damages suffered by the patron, and the amount of such damages shall be ascertained by him in a sworn affidavit that will be accepted as valid proof.

This article is written for this reason: no one is able to overcome the obstacles placed in his path by God, the sea, winds, or authorities. Therefore, let all beware to proceed in a manner by which they could avoid causing harm to themselves.

261-Death of a Merchant Who Contracted for a Shipment of Cargo in a Foreign Country

If a merchant engaged a vessel while in a foreign country with the understanding that such a vessel would arrive at a specified time at a specific destination to pick up such cargo, and if the merchant should die in the location where he had engaged such a vessel, regardless of whether or not the merchant left a will, the patron of the vessel that had been engaged should before sailing out from the place where he had been engaged and where the merchant who had engaged him had died, and before the patron incurs any expense, proceed to the partner of the merchant whether he lives in that vicinity or nearby and demand in writing or through a special messenger whether the partner wishes that the vessel engaged prior to the death of the other partner shall proceed on the agreed journey.

If the partner should approve of the agreement, the vessel shall sail, because the second partner had agreed to honor the original contract, which the deceased had concluded and obligated himself to before his demise.

If the patron should have proceeded to the place agreed with the deceased to pick up cargo without first receiving the approval of the partner of the deceased merchant, the latter shall not be obligated by the contract signed by his deceased partner, for a deceased person has no partners, and on the day of his death a partnership is dissolved. However, if the deceased merchant had obligated his partners in any agreement with the patron relating to shipment of cargo, and such an agreement had been executed in writing, such partner or partners must fulfill the terms of the contract.

The above should be interpreted in the following way: that the deceased merchant had been authorized by his partner to conclude shipping contracts in his name also, that is to say, that the latter gave him the power of attorney in writing or in the presence of witnesses, that he shall be obligated by everything his partner would do. If the patron would be able to substantiate such an arrangement either in writing or by creditable witnesses, the remaining partner shall be obligated in the same degree as the deceased partner who had engaged the vessel if he would still be alive.

Should the patron be unable to prove this either by written documentary evidence or witnesses, the remaining partner shall not be bound by any agreements concluded by the deceased, even if the patron could prove that the deceased had mentioned his name in the agreement made when the shipment of cargo was contracted, because the deceased had acted without authority from his partner. It would certainly be an injustice that any person could obligate another without his knowledge and agreement, and it would be evil if such a statement of obligation should be binding, because if this were allowed, one person could ruin another. It would be unjust and in defiance of all customs that anyone could legally obligate another, as has been stated above.

If it should happen that the deceased merchant who had contracted for a shipment of cargo should leave a testament by which he would leave his wealth to his sons, relatives, or some other persons as he had pleased, and had named one of these his beneficiary, the patron of a vessel, aware of the fact that the merchant who had concluded an agreement with him is ill and has made his last will, should, in the presence of witnesses, if he is able, ask the merchant before he dies what should be done with the agreement they had concluded. If it pleases God the merchant will be called to Him, and persuade the merchant to decide on a course that would not be a source of trouble, should God please to take him unto Himself.

If the ailing merchant would inform the patron to proceed quickly on the agreed journey and assured him that with the help of the Almighty he shall protect the patron from any losses, and that his illness will not prevent him from carrying out all of the promises made, and the patron departs from the ailing merchant with such assurances and a document, that is, a written statement sealed and directed to the living partner, if he had one, or to a person who in his place will accept the cargo at the designated location where the vessel will deliver it, and after this had been accomplished, news is received that the merchant had died, and the person who had been authorized by the merchant to provide another shipment of cargo for the vessel declines to do this, any damages and expenses suffered by the patron shall be paid out of the estate of the deceased merchant. This procedure must be followed because the patron had made an agreement with the merchant before the latter died and before the patron had undertaken the original journey, therefore he acted with the approval and consent of the merchant and had received a letter from him, in which the merchant had called upon his partner or some other person authorized by him to expedite the shipment of cargo in conformity with the promise he had made to the patron.

If it should happen that the patron of a vessel engaged by a merchant had not sailed before the merchant died from the locality where the agreement had been concluded, he shall not begin the voyage until

170

he has notified the partner of the merchant or the party whom the merchant authorized to act in his name by letter or a messenger, asking him to come to the location where the vessel is berthed and make arrangements to dispatch it, as had been agreed. Only after one of these persons mentioned had fulfilled the terms of the agreement made by the deceased by notifying the patron through a special messenger or a written letter sealed with their official seal that the vessel should attempt the voyage and that these persons or one of them are ready and willing to fulfill all the terms of the agreement entered into by the deceased in writing relating to the shipment of the cargo, the patron shall depart with his vessel to fulfill his obligation.

If the patron should suffer any damage or losses due to the fault of the parties who notified him by letter or messenger, the guilty parties shall be liable for the damage and shall also provide him with the cargo, because he journeyed only upon their demand and approval.

If a patron had arrived at the place where he was to pick up the cargo or left the locality where the vessel was engaged to carry cargo after the death of the aforementioned merchant, and the latter had left a will in which he named his beneficiary, the patron, as had been stated, will arrive at the locality where he was to pick up the cargo on the date designated in the written agreement concerning the shipment of cargo; and if in addition the deceased merchant had made a change and had ordered his beneficiary to release the cargo that he had himself promised to provide for the vessel, the beneficiary named by the merchant shall fulfill his wishes. Should he refuse to do this, he shall be forced to do this by the local courts. It is absolutely necessary that the will of the deceased be carried out.

Further, if the deceased had not made such a change and did not specify this in his last will, the party whom he named as his beneficiary will not be obligated if he does not wish to carry out the terms of the agreement. The above resolution should be understood in the following way: that the beneficiary will not attempt to ship the cargo elsewhere but will sell it where it is located, in order to carry out the wishes of the deceased as expressed in his last will, and also because the patron had arrived with his vessel without the knowledge and approval of the party who had been constituted the beneficiary.

Further, if the party who had been designated the beneficiary would not wish to sell the cargo where it was located, but rather to ship it to the location where the deceased had intended it shipped before he died and for which he had made the necessary arrangements, if, in addition, the beneficiary refused to load the cargo aboard the vessel that had been contracted for by the deceased who had summoned the vessel, and instead loaded the cargo aboard another vessel, the estate of the deceased shall be held accountable for the obligations he had assumed during his life with the patron of the vessel that he had engaged to ship this cargo, if the patron on his part had fulfilled all the provisions that he had promised to fulfill at the time he agreed to carry this cargo.

However, if the patron of this vessel failed to carry out his promises, neither the estate of the deceased nor his beneficiary shall be obligated in any manner to the patron, unless the patron shall be able to show and prove that his inability to carry out the terms of the agreement was not due to any negligence on his part and that these obstacles prevented him from the fulfillment of his responsibilities. If the patron should be unable to show and prove this, the estate of the deceased merchant as well as his beneficiary shall be freed from any obligation toward the patron, because it was the patron who failed to fulfill his obligations toward the merchant. If, however, the patron shall demonstrate and prove that this did not happen due to any fault of his, the estate of the deceased as well as his beneficiary shall be held liable.

262-When Illness Prevents a Merchant from Fulfilling His Agreement to Ship Cargo

If a merchant who engaged a vessel and promised to dispatch it cargoed on a specified day had become ill and notified the master of the vessel that due to his illness he will not be able to fulfill his promise and advised the master to seek another cargo wherever he can, and further informed him that had not illness interfered, he would have gladly fulfilled his contractural obligations, and the patron of the vessel shall demand a reimbursement for the expenses he had incurred, the merchant shall not be required to reimburse him for these expenses, because the inability to carry out the terms of the agreement had not occurred by neglect on his part, and also because he had notified the patron about this matter before the date they had agreed on for dispatching of the vessel, and finally, because it was his full intention to carry out this agreement if on his part the patron would be willing to wait for the cargo until he would recover from his illness; there is still another reason why the merchant is no longer obligated to carry out the terms of the agreement, namely, that no one can interfere with the will of God.

Further, if the former merchant had become ill after making arrangements to ship cargo and failed to notify the patron within the time limit that the latter was to wait for the cargo, but after the expiration of that time informed the patron that he should look for work wherever he can find it, and the patron of the vessel had incurred some expense because he was not notified within the period of time agreed between them, the merchant shall reimburse him for the full amount he expended because he had waited without being notified. If the patron suffered other damage or loss, the merchant will not be required to reimburse him because he did not fail to embark on the journey by his own will or with the intention of causing harm to others, but fate visited illness upon him.

Further, if the merchant had been ill at the moment he had contracted to ship cargo and on this basis he wanted to withdraw from this obligation, notifying the patron within the agreed period of time during which the patron was to wait for his cargo, he will be allowed to do this only in a situation where his illness had become more severe and when he is doing this in good faith; otherwise he shall be compelled to reimburse the master of the vessel for all the damages and expenses that the latter had suffered at the hands of the merchant, the amount of which shall be made in a deposition under oath by the patron of the vessel, and accepted as binding. It is the merchant's fault that while ill he was engaging a vessel to ship cargo and obligated himself in this manner by concluding an agreement with the patron.

In addition, if the merchant did not notify the patron within the period of time the patron was to wait for the cargo, but only after the time agreed upon had elapsed he had informed him that he will not undertake the voyage, the merchant shall be held liable and will be required to repay the patron of the vessel all the costs, losses, and expenses incurred by the patron.

Further, the amount to be awarded in damages to the aggrieved party shall be given to arbitration by two Elders of the Sea Guild, who will arbitrate the matter justly, taking into consideration the worsening illness of the merchant as well as other circumstances. If the merchant had not suffered a relapse and his illness was no worse than at the time he made the agreement, the issue should not be given to adjudication by anyone, and the patron should be reimbursed by the merchant for all the damage he had suffered, and this should be done without any opposition, because he had suffered such damage by action of the merchant.

The patron of a vessel is obligated in same manner toward the merchants with whom he makes agreements for the shipment of cargo, as had been discussed in the previous article.

263-If a Merchant Should Die After Engaging a Vessel but Before He Had His Cargo Loaded Aboard the Vessel

If a merchant who had engaged a vessel to carry his cargo should die before all or part of his cargo is loaded aboard the vessel, both the merchant and his estate shall be free from any liability toward the patron of the vessel engaged, because a deceased person cannot be obligated by any contract that he concluded while alive, with the exception of a loan or some action that would cause damage to another person. In such cases these obligations shall be met from the proceeds of his estate, if he left any property, regardless where such property may be located.

Further, if the merchant died after cargoing the vessel partly or fully within the period of time agreed upon, he shall not be held liable for any damages or losses suffered by the patron of the vessel, because it should be anticipated that had he remained alive, he would have most likely wished to fulfill all the provisions of the agreement he made with the patron. It is not his fault that death prevented him from carrying out such obligations, for no one can be held responsible for the consequences of death.

However, if the latter merchant had cargoed the vessel completely after the date agreed upon and then died, any damage suffered by the patron of the vessel shall be paid out of the estate of the deceased, because the merchant had failed to cargo and dispatch the vessel within the time agreed and thus had failed to provide the patron with an opportunity to look for other cargo, while he was unable and did not intend to carry out his promise to the patron.

Further, if the merchant had loaded the vessel with his cargo, and the vessel had set sail, and subsequently the merchant died, the patron shall, depending on where the death of the merchant occurred, return to the place where he picked up the cargo and return the cargo to the relatives of the deceased, if there are relatives resident in that locality. If, however, there are no relatives there or other persons from whom the deceased merchant accepted the cargo in his care, the patron shall unload the cargo that had belonged to the dead merchant and store it in a safe place on land. After the cargo had been stored ashore, the patron of the vessel shall dispatch a letter or a message by a trusted messenger to the locality where, as far as he knows or can tell, the persons from whom the patron had received the cargo or his relatives reside. All the expenses that the patron had incurred in unloading the cargo shall be assessed against the cargo.

In addition, if some relative of the merchant or one of the parties who had entrusted him with the cargo should reach the locality where the patron of the vessel had unloaded the cargo, the former shall pay all the expenses of the patron in connection with the necessity of making the return voyage.

If the patron was unable to reach an agreement with the relatives of the merchant or the parties who had entrusted their cargo to the deceased merchant, any dispute arising due to such a misunderstanding shall be submitted to the examination and arbitration of two reliable Elders well versed in the matters of marine commerce, and whatever these two declare shall be accepted as valid and carried out.

If the patron had been paid part of the lading charges for carrying such cargo, the wages of the crew shall be paid proportionally to the amount he had received.

Further, if the relatives of the deceased merchant or the persons who entrusted their cargo to his care should be living at the place from which the patron had undertaken the journey and to which he had returned to unload the cargo and should decide that the vessel that had been cargoed by the merchant while he was still alive should complete the journey as had been agreed by him, the patron of the vessel is required to complete such a voyage provided that the above mentioned persons reimburse him for all the expenses and losses due to the fact that he had to return with this cargo due to the death of the merchant, or they may reach a new agreement with the patron. In addition, they shall give the patron a written promissory note that each of them and all of them shall fulfill all the terms of the agreement made by the deceased merchant while he had been alive. The patron shall be required to proceed on the journey previously mentioned only after all these conditions had been met by all or even one of the parties mentioned above.

Further, if the patron cargoed his vessel in the territory of the Saracens or other dangerous location and was to proceed to a friendly territory to unload such cargo, he cannot be forced to return to the territory where he had loaded the cargo aboard his vessel. He shall rather be required to sail only to the port of destination agreed upon with the merchant while the latter was still alive. However, before he unloads such a cargo, he shall notify the local judicial authority about this matter, and in the presence of merchants and a representative of the local court he should store the cargo in a safe place in the name of the parties having an interest in the cargo.

The judicial authorities, after taking counsel with the local merchants, shall order that a portion of the cargo be sold in order to pay the patron of the vessel all the lading charges due him as well as all other expenses connected with this cargo; the above procedure shall be followed only if in that locality none of the relatives of the deceased merchant or any of the parties who entrusted their cargo to his care reside.

If none of these persons reside at the port where the patron had brought the cargo, the local authorities and the patron should dispatch a letter concerning this matter to the place where they believe his relatives or cargo owners reside; and the local authorities with the approval of the Elders of the locality where the cargo had been unloaded shall safeguard such cargo until the relatives or the parties, whose cargo they are holding that had been entrusted to the deceased merchant, shall arrive to claim the cargo or send their representative to claim it.

Further, if the cargo was of the variety that it was feared that it might spoil, it should be sold, and the amount received shall be deposited in an institution where it will be readily available to its rightful owners if they come to claim it and shall be able to prove that they have a rightful claim to it.

This article was written for the reasons mentioned above.

264-Death of a Patron of a Vessel That Had Been Engaged but Had Not Been Cargoed

If a master of a vessel died before it had been partly or fully cargoed by the merchant who had engaged the vessel in order to ship his cargo, such a vessel will not be required to proceed on the agreed journey, unless the relatives of the deceased master or the shareholders in the vessel express a desire that this be done, or if the majority or all of the shareholders were present at the time the agreement was made and all of them or even a single one had obligated himself to the merchant who had engaged the vessel that the cargo will be shipped, this must be done, because a deceased person is not and cannot be considered a patron of a vessel anywhere in this wide world, with the provision that all the damages and injustices the deceased had been guilty of shall be remedied, if such a patron left a sufficient estate to make this possible.

Further, if such a vessel had been partly or fully cargoed before the death of its master, it shall proceed and complete the voyage contracted for by the merchant who engaged the vessel for this purpose. This is due to the fact that neither the shareholders in the vessel nor the relatives of the patron had made any objections when the vessel was being cargoed; for this reason the vessel shall complete the voyage contracted. In addition, the shareholders are required, after taking counsel with the relatives of the deceased patron, to appoint a person who shall take command of the vessel and replace the patron, and who shall take upon himself all the obligations that the original patron had assumed, and shall in the presence of the merchant make these commitments that he will carry out all the agreements that the deceased would have carried out had he remained alive, and this must be done because neither the relatives nor the shareholders had made any objection to the vessel being cargoed although they knew that the patron was ill and actually was fatally ill.

Further, had the shareholders or the relatives of the patron who had been in command of the vessel while he was alive informed the merchant that they were opposed to the cargoing of the vessel because they feared that the patron will die, and in case of his death the vessel will not undertake the journey, but in spite of the warning that, "If the patron dies, the vessel shall not be able to undertake the voyage," neither the shareholders, nor relatives, nor the beneficiaries of the deceased patron shall be liable for any damages to the merchant who had engaged and cargoed the vessel, regardless of the amount of damages, simply because he had refused to stop the cargoing of the vessel in spite of the warnings and protests that had been made and given to him.

Further, if a vessel after being cargoed unfurled its sails and departed from the place where it had been cargoed and then the patron should die, regardless of the fact if he was or was not in good health prior to the departure of the vessel, his death shall not prevent the completion of the voyage. If aboard this vessel one of the shareholders or relatives was present, he should be designated the new patron of the vessel, provided that the navigator, clerk, the merchants aboard, and the whole crew will agree that he is a fit person to assume the command of the vessel. Should they decide that he is incapable of such a task, and there is aboard the vessel either an officer of the prow or an officer of the stern, adjudged to have proper qualifications for this position, one of them shall be constituted the patron of the vessel. This should be understood in the following manner: that the newly appointed patron shall only exercise this position until the journey is completed, as had been agreed with the merchants by the deceased patron.

Immediately after the completion of this journey, the vessel shall be surrendered to the shareholders and relatives of the deceased patron, and the clerk of the vessel shall make an accounting of all the profits and losses, if there were any losses, to the relatives and shareholders of the vessel, as would have been done by the patron of the vessel had he been alive at the time the vessel left the port where it was cargoed and where the relatives and shareholders resided.

Further, if the vessel had picked up cargo in a location where none of the relatives or shareholders of the patron resided, they shall return, after making the voyage, to the place where the voyage had originated, provided this was not a dangerous territory. If the port of origin should be located in a dangerous domain, they shall proceed to another, a safer location, after which the clerk together with the navigator shall write a letter and send it by a trusted messenger to the place where according to the information they have on hand the relatives and the shareholders of the deceased patron reside, in order that these parties could come and take possession of the vessel whose patron had died.

The clerk and the navigator are not permitted to leave or abandon this vessel until the relatives and the shareholders of the deceased arrive to claim it, and until they had been reimbursed for all their expenses and paid for all their care and trouble to maintain the vessel.

This article was written for the reasons listed above.

265-Engaging a Vessel Without Agreeing to the Date on Which It Will Be Cargoed

If a merchant or several merchants engage a vessel, and had made an agreement in writing or in the presence of witnesses, but had not specified the date the vessel would be cargoed and dispatched on its way, and then keep on delaying the day of sailing that the patron of the vessel had taken for granted would have been soon, the merchants shall not be liable for the damages claimed by the patron unless he can prove that this delay had been caused by their negligence. Therefore, every patron should be most careful, when making agreements to take on cargo, that he suffer no damage.

Further, if these merchants, having engaged the vessel as had been stated above, did not cargo and dispatch it in the shortest possible time, and the vessel had to wait because of their indifference, and the patron of the vessel shall be able to show and prove that due to their neglect he had suffered some damage, the merchants shall be liable for such damage because it occurred due to their negligence.

On the other hand, regardless of whether the vessel engaged in this manner was to pick up the cargo at the place where the agreement had been made or if it had to sail to pick up such cargo at another location, merchants who can prove that their inability to deliver such cargo as had been agreed, either at the place where the agreement was concluded or any other place, was not by their fault or negligence shall not be held liable to the patron even in a smallest degree for their inability to provide him such cargo, because the situation developed without any fault of theirs.

However, if these merchants had been able to obtain lower lading charges for the shipment of their cargo than they had agreed on with the patron of the first vessel, and advantageously engaged instead another vessel to carry their cargo, leaving the first vessel engaged without a cargo, they shall be required to pay for all the damages and expenses suffered by the patron of the vessel that they had originally engaged, and shall also be required to furnish him the cargo they had agreed upon. Should they refuse to do so, they shall be required to pay the patron of the first vessel they engaged the full amount of the lading fees they had agreed to pay him, because otherwise he would lose, by their fault and the fact that they found another vessel that would carry their cargo at a cheaper rate, all the income he was expected to make, for his damage would not have occurred otherwise. It is, therefore, justifiable that the party acting or attempting to act in a manner that would subject another to a damage, which he does not deserve, should bear the consequences of such an action himself.

For the reasons explained above, a patron who would, after an agreement with one group of merchants to carry their cargo, enter into an agreement with another group of merchants to do likewise, because the latter offered him a higher price than the merchants with whom he had concluded the original agreement, shall be required to repay them for the damages, costs, and losses incurred by his fault, because they had suffered as result of his neglect. In addition, he shall be required to carry the cargo he had originally contracted for, even if it became necessary to sell the vessel in order to accomplish this, for it is only proper that patrons of vessels shall be obligated toward the merchants who engage their vessels in the same degree as the merchants are obligated toward the patrons of vessels they engaged.

This article is written for the reasons given above.

266-When a Vessel Is Prevented from Sailing by the Local Authorities

If a merchant or several merchants had engaged a vessel in a given locality, and regardless of the fact that this vessel is to take cargo aboard in the locality where the agreement was made or is to proceed to another locality to pick up the cargo, if during the time it is anchored at the spot where the agreement was signed, the local civil authorities impose some restrictions against it leaving such a locality (let us assume for the moment that the vessel was to take on cargo at the place where the agreement was concluded), and the patron of such a vessel approaches the merchants who had engaged the vessel to annul the contract that had been concluded in writing, that they free him from the responsibility of fulfilling the obligation to carry their cargo, in order that he might be able to sail to another locality to look for cargo that other merchants may want him to carry, and if the merchants who had engaged his vessel refuse to annul the contract and free him from the responsibility of the obligation that he had taken upon himself to carry their cargo, but rather inform him that he should not trouble about this matter, that they will take care of this legal restriction, and that they are positive they will be able to furnish him the cargo agreed upon, and if they are able to settle everything and furnish the promised cargo, they shall nevertheless be obligated to reimburse the patron for all the expenses he incurred from the date he had requested that they annul the contract and free him from his obligations. They are not, however, compelled to do this because of any negligence on their part, but rather because of obstructions invoked by the authorities, for they had provided him with the cargo as had been promised.

Further, if on the other hand, the merchants could not furnish him the cargo promised or any other cargo, they shall be required to reimburse him for all his expenses and pay all the damages and costs. The above should be understood in the following manner: that the amount to be paid the patron for his damages and expenses shall be arbitrated by two Elders well versed in the art of sailing, because the merchants wanted to provide the patron with the cargo as they had agreed, but could not do this due to no fault of their own. Regardless of the type of an agreement the patron had concluded with the merchants, the crew shall abide by it.

Further, if the vessel was to proceed to pick up the cargo at another location, and before the vessel could sail from the place where the agreement was concluded, some restrictions were imposed against the vessel, if the merchants informed the patron of the vessel that they engaged that fear of these restrictions should not prevent him from proceeding to pick up their cargo, because they are convinced and have no doubt or fear that these imposed restrictions will either affect or delay their cargo or them personally, and if the patron assured by these statements made by the merchants should set sail for the locality where according to the agreement with the merchants he was to pick up the cargo, and the merchants shall not be able to supply him with the cargo promised, they shall be required to reimburse the patron for all the damages and expenses he suffered due to their negligence and the restrictions imposed by the authorities, as well as pay him the full lading fees he would have been paid had he carried their cargo, because it was their fault that he did not carry their cargo.

This matter cannot be submitted to arbitration by the Elders without the consent of the patron of the vessel, for this reason: because in conformity with what has been stated in one of the previous articles, any vessel that had already unfurled its sails, even if it was detained from sailing, shall be paid the full lading charges without an imposition.[78] If the patron agreed to make some concessions in this matter,

78. Reference is made to Article 84.

the crew shall abide by them.

Further, if during the time that the merchants were in the process of engaging a vessel, there were in force certain restrictions, and the patron of the vessel informed and instructed the merchants that they should not enter into any agreements in relation to the engagement of his vessel, if these merchants tell him that he should enter into an agreement with them, that he should not refrain from such action because of any restrictions that may exist, and that they shall protect him from any damages, if the patron relying on these assertions concludes such an agreement, the merchants under such circumstances shall reimburse him for all the damage, expenses, and losses that occurred as result of their neglect.

A patron of a vessel is obligated to the merchants in similar manner and degree, and even under other circumstances.

This article has been written for the reasons mentioned above.

267- A Sailor Should Not Leave the Vessel Immediately upon His Discharge from Service

If a patron of a vessel discharged a sailor for any reason whatsoever, he should not leave the vessel merely because the patron discharged him but wait until such a time as his rations of bread and other provisions are cut off.

If the sailor left the vessel merely on an oral statement made by the patron and before his rations were cut off, the patron shall be freed from all his obligations toward the sailor, regardless of the kind of claims the sailor may make.

Further, if a patron discharged a sailor, and by this we mean that he cut off or ordered that his rations be cut off before the voyage was completed and without well-founded reasons, he shall pay such sailor his full wages in the amount promised him at the time of the enlistment. If the sailor had enlisted with the stipulation that his wages would be determined at a later date, the patron of the vessel shall pay him the amount that shall be determined by the clerk and the navigator of the vessel under oath, and the amount shall be identical with the amount he would have received had he remained in service of the vessel for the duration of the voyage.

In addition, if the patron discharged a sailor in a foreign country and the latter did not wish to remain there, the patron shall be required to make arrangements for the sailor to return to the place where he had been hired, aboard some other vessel, unless he makes a different agreement with the sailor, providing that such a sailor is willing to make such an agreement.

Further, if a patron discharged a sailor in the manner stated above or for reasons that had been explained and discussed in one of the previous articles, he shall not be obliged to pay him his wages nor to provide for his passage and maintenance aboard another vessel in order that he could return to the locality from which he had originally sailed. [79]

For the reasons mentioned above, every patron should be careful when he is discharging a sailor, to do this only upon well-founded principles, otherwise this may turn to his disadvantage; the sailors should also be careful when they accept dismissal from service, how they go about this matter, in order to avoid charges being brought against them and to avoid suffering any losses.

For these reasons this article has been written.

268-Desertion[80]

If a sailor deserts his vessel wherever the vessel may be after receiving his wages and before the term of service he enlisted for is completed, that is, before the vessel shall have completed the voyage for which he had enlisted, even if he had completed part of his enlistment, he shall be required to repay the patron the amount he had received in wages without any opposition; he shall not be paid anything for the period he had served aboard the vessel, because, as had been stated above, he had deserted. Otherwise, wherever he shall be apprehended he shall be jailed and shall remain in jail until he has repaid the patron the amount he had received in wages and shall reimburse the patron for all the damages and losses borne by the patron, and the patron's deposition in this matter shall be given full credence without the need on his part of presentation of witnesses to this affair.

This article was written for the reasons listed above.

269-Cargoing a Vessel with Unmeasured Load of Grain

If the merchants had engaged a vessel and are cargoing it with a load of grain, and neither the patron nor his representative have been able to ascertain the exact amount being loaded aboard, but had accepted the measurement given by the merchants or some other person acting in their stead, if later the patron would wish to remeasure the amount of the grain or order some other person to do this before the cargo is unloaded at its place of destination, he shall be able to do this, and none of the merchants can oppose this or take any steps to prevent

---

79. Reference is made to Article 125.

80. Reference is made to Articles 157 and 158.

this being done or make any accusations against the patron.

If the patron had remeasured or ordered that the grain be remeasured and was able to ascertain that there was more grain aboard than the amount that had been given to him by the merchants or their representative, he shall be paid the full amount of the lading fees for the amount of grain given by the merchants or their representative as well as for the amount he found above the figure given him, regardless of whether the additional amount of the grain aboard the vessel was due to a mistake in measurement or had been given in an attempt to cheat the patron of the actual amount in the lading fees that were due to him, or even if the increase in the amount of the cargo was due to the swelling of the grain. [81]

In assessing the additional amount of lading charges, the patron should apportion it proportionally among the merchants, depending on the amount of grain each merchant had loaded aboard the vessel, each paying the portion due from him. Each merchant shall be required to pay the patron the lading charges not only on the amount of grain he had specified but also on the additional amount found aboard the vessel, because it is only proper that if the merchants make additional profit, the patron should not incur a loss. In addition, there is still another reason, namely, that the patron or anyone appointed as his representative had not accepted the quantity of grain as cargo according to the figures furnished by the merchants.

If the patron or his representative had measured the grain, or had accepted the figure submitted by the merchants as to the quantity of their cargo, and after arrival at the place of destination, the amount of the shipment would be in excess of the amount given by the merchants, the latter shall not be required to pay the cargo charges on the additional amount of grain found aboard the vessel because the patron had not been willing to accept the figures submitted by the merchants.

If God in His charity aids the merchants in increasing their cargo, they shall benefit by this in the same manner that the patron would have benefited had he trusted the merchants. It is therefore proper that the increase, which God made possible, should accrue to them, because the patron of the vessel refused to believe what they told him.

Further, if the patron had ordered that the grain aboard be remeasured or if he had accepted the cargo without having it measured, and later the merchants prove that there are shortages in their cargo,

81. Due to the inability to control moisture-laden air aboard such vessels, this appears to have happened frequently.

the patron shall be responsible to pay for such shortages. This proposition should be understood as follows: that the type of grain being shipped is taken into consideration, for there are grains in existence that never have the same measurement at the time of unloading as they had at the time they were loaded aboard the vessel.

Further, if the patron or his representative was present at the time the grain was measured, but neither he nor anyone he would designate ordered that the grain be remeasured, and did not accept the figures on the amount of the grain from the merchants, but just believed what the merchants had told him concerning the amount they were shipping, he shall be paid additional lading fees for any amount of the grain in excess of the amount declared by the merchants. In addition, if it could be proved that there were shortages after unloading the grain, the patron shall not be held accountable, because neither he himself nor anyone acting in his stead had measured or ordered the grain measured, and did not officially accept the amount declared by the merchants.

This article was written for the reasons given above.

270-Payment of Lading Charges

If a master of a vessel had reached an agreement with a merchant or several merchants to carry their cargo, had arrived at the location where he was to discharge this cargo, but there had been no date or period of time set as to when this was to take place and the merchants were to pay the lading fees, the patron may refuse to unload any of the cargo and retain it all aboard the vessel until the merchants guarantee him that the amount of lading fees set in the agreement shall be paid him on a specified date.

Further, if the patron made an agreement with the merchants that he would discharge the cargo and that they would pay him the shipping charges due on a certain day or within a certain period of time, he cannot and should not attempt to prevent the unloading of the cargo, unless he fears that the above mentioned merchants are deceitful brigands and will do everything to bring about the loss of his lading fees. If the merchants would give the patron sufficient security that will guarantee his lading fees, the patron should allow them to unload their cargo.

If it should happen that these merchants approach the patron and offer him part of the cargo in lieu of the lading charges, at the price they would be able to sell such cargo or at the value it has at the place where it is to be unloaded, and that they shall unload their cargo leaving enough of it to pay for his shipping charges, the patron may, if he wishes, accept such an offer; however, he cannot be forced by the merchants to accept such a proposition if he is unwilling to do so.

If the patron shall agree to such a proposal freely, and he is allowed to do this, and he shall profit by such an arrangement, all the profit shall belong to him. Should he, however, lose money by such an arrangement, he shall bear the loss alone, as none of the shareholders in such a situation shall be liable for any agreement of this kind. The patron shall be required to pay each of the shareholders his proportionate share from the total amount he had received for carrying such cargo.

Further, if the merchants left all their cargo to the patron in lieu of the lading charges due him, he shall be forced to accept this and cannot make any other demands upon them. If the patron, as had been stated above, was forced to accept the above cargo, none of the shareholders shall reproach him and each of them will be forced to share in any losses as well as in profits, if God enables them to make a profit.

In addition, if the shareholders had agreed with the patron that regardless of where he sails or from whence he returns, he shall be authorized to invest their money that he had received for the lading fees, and if this agreement had been made by the majority or all of the shareholders, and the money invested by the patron shows profit or results in a loss, each of the shareholders shall share in the losses in the same manner as he would have shared in the profits, if God had allowed profit to be made. In such circumstances the shareholders shall not reproach the patron, because he has acted in conformity with the instruction of all or most of them.

In addition, if the patron invested the money he had left over from the lading charges several times without the permission and authorization of these merchants, they shall share in any profit he had made in these investments, but if they had instructed and ordered him not to invest the money he had left over from the lading fees, they will be glad to share in any profit, which God allowed them, but if there should be any losses, the patron alone shall bear them. If the shareholders had instructed and ordered what had been stated above, and in spite of this the patron had invested the money he had left over from the lading fees, he shall pay the shareholders the proportionate amount due each of them out of the profit God had allowed him to earn. Should he suffer losses, he shall assume them alone.

If it should happen that the patron while making several voyages had invested the money he had received in lading fees, and the shareholders had taken their share from the profit God had allowed him to earn, but had given the patron no instructions or orders regarding such investments, which had been discussed above, they shall share in the losses as they had shared in the profits when God made that possible, until such time when they had given proper instructions to the patron regarding these matters.

This article was written for the reasons given above.

271-Cargoing a Vessel during a Storm

If a patron had been contracted to cargo a vessel in a specified location, and his vessel is ready to take on the cargo, and the weather changes so quickly that a storm can be expected momentarily, and due to this the patron would incur some expense, such as rental of additional lines to moor the vessel more securely, the merchants who had leased the vessel shall not be liable for such an expense, because they had not actually loaded any cargo aboard, unless the patron had reached an agreement with them at the time they were arranging for the shipment of their cargo that they shall share in all the expenses incurred by the vessel due to some unfortunate incident.

If it should happen that the patron partially cargoed the vessel with the goods that the vessel was to pick up, part of the cargo together with the owners of the vessel shall proportionally pay for the expenses suffered by the vessel due to some misfortune, unless there had been an agreement concluded with the majority or all of the merchants that in case of such a misfortune the cargo remaining on shore shall share with the cargo aboard the vessel in an assessment to pay for such expenditures. If the vessel was completely cargoed and then the misfortune occurred, such expenses shall be covered proportionally by all the cargo aboard as well as the vessel.

The above provisions shall be understood in this manner: that the vessel was properly and sufficiently equipped and that the equipment aboard was of good quality and in proper quantity. If the equipment aboard the vessel was insufficient even for a smaller vessel, and the misfortune mentioned above overtook the vessel, the merchants and their cargo cannot be held liable for the expenses that the patron of the vessel shall bear because of such a misfortune; in fact the patron of the vessel shall be required to pay the merchants damages for all their losses that happened due to the lack of proper equipment aboard the vessel.

Nevertheless, it should be remembered that no credence shall be given to the claims made by the merchants merely on their depositions. The matter shall be entrusted to two Elders of the Sea Guild who will determine whether the equipment aboard was sufficient for the vessel of that size, and whatever they decide shall be carried out, for the simple reason that at times, and often most frequently, when an unfortunate misfortune overcomes a vessel, after the claims of the merchants were accepted, it was discovered that they always claimed

186

that they sustained damage due to insufficient equipment aboard it; therefore, if such claims were not properly examined and arbitrated by the Elders, the patrons of vessels would always suffer damages.

This article was written for the reasons given above.

272-Concerning Carpenters and Shipwrights

In one of the earlier articles it was explained and shown what are the responsibilities of carpenters and shipwrights toward the patron who had entrusted them with the performance of a certain task or work for which they were hired, as well as of the responsibility of the patron toward these master mechanics. It was not, however, made clear the degree of obligation of these craftsmen, if after reaching an agreement to perform this work, they should refuse to carry out the provisions of such an agreement. [82]

For these reasons, our ancestors who first circumnavigated the earth enacted these amendments in order to prevent the possibility of disputes that could arise between the masters of vessels and these craftsmen. They, therefore, decreed that every carpenter or shipwright who had contracted for work with a master of a vessel is required to complete such work, whether he had agreed on the price or not, because he had assumed the responsibility.

If any such tradesman refuses to fulfill this responsibility, he shall be required to pay for all the losses and damages suffered by the patron for whom he had promised to perform such work, provided that the patron can prove such damages. There is only one exception to this rule, namely, if the latter tradesmen were unable to fulfill their obligations due to some obstacles placed in their path by God or the local authorities.

For the same reason, a patron who had promised employment to one or several of such tradesmen and failed to live up to his promise shall pay them the wages that had been agreed upon between them. If it should happen that they did not agree on any specific amount of remuneration, the patron who hired them shall pay them the same amount paid other tradesmen for the same type of work, taking into account their skill and efficiency.

In view of this, a master of a vessel who had broken the contract with these tradesmen shall be required to pay all the losses and damages they incurred or that they will bear and that they can show and prove, taking into consideration, however, the size of the job that the

---

82. Reference is made to two, not one, articles, specifically, Articles 53 and 54.

patron intended to give them. There is only one exception to this rule, namely, if the patron was prevented from carrying out the agreement by the will of God or the local authorities.

This article was written for the reasons given above.

273-Rights and Obligations of Servants

If a patron hired a servant for a specified period of time, the servant shall fulfill all his obligations that he had promised the patron to fulfill. It is only proper that similarly as the servant shall be required to fulfill all his obligations toward the patron, the latter must also fulfill all his obligations toward his servant. [83]

If such a servant should die before the expiration of his term of service, the patron shall be required to pay the relatives of the deceased his entire wages for the full period of his service, without any opposition.

If it should happen that the patron of the vessel shall die, his former servant shall continue in the service of his relatives and beneficiaries for the whole period that he was obliged to serve the patron on the day the agreement was made, and he must do this without any opposition. The patron's relatives and beneficiaries are obligated to fulfill all the terms of the agreement entered into by the patron while he was still alive and that he had promised the servant he would carry out.

Further, the following shall be understood in this manner: that this servant shall be required to serve the relatives and beneficiaries of the patron only if the vessel will continue to be under the control and disposition of the relatives and beneficiaries of the deceased patron. If these relatives and beneficiaries of the patron sell the vessel before the expiration of the time for which the servant had agreed to serve for the deceased, the servant shall be free from the moment of the sale of the vessel, while the aforementioned relatives and beneficiaries shall be required to pay him for the time he served them as well as the time he served the deceased, and this shall be done without any dispute.

If it should happen that these relatives and beneficiaries were without means to pay the servant, he shall be paid from the proceeds of the sale of the vessel. If, however, these relatives and beneficiaries refused to pay from the amount they had received from the sale of the vessel, the servant can and shall pursue his claim upon the vessel legally, because it is proper that if a person devoted his time to

---

83. Reference is made here to Article 145.

some pursuit he should be paid from such pursuit. Let, therefore, the party who is buying such a vessel be most careful that when he is acquiring it he would not also become subject to any losses or damages. [84]

This article was written for the reasons listed above.

274-Loading Aboard a Cargo of Empty Casks and Barrels

If the master of a vessel is to sail for the Barbary Coast or for Spain or into any other waters, and if the merchants load a cargo of assembled casks or barrels in order to ship them to a designated destination without having reached an agreement with the patron as to the amount due him for carrying this cargo, the patron of the vessel shall be free to decide on the amount due him when he has reached the port of destination or he may keep half of the cargo in lieu of his lading fees, because no agreement had been made concerning this matter.

If, however, the patron had reached an agreement concerning the lading fees on such a cargo of barrels, he shall be bound to carry out the terms of the agreement.

Further, if this shipment did not consist of assembled barrels but rather of barrel staves and parts, the patron of the vessel shall not receive half of the cargo in lieu of the lading fees. If there had been no agreement concluded relating to the shipping charges he would have received, he can only demand payment of the customary lading fees. Why should he not be able to retain half of the unassembled barrels when he is able to take half of the cargo of assembled barrels in lieu of the lading fees due him? Because if he had accepted a cargo of assembled barrels, he would have been unable to take any additional cargo aboard his vessel at the location where the barrels were loaded aboard his vessel and thus would have lost an opportunity to earn additional money for his vessel, because a load of assembled barrels would have made it impossible for him to have room for any additional cargo. There is another reason for this, namely, if he had ordered the barrels disassembled, to assemble them again would have probably been more expensive than the amount he would have been able to earn from taking additional cargo aboard his vessel; therefore, it is proper that he receive half of the cargo of assembled barrels but not half of the unassembled barrels. There is still another reason for

---

84. The only protection a buyer had against claims and loans was to get a written deposition under oath from sellers that the vessel was not encumbered and that if any claims should appear they would honor them.

this: if he would happen to carry a cargo of unassembled barrels, he might have been able to pick up additional cargo in some places along his course; thus he would have stored the unassembled barrels on the bottom of his vessel and the other cargo on top of that. However, if the staves had been tied in bundles, he would have to bear the cost of retying them in bundles before delivering them.

For the reasons explained above, the patron should not have the right to retain half of the cargo if it consists of staves, as he does when he carries a cargo of assembled barrels.

275-Merchandise Can Be Accepted or Refused As Payment for Lading Charges

If a vessel was cargoed to proceed beyond the seas to Alexandria, Armenia, or some other distant shore, the merchants are required to pay the full lading fees as they had agreed to do with the master of the vessel. Should they refuse to do this, the patron may retain sufficient amount of the cargo in lieu of such fees, and even a bit more, and the clerk is also required to follow this course when acting as a representative of the patron, as had been discussed in one of the preceding articles. [85]

Further, if the merchants wish to pay him with their cargo for the amount due him in lading fees, he shall accept their proposal, but he cannot force the merchants to give him anything additional, unless there had been some special agreements and promises concluded between them concerning this matter.

Further, the above provisions shall be interpreted in the following manner: that if this cargo was to be carried for a set fee, and the cargo consists of various kinds of merchandise loaded aboard the vessel, such as some chests of silks, saffron, spices, and other valuable merchandise, and all the other cargo that they wish to leave to the patron in lieu of the lading fees, and does not have the value equal to the amount due him, the patron shall not be required to accept such a cargo if he refuses to do so, because there had been cargo aboard the vessel that had been of higher value.

Further, if the merchants should find themselves in a location where they will be unable to sell their cargo and will be forced to exchange their cargo for other merchandise, they shall be required to give the patron of the vessel, if he will agree to accept it, enough

---

85. Actually, reference is made here to three previous articles, Articles 60, 83, and 139.

cargo to pay for the lading charges due him. If the patron should refuse to accept any of their cargo in lieu of cash, if necessary, all their cargo shall be sold to pay him; for it is necessary that the patron receive his lading charges, provided this is done in conformity with the prevailing customs.

If the patron would wish to make a concession to the merchants and delay this payment till they return to the place from which their voyage originated or until they reach a location where their cargo can be sold, he may do so, and neither the crew nor anyone else can attempt to interfere in this matter, unless the patron had made some other promises to his crew.

If the patron should make such a concession to the merchants, they shall share with him all the profit made in selling their cargo, proportionally to what they owe him for the lading charges. Should the merchants fail to make profit in selling such a cargo, they shall nevertheless be obligated to pay the patron the full amount due him for his services, for it would be improper that a patron would suffer damages because he wanted to be helpful to the merchants, and also because the merchants had not failed to make profit cannot be attributed to any fault on his part.

The patron shall share the amount of the profit he had received from the merchants, proportionally to the amount of wages due, with the sailors, unless there were some special agreements made with the sailors and the merchants.

Further, if the merchants had arranged to ship cargo and the lading charges were based per hundred weight, and they had not stated that one type of cargo shall be assessed for another type of cargo in paying for the shipping charges, the patron shall not be able to keep any part of one cargo, because no such agreement had been made between them. Therefore, every patron should be most careful at the time he is negotiating an agreement to carry cargo, in order that he would not suffer any loss; he should also be careful from whom he accepts such cargo, to make sure that the crew shall be paid, even if he would not be paid for carrying such cargo, because the crew had earned its wages by working aboard the vessel during such a voyage.

This article was written for the reasons given above.

276-A Merchantman Intercepted by an Armed Vessel

There is no need to discuss a situation when an armed vessel sets out on a journey, is cruising around, or is returning to its home port and intercepts a merchantman, and the latter vessel and its cargo belong to enemy nationals, because all informed persons know what will happen under such circumstances, and what is to be done, and therefore it would be misleading to try to set some sort of a rule about this.

However, if an intercepted vessel belonged to friendly nationals and the cargo aboard it belonged to unfriendly nationals, the admiral in command of the armed vessel may force the patron of the merchantman to surrender all the enemy goods to him, or to keep these goods aboard the vessel until they reach safer waters. This provision should be interpreted in the following manner: that the admiral or a person designated by him shall attach a line to such merchantman, if the vessels are located in waters where there is no possibility that an enemy craft would be able to take such a vessel away from him. The admiral shall pay the patron the full lading fees he would have been paid for such confiscated cargo had it been delivered to its destination, as confirmed by the entry made in the ship's register. Should such a register not be located, the patron's deposition under oath as to the amount of lading fees due him shall be accepted as valid.

In addition, if it should happen that the admiral or the party designated by him to act in his stead are in waters where the booty can be easily stored nearby, and he should decide to do that, the patron of the vessel that has the enemy cargo aboard shall transport it to such place as ordered. However, an agreement should be concluded with the patron concerning this; and it shall be absolutely necessary that the admiral or the party designated to act in his stead fulfill the terms of such an agreement in every detail.

If they should have failed to conclude such an agreement concerning the lading fees, it shall be necessary that the admiral or the party designated to act in his stead shall pay the patron of the vessel, who will carry the confiscated cargo to the location ordered, the same amount of lading fees that any other vessel would be paid for doing this, and even if necessary a bigger amount, provided that the vessel shall reach the locality where the admiral or some other party designated by him shall be able to store the cargo safely, and provided that the location designated by the admiral or his representative for the delivery of this cargo shall not be in an enemy territory.

If aboard the vessel intercepted by a man-of-war there is some cargo that is claimed to be the property of the patron or some members of the crew, their claims will not be recognized as valid, but a search will be made in the entries of the register, provided such a register can be found. If no register is found, the patron and the crew members claiming ownership of such cargo shall make their depositions under oath. If they testify under oath that such cargo belongs to them, the admiral or the party designated to act in his capacity shall return such cargo to them without any opposition, taking into consideration the reputation and respect the parties who had made such depositions enjoy.

If it should happen that the master of the intercepted merchantman, in spite of the orders issued by the admiral, should refuse to carry the enemy cargo he had aboard his vessel to the place designated, in order that those who seized this booty could store it safely, the admiral may sink or order such a vessel sunk, provided he takes measures to protect the lives of those aboard the merchantman; no authority in the world can hold him responsible for such action, regardless of the type and kind of accusations that would be made against him. The above should be understood as follows: that the major portion or all of the cargo aboard the merchantman had belonged to enemy nationals.

If it should happen that such a vessel belonged to enemy nationals and the cargo aboard it belonged to friendly nationals, the merchants who are aboard the vessel, and to whom all or most of this cargo belongs, should reach an understanding with the admiral as to the amount of ransom the vessel shall pay, the value of the booty, and the amount they are able to pay him, and the admiral shall conclude a sensible agreement with them, which will be possible for them to accept.

Further, if these merchants should fail or would refuse to reach an agreement or an understanding with the admiral, the admiral shall put a prize crew aboard this vessel that will sail the vessel to the location from which he had sailed forth, while the merchants shall pay him the lading charges equal to the fees they would have paid had the vessel delivered the cargo to its original destination, but not anything more.

Should it happen that these merchants shall be damaged and wronged by the terms imposed upon them by the admiral by force, the admiral shall not be held accountable because these merchants had refused to enter into negotiations and reach an agreement with him regarding the ransom of their vessel. There is yet another reason for this, namely, that often the vessel is worth more than the cargo it has aboard.

If, however, the merchants were willing to conclude an agreement or reach an understanding with the admiral, as has been discussed above, but the admiral due to pride or arrogance would take control of the vessel, as has been mentioned above, and took possession of both the merchants and their cargo, which he had no legal right to do, the merchants shall not be liable for any part or all of the lading charges; rather, the admiral shall reimburse them for all their damages and losses that they had suffered or expect to suffer due to the forcible manner in which he dealt with them.

Further, if it should happen that the man-of-war would intercept a merchantman in a place where it will be impossible for the merchants to reach such an agreement or understanding with the admiral, and these merchants will be man of good reputation and able to guarantee the fulfillment of any agreement, the admiral is prohibited from using force against them. Should he resort to force, he will be liable for all the damages they incur. If it should happen that such merchants are not well-known and cannot pay the ransom, the admiral may resort to the use of force against them, as has been stated above.

277-Necessity of Unloading Cargo Due to Unforeseen Circumstances

If a patron has cargoed his vessel partly or fully, at the shore, in a port, at a dock, or at any other place, and then an unfortunate accident occurs that necessitates the unloading of part or all of the cargo —and by an unfortunate accident we mean a loss of herds, equipment made out of wood, chains, or any other equipment, thus endangering the vessel, or the arrival of armed enemy vessels, if his vessel is located in an area where there are lifeboats that could be used to unload such cargo, the patron of the vessel shall rent these boats to unload the cargo, until such time as the cause of alarm would have passed, that is, until the damage has been repaired or other matters endangering the vessel no longer exist.

If he could not find such boats to unload and save the cargo, and nearby there are other vessels that are not engaged and not under sail, the patron of the vessel in danger should approach the patrons of these other vessels or persons who are in command of these vessels, explain his dangerous situation, and ask their help in saving his vessel and the cargo aboard it. If these patrons or persons in command of these vessels offer to help him without any compensation, he should accept their help and assume all the damages they may suffer due to this. If, however, the above mentioned patrons demand a reward or payment for their help, he shall meet their requests depending on the terms of the agreement he is able to reach with them.

If, however, these patrons demanded too much for their help, but he nevertheless agreed to meet their price, he should not pay them the full amount promised, but should turn this matter over to the arbitration by the Elders, who shall render a decision. What is the reason for turning such matter over to the arbitration of the Elders if both parties had agreed on the terms beforehand? Because if these people demanded half of the cargo and half of the vessel in order to help, the patron of the vessel in distress would have promised them what they asked for, even if it were not just that they should receive so much; for this reason such a matter as has been indicated shall be turned over to arbitration by the Elders.

Further, if a vessel that had been rewarded for helping was damaged in some way, the party who paid the award shall not be held liable for any such damages.

If it should happen that aboard such vessels there would be no one who could help the distressed vessel, the patron of the latter vessel should approach the civil authorities where the misfortune took place, and with the approval of these authorities he may and can use these vessels to help his own, but he shall be liable for all the damages these vessels may suffer while he used them; in addition, he shall pay the owners of these vessels a reward in the amount determined by the local authorities.

If a misfortune overtook the vessel in a locality where it would be impossible to locate the local civil authorities quickly, and a complete loss threatens the vessel, the patron may use other such vessels without receiving permission from the civil authorities. However, he must assume full responsibility for any damages and losses that such a vessel may suffer due to this, and shall pay such indemnities and rewards as established by the Elders of the district where such a vessel is located.

This article has been written for the reasons given above.

278-Inability of the Patron to Undertake a Voyage Due to His Indebtedness

If a master of a vessel is indebted to anyone and if he remains in the locality where he had become indebted, together with his creditor for a period of a month, two months, or even a longer period, and the latter did not press for the repayment of the loan, and did not take this matter before the local judicial authority, until the moment he realized that the patron was about ready to sail in order to earn money, and then, when the patron was about to hoist anchor, this creditor would petition the court to issue an order forcing the patron to repay the loan, the court shall not interfere in this matter and attempt to force the patron to repay his loan, nor interfere with his date of departure, because as has been mentioned before, both the patron and his creditor were in the vicinity together and had ample opportunity to attend to this matter. If the debtor is able to procure a guarantor for such a loan, the court shall order that he do so. [86]

Under such circumstances the guarantor of the loan shall not be harassed by the court concerning the repayment of the loan until the borrower has returned from his voyage, that is, until he has returned to the place where the loan was to be repaid and where he had provided a guarantor, unless the latter accepted the responsibility for this

---

86. Writ *ad rem.*

loan without any reservations.

A person who had accepted the responsibility for the repayment of a loan under such circumstances shall not be harassed by the courts or by the creditors until the liquidation of the property of the debtor has been completed. If the property of the original debtor is insufficient to repay such a loan, the courts as well as the creditor may take legal action against the guarantor for the repayment of the loan out of his own property.

If, however, the wealth of the original debtor was sufficiently large to repay the loan, under no circumstances shall the property of the guarantor be attached to guarantee the repayment of the loan unless he himself had agreed to such an arrangement.

Further, if a patron could not find a co-signer or guarantor, the court shall not delay the departure of his vessel. He shall testify under oath that he does not have and cannot find a co-signer. In addition, he shall be required to make a deposition under oath that he will return to the locality where the loan was made, and shall reach a satisfactory agreement with his creditor. The courts shall not be able to delay his departure if he fails to produce a co-signer, because his creditor failed to petition the court for such action before his departure, when both parties were readily available at the same location, but the creditor had waited until he learned that the debtor was about to leave the country before taking any action. In addition, it would be a very serious injustice to the merchants who had their cargo loaded aboard if this vessel would be delayed, and could possibly lose their cargo due to such negligence on the part of the creditor, who had made no attempt to have his loan repaid until the vessel was ready to set sail.

Let therefore all creditors be very cautious and watchful and not wait till the last moment to settle such accounts, or they shall suffer the consequences described above.

This article was written for the reasons given above.

If it should happen that the master of such a vessel would die before he was able to return to the place where he had found the co-signer and before the loan was liquidated, the co-signer of the loan who had accepted full responsibility for its repayment, that is to say, he had agreed to be responsible for the repayment of the full amount of the loan after the voyage was completed, will be required to repay the loan, whether the debtor failed to return from the voyage, had died, or is alive, unless there had been some other agreements made by the interested parties, in conformity with well-founded customs.

If a party entrusted his cargo to another for trading purposes and had concluded an agreement in respect to this, that he shall deliver such cargo to a mutually agreed destination, and carry it aboard during a specific voyage or voyages he will undertake, he shall fulfill all the terms of such an agreement; such an agreement shall be binding whether it had been executed in writing, or orally, as long as it can be proved, if the necessity requires such proof.

If after the completion of such an agreement, containing the provisions mentioned above, the party who accepted the care of the cargo should release these goods to another party or send them aboard another vessel without the knowledge and approval of the party who entrusted such cargo to him, and if such cargo should be partly or totally lost, the party who had been entrusted with such cargo shall pay all the damages for the cargo lost as well as the profit that would have been made had the cargo been merchandised, because the latter had failed to live up to the terms of the agreement.

If, however, such cargo was not partly or completely lost, and had reached the destination specified by the party who had accepted such cargo under his command, and while at that place the cargo is allowed to remain so long that it is spoiled or damaged by the negligence of the party who had care of it, the latter shall pay all the claims due from spoilage or damage of the cargo.

If the party to whom such cargo was dispatched by the party who had accepted care of such cargo sold it at a very low price because of carelessness or lack of business acumen on the part of the merchant, that is, if this person failed to take proper precautions and care of such cargo, as he should have had done, and as would have been done by the party who had accepted care of the cargo, who would have accompanied it as had been set forth in the agreement, or if such a commission merchant had failed to sell it at the market price, that is, at the price that the cargo could have been sold at that time in that location, and had sold this cargo at a much lower price or even at loss, the party who had originally accepted care of the cargo shall pay the owner of the cargo the amount due him for the difference in the prices he sold the cargo and the actual amount that this cargo should have been sold at the destination to which he had shipped it, provided that the owner of such cargo can prove that there was a difference in the amount the cargo had been sold for and its actual value on the market at the place where it was sold.

The above resolutions should be understood in the following manner: that the destination where the cargo had been sent by the party who had accepted care of it was the same destination agreed upon between himself and the owner of the cargo. However, if such cargo had been dispatched to another locality not specified in the agreement, it should be determined what were the prices on the market of some of this cargo and also of all varieties contained in this cargo, at the time and during the period when such cargo was placed on sale in that locality, and this determination shall be made by the owner of the cargo arbitrarily. Everything that has been stated above must be accomplished without any attempt at deceit and fraud.

The party accepting the cargo under his care shall therefore be required to pay the party who entrusted such cargo in his care all the damages due without any hesitancy and opposition because of his failure to fulfill the terms of the agreement, and in fact he had acted contrary to its terms and therefore it is only proper that he pay for all the damages that had resulted. There is another reason for this, namely, it would not be proper or just that anyone should have more right to the property of another than the owner of such property. Any person who would claim that he has such rights, or try to usurp such rights, should not call himself a merchant or a commission man, but rather a common thief; such person should be dealt with as a common thief and the prescribed punishment shall be the same as prescribed for a thief, because he can actually be called a thief because he had taken property belonging to another person without that person's knowledge and permission. If, however, the party who had accepted command of such cargo could show justifiable reasons why he acted in such a manner, he shall be absolved from all charges.

In addition, the agreements and promises that the parties had concluded should be taken into consideration, unless either of the parties involved shall be able to demonstrate that some circumstance or a well-established obstacle prevented him from fulfilling the terms of such an agreement or promise.

This article was written for the reasons given above.

280-Credence Shall Be Given to a Middleman Making a Deposition Under Oath

If anyone entrusted a patron of a vessel with money or cargo that was to be used in trading, he shall accept the accounting made of this transaction by the patron without any question whether a profit or a loss resulted from such an undertaking. If, however, the parties who had entrusted him with such an undertaking suspected that the accounting he had submitted to them of such transactions was suspicious and did not appear to reflect the true situation, they can demand that he make a deposition under oath that he accounting he made is factual and had been carefully and accurately prepared.

If the party who had accepted such a commission shall testify under oath that the accounting he had rendered of this transaction is accurate and properly made, those who entrusted him with such commission shall have no right to make any further demands upon him, unless they can prove something to the contrary; they shall then accept his accounting whether it has shown profit or a loss. This is only proper, since anyone entrusting another with such a commission should have sufficient confidence in him, otherwise he would have not trusted him with the execution of such a task. It is also proper and just that those entrusting care of their property to others should have proper confidence in them, whether they earn a profit or suffer a loss in such a transaction, as much confidence as they had in them at the moment they were entrusting them with such a commission, unless as had been stated above they can prove something to the contrary. If they shall not be able to prove anything to the contrary, the deposition made under oath by the party who had been entrusted with their property shall be accepted, and he shall have no other obligation toward them.

Such are the customs in matters relating to marine commerce, regardless in what manner a commission had been entrusted to another party. Let, therefore, all be careful with whom they enter into such an arrangement and in what manner they go about it.

This article was written for the reasons listed above.

281-Agreements Concluded Between Merchants and the Patron of a Vessel Regarding a Shipment of Cargo

If the merchants conclude an agreement with the patron of a vessel either in writing or in the presence of witnesses to carry their cargo, he shall fulfill all the terms of such an agreement, as written or heard by the witnesses who were present when it was concluded.

If, however, the patron did not see the cargo personally or it was not identified in the written agreement or specifically mentioned in the presence of the witnesses, and the patron merely accepted the word of the merchant who had informed him that he had loaded a particular cargo aboard the vessel, and actually had loaded some other cargo aboard, that is, that the merchant had loaded aboard bags, crates, or bales, telling the patron or leading him to believe that in those aforementioned crates, bales, and bags are contained a certain number of hundred weight of cargo, but it appears to the patron that the contents of these bales, crates, and bags contain many more hundred weight of cargo than he had been informed by the merchant in the written agreement or one made in the presence of witnesses, the patron may reweigh such cargo.

If the patron would be able to prove that the amount of cargo declared by the merchants at the time they arranged for shipment was smaller than he had been able to ascertain, he shall be able to demand additional lading charges in the amount determined arbitrarily by himself. In addition, if in the process of reweighing the cargo he found it was heavier than had been declared, and he had suffered some expenditures, the merchants shall reimburse him for this expense.

If he found that the amount declared was correct, he shall bear the cost of reweighing the cargo. If the merchant had been forced to bear some expense in reweighing his cargo, the patron of the vessel shall reimburse him because it had been proved that the amount of cargo he had declared had been accurate.

Further, the patron may order that the cargo be reweighed before it is loaded aboard the vessel or after it is unloaded at the port of destination.

If, however, the patron of the vessel had seen the cargo once or twice before it was loaded aboard the vessel and before it was specified in the agreement he had concluded, he shall not be allowed to make any stipulations or reservations about it. Nevertheless, if it should appear to the patron that the merchant had added some cargo into the crates, bales, bags, or chests mentioned above, after he had made arrangements for the shipment and after he had signed the agreement, the patron may force the merchant to swear an oath that he did not add any additional cargo, because the patron can order that the cargo be reweighed when the merchant claims that he only had a specified number of hundred weight of cargo.

Further, if the merchant had informed the patron that he will ship a specified number of crates, bags, bales, or chests of cargo without specifying their weight, and the patron had not asked him the weight of these crates, bales, bags, and chests, he will be unable under any circumstances to order that the cargo be weighed.

Nevertheless, if the patron suspected that the merchant had added some merchandise after arranging for its shipment and after showing the cargo to the patron, he can force the merchant by a court order to make a deposition under oath relating to this matter; if the merchant shall testify under oath, credence shall be given his testimony unless it can be proved that he perjured himself.

Should the patron be able to prove that the merchant had perjured himself, the latter shall be required to pay double the amount of the lading charges due on all the excess cargo that he has secretly added to his declared shipment, or the number of hundred weight of cargo in excess of the declared weight at the moment he had concluded the agreement to ship such cargo; in addition he shall be turned over to the local court for having committed perjury.

Further, there is no need to discuss a situation when the cargo was shipped per hundred weight and the lading charges were levied on each hundred weight of cargo; it is certain that everyone knows well what should be the proper procedure under such circumstances, and what cannot be done.

This article was written for the reasons listed above.

282-When a Vessel That Had Been Engaged to Take on Cargo Is Restrained from Leaving By the Civil Authority

If merchants had engaged a vessel in a particular locality and after making arrangements for shipment of cargo, the vessel is restrained from sailing by local authority, the patron of the vessel shall be required to wait for the merchants as long as had been agreed between them when they engaged him.

If after the time they had agreed upon that he would have to wait for their cargo, the restrictions shall be removed by the local authority, the patron must take their cargo aboard and cannot demand any additional lading charges. The merchants shall be required to pay part of the expenses suffered by the patron while he had waited for their cargo. This is done so that neither the merchants nor the patron of the vessel would suffer any damage.

If it should happen that in the locality where the patron was to take the cargo aboard, the above mentioned restrictions imposed by the local authorities have not been removed after the expiration of the time that the patron had agreed to wait for the cargo, the patron shall not be required to wait any longer for the cargo, unless he would want to, and neither shall the merchants be required to wait for the patron if they do not wish. Nevertheless, the merchants shall reimburse the patron for his expenses while he waited for them, according to the decision made by two Elders. After this had been done, each party may proceed according to his own choice unless there had been some agreement made that one would wait for another.

If there had been no such agreement concluded, and as soon as the restrictions imposed by the local authorities where the vessel was to be cargoed are lifted, the merchants who had engaged the vessel may approach the patron and propose that he make preparations to take on the cargo. He shall not be required to do this unless he chooses and unless the merchants make a new agreement with him; the merchants on their part shall only be required to pay the expenses he had incurred due to such delay, unless they had promised him other things.

If it should happen that the merchants had made arrangements to ship cargo but had not set a specific date or a period of time for the patron to wait for this cargo or for them to dispatch the vessel, and the above mentioned restrictions are invoked against the vessel, the patron shall not be required to wait for the merchants, nor shall they be required to wait for him, provided that the above mentioned expenses are paid.

If after the merchants had taken proper steps to remove the restrictions imposed by the civil authorities against the vessel, and they inform the patron that such restrictions had been removed and that he should begin to cargo the vessel, he is not obligated to do so unless he chooses to please them, unless the merchants reach an agreement or have reached an agreement with him, as had been stated when we discussed the situation when the vessel had to wait for the merchants, or in the case where the merchants had agreed to cargo and dispatch the vessel on a psecific day or within a set period of time, and this is due to the fact that by all that is right, just, and proper, the patron would be burdened by such responsibility. It would not be just that a vessel should await the merchants until all the legal restrictions are removed, for such restrictions could last for such a long time that the vessel would no longer be seaworthy, unless the merchants had specifically agreed with the patron that he wait that long. [87]

If in case the merchants had told the patron to wait for them and that they will assume all damages, expenses, and losses that he will suffer, the patron should wait under the above provisions. If the master of the vessel continued to wait for them under the conditions and circumstances mentioned above, the merchants are liable, regardless of the continuance of such restrictions against the vessel, or whether these restrictions had been removed, whether they had cargoed the vessel or not, to reimburse the patron for all the damages, expenses, and losses that he suffered or may suffer without any dispute.

If the merchants should attempt to enter into disputes regarding the above stated conditions and circumstances, they shall be required to reimburse him for all the damages, losses, and expenses that he suffered or expects to suffer due to such disputes. If, on the other hand, the patron should attempt to enter into a dispute with the merchants because he is unwilling to carry out their agreement or the promises that he made to the merchants, and the merchants suffered damage, loss, or expenses due to this, he shall reimburse them for this, even if it became necessary to sell his vessel to satisfy their

87. Reference is made to Article 80.

claims.

This article pertains to a vessel that had not been cargoed partially or completely, because there are explanatory articles about the responsibility of the merchants toward a patron of a vessel that had been cargoed. However, this article shall be understood in the following manner: that if the merchants had informed a patron of a vessel that he wait for them, they shall be required to carry out all the provisions that had been stated above, because they had mutually agreed on the day or a period of time in which the merchants had promised to dispatch the vessel; thus there is no chance for any dispute among them in this matter.

This article has been written for the reasons listed above.

283-Liability of Shareholders

If a party undertakes to build a vessel and asks others to buy shares in such a venture, and these persons agree, they shall be required to keep their promise. If the party who had undertaken this venture by others had failed to inform these shareholders whether the boat shall be large or small, or the shareholders had failed to ask him about the size or cost of such vessel, or the length or capacity of such vessel, they shall be required to participate as they had promised regardless of the size of the boat that will be built, whether it shall be small or large.

Further, if the party who had undertaken the construction of a vessel, or will undertake it, had informed the prospective shareholders about the type of vessel that shall be built and had given its dimensions and cost, and then would order a larger sized boat be built without informing the shareholders about this change, the shareholders shall not be required to increase their holdings in such vessel but shall only be liable for the amount they had originally agreed to invest.

If the vessel would appear to be bigger and costlier than it had been estimated, the shareholders shall only be liable for the amount they originally agreed to invest in it; they are entitled to this because the patron had caused a larger vessel to be constructed without their knowledge and approval. If, however, the patron ordered that a larger vessel be built with the approval of the majority or all of the shareholders, they shall be liable for all the additional expense, as has been explained and discussed in one of the earlier articles. [88]

Further, if the party who intended to construct a vessel had informed and explained to the prospective shareholders that he intends

---

88. Reference is made to Articles 50 and 51.

to construct a boat but instead he ordered a smaller vessel be constructed, without the knowledge and approval of the persons who had promised to invest in a boat, they shall not be obligated to fulfill their promise, because the party who initiated this undertaking failed to fulfill his part of the agreement. It is, therefore, only proper that since he failed to keep his promise, his partners be released from fulfilling their obligation.

Further, if, however, this party had a small vessel constructed with the full knowledge and approval of the majority or all of the investors, the latter shall be liable for the full amount of their investment, because the patron had acted with the consent of the majority or all of them.

If it should happen that a party had promised the prospective shareholders that he shall have a small vessel constructed, but actually he shall proceed to have a large vessel constructed, undertaking this without the authority of these shareholders, the latter shall not be required to fulfill their obligation to invest in this venture, unless it should happen in this manner, that for the same amount they had promised to invest in a small vessel they shall have a large one constructed. We should exclude a situation that had been anticipated in one of the previous articles in which we discussed the patron who attempted to build a small vessel; we should also keep in mind the explanation given in that article.

The above information relates to every vessel, small or large, that will be newly constructed, and pertains to it until the newly constructed vessel leaves the locality where it had been constructed.

This article was written for the reasons given above.

284–Cargo Tossed Overboard

If a master of a vessel, upon the demand of the merchants, drops anchor in some locality, and while at anchor the vessel is overtaken by a severe storm, so that the vessel will be not only unable to hoist anchor and sail away from that locality, but it will be necessary to throw overboard most or all of the cargo aboard in order to save the vessel, under such circumstances of the necessity of throwing cargo overboard, neither the patron shall have any responsibility toward the merchants nor the merchants toward the patron, regardless of whether the merchants order that the cargo be tossed overboard or whether they personally tossed the cargo overboard without notifying the patron about it, or whether the patron orders that the cargo be thrown overboard or throws it out himself without informing the merchants about it, for this reason, tossing of cargo overboard under such conditions cannot be considered in the category of an ordinary

situation when cargo is thrown overboard, but in the same sense as
if the vessel was wrecked and the cargo was lost; therefore, under
the conditions described above neither party can make any claims regarding the cargo. [89]

The value of the cargo thrown overboard under such circumstances
shall be evaluated proportionally as to quantity and quality, and the
vessel shall share in the loss of such cargo in the amount up to two-
thirds of its value. If the incident of the necessity of throwing cargo
overboard was not of this category, the vessel would have been liable
up to half of its value for the damages, but in the situation explained
above, it shall share in the damage up to two-thirds of its value, because this was not due to the total destruction of the vessel. If the
vessel had suffered complete destruction, it would be required to
share in the damage up to its full value.

Why should a vessel share in the damages up to two-thirds of its
value under such circumstances? Because there was no shipwreck
nor an ordinary instance of throwing of the cargo overboard, but
rather a situation that closely resembles a shipwreck, rather than
some other reason for throwing of cargo overboard.

If it should happen that a vessel should lose some equipment, such
as anchors, lines, boats, or any other equipment, all this shall be
proportionally evaluated, because this is not a matter of simply throwing of cargo or equipment overboard, and therefore the matter cannot
be treated in the same manner, for such a situation more closely resembles a shipwreck than a mere throwing of cargo overboard. In a
typical situation when the cargo must be thrown overboard, a loss of
a boat tied aboard the vessel or tied to its gunwales, due to the break
of its lines or lack of sufficient ropes to tie it securely, would be the
patron's responsibility, as he is to see that proper ropes are used to
secure such boat. Similarly, in a case of an ordinary necessity of
throwing cargo overboard due to the loss of anchors because of weak
anchor chains or lack of enough anchor chains, the loss would have to
be assumed by the vessel, and no merchant or any of his cargo left
aboard the vessel would be under such circumstances assessed for
the damage that had taken place.

Further, if any merchant would throw overboard or order anything
thrown overboard without informing the patron and without the patron's knowledge, neither the patron personally nor his vessel shall
be liable to share in such damage, unless he would wish to do so, if
the patron can show and prove that this was a case of an ordinary instance of throwing cargo overboard, regardless of the fact whether

---

89. Compare Articles 95, 99, and 195.

the vessel was at anchor or was under sail.

If it should happen that the patron of a vessel, in spite of the fact that the merchants are aboard his vessel, or even just one merchant is aboard, throws overboard some cargo without their knowledge and approval, he shall be liable for the damages the merchants had suffered due to his action of tossing cargo overboard. The above should be interpreted in this manner: that it can be proved that this was just an ordinary case of throwing cargo overboard, and this happens when there is no storm endangering the vessel and that all parties concerned are able to communicate with each other about such matters.

Further, if there are no merchants aboard the vessel, the patron may order the cargo thrown overboard with the approval of the majority or all of the crew members, if he has time to ask their assent to this. If, however, a storm should overtake them suddenly, and the patron ordered the cargo tossed overboard without being able to get the assent of the persons mentioned above, this action will have the same validity as if the patron had been able to get such assent from the crew or if the merchants were aboard, or if all the cargo belonged to the patron personally; the cargo aboard his vessel can actually be considered as his property, as it was entrusted to his care.

Further, after the cargo had been thrown overboard, and regardless whether the storm had somewhat abated or had completely spent itself, or if it is still continuing, and the vessel departs the locality where the misfortune happened with the consent of the merchants, and with their consent the vessel also abandons part of its equipment, the value of such equipment, if it is lost, shall be paid for by the merchants upon the evaluation of their cargo aboard the vessel as well as the vessel that shall share in this damage to the extent of half of its value, regardless of the fact whether aboard the vessel there is enough equipment left to enable the vessel to sail safely to the locality where it was to unload its cargo.

If it should happen that the above mentioned equipment is not lost, but is recovered, and that it had been salvaged at some cost, these expenditures shall be borne in the same manner as had been prescribed in the situation when such equipment had been lost; however, the above stipulation should be taken to mean that the tossing overboard of such equipment was not of the ordinary kind, but rather similar to a situation of a shipwreck.

If this had been an ordinary incident of dumping cargo overboard, and not a situation closely akin to a shipwreck, and if under such circumstances the patron of the vessel, upon the demand of the merchants had left such equipment aboard, as had been discussed above, [90] re-

---

90. Reference is made to Article 109.

gardless whether such equipment will be lost in part or completely, or if in order to salvage it some expense will be incurred, all the expense connected with this salvage shall be apportioned against the quantity and quality of cargo left aboard, and the vessel shall not share in such expenditures, because the vessel had already been sufficiently damaged, due to the fact that upon the insistence of the merchants it had left the locality and exposed itself to dangers sailing to the destination where the merchants demand that it proceed and to which the crew had agreed to proceed.

If it should happen that aboard the vessel there would not be sufficient equipment in order that the vessel could undertake to sail to the locality indicated by the merchants, the vessel shall return to the locality from which it undertook the voyage and at which it had been cargoed, and all the financial matters between the patron and the merchants shall be made at the location where the vessel took on the cargo and to which it subsequently returned.

The above shall be construed in this manner, that if the misfortune took place after completion of half of the journey, the financial transactions shall be made at the destination of the cargo at the prices prevailing in that locality, in spite of the fact that the vessel may have returned to the locality where it had taken on the cargo. If the misfortune happened before the vessel completed half of the distance to the location where the cargo was to be unloaded, the financial accounting shall be made at the location where the vessel had picked up the cargo, if the vessel returns to that place with whatever cargo remained aboard it. [91]

If the patron of a vessel demands payment of the lading fees for the cargo that had been lost as well as for the cargo salvaged, he shall be paid as requested. However, these lading fees shall share in the payment for the cargo thrown overboard and lost. If, on the other hand, the patron does not demand payment of lading fees, and refuses to accept it even if offered, the patron shall not share in the resulting damages.

If the patron expects payment of the lading fees for the cargo that had been saved, he shall complete the journey with such a cargo, if he demands payment of the lading fees from the merchants.

If, on the other hand, the patron of the vessel does not demand payment of the lading charges for the cargo saved nor for the cargo lost, he will not be forced to complete the voyage if he shall not desire to do it, and this is only proper, as he had already lost enough on such a venture, expending his energy, his time, provisions, and

---

91. See Article 97, and compare Articles 98, 196, and 296.

using his vessel. This shall be understood to mean the following: that the merchants are located in a territory free of any danger, in a friendly territory where they will be able to find another vessel that will be willing to take their cargo for a payment. An agreement reached by the patron with the merchants under such circumstances shall be binding upon the crew of his vessel.

This article was written for the reasons given above.

285-When a Vessel Is Forced to Hoist Anchor Due to Ill Fate

If an engaged vessel was to proceed to a designated locality to pick up cargo, and after the arrival of the vessel at this destination a violent storm would intervene before the cargo can be loaded aboard, that in order to save the vessel it will be necessary to hoist anchor, or this must be done because of the appearance of armed enemy vessels, or due to the information that had been received that enemy vessels are on the way toward the spot where the vessel was anchored; if because of one of these circumstances the vessel will be forced to sail without taking on the cargo in order to return to the place from which it had sailed and where it had been engaged to take on cargo, and the patron refuses the pleas of the merchants that he return for their cargo, when the storm had abated or a safe report is made concerning the movement of enemy vessels, but he demands payment of the lading fees agreed to at the time the contract was made, he shall be required to return for such cargo.

Should he refuse to return, he may be forced to do so by the legal authorities. If he still continues to refuse to return for the cargo, the merchants can engage another similar vessel to carry their cargo; if the lading fees charged by the second vessel the merchants hired are higher, the patron of the first vessel they engaged shall reimburse them for the amount of the difference in these fees. Should he refuse to pay for this difference in the lading fees, he shall be compelled to do this by the judicial authorities, even if it were necessary that his vessel be sold to satisfy such a claim.

In addition, the merchants shall not be obligated to pay the patron of the original vessel anything because he had failed to carry their cargo, and this situation had not developed of any fault of theirs. This should be understood to mean that if the merchants who had engaged the vessel failed to fulfill their obligations, which they had agreed to at the time the vessel was engaged to carry their cargo, or if the patron had to return from the voyage without a cargo by their fault or negligence, he is not obliged to return, but rather they shall pay him the lading fees, because he had to make the return trip for the cargo as result of their carelessness.

If the merchants were not at fault, and the patron wished to return, but his crew is opposed to this and refuses to return, the crew cannot and should not act in this manner, because this situation had not come about out of the neglect of the patron or the merchants, but because of circumstances described above.

Further, if the vessel due to the circumstances mentioned left on the shore part of the cargo or some equipment or a few members of the crew at the location from which it had to depart, the patron should substitute other equipment and sailors for those left behind. If he refused to do this, the sailors cannot be forced to make the return trip against their own will, and the patron cannot force them to do this under any condition, by the fact that he himself refused to complete the necessary equipment and provide a full crew, as it has been stated above.

This is why the above article was written.

286-Convoys

If a master of a vessel had decided to sail in convoy with one or several other vessels of similar or smaller or larger size, all the terms of the agreement relating to this arrangement whether entered into in writing or orally must be carried out.

This should be understood to mean that the existence of an agreement to sail in convoy shall be proved, and this can be done by the testimony of witnesses who had been present at the signing of such an agreement, or by an entry made by a clerk under oath, or by the introduction of the letter of agreement, provided that the date, the hour, and the place where such document was executed are contained within it. In addition, the document of agreement shall bear the seals of the parties who had agreed to sail in convoy if they were able to do so.

If the parties concerned were unable to formalize such an agreement in writing at the place where they were located at the time the agreement was concluded, and merely agreed orally to sail together in convoy, such an oral agreement shall be valid if the interested parties had agreed to everything that had been stated, as valid as if it had been executed in the presence of a clerk acting under oath, or if it had been made in writing according to private legal concepts, or if it had been entered into the ship's register. In case some dispute should arise concerning the interpretation of the terms of the agreement, it will be possible to ascertain its existence and its provisions by calling of witnesses.

If it should happen that one of the signatories to the agreement should refuse to carry out its terms, promises, and obligations relative to sailing in convoy, the latter party, regardless of whether the agreement was made in writing or entered into orally, shall be liable for all the damages and losses of the other parties, provided that the aggrieved parties can prove the existence of such damages and losses.

In all circumstances where the fulfillment of the agreement had been frustrated by the intervention of fate, due to which one of the signatories could not remain sailing in the convoy, he shall not be held liable if he can prove his inability to fulfill the terms of the agreement because of intervention of forces beyond his control.[92] If, however, he could not prove the existence of such a fateful intervention, the party or parties claiming this in self-defense and being unable to prove this will be liable for all the damages as had been stated above, and shall reimburse the party or parties aggrieved without any dispute.

This article was written for the reasons given above.

287-When the Shareholders of a Vessel Entrust It to the Care of Another Party

If responsible people or merchants express a desire to invest in a vessel and entrust the party from whom they purchased their share in the vessel with its command, regardless of whether such a person has any investment in the vessel or not, he shall sail into all waters where he will have an opportunity to earn profit with this vessel, unless there had been other arrangements made between the party commanding the vessel and the merchants who entrusted the command to him at the time the agreement was made.

If the party who was entrusted with the command of the vessel made any profit, he shall be required to make an accounting of his transactions and pay these merchants and the above mentioned respectable people all the profit he made with the exception of the amount due him, proportionate to his investment in this venture. If he had no investment in the vessel, he shall receive the amount due him as the commander of the vessel, similar in amount to that received by masters commanding the same type of vessels.

If the patron or the person who was given command of the vessel failed to earn any profit, but on the other hand suffered some losses, the above mentioned worthy personages who had entrusted their vessel to him and made him its master must accept the liability for these losses unless they could prove that they occurred by his negligence, that he gambled the money away, wasted it, stole it, or man-

---

92. Reference is made to Article 94.

aged it very poorly. If they should be able to prove these charges against him, the above patron whom they entrusted with their vessel, shall be required to reimburse them for all their losses without any opposition in the amount to be determined by these worthy people arbitrarily who had entrusted their vessel to him or made him a shareholder of the venture.

If, on the other hand, they could not prove any such charges against him, as he had done everything that was within his power and had acted prudently and honestly, he cannot bear the responsibility for such consequences, and the accounting he makes of these transactions shall be accepted as valid.

If such a patron or person who was entrusted with the command of the vessel would take aboard his vessel a trusted clerk, who took an oath upon accepting this office, for if he did not take such an oath of office, the shareholders may question him and order him to testify under oath, and if the expenditures and losses shall be accounted for and in agreement with his testimony, or if the clerk states under oath that the accounting made is in agreement with his entries, his testimony shall be accepted as final, unless it could be proved that he testified falsely.

If it should be proved that the clerk testified falsely, he should be punished according to the penalty prescribed in one of the earlier articles, [93] while the patron or the party who had been entrusted with the command of the vessel shall reimburse these worthy people for their damages if the clerk had no means with which to pay these damages, regardless of whether the damage resulted due to the negligence of the patron or the party who was trusted with the command of the vessel, for this reason, because the patron as had been stated above had personally picked the clerk to serve aboard the vessel.

If, however, it could not be proved that the clerk had made false entries in his accounts, he shall not be punished as stated above, and neither he nor the patron of the vessel shall be liable for these damages suffered by the shareholders, if any damages can be proved, for the damages did not arise out of their negligence.

If it should happen that the patron did not hire a clerk who had taken an oath of office, or he lost the clerk and made the entries himself or ordered that some other person make these entries, the shareholders who had entrusted the vessel to his care, may, if they suspect any irregularity, require that the patron swear an oath to the effect that whatever statements he will make concerning the expenses shall reflect the true situation, and that these expenses actually amounted

---

93. Reference is made to Article 57.

to the sum he had entered or caused another party to enter in the register and reported to the shareholders.

If he makes these depositions under oath, they shall be accepted at face value unless it can be proved that they were falsehoods. In such a situation he shall be forced to pay all the damages in the amount decided by the parties mentioned before. If no attempt in deceit can be proved, his statement shall be accepted and his account judged accurate, regardless of whether it shows a loss or a gain, because it had not been his fault that he was unable to earn a profit.

It is only proper that if the shareholders had confidence in him when they made him master of the vessel, they should also have confidence in his accounts, whether these accounts show losses or gains, unless as had been stated before, they can substantiate the falsehood of his statements.

Thus, whether a patron of a vessel take on or not take on a clerk who had taken the oath of office, he shall not and should not suffer any damages, for the reasons explained above. Nevertheless, in every instance when the patron does or can take aboard a sworn clerk, it will be of great aid and relief to him; therefore, every patron should take aboard a clerk, if he can. This article was written for the reasons mentioned above.

288-When a Merchantman Is Intercepted by an Enemy Vessel

If a merchantman is about to be intercepted by an enemy vessel, and aboard the merchantman there is one or more merchants, the patron shall inquire of them if it is their desire that he attack, capture, and take over the enemy vessel. If a merchant or all the merchants or the majority of them express approval to his proposal, the patron may proceed to take this action and shall not be liable in any degree toward the merchants no matter how extensive their losses and damages may become, because these merchants had expressed their consent and approved the attack.

If the patron took the action mentioned above without the approval of the majority or all of the merchants, and if these merchants should suffer damages and losses or may suffer them later due to his actions, the patron shall be liable for all such damages and losses and must reimburse the merchants for them without any disagreement, even if it became necessary to sell the vessel and all his possessions wherever they shall be found, and this shall be done because the patron proceeded in this manner without the approval of the majority or all of the merchants.

If it should happen that the patron took such action, as had been described above, with the approval of the majority or all of the merchants, promising them a share in the booty he will capture, he shall fulfill this promise without any disagreement or protest.

If it should happen that between the patron of the vessel and the majority or all of the merchants there had been no agreement made or any promises made regarding the booty, but some booty shall be taken under the circumstances described above, it shall be divided in the following manner: the patron and the vessel shall be entitled to and shall take one-third of the booty; the merchants with their cargo are entitled to one-third part also; the remaining third shall be taken by the navigator, officers of the prow, sailors, and the rest of the ship's personnel serving aboard the vessel and drawing wages.

Further, from the three parts of the booty shall be subtracted the amount that is due as a reward and a prize for personnel of the vessel; these rewards shall be apportioned according to the judgment of the merchants, the clerk of the vessel, one officer of the deck, and two sailors of the prow. It should be understood that the booty whether large or small shall be divided proportionally. Under all circumstances, however, whether the booty is large or small, the patron and the vessel shall receive one-third; the remainder shall be divided among the persons mentioned above.

If the patron had taken the action discussed above without the knowledge and approval of the majority or all of the merchants aboard his vessel, but these merchants had not been damaged in any way, the patron shall not be obligated to give them a third of the captured booty, but only such a share as he considers proper, with the approval of the navigator, the clerk, and two sailors of the fore deck, and they shall apportion the part of the booty the patron decided was the proper share for the merchants according to the amount of cargo the merchants have aboard his vessel and according to the worth and status of each of them.

It appears absolutely proper that the merchants be satisfied with the share the patron had decided was due to them in the manner mentioned above, for this reason, that the patron would have been held responsible for all the damages suffered by the merchants, had they suffered such damages.

If it should happen that aboard the vessel there had been no merchants present when the patron had taken the action mentioned above, he shall not and cannot take any such action, for he legally has no right to do it. Should he dare to do this, nothing shall be said, if he had been successful in such an attempt. It will, however, depend on his generosity and good will what share of the booty he will be willing to assign to the merchants who had their cargo aboard his vessel; this will be a matter left entirely to his good disposition.

Further, should he fail in the attempt of his undertaking, he shall be answerable with his person and his property to the merchants for damages they suffered, in agreement with what had been stated above, because these merchants were not aboard the vessel. There is still another reason for this, namely, a patron under such circumstances should not attempt any such action without the knowledge of the merchants, and it would not be proper that he would have the authority to do this, for he already has enough authority in regard to the cargo, and that is that he may in a case of necessity throw it overboard, or in case the vessel is wrecked if these incidents happen when the merchants are not aboard the vessel.

Further, if the above mentioned patron can show and prove that he had a misfortune brought on by act of fate, and by this we mean that he could not escape, that is, that the enemy vessel overtook his craft and held it with grappling irons, and if under such circumstances the merchants suffer damages, the patron shall not be responsible to pay them any damages whatsoever, because the damages were not the result of his negligence. It will make no difference in such circumstances whether the merchants are or are not aboard his vessel. There is still another reason for this, namely, that no person can circumvent acts of fate.

Therefore, for the reasons listed above this article has been written.

289-Agreement Concluded by a Party Entrusted with the Command of a Vessel

If an owner of a vessel entrusts another party with its command, and the party accepting the command reaches some agreement or makes some promises to the person or persons who entrusted him with this command and then fails to fulfill these promises, and the parties from whom he had accepted the command suffer by his neglect any losses or damages, he shall reimburse them for all such losses and damages, even if it became necessary to sell the vessel. This provision obtains only if the issue involves the vessel.

Further, if the party who gave the vessel to another to command had suffered or was in danger of experiencing some damage by the negligence of the party who accepted the command, the latter shall pay all the damages and losses, if he has the means to do this. If the party who had taken the vessel under his command had no property and was unable to pay for such damages, he shall be turned over to the legal authorities, and shall be detained for so long until he is able either to pay such damages or to reach some agreement regarding this matter with the aggrieved party; everything that has been stated above should be done without any deceit or fraud.

Further, if the party who had accepted command of the vessel concluded some agreement or promised someone to do something and had failed to live up to his promises not to some fault of his own, neither he nor the party who entrusted the vessel to his care shall be liable for any damage to such a party to whom such promises were made, because the inability to carry out these promises happened without any omission on his part.

Let, therefore, everyone be most careful to whom he entrusts the command of his vessel and in what manner he does this, in order to avoid damages and not be liable in any manner whatsoever.

This article was written for the reasons given above.

290-Retaking a Captured Vessel

If a vessel after having been captured by an enemy craft is intercepted by a friendly vessel that had come upon the enemy vessel that had made this capture and as a result of this encounter the captured vessel is freed by the friendly unit, regardless of how this had been accomplished, the retaken vessel shall be returned to the owner or owners, together with all the effects aboard, provided the owners are alive, under the condition that the owners reward those who had rescued their vessel sufficiently and proportionally to the amount of trouble and expense they had suffered in doing this.

Further, the above should be taken to mean that the friendly vessel had recaptured the prize within the territorial waters and within the jurisdiction of the nation to which the prize belonged, or in some other waters or territory where the captors had not been able to moor the vessel, that is, to cast an anchor in a safe place; under such circumstances the procedure outlined above shall be followed.

If, however, the friendly vessel was able to retake the captured vessel from the enemies at a location where the friendly vessel had been properly moored and safeguarded, they need not be given a reward unless they themselves wish it, for the whole prize belongs to them, with everything aboard it, and no one can oppose this, and neither the local court of law nor anyone else can and should make any charges or claims against them.

Furthermore, if the enemy vessel that had taken such a prize noticed another vessel approaching and, fearing an encounter with such a vessel, abandoned the vessel that they had captured, and the vessel that caused the enemy craft to flee put aboard a prize crew on a vessel that had been abandoned, or took this vessel in tow in order to keep the booty, they shall return the retaken vessel to its proper owners provided these are still alive or to their relatives without any delay and reluctance, provided that these relatives will pay those who saved the vessel and all the cargo aboard it a suitable reward, in agreement to what had been stated above, if they can reach a mutual understanding. If the two parties could not reach a compromise, the matter shall be given to the Elders for disposition.

Further, if anyone abandons his vessel due to the fear of enemy craft, and another vessel intercepts such an abandoned craft, puts aboard it a prize crew, and sails it to a safe location, this is to mean that those who took such a vessel did not recapture it from an enemy, and the latter had not yet succeeded in taking it away from its rightful owners, such a vessel and its cargo shall not belong to the party who found it; however, the party who found such a vessel under such circumstances may demand a suitable reward in conformity with the well established marine customs. If the two interested parties could not reach an agreement, the dispute shall be given to the disposition of the Elders, because dependence upon the wisdom, sense of justice, and honesty of the Elders is always beneficial. It is also proper that one party would not wrong another, which one of the parties would be capable of doing, because no one knows, cannot know, and cannot be certain when he himself may be exposed to danger and ill treatment at the hands of others; therefore everyone should bring disputes before the Elders for their arbitration and especially in cases such as we have mentioned above or similar matters, in order that neither God nor people could ever and under any circumstances accuse him of any wrongdoing.

Further, it should be remembered that everything that has been said above shall be done without any deceit or fraud because very often he who believes that he has cheated and wronged another actually wrongs himself, for no one knows what can happen to him and his kin; let, therefore, no one under any circumstances cheat, defraud, or damage another, for he does not know what fate holds in store for him.

Further, any person aware of the fact that a given vessel is to proceed or had sailed to a territory where danger from an enemy can be expected would sail such a vessel in hope of doing damage to it or any other vessel for the reward he might receive or in order to take over such a vessel with all its cargo, or for any similar reason, should it be proved that he sailed out for the reasons and purposes mentioned above, shall not in case of an incident be given any reward or any part of the cargo from aboard such a vessel, even if the owners of the cargo had thrown and abandoned such cargo, or if their enemies had captured such a cargo, unless he can prove that he had not sailed for the purposes and reasons stated above.

Further, if it shall be proved that the latter sailed in order to wrong some specific person or any other party, whomever such a misfortune shall befall, for he is acting as an enemy would act, and even if he should bring in the vessel to a safe place, with or without the cargo, whether he found it abandoned or recaptured it from the enemy, as had been said before, he shall return everything to its rightful owner. Those who had sailed with the objectives mentioned above shall be imprisoned and turned over to justice, and they shall be treated as ordinary brigands, provided of course that the circumstances mentioned above shall be proved against them.

If it had been proved that they had not sailed with such evil intentions, and should they be able to retake a captured vessel from the enemy, or if they found an abandoned vessel under the circumstances mentioned above, their rights of salvage and reward shall be adjudged valid.

Further, should there be any doubt that these parties had sailed with evil intention mentioned above and if the accused were forced to disprove accusations made against them, neither the accused nor any of their fellow travelers or any other parties who could benefit or suffer in this issue, and finally, no person who is known by reputation of being avaricious, who could also be suspected of being easily bought, shall be allowed under any circumstances to offer any testimony in such an issue.

Further, if it should happen that the enemies after capturing the vessel or cargo abandon it of their free will and not from any fear of another vessel that they see approaching or that they expect will approach, anyone who finds such a vessel or cargo in a safe zone and takes possession of it shall not be allowed to keep all of the prize if he can find its owner. He shall, however, be properly rewarded according to the judgment of the local Elders at the location where he had brought in the vessel or the cargo, all circumstances and conditions mentioned above being taken into consideration.

If, on the other hand, the owner of the vessel or the cargo could not be found in proper time, the parties who had found this vessel or its cargo shall be given half of the total value as their reward; the other half of the salvage shall be disposed of in the manner explained and discussed in the article related to salvaged cargo. [94]

If the enemy craft that had captured such a vessel or its cargo and abandoned it not by their own volition but because they were forced to do so by a storm or fear of other vessels, the matter shall be adjudi-

---

94. Reference is made to Article 252, which in turn refers to Article 160.

ciated in the same manner as in a case where the enemy vessel forced them to surrender such captured prize; everything shall be done without any attempt at deceit or fraud in such matters.

If it should happen that the enemy arrived at a place where they would offer the captured prize for sale, the party or parties who would purchase such a vessel or cargo shall be required to return the items purchased to the parties from whom it was stolen, provided that the latter demand the return of such property and provided that they shall agree to reimburse the buyers of such property for the amount they paid for such cargo and even the profit that could be made on it, if the buyers demand that.

If, on the other hand, the enemy who captured the vessel or the cargo should present it to someone as a gift, such a gift shall not and cannot be considered as proper. If, however, the enemy should offer it back to the owner from whom they had taken it away without demanding any ransom, such a gift shall be proper and must be considered proper; in such circumstances no one can oppose this.

If it should happen that the enemy inform the patron of the vessel that they had captured, "We are returning your vessel without any ransom, but we demand you pay a ransom for the cargo aboard it," such a gift shall not be considered proper if the enemy was not located in a place that can be considered safe enough for them, so that they feel certain that they cannot lose the booty until they reach a place of safety. They could of course burn or drop the cargo into the deep waters if they wanted to do this; however, a vessel or cargo that is burned is of no value to anyone and no one can profit from it, neither friends nor enemies, thus both sides lose it.

Whatever had been said above about the vessel shall also apply to the cargo.

If it should happen that merchants or their friends shall pay the enemy ransom for the cargo aboard their vessel, the patron and his friends will be required to share in the payment of the ransom in proportion to the quality and quantity of their cargo as well as the full value of the vessel, and this must be done without any dispute; the above rules as had been stated above shall apply equally to a vessel in its relation to the cargo as well as the cargo in its relation to the vessel.

Further, if the enemy locate such a captured vessel or its cargo in a safe place, that is, if they took the prize out of the waters of their enemies, this means waters in which help could come to the vessel that they had captured, and then they sell or give the vessel or the cargo to someone, such a sale or a gift shall be considered valid and it must be so considered without any dispute or by action of any court, and no person can consider such action doubtful or suspicious. The person who had been so gifted by the enemy may make some concessions to those from whom the vessel was taken, if he so choose. However, no court or any other person can force him to do this, unless the party from whom the vessel or the cargo was taken can prove that deceit or fraud was used to accomplish this.

If fraud or deceit can be proved, such a gift cannot be adjudged legal or have any lasting effect; in fact, the deceit could have taken place under such circumstances that the party who accepted such a gift shall be jailed, and the court shall decree a judgment against his person and property, regardless of the deceiving method he adopted to accomplish this. If such a deceit is revealed, the vessel or the cargo shall be returned to the party from whom it was taken without any opposition whatsoever.

If it should happen that such enemies sell the captured vessel or its cargo, such a sale shall be considered valid and must be so considered, provided that the buyers will be able to prove that such a sale took place when the enemies were located in a safe territory, this is to say, that they had the vessel moored.

If it should happen that the buyers of such cargo would state that they bought the cargo under justifiable and proper circumstances, but will be unable to prove this, such a sale cannot be considered valid; and, if the patron of the vessel or the owner of the cargo that had been captured should appear and can prove that the vessel belongs to him, it will be necessary to return the vessel to him. Should any dispute develop over this matter, it shall be submitted to arbitration of the Elders or the courts in order to avoid any deceit. Should any deceit and fraud be proved, the party guilty of such conduct shall be required to repay the aggrieved party all the damages, costs, and losses suffered, while the party guilty of such deceit shall be turned over to justice.

Further, if a patron of a vessel or his representative regain the vessel or the cargo, regardless of the conditions under which he regained them, he shall be required to pay all the interested parties their share of the investment they had in the vessel or the cargo at the moment it was seized by the enemy, provided that they share in the cost expended in regaining these possessions, each of them in proportion to the value of his investment.

If the patron had been able to regain some of the cargo and had made an agreement to regain the vessel and the rest of the cargo and he had done this with the approval of the majority or all of the shareholders, in case it will become necessary he shall force them through legal channels to fulfill their part of the obligation in this matter.

Their promises in this matter are as obligatory and valid as when they make a promise to invest in purchasing a vessel or constructing a new vessel.

Further, if the patron made such an agreement without the approval of the majority or all of the shareholders, they shall not be obligated to any action that would be against their will. On his part the patron will not be obligated to acknowledge their share in the vessel and its contents that they had possessed when the vessel had been taken by the enemy, as long as he will make an accounting of the matter relating to the vessel and the cargo as of the moment before it was taken as a prize by the enemy.

Further, if these shareholders wish to ransom their holdings and the patron opposes this, he shall be ordered to proceed to ransom their holdings by a court order. The patron should not hesitate or refuse to accomplish this for any reason whatsoever as long as these shareholders agree to pay the full amount due for the ransom, proportionately to the amount of their investment. It would, therefore, not be proper and just that another party should have any more right and privilege to the property of a person than the owner of such property who wishes to make some disposition of that which belongs to him.

The above restrictions should be understood in this manner, that if a patron or some other person acting as his representative should ransom or repurchase the vessel or the cargo from the enemy or from other parties who may have acquired such property in a legal manner, and if the shareholders of such property would refuse to pay the expenses incurred, the patron or person who had acted as his representative in such a transaction should appeal several times to the shareholders to reconsider this matter. If they should absolutely refuse to pay for such expenses, the patron should if he so wishes sell such property with the permission of the court at a public auction to the highest bidder.

If it should happen that the investment the shareholders had in the vessel or the cargo shall exceed the cost of the ransom or repurchase, they shall reimburse the patron of the vessel for the difference in the amount, each of them in proportion to the amount of his investment.

The above should be taken to mean the following: that the patron is willing to proceed in this matter, for he cannot be either forced to do this, nor is he obligated to do this. The patron of the vessel, or the actual owner of such property, or the person who acted in his stead and ransomed or repurchased such property, has a prior claim to keep such goods at the price he paid for them, if the patron should not agree to sell such property at a public auction.

If it should happen that the amount received for the vessel or cargo was insufficient to pay for the ransom or repurchase of either, the patron or his representative who ransomed or repurchased such property without the approval of the shareholders cannot force them to reimburse them for the difference, unless they willingly agree to do this. It is, therefore, just and proper that the patron or the party acting as his representative who had ransomed or repurchased such property should be able to have prior claim to keep such property and sell it to anyone who offers a bigger price for it, because he had taken a risk that he would have been required to assume the consequences of, had there been a loss in such a transaction. It should be remarked that if some of the shareholders would express a desire to retain possession of such property, they shall also be required to share in any possible losses in the amount proportionate to the amount of their investment.

Everything that has been stated above as well as all the reservations and circumstances enumerated shall be carried out in good faith. This refers to the situation when the enemy had accepted the ransom in a safe location and remained in such location while the deal was negotiated, and there was no attempt to deceit and fraud in all these negotiations.

291-A Cargo of Lumber

When a vessel takes aboard a load of lumber in order to deliver it to some destination, and there has been no agreement concluded between the master of the vessel and the merchants as to the amount that will be charged for transporting such a cargo, the patron may retain half of the cargo in lieu of the lading charges, and neither the legal authority nor the merchants nor anyone else can under any circumstance oppose this, because it had been so decided and it had been the custom to do this from the moment our ancestors began to sail throughout this world, and had decided and ordered that such a procedure be adopted and followed; therefore, all should act as had been decreed from time immemorial, and in no other manner.

However, if the merchants to whom the lumber belonged had informed the master before the vessel was cargoed that they wished to reach a decision on the amount of the lading charges, and the patron answered them that this will not be necessary because he will agree to accept any just amount they determine should be paid him, and the merchants relying on his assurance in this matter load their cargo aboard, they will not be required later on to give him half of the cargo in lieu of the lading fees, because they had cargoed the vessel under the condition indicated above and the patron cannot demand that they allow him to keep half of the cargo because he had agreed to the conditions mentioned above. The merchants shall be required to pay him an adequate lading fee, equal in amount to the fee paid for such cargo at the place where it had been loaded aboard, or the amount that can be agreed upon with the patron.

If it should happen that the merchants cannot reach an agreement with the patron as to the amount that should be paid for his services, the matter shall be submitted to arbitration by the Elders, and whatever they decide shall be carried out. The above shall be interpreted to mean the following: that the merchants will be able to substantiate their claims by witnesses under oath or by a written document, that they had relied on the conditions and stipulations made by the patron in this matter. If they are unable to prove this, they shall be forced to give the patron half of their cargo of lumber in lieu of the lading feeds due him.

292-Contractual Validity

If an agreement had been concluded between specific parties fully conversant with the issues involved concerning any matter, and such an agreement was entered into in the proper location, [95] all parties concerned shall abide by its terms and carry them out completely. Therefore, any agreement concluded in a proper place between people fully aware of its terms and entered into for justifiable reason shall be carried out by all parties concerned.

If it should happen that one of the parties to the agreement should fail to fulfill its obligations, and the second party or parties to such an agreement should be damaged due to the unfulfillment of the agreement by the party of the first part, the latter shall be required to repay all such damages suffered without any opposition.

Further, excluded from this obligation shall be a situation in which the party that had failed to carry out such an agreement did this for justifiable and well established obstacles; if these impediments can be proved, that party who had failed to carry out the terms of the agreement shall not be liable for any damages suffered by the party of the second part, because of the impossibility of carrying out such an agreement. If, however, no such impediment could be proved, the guilty party shall pay the damages as mentioned above.

If, on the other hand, the party that had failed to carry out the terms of the agreement can prove that this happened due to the fault

---

95. Reference is made to Article 252, in which agreements are more fully discussed.

or carelessness of the second party to the agreement, and if due to this the party of the first part would suffer any damages or losses, the party or parties who had been negligent in this matter shall pay for all the damages and losses and shall do this without any opposition.

Everything that has been stated above shall be executed without any deceit or fraud, provided that neither of the parties was prevented from the fulfillment of its obligations by some well established impediment.

For this reason the above article has been written.

293 –Substitution or Falsification of the Bill of Lading

If a merchant sold some cargo to another, and the buyer did not see and did not wish to inspect such cargo, trusting the seller's description of the merchandise, who had informed him that he is selling him premium quality merchandise, and after being so reassured, the buyer purchased such merchandise, but later it is discovered that the cargo was not of the quality as represented and actually is of very poor quality or spoiled when it is unpacked at the site where it had been delivered, the seller shall be forced to pay the buyer the full amount such cargo would have been worth at the place where he had taken it to sell, had it been of the quality described by the seller.

In addition, if any buyer should suffer any damages, losses, and expenses by such misrepresentation of cargo, the seller shall be liable for any damages resulting, and must pay for them without any delay. In addition, if the buyer had suffered other losses due to the fact that he could not regain his money from such a misrepresentation and invest it in some other venture, the seller shall be forced to pay him the full amount, proportionately to the amount and value of such cargo, had he been able to sell it and invest the money he had received for it in order to make additional profit by trading in goods that were not misrepresented as to value and quality, and a deposition made by him under oath shall be accepted as prima facie evidence of the possibility of such an accomplishment. Everything that has been stated above shall be carried out without any attempt at deception or fraud.

Further, if, on the other hand, the seller informed the buyer that he is selling him the cargo as is, and stated: "Inspect this cargo, or order someone to inspect it, and either take it or leave it," and if the purchaser agreed to take the cargo, either after inspecting it or not inspecting it, the seller shall be free from any other responsibility or liability toward the buyer, regardless of the fact that the buyer may lose or profit on such a transaction, unless the seller would be willing to accept some liability in this matter for the transaction took place in the manner and under the conditions described above. If it should become necessary, however, the conditions under which such a transaction was made shall be proved.

This article was written for the reasons stated above.

294-Charges of Misrepresentation Brought Against the Beneficiaries of the Patron by the Shareholders

If the patron of a vessel or the clerk acting in his name makes an accounting of all the profits and losses with the majority or all of the shareholders, or if such an accounting is made for some other reason, the party who prepared such a statement and the shareholders who had accepted it, whether all of them or a majority, and regardless of whether the patron of their vessel shall remain alive for a long or a short time, and shall reside in the same location as the shareholders, or shall continue to sail and shall return to the place of the residence of the majority or all of the shareholders after completing each journey or several journeys, or after giving them an accounting of his transactions shall proceed on a journey, and after a short or a long period of time while sailing, due to the will of God, shall die, when his vessel returns from the journey during which he died, the majority or all of the shareholders shall be able, if they claim that they found some mistakes or misrepresentations in the last statement given them, take action against the property or the beneficiaries of the patron or other persons who have control of his estate.

If the deceased had made an accounting to the shareholders and had left a last will in which he had indicated that he was aware of the mistake or misrepresentation in such an accounting, and would admit wronging the shareholders, such mistakes or misrepresentations shall be remedied without any hesitance and dispute, even if it was necessary to sell all the property left by the deceased, and neither the beneficiary nor anyone else can object to this, with the exception of the sailors, if they had not received their wages.

If it should happen that the deceased as had been mentioned above left a will but did not mention such a mistake, his beneficiaries shall not be obliged to pay the shareholders anything whatsoever, unless it can be proved that in the entries the patron had made in the register there had been mistakes or misrepresentations. It would have to be proved that such entries were made in the register by the deceased personally and not by another party. If the entries were made by the clerk, he shall be summoned, if he is alive, in order to ascertain if there actually had been any errors or misrepresentations made. No other records can be accepted as valid evidence in this matter.

If no such register could be found in which the deceased while still alive had made entries regarding the accounting he had made to the shareholders, but the latter could produce a bona fide copy of such a register prepared by the same clerk, but not any other register, it would be immaterial whether such a clerk is alive or deceased, if on the basis of such a register it could be demonstrated and proved that mistakes or misrepresentations had been made, the estate of the deceased and his beneficiaries shall be liable to its full value for the amounts due to the shareholders caused by such error or misrepresentation.

If it should happen that the deceased after having made an accounting to the shareholders and while still alive had not prepared any last will, but there should be found a register or an authentic copy of it, as had been stated above, and on the basis of its contents corrections can be made, such corrections shall be made in the manner indicated above.

If he had not left a will and no register is found, there may arise serious disputes and troubles. In such situations the matters at issue shall be turned over to those who care for the welfare of the soul; an attempt shall be made to discover if the deceased had a confessor to whom he confessed his sins;[96] should such a confessor be found, the matter shall be given to him for arbitration. If, however, his confessor cannot be found, the matter shall be given for arbitration to people who live in love and fear of God, who are religious, trustworthy, and of high reputation. If such persons accept this matter for adjudication, they shall summon all the shareholders and administer an oath to each of them that they will testify truly about the erroneous entries in the accounts, explain what they based their reason for making such a statement, and also explain how such irregularities could have arisen; the Elders who will be arbitrating this issue must take in consideration the reputation and the status of the shareholders being examined.

Furthermore, they shall not accept the mere testimony of the shareholders; the latter shall be able to present creditable witnesses to substantiate their claims, and such witnesses shall be disinterested parties to the dispute and cannot profit or lose anything due to the outcome of such an issue, and this is proper, and justice demands that no one be allowed to offer testimony in a case that could in some manner benefit him or cause him damage, unless the parties to such a dispute agree to allow these persons to testify. Whatever the

---

96. The "seal of confession" would have prevented a Roman Catholic priest from revealing any matter heard in the confession.

Elders decide in such a case shall be carried out and no other action shall be allowed to be taken.

For these reasons this article has been written.

295-Removal of Equipment from a Vessel after It Had Been Cargoed

If a master of a vessel took aboard a cargo of some merchants at some designated location, and subsequently at the same location or some other location for whatever necessary reason will be forced to reduce the load of the cargo aboard as a safety measure for the vessel, and will also command that in order to further lighten the load, sails, anchors, or some other equipment be taken off the vessel, and this is done before the cargo is completely stored aboard, and due to this some damage or destruction takes place, if it can be proved that such damage or destruction happened due to the negligence of the patron, he shall be liable for and must pay the damage.

If the patron was without any means and was unable to pay the merchants for the damage suffered, it shall be proper, if he can be apprehended, to turn him over to the legal authorities, as would have been done in a case when the cargo had been specifically entrusted to his care, for every patron of a vessel must be treated and considered similarly to a party who had assumed control over all matters that occur in the relationship between the merchants and the owners of the vessel, of which we need not speak here.

This article was written for the reasons given above.

296-Lading Fees Assessed for Loss of Cargo Thrown Overboard

There are many opinions regarding the manner in which lading fees should share in the damages due to cargo being thrown overboard, one side arguing that all of the lading fees received shall be used for that purpose, the other side claiming that if the patron of the vessel had been paid lading fees for the cargo salvaged as well as for the cargo thrown overboard, he shall only share in the damage with the fees he had received for the cargo saved, and finally, still others maintain that if the patron had not taken charges for the cargo thrown overboard, he should not be forced to share for the loss of the cargo thrown overboard in any degree. Every merchant or any other person who has expressed such convictions has been fully convinced that his interpretation is proper and should be adhered to.

For these reasons our ancestors who first sailed throughout the world to many places and localities, having become aware of the diversity of opinions, had mutually agreed and determined the method that shall be used in order to satisfy all concerned, and to prevent disputes and misunderstandings that could arise between the merchants and patrons, as well as other persons who may be the interested parties in such matters. With this objective in mind they unsparingly and with much effort and in order to reap the blessings of God and to gain the love and gratitude of the people, and in order to put an end to disputes and differences of opinion had declared and proclaimed what has been written and ordered in this article.

The full amount of the lading charges that the merchants or other persons had agreed to pay the patron shall be paid to him without any opposition, unless there were some agreements or special restrictions made between the patron of the vessel and the merchants or other persons, while the patrons of vessels shall share in the damages resulting from the cargo being thrown overboard to the full extent of the money they had been paid for carrying such cargo on a specific journey by the merchants or other persons.

Further, the above shall be taken to mean this, that the patrons of vessels shall be allowed to subtract from the full amount received in lading charges the wages of the crew, the cost of feeding the crew, and other legitimate expenses incurred during such a journey. Whatever is left over shall be accounted for by the patron or his representative acting together with the merchants or their representatives; if, however, the merchants are willing to accept the statement of accounts issued by the patron, they may do so.

In this manner, therefore, patrons of vessels are required to share in the damages due to the fact that cargo had to be thrown overboard in the net amount of the lading fees they had received from the merchants for the journey during which the cargo had to be thrown overboard, proportionally and in the same degree as the cargo saved shall share in the damages for the cargo lost.

If it should happen that some or all of the merchants demand that the patron share in the damages for the cargo thrown overboard on the return voyage, that is, with the lading fees he had received from the same or other merchants, for other cargo, or even the same cargo if he is taking it back, the patrons shall not be required to do this under any circumstances, because the damage due to the cargo being thrown overboard had already been adjusted in the previous voyage, and also because the cargo carried on the return voyage is neither the same cargo nor does it belong to the same merchants, and thus they are not obliged to share in any damage that had taken place on another voyage, and there is no logical reason why they should be forced or obligated in any manner. Thus, for the reasons listed above and many other reasons, a patron is not obligated under any circumstances to share in the damages resulting from cargo being thrown overboard on one voyage to pay such damage from the lading fees he received for carrying cargo on a return voyage.

This article was written for the reasons listed, which in no way are contradictory to reasons listed in some of the previous articles.[97]

297-When a Patron and His Crew Attempt to Withdraw from Proceeding on a Voyage

If a master had hired or shall hire a crew to serve aboard his vessel for a specific voyage, the crew must undertake and complete such a voyage, unless they can refuse to undertake such a voyage upon the conditions and circumstances already stated in one of the preceding articles, which had discussed this matter; everything stated above shall be carried out without any deceit or fraud.[98]

If it should happen that the patron of the vessel after hiring the crew aboard his vessel would wish to excuse himself from undertaking the journey, without justifiable reason, and actually because he wants to remain behind, and if the voyage for which he had hired the crew and leased the vessel had as its destination a dangerous and a suspicious area, the crew may if it wishes refuse to proceed on such a journey if the patron of the vessel had refused to undertake it, as stated above.

Further, if, however, the patron wished to remain behind for some well established and justifiable reasons, of which he had informed the members of the crew at the time they were being hired, he may remain behind. The crew, however, shall not be able to refuse to proceed on this journey, unless they have reasons that had been discussed in the article mentioned.

Further, if the patron wishes to remain behind and does remain behind for justifiable or not justifiable reasons, and the crew is willing to undertake the voyage and is ready to sail, the patron is required to provide a capable person to replace him aboard the vessel, who shall be required to fulfill all the obligations toward the crew as had been agreed at the time of the enlistment. Such a statement shall be read in the presence of the party who hired the crew as well as the crew itself and the person who is replacing the patron as master of this vessel. In this manner the sailors shall be obligated to obey the commands and carry out all the reasonable orders of the party who had been given command of the vessel, and who had replaced the pa-

---

97. Reference is made to Articles 70 to 99, 111, 112, 131, 132, 187. 257, 284, and 295.

98. Reference is made to Article 156.

tron, in the same manner in which they had obligated themselves to serve the party with whom they had reached an agreement to serve aboard the vessel.

If it should happen that the party who had hired the sailors and who had been the patron of the vessel at that time, should say the following to the sailors: "I give command of my vessel to such and such a person and give him to you and make him a patron, that you will act toward him in the same manner as you had promised to act toward me, if I would undertake this voyage myself," at the moment these words are uttered and without renouncing his obligations to the sailors, but obligating the sailors to carry out all the agreements that had been concluded between them, the sailors shall thereafter carry out all provisions to which they had agreed and obligated themselves toward him, toward the person whom he had constituted as a patron of the vessel.

Further, should the sailors fail to carry out their obligations toward the party who had been appointed their patron, which they had promised they would do to the party who hired them, the latter may demand at will and at any time that they carry out these obligations and see to it that they are carried out.

If, however, the sailors fulfill and carry out all their responsibilities toward the party who had been appointed their patron, as they had agreed, and while they are aboard the vessel, the party constituted their patron shall conclude some agreement with them regarding the direction of the journey or some other matter, and this new agreement should become a cause of dispute between them, that is, between the party who had been appointed the patron and the sailors, he who had renounced his authority and entrusted it to the party who had negotiated a new agreement, the former cannot take any action against the sailors in his own name in reference to the newly made agreement and should not attempt to do this under any condition. The sailors shall not be accountable to him, and no person or judge can force them to do this for the reasons mentioned in this article.

Nevertheless, if the person who had been given command of the vessel surrendered it to the party who had given him the command, he may act upon the dispute but not in his own name, but in the name of the former master of the vessel. If he acts in the capacity, as had been mentioned above, the sailors shall be accountable to him, but they shall not be accountable under other circumstances.

Further, if the party who had accepted the vessel under his command had caused some damage to the vessel, in any manner whatsoever, the party that had given the latter party command may take action against him; we will not discuss or explain such a situation in

229

detail, as everyone knows very well what he should do and what he should not do in such circumstances.

This article was written and explained for the reason given above.

Thus far we have discussed laws and ordinances relating to sea and commerce; now we will present ordinances relating to laws and rights of armed naval units.

PART III

ORDINANCES RELATING TO ALL ARMED SHIPS ENGAGING

IN PRIVATEERING AND ARMED NAVAL EXPEDITIONS

298-The Admiral, the Captain, and the Outfitters

Firstly, the admiral, captain, and the outfitters[99] shall pledge an oath that they shall render an honest accounting of the prizes captured by the ship to the owners of that ship, owners of galleys and assault boats[100] and that after paying for the provisions and equipment that had been bought on credit and after paying off the loan that had been taken out in the name of such a ship, they shall pay out each of the naval units its proper share of the booty and that in this manner they shall pay for all the expenses of each of these units out of the proceeds of the prize.

If it should happen that aboard such a ship there should be a party who had extended credit to the ship or made a loan beneficial to the ship, and had done this on the orders of the admiral and the outfitters providing such money from his personal possessions, the admiral should repay him the amount he had advanced from the proceeds of the first capture made by the ship and its auxiliary naval units.

This article was written for this reason, that many such ships would have to be disarmed if their commanders did not procure a loan and give proper guarantee of repayment of such loans, thus making it impossible for such ships to undertake such voyages.

299-Procedure to Be Followed Aboard Armed Ships in Dividing Spoils and Expenses

It should also be made known how to treat people sailing aboard such ships; they shall be required to pay their share of the expenses of the ship, as if they remained permanently aboard the ship. De-

---

99. An outfitter leased a ship from its owner, fitted it out with guns, armaments, armor, and other necessities, and paid its owners an agreed portion of the captured booty.

100. This craft, corresponding in size to a modern life boat, was usually armed with one cannon and used as an assault or diversionary weapon.

pendent upon the position of such a person, he shall share in a large or small degree in the booty, depending on the time he remained aboard the ship. For example, if a person came aboard the vessel and remained aboard for ten days or a month or two months, or a similar period of time, and other persons had remained aboard for a year or longer, and on two or three occasions outfitted the ship from captured booty or made loans to the ship, it is only proper that those who remained aboard the ship longer receive a larger share of the prizes.

Nevertheless, the admiral, captain, chief navigator, steward, and the clerk shall remember that they shall be under oath to consider the status and the services rendered by those aboard when they divide the booty. There could be aboard someone who had distinguished himself by bravery and had become such a good soldier that he should actually receive a larger portion than a person who may have been aboard the ship a longer period of time.

300-Commanders of Galleys and Other Smaller Armed Vessels[101]

Any commander of a galley or a smaller craft privateering alone and not in a convoy or an armada belonging to a state, and paying his own expenses, shall receive one-fifth of the booty captured, and all members of his crew shall obey him as if he were a subaltern of an admiral.

On the other hand, if such a vessel is sailing in the wake of a ship or in convoy with other ships, and if such a craft had received a subsidy of ten bezans from the official ship,[102] the subaltern in charge shall keep three bezans. If he had been given a subsidy of five bezans, he is entitled to keep two. If the subsidy consisted of five bezans, the subaltern shall keep two, the captain of that vessel one, and the navigator the remaining two bezans.

If the subsidy consisted of more than five bezans, the division shall be made by the admiral and the crew of the vessel receiving the subsidy, but in all cases where the subsidy was over five bezans, the

---

101. The position of these subalterns or junior commanders had been established in 1266 by an ordinance promulgated by King Alphonse of Castille, which stated in part: "Subalterns are called persons who command under the authority of an admiral. Each of them may command the people aboard his own ship..."

102. Flagship.

sub-commander shall receive three. Whether the subsidy amounts to more or less, the procedure of dividing it shall be the same.

If, in addition, the above sub-commander shall capture a vessel in a battle, and this had been an armed vessel, he shall be entitled to keep the personal arms of the sub-commander of the captured vessel, or may even change such weapons for some of better quality until the completion of the journey.

In addition, out of each prize taken in battle, regardless whether the captured unit was a galley or some other type of vessel, he shall be allowed to keep one anchor and the flag that the vessel flew. In addition, he shall receive one and a half portions of the cargo of such vessel.

All persons aboard the galley or other craft shall be subject to all the orders of the sub-commander.

301-Junior Commanders

A junior commander shall take an oath pledging to the admiral and the crew of the vessel that he will command that he shall not sail against their will upon his own volition, and that he shall not cut the tow line attached to his vessel, unless this would make it impossible for him to navigate the vessel. Should he be forced to cut the tow line, he will replace it immediately with another.

Should he cut the line or order it cut for some other reason, he shall be adjudged a deceitful and disloyal person. Should it happen that he cut such a tow line because of hate or betrayal, and anyone can prove his motivation, he shall be impaled on a stake.

302-Agreements

Let us begin with the ship and provisions aboard it. The admiral, outfitters, captain, and all the rest who had equipped the ship shall act in accordance with the terms of their agreement and understanding. Upon demand, the admiral and the captain shall announce the terms of these agreements; however they need not do this if no one demands it.

Further, the admiral shall authorize the clerk to announce these terms, and the clerk shall inform all those on shore or aboard the vessel who are enlisting for service aboard such a ship. Just as the outfitters of the ship may enter into any agreements that they wish, similarly, people who are enlisting for service aboard such a vessel should be aware of these agreements, in order that they may decide whether they wish to sail aboard such a ship or not.

It should also be known into how many parts the ship shall divide the captured prize.

If a ship is sailing in convoy with small galleys or some other small armed units, and if aboard all the units in this convoy there are one thousand in the crews, there shall be a provision made for dividing all captured booty into six thousand two hundred shares. If the ship and all the other armed units in the convoy have a combined crew of five hundred men, the booty shall be divided into three thousand and one hundred shares. If the combined crews number two hundred and fifty men, there shall be fifteen hundred and fifty shares provided. Finally, if the ship with all the auxiliary units had the combined crew of one hundred and fifty persons, there shall be seven hundred and seventy-five shares created; and in the proportion to the number of the crew shall be created the number of shares.[103]

These shares shall be awarded to the personnel aboard depending on their bravery and on the efficiency with which they carried out their duties.

Further, the captain, the chief navigator, stewards, and ranking officers of each division aboard the ship shall swear[104] an oath that they shall conduct themselves according to a code prescribed by the three best navigators aboard the ship, as well as that of the three sailors of the prow, two stewards, two crossbowmen with their leader, that they shall do nothing while in the exercise of their office to favor any of their relatives, or in expectation of receiving some gifts from anyone, or for having received a gift, that in agreement with the wishes of the whole crew aboard the ship, they shall tell the truth to all parties and that they shall divide the spoils honestly in the presence of the admiral and reward those who deserve to be rewarded.

They shall be required to award such portion to the admiral, as they do to all others, if he is worthy of such an award, and if there is any booty, they shall also reward the stewards, the navigators, crossbowman, or anyone else.

---

103. There actually is an error in the original manuscript. It should read 125 persons, instead of 150.

104. Actually, a section leader, similar to a position of a Petty Officer in present day U.S. Navy.

Aboard every privateer ship having a crew of one thousand men, there shall be one hundred sailors, sixteen navigators, and twenty-four sailors of the prow; if the crew numbers five hundred, there shall be twelve navigators; if it should number two hundred and fifty, there shall be eight navigators.

The clerk and the chief navigator shall receive the same pay as the other navigators, dependent upon the agreement made by the admiral and the chief navigator; thus if the admiral had promised him one thousand morabatins in addition to the ten shares of booty due him, he shall be given his due. It will be necessary, however, that the captain and the chief clerk be present at the time they made such an agreement, and that the navigator would be proficient in his calling, or he may be removed from his post and another navigator put in his position. In addition, the clerk, similar to the navigator, shall receive ten shares of booty, and the shares received by the chaplain and the doctor aboard the ship shall equal those of the navigator. [105]

If it should happen that the navigator or a sailor or any other member of the crew is actually not versed in the work for which he had enlisted or does not know how to perform it properly, he shall be dealt with as had been ordered above in dealing with a navigator guilty of the same indiscretion.

And now let us return to the division of spoils. After the amount expended on provisions and the share due to the ship had been deducted from the captured booty, the commanders, that is to say, the admiral, captain, and the outfitters shall proceed to sell at auction, under the penalty of losing their own shares if this is not done in eight days, all the captured booty, and after the sale has been completed shall divide the proceeds within a period of four days.

This article has been written in order to prevent the admirals, captains, and other outfitters from telling their crew members to wait on the shore for their share so long that they could suffer many losses and incur many expenses.

---

105. *Morabatin, morabatine,* or *almorabitino* was a gold coin minted in Spain and Portugal very similar to a gold coin in size and appearance minted from the year 1087 in the Arab territories. It weighed 3.83 to 4.18 grams and was made of pure gold. Even though minted in Christian states, it often carried Arabic inscriptions and legends written in Latin but in Kufic alphabet.

Further, the admiral shall authorize the clerk and the chief navigator to procure the necessary amount of supplies and to keep these supplies in reserve until the moment the vessel shall be auctioned off, for this reason, in order that the clerk would be able to pay them an advance on their share of the booty to provide them with means of livelihood. If the ship had captured prizes that will permit this after payment of the loans and obligations, the navigator and the clerk, depending on the evaluation they place on the booty, shall be able to sell more of it in order to disburse larger amounts of money among the crew members in order that they may not only pay for the sustenance but also clothe themselves; it is necessary, however, that the booty be large enough to pay for the above mentioned payments. For this work the clerk shall be paid two millares, of which half will belong to the navigator.

The clerk is required to keep an account of the sum each member of the crew received. If anyone had received more than he should have, the clerk shall be held accountable, because it was for this reason that the clerk and the navigator had received two millares. Both of them, therefore, should keep accurate records for all aboard the vessel as well as for the outfitters of the ship.

Such are the functions of the clerk and the navigator in all privateering expeditions as well as aboard all armed ships and other naval craft.

305-The Admiral

The admiral may reward any one he selects with two, three or five, or even ten shares of the booty, and the number of persons selected for this may be from five to eight.

The admiral may summon the section leaders and declare that they shall receive one more share than the rest of the crew, but only after a consultation and agreement of those who had apportioned the shares among the crew.

The admiral may reward each of the officers provided that each of them was a good officer and that the crew will agree to this. Everything that has been stated above was written and decreed in the same manner as the contents of other articles.

306-Ordinances Governing Privateering Expeditions

In conformity with customs relating to privateering by vessels or by galleys that carry oars (it shall be understood that a vessel that is not equipped with oars, but has a crow's-nest, is classified in the same category as a ship) it has been ordained as follows:

Let us begin with an admiral who commands the armada. First of all he shall pledge an oath to the outfitters that he shall exercise all caution, that he will loyally perform his office, and that he shall take proper care of the ship and the interests of the shareholders who had outfitted him, that is, both the ship and the equipment, which he had faithfully promised to do to the outfitters.

The party who owns the ship, or who had given the admiral his position aboard such ship, shall order the navigator, under the penalty for perjury, that he should give him a list of all essential needs of the ship in order to undertake such an expedition. The above mentioned navigator together with the officers of the stern, called navigators aboard all privateers, numbering three to eight, shall inspect the ship and inform the admiral under oath, in order that they tell the truth, what is needed aboard the ship. Everything that the chief navigator in company with other navigators state under oath shall be relayed to the outfitters by the admiral, who shall also be under oath, in order that he too would not tell them more or less but only the truth. If the admiral should proceed in any other manner, he shall forfeit the ten shares of spoils that were due him and that shall be added to the share the crew will receive, regardless of whether the ship belongs to him or to other parties. In addition, he shall be punished, and the penalty shall be the usual penalty given aboard a ship to anyone who commits perjury, for such penalty must be imposed on any guilty party, from the most important to the humblest.

In addition, if the navigator entered into a conspiracy with him to lie about the equipment and other effects, such a navigator shall lose all his shares of the booty that would be due him as well as all weapons captured that will rightfully accrue to the crew.

In addition, the admiral shall order that everything that has been stated about the equipment by the navigator shall be reduced to writing and shown to the outfitters; if the navigator failed to tell the truth, he shall be liable to the punishment mentioned above.

The admiral shall conduct himself in a similar manner toward the merchants, under the penalty mentioned above.

The merchants shall be responsible for carrying out all the obligations they had assumed toward the admiral under the threat of payment of a double fine.

The admiral is required upon the demand of the navigator and any other person aboard to tell how much money he had received for the expenses of the vessel and for the provisions of all aboard and also whether he had taken out any loan.

In addition, the admiral shall not engage any of his relatives as a navigator under the penalty mentioned above, unless he does this with the approval of the outfitters, the captain, and the shareholders in the vessel.

Let it also be known that the admiral cannot commission a captain nor can a captain commission someone an admiral without the approval of the outfitters.[106]

In addition, neither the admiral nor the captain can discharge any person from a responsible position because of spite, but only for improper behavior or brawling, or for his inability to perform his duties, which must be attested to by the whole crew; only under such a circumstance can such party be removed from his position and another take his place. However, the admiral may take on a less qualified person, after consultation with the crew.

The admiral shall state under oath that he shall carry out all the promises he shall make to anyone, whether that be a shareholder in the ship, an outfitter, a navigator, a section leader, an armed sailor, servant, merchant, whether such party be a Saracen, a Christian, or a Jew. Everything that he had promised to some officer of his ship, whether he had made such a promise aboard the ship or on land, he shall fulfill, as he had promised, provided that such an officer shall be capable of fulfilling the obligations of his office as he had promised the admiral he was capable of doing. Should he be incapable of fulfilling these responsibilities that he had taken upon himself, the admiral shall not be obligated to carry out the terms of the agreement he had made with such officer, and shall be able to replace him aboard his ship with another more reliable officer.

In addition, the admiral shall ask the advice of the whole crew when he is about to depart from a given locality.

He shall also do this when he attempts to negotiate a loan while on the high seas or wishes to accept anything from friends.

Similarly, when he is about to attack another vessel, when he changes vessels, or barters for other supplies.

Similarly, when it pertains to some equipment or other essential items.

An admiral sailing on the basis of share of booty may replenish his supplies, but only with the approval of the outfitters and shareholders.

Further, an admiral or any commander of any vessel cannot sell

---

106. A captain could not elevate someone to a higher rank than his own. The above probably refers to a situation when an admiral died or resigned, and the captain took over his functions temporarily and proposed someone to the outfitters of the ship as a candidate for that position.

or give away any equipment valued at more than five bezans without knowledge of the outfitters and shareholders. If the value of such items exceeded five bezans, he should ask the consent of the whole crew; if the majority and one more of them agree, he may proceed, even though the other smaller half of the crew objected.

However, the above shall be agreed to by all those who are navigators, officers of the prow, but especially of all, the shareholders and outfitters who will together with the crew constitute the majority of all interested parties.

Further, the admiral shall summon the stewards with the approval and knowledge of the navigators, sailors, crossbowmen and armed sailors, that is, one navigator, one of the shareholders who is also an outfitter, one sailor, and one crossbowman, or one sailor armed with pickaxe. In conformity with what the majority of these decide, the stewards and authenticators shall be summoned. [107]

The admiral may summon the officers of the bow after seeking the opinion of the navigator, for the navigator is well versed with the opinion of the sailors.

The admiral may summon and appoint one of the crossbowmen their section leader with the approval of the captain.

The admiral may appoint a standard bearer with the approval of the captain.

The admiral may appoint personnel to guard the Saracens and the food supplies.

The admiral may appoint the lookouts, rudder tillers, and the senior guards.

307-The Navigator

The navigator should receive a reward, that is to say, should he capture any weapons, he may use them until the journey is completed; wherever he procures food, it shall belong to him. All the items that he has taken while capturing a vessel and that are worth less than five bezans shall belong to him. Should he capture any animals, he shall be entitled to one as his reward.

The navigator can demand that all necessary equipment aboard the vessel be furnished.

In the event new supplies are loaded aboard the vessel, the navigator is entitled to one and one-fourth shares as part of his reward.

The navigator shall receive ten shares of the booty, and when ad-

---

107. Authenticators were official witnesses with power but no seal of a notary public.

ditional booty is shared, he may get more, dependent on the approval of the crew.

The navigator may buy the vessel that is offered by bidding for one bezan less than any other bidder.

The navigator is entitled to receive one mainsail unfurled at the sailing yard; if there is no such sail aboard, he shall take any sail he chooses.

308-Sailors of the Prow

The sailors of the prow should be under the command of helmsman of the stern; they shall care for all the equipment and guard it.

They should receive one anchor chain and one anchor. The anchor chain they receive shall be the best of all the chains attached to the anchor. If there should be no chains attached to the anchor, they should be given the best anchor found aboard the vessel, and each of them shall receive five shares of the booty.

When the matter of division of spoils as a reward for services rendered is undertaken aboard the ship, the navigator, two sailors of the prow, and two stewards shall take an oath that they shall designate as recipients of such rewards only the best of the personnel and that they shall not be motivated in this matter either by any monetary considerations, friendship, or amity.

Should some sailor of the prow fail to take the arms he was to have been equipped with, the admiral and the captain may supply such weapons for him, at the price they decide arbitrarily and that shall be deductible from the amount of his future share in the spoils.

309-Crossbowmen

The crossbowmen should receive everything that had been agreed to with the outfitters, the admiral, and the captain; they should be armed with two large two-legged crossbows, and one crossbow with a strap, three hundred arrows, a bodice, coat of mail, a helmet, sword, helmet liner, and two curved iron hooks. Anyone who had obligated himself to have this equipment and had failed to bring it aboard with him shall be left to the disposition of the admiral, who may procure these items for him, even at double the price, and put it on his account, if it is so determined by the admiral, the captain, and the outfitters.

A crossbowman shall receive five shares of the booty. As to any reward that shall be given to him, it shall be done on the evaluation of his services by three crossbowmen and their leader, who will testify to this effect under oath, similarly as the navigator does in the instance of the sailors; the captain should also give his opinion in this matter under oath.

The crossbowmen shall receive all the ropes that are found on the deck of the captured vessel as well as all the winches found aboard.

310-Armed Personnel

All armed personnel shall come equipped in the manner they had promised to the admiral and his aids; if they should fail to do this, they shall be left to the disposition of the admiral, similarly to the crossbowmen. They should be able to keep everything that they will find on the persons of other armed personnel whom they have captured; they are not allowed to take anything after the vessel has been captured; they shall receive four shares of the booty.

Nevertheless, everything that the admiral had promised them for attacking and getting on the deck of the attacked vessel and hand-to-hand combat, he and the captain shall give them; they, on the other hand, shall conduct themselves in accordance with the promises and obligations they had made to the admiral. If the admiral carries out his promises, they are required to watch and defend him even at the loss of their own lives. Should he fail to carry out his promises, they are not compelled to carry out theirs.

311-The Lookout

The lookouts must bring all the equipment they had promised and obligated themselves to bring with them; there should be two of them at the prow of the ship and two in the middle of the ship; they are entitled to receive the weapons of the lookouts of the captured vessel.

312-Weights and Measures

If anyone uses false measuring or scaling devices, or dilutes wine by adding water to it, after he has announced that he is selling wine, he shall lose the barrel with all the wine in it, as well as all the money he had received for selling it; the consuls shall confiscate such wine and distribute it among the crew of the ship. If the consuls were in conspiracy with such a party, they shall be branded with a hot iron on their forehead.

313-Senior guards

There should be eight senior guards aboard the ship and each of them shall receive a wage of eight bezans as well as all bows, boots, and bast-shoes of those captured in any raids made on the shore.[108]

314-Ruddermen

Ruddermen shall receive what had been promised them by the admiral, captain, and the navigator. The admiral is required to pay them their shares regardless of the number of shares of spoils they are entitled to.

315-Barbers

Barbers are treated in the same manner as the ruddermen; the crew members in charge of loading winches shall be paid according to the agreement they had made.

316-Ensigns or Standard Bearers

Every standard bearer shall receive five bezans; if there was a flag flying at the prow of the captured vessel, they shall be entitled to keep it.

317-Jolly-Boat Crew

Crew members of the jolly-boat shall be entitled to the knives and daggers of the oarsmen of the captured vessel, and as a reward, the heads of the animals that were being eaten aboard the vessel.

318-The Attack Force

Members of the attacking force shall receive whatever they were promised by the admiral, whether that be fifty or one hundred or ten bezans; and all aboard the ship shall recognize such a promise as binding.

319-Grappling-Hooks Men

The men handling the grappling hooks should receive five bezans and all the chain hooks from the captured vessel.

320-Guarding the Admiral

All personnel aboard the ship are required to protect the admiral with their lives until their death and to perform all the duties agreed

---

108. Bast-shoes were made of cordage that was made out of the inner bark of trees. They were used for wading.

to at the time the journey was undertaken until it is completed. The admiral is required to fulfill, if at all possible, all the promises he had made to them, provided they carry out their promises to him.

If the admiral failed to fulfill his obligations, they shall not be required to fulfill their responsibilities, because he had already broken the agreement; it is, however, essential to consider that the admiral was able to fulfill his obligations; if it had not been in his power to carry out these promises, they shall be required to fulfill their responsibilities even though he was unable to fulfill his promises.

321-Authenticators

Each authenticator shall be paid five bezans. Should they conduct themselves in a biased manner, they shall lose their shares of the spoils, provided that such prejudice can be proved against them. From the money found in the safe of the captured vessel they shall receive five millares for every hundred bezans found, as well as five lengths of cloth for every one hundred captured.

If it should happen that they overlooked some booty, claiming that they did not see it and that they were searching and looking for booty somewhere else and that is why it had been removed without their being able to make a record of it, they shall lose one eye.

322-Servants

Servants shall receive two shares of the captured booty. They shall nurse the ill Saracens and others who are ill aboard the vessel, as well as clean the ship. If the servant is employed by the armed personnel, the captain shall properly adjudge him a reward in conformity with the oath he had taken.

323-Ship's Carpenter

The ship's carpenter shall receive the tools used by the carpenter of the captured vessel.

324-Commander of the Crossbowmen

The commander of the crossbowmen shall receive all the equipment of the crossbowmen of the captured vessel. He is required to make the bow strings and repair the crossbows of the crossbowmen aboard the ship as well as to teach those of them who do not know how to make such repairs that are necessary to their profession, such as, attach feathers to the bows, pare the wood for arrows, stretch tongs for bow strings, and to fashion the arrowheads. That is why he should receive the tools of the master bowman of the captured vessel as well as all the materials that belonged to him, and the various parts for the crossbows.

325–Ship's Caulker or Sealer

The caulker shall receive the tools and the rain cloth of the caulker of the captured vessel.

326–King of the Servants[109]

The king of the servants shall receive the best kitchen utensils that are found aboard the captured vessel plus one cooking kettle for himself and his helpers. He shall be given five shares of the spoils and is forbidden to sell anything without the approval of his helpers.

No one aboard the ship may use the dining table to play dice without his permission; should anyone attempt to do this, he may destroy such dice.[110]

327–Consuls

Should the admiral wish to engage the services of Consuls aboard his vessel, he may only do so with the understanding of the whole crew. They shall be required to pledge an oath that they will abide by all the rules regarding the distribution of the booty; they shall be entitled to receive one-half of all the fines and assessments levied aboard the ship.

328–Agreements

The admiral must fulfill all the promises and obligations he agreed to fulfill with the officers of the ship or other members of the ship's personnel. If he fulfills all his agreements, those mentioned above must fulfill theirs, in a manner as if they were his charges in life and even unto death, and they shall aid him against all with whom he shall engage in combat. Should the admiral fail to live up to his obligations, the others need not carry out their promises, because it was he who had broken the agreement. Therefore, it has been decreed that the admiral must fulfill his obligations provided that a

---

109. In the original manuscript, *Rey de servicials* . Most probably a person in charge of the kitchens aboard the ship, a chef.

110. This provided added income for the chef, who charged a flat fee or take percentage of winnings for the privilege of the use of table.

given person aboard the vessel is capable of doing his work, that he is able to carry out his responsibilities as he had agreed with the admiral that he would, otherwise the admiral shall not be required to fulfill his responsibilities toward such a member of the ship's personnel.

The admiral and the captain shall deduct from the booty taken by the ship, first, all the expenses for the provisions and equipment aboard the ship and for the repayment of any loans that had been negotiated; they may make all these deductions without receiving the approval of the crew.

The admiral and the captain shall replace the merchandise taken from any member of the ship's crew or any other person aboard, provided that the party from whom such merchandise was taken can prove this; the justification for such requisition of goods lies in the fact and shall be resolved by the repayment of such merchandise from the first prize taken. If the owners of the goods requisitioned by the admiral and the captain shall not be aboard the ship when this took place, a sum equal to the value of the requisitioned goods shall be set aside to reimburse the owners upon demand. The admiral and the captain shall dispatch letters to them, asking them to present themselves to receive payment for such goods. Should the crew testify that such merchandise had been taken, and the admiral and the captain fail to follow the procedure outlined above, they may be punished by the legal authorities.

All the expenses incurred by the admiral for the food and maintenance of the people he had taken aboard his ship after he was installed as an admiral and undertook the expedition shall be shared by the whole crew until the completion of the voyage.

The admiral has the authority to administer justice and to mete out punishment by ordering that the offender's ears be cut off or that the guilty party be whipped, while the ship is on the high seas or if a vessel is moored next to a small island and there is no civil government on such an island.

The admiral cannot hire a clerk without the approval of the ship's outfitters.

The admiral shall summon the stewards and order that each of them have a lock on the door of his cabin and on all the sea chests.

The admiral may punish any person who should break open any bale, crate, or chest filled with merchandise.

The admiral may punish all who fail to carry out the orders of officers duly appointed aboard the ship.

The admiral shall receive from twenty to forty shares of the booty, depending on his agreement with the outfitters of the ship, therefore,

247

twenty, twenty-five, thirty, or forty shares, as many as had been agreed upon.

The admiral shall receive, upon his own volition, all the garments or clothing of the most distinguished person of the captured vessel.

The admiral shall be entitled to receive the linen off one bed of every captured vessel.

The admiral shall receive one silver goblet from the captured vessel.

The admiral shall retain all the shields taken off the captured vessel with the exception of the shields that belonged to the lookouts aboard such a vessel.

The admiral shall take one of the rings worn by the persons aboard the captured vessel that shall be valued at less than twenty bezans.

The admiral may take one jewel worth less than twenty bezans without violating any ordinances or regulations set for the expedition of the armada; should such a jewel be worth more than twenty bezans, it shall be included in the rest of the booty taken.

The admiral is required to pay the owner and the shareholders of the ship the agreed share of the prizes taken by his ship.

If the ship takes prizes, the admiral should receive a reward in addition to the share of the booty he is entitled to, with the knowledge and approval of the crew. He shall swear an oath that the ship shall set sail and leave the port where it was outfitted and that he will loyally and honestly carry out all the responsibilities that he had taken upon himself, with the exception of a situation when a given member of the crew shall not be able to fulfill the obligations for which he had enlisted aboard the vessel.

The admiral shall loan money to the members of the crew in the same manner that he negotiates loans from them. If he negotiates any loan, he shall inform the crew about it. The sailors and all the rest of the members of the crew should continue to sail with him until the expedition has been completed, if they are serving aboard the ship for share of the booty, and the admiral shall have the right to put into any port or any locality as often as he shall wish in order to reprovision or refit the ship. If the sailors remain in his service without any opposition till he had completed the expedition, the admiral cannot demand from them or any other members of the ship's personnel repayment of any loans he made to them, even if he made such loans to them when the ship was in some specified locality, not upon the demands and needs of the crew but actually to accommodate himself.

If a member of the ship's personnel wishes to leave the service before the completion of the expedition, he shall return to the admiral whatever he had received from him and also leave aboard all his personal weapons; he cannot do this without the permission of the admiral until the ship had docked at two ports in order to be refitted. Only after the ship had been refitted twice, the sailor can terminate his services, as had been stated above, returning all the money that he had received and leaving his weapons.

This article has been written in order that those who borrow money shall not be required to pay interest on such loans, because the admiral does not pay any interest on the money he borrows from others, that is, he does not repay two pennies for one that he borrowed, and because the admiral returns to the outfitters the same amount that he had borrowed from them.

329-Duties of a Captain

The captain shall fulfill all his undertaken obligations and shall see to the enforcement of justice aboard the ship.

The captain shall inform the admiral and the outfitters of all matters known to him that may be harmful to the ship.

When he metes out justice, he shall be impartial toward all aboard the ship and should make certain that all the obligations that he and the admiral had undertaken shall be carried out.

The captain shall order the clerk to render an account of all vital matters relating to the ship as soon as the ship sails out of a port where the expedition was undertaken, or if it has reached a port for provisioning, if anyone aboard the ship shall ask that such an accounting be made; such an accounting shall be made in the presence of three navigators, four stewards, four sailors of the prow, two other armed members of the expedition, and three crossbowmen.

The captain shall explain and announce what the admiral's responsibilities are toward each individual aboard the ship; if the admiral should do something evil or improper, the captain together with the whole crew shall inform him about this and insist as long as is necessary that the matter be rectified.

The captain shall care for the welfare and show concern for the problems of the humble as well as influential people who are aboard the ship, in order that each of them would be helped by the laws that protect them; he shall also see to it that neither the consuls nor the officers take any action that might be harmful to the admiral or the ship.

The captain, when authorized, replaces in authority the admiral when the latter is not aboard the ship.

The captain shall order boats dispatched to any place or locality if the admiral advised or ordered that this be done.

The captain shall proceed as a representative of the admiral, in his own right as well as a representative of the crew aboard the ship, to meet with and negotiate with any other vessels met on the high seas, and whatever action he had agreed to shall be valid.

The captain shall appoint his representative aboard all galleys and other units of the armada. This representative shall be of his own choosing, and then he shall present him to the admiral, and whatever orders such a representative shall give must be carried out.

The captain assigns the crews of the smaller units of the armada, appoints all to specific tasks or ranks, and discharges them at will.

The captain shall deal in the same manner with boats equipped with oars as he deals with sail boats, and shall do everything that shall be necessary.

The captain shall apportion food in the manner and for a period of time he feels shall be proper.

The captain shall assign all battle stations aboard the ship and properly apportion all armed personnel aboard.

The captain shall bear the responsibility for all section leaders and shall watch them carefully. Should they fail to conduct themselves properly, he shall notify the admiral of this matter, and whatever the admiral will decide shall be carried out.

The captain shall inspect, order repairs made, and divide the arms held in common aboard the ship.

The captain shall designate the parties who shall go ashore, and when he is away from the ship, he shall exercise the same degree of authority over such a party as the admiral does when they are aboard the ship, and the latter must invest him with such an authority.

The captain has the same authority as the admiral when the latter is absent and the former is acting in his stead; the captain, however, shall make a complete report of everything that happened when the admiral returns aboard.

The captain shall station the standard bearers at any location he believes they should be stationed.

In case of necessity the captain shall assemble all the personnel and shall force them to assemble as ordered.

The captain shall receive one fourth of all the fines and assessments levied aboard the vessel.

The captain shall be an arbitrator in any disputes between the consuls; if, therefore, one of them has a dispute with another, he shall arbitrate it.

The captain shall deliver all the effects of a deceased member of the crew to the wife or relatives of the deceased; should any such effects be lost, he shall pay them damages.

The captain may auction off the effects of the deceased if in his judgment this should be done.

The captain shall supervise the distribution of food aboard the ship.

The captain, with the agreement of the admiral, may give his armed servant one half of one share of the spoils.

The captain shall apportion, with the approval of the admiral and the outfitters, suiting material to persons aboard the ship who are in need of clothing, as well as other things that shall be distributed.

The captain shall see to it that the weights and measures used by the consuls are accurate; should they act dishonestly and thus cause damage to anyone, they shall be branded on their foreheads. This paragraph was written so that consuls would conduct themselves loyally toward the crew of the ship.

The captain is required to prevent the sale of any collateral given for the delivery of wine and food aboard the ship, until the expedition is completed.

The captain shall see to it that no one aboard the ship is allowed to sell any wine, meat, or other food measured on scales or containers unless verified by him to be accurate; should the captain be able to prove that these instruments were inaccurate, he shall together with the consuls confiscate all the merchandise offered for sale and distribute it among the crew of the ship.

The captain shall see to it that if the down payment made for food aboard the ship was insufficient to pay for the amount used, that the debtor pay his debt to the creditor in order that the latter shall not be damaged, and that this is done while the booty is being auctioned off aboard the ship.

If, after an announcement had been made that wine is being sold aboard the ship, water had been added to the wine, the captain shall bring this to the attention of the consuls.

The captain shall receive twenty-five shares of the booty or more, depending on the amount promised him by the outfitters who in consultation with the admiral promised him such a share at the start of the expedition; under no circumstances can he be given fewer than twenty-five shares.

The captain is entitled and shall receive all the broadswords taken off the captured vessels; it shall be taken for granted that all broadswords that are bundled and are carried aboard such a vessel as part of cargo designated for sale shall not be taken by him; he shall only receive broadswords that are carried by the personnel aboard such a vessel as side arms, and only those.

The captain shall receive all the flags carried aboard such a vessel that are attached to the ropes by pins or with thread.

In addition, he shall be paid one-half bezan for each Saracen sold, whether he be an adult or a child. In addition, he shall be paid five bezans for every Saracen who is capable of ransoming himself for over one hundred bezans, and two bezans for each of them who has ransomed himself for one hundred bezans or less.

In addition, he shall receive all the rain garments that they wore, whether made of the gelling material, azure cloth, or any other worn by the Saracens.

He may also take any weapons that he may need in order to be properly and suitably armed. He shall, however, in such a case turn over his own weapons for the use of the personnel of the aramada, that is, he shall surrender his own knives, weapons, retaining one of each variety for personal use.

330-The Clerk

The clerk shall conduct himself loyally towards all and shall take an oath of his office in the presence of the admiral and the outfitters of the ship; if the vessel should be under sail on the high seas, he shall take his oath of office in the presence of the entire crew of the ship.

Immediately after the sails of the ships shall have been unfurled, he shall make an accounting of all matters to the sailors of the prow, the navigators, the crossbowmen, and the rest of the armed personnel; he shall do this in the presence of four navigators, four sailors of the prow, three crossbowmen, two armed crewmen, and four stewards, who after examining his report shall certify in the name of the whole crew that his ledger entries are accurate.

The clerk shall keep a ledger or a register, and no other person shall make any entries in it, cannot examine and read it, or keep it in his possession. If any other person besides the clerk handled such a ledger, it shall no longer be considered as authentic, and the clerk shall lose all his possessions as well as his share of the spoils, and shall be removed from his position. If it should be proved that he had acted in bad faith, the court shall order that his hand be cut off.

The clerk is taken aboard the vessel in order that loyalty will be maintained by all and that he may observe this, for the clerk's testimony is equal to that of three other witnesses, and the ship is held accountable for all his acts.

The clerk should be present when the admiral makes any promises to any member of the ship's personnel, and whatever the admiral would promise to anyone within his hearing, he should write down, but he should only state what he had heard and nothing else. Should he fail to write this down, and he is called to give testimony in some dispute, he shall tell the truth about everything he had heard or seen. He should act in this manner in all commercial matters as well as matters pertaining to privateering, as all evidence aboard a ship emanates from the clerk.

The clerk should not make any entries aboard the ship when the ship is not moored, that means, when the ship is under sail on the seas, for such entries shall not be valid. [111]

The clerk occupies a position of trust, and thus all his actions, whether he concludes an agreement regarding lading of cargo, whether he buys or sells something or whether he divides the food among the crew, shall be binding. After he has taken his oath of office, any deposition he makes regarding any matter shall be accepted at face value.

The clerk enjoys other privileges; any agreement concluded aboard the vessel shall not be legal if the clerk was not present when it was concluded. In addition, if the clerk had heard the statements made by both of the parties, he may be able to set this down in his ledger when the ship is moored; such an entry will be binding, even if neither of the two parties to such an agreement were present when he entered this matter in the ledger.

In addition, if the clerk did not give an order to the guards, they shall not be allowed to take anything aboard or to give anything away, without a written statement prepared by him and sealed with his seal of office. Unless this is done, the clerk shall not be responsible for anything that may be lost. Further, the patron of the vessel shall not give anything to anyone contrary to his will or without a written authorization from him.

None of the sailors is permitted to take anything under the penalty prescribed in former articles. [112]

Further, if the clerk was not present when an agreement has been made with the patron regarding the amount of the lading charges and the clerk had not made a written record of this, the party refusing to pay such shipping charges cannot be forced to do it. If, however, the clerk had been present, such an agreement shall have binding force, because the clerk heard it and can set it in writing at any moment.

The clerk may in addition hire sailors with the exception of the sailors of the prow, and the patron of the ship must recognize such enlistments as if he had concluded them himself.

The clerk shall be present at all the negotiations related to the

---

111. Reference is made to Articles 60 and 253.

112. Reference is made to Articles 167 and 173.

ship, whether they pertain to the provisions of the vessel or any other matters. If it should happen that some foodstuffs were captured, the clerk shall immediately divide it, and may reward someone in doing that as he wills.

The clerk may take the best accommodations between the middeck and the prow of the ship and dispose of it as he shall wish. He may also take into his service an assistant clerk; however, the latter cannot make any entries in the ledger; if he does, the clerk shall suffer the penalty described above.

A clerk aboard an armed ship receives ten shares of the booty, the same amount as the officer of the stern deck, who is called a navigator. In addition, he shall receive all the books off the captured vessel whose value does not exceed five bezans per book, but no other books even if they are crated in small boxes. On the other hand, all the papers found in chests or elsewhere shall belong to the clerk, as well as all the inkwells and other clerical supplies that belonged to the clerk of the captured vessel.

In addition, at the sale of all prisoners the clerk shall receive two millares for each prisoner sold, and for each prisoner able to ransom himself he shall receive five millares; and wherever he and his assistant happen to find themselves, they shall be reimbursed for their maintenance and footwear from the time they had been hired.

The clerk may discharge the person from service of the ship who had served the amount of time he had enlisted for, and no one can detain this person by force, if the enlistment had been made under these stipulations when such a person enlisted to serve aboard the ship or the ship had sailed on its expedition; and this shall be binding and not subject to any speculation.

The clerk is required to deduct from the first prize captured by the ship any loans that were made and repay such loans that had been made when the ship had to reprovision at any locality. It shall not be proper to commence distribution of the spoils until such loans are paid off, and the clerk shall have a right to demand that this be done.

331-Stewards[113]

In there had been stewards hired aboard the vessel, they together with the clerk are required to guard faithfully the common property aboard the ship and to make inventory of it, and each of them shall have a copy of such inventory, and each of them should have his own lock, so that one cannot open the chest of another and cannot be able

---

113. In modern terminology, Quartermaster.

to put anything into it or take anything out; and the clerk shall be present each time any valuables are put in or taken out of these chests.

If it should happen that any of the stewards takes out or issues anything on the orders of the admiral or some other party in command of the ship without the knowledge of the other stewards aboard the ship or of the clerk, he shall lose his hand, and he shall be removed from his office and shall be given over to the mercy of the crew and lose his shares of the booty.[114]

Stewards are paid a silver mark for every privateering expedition.

Stewards are given one chest from each captured vessel, the best that shall be found aboard, without any merchandise that it may have contained, just the wooden part of it.

Stewards receive all the locks that shall be taken off a captured vessel or ship.

Stewards shall receive all the ropes taken off the crates from the captured vessel.

Stewards shall receive all the nails found aboard the captured vessel that are not in chests, packs, or baskets.

Stewards receive two millares for every Saracen captured; but they shall be required to furnish the rivets needed to fasten the fetters of the prisoners.

Stewards receive all the chisels found aboard the captured vessel with the exception of those that belong to the carpenter, but they shall make them available for use aboard their ship.

They shall be required to furnish the ropes necessary to tie up the crates until these are sold at auction, and the chisels for putting on the fetters on the prisoners and for taking them off. They shall also furnish ropes to tie up the prisoners and fasten the sails, if there are no such ropes aboard the vessel.

332-Chief Navigator

The chief navigator of a ship is required to be loyal to the admiral, the captain and the outfitters, and not to delay accomplishing anything that is necessary; if such matters can be done in one day, he shall not use additional days for this task, for a battleship must be ready at any day or hour to take pursuit of an enemy vessel, or in case of necessity to be able to flee; therefore, the navigator shall perform all the tasks that he is to perform as quickly and efficiently as pos-

---

114. Punishment was severe and administered on the spot.

sible, and he shall pledge an oath that he will do this.

In addition, he shall also swear an oath that he shall not be swayed by any ties of relationship or because he has received some gifts refrain from issuing orders to those who can carry out these orders satisfactorily.

In addition, he shall swear an oath that he shall not assign any person a job that he knows another person could do better.

In addition, he shall inform the proper authority of the lack of masts, sailingyard, anchors, or other equipment aboard the ship. Should he fail to reveal such shortages, and it shall be proved that he withheld such matters, he shall be deprived of his shares of the booty and his weapons.

In addition, should he witness a theft, a fight, or any other violation, he shall make this public and punish the culprit; if the guilty party refused to reform, he shall inform the admiral and the captain about this matter.

In addition, he should not hire a stranger for a member of the crew, nor state that anyone is a good sailor if he actually does not know this; should he do that, he shall be responsible for all the damage that the ship will have suffered by his misstatement of facts.

Should the person he hired become seasick and unable to perform his obligations, and if it became necessary to hire another to replace him, the navigator shall have to pay his wages.

In addition, he shall perform all the services that are part of his obligations. Should it happen that he cannot perform such services and it will become necessary to hire another in his stead, he shall have to pay the wages to his replacement; by the above it should be understood that he will not know what is necessary to know aboard the ship regarding its sailing. He is not required to know other matters that are not related to sailing of a vessel, but he shall know that which had been mentioned previously, as it was for this knowledge that he had been made the chief navigator. In addition, should he not know the matters essential to his position, he shall be removed from his position and forfeit the rewards he had been promised; on the other hand, if he fulfills everything that he had promised, he shall be given what had been promised him.

In addition, he shall not sail out of or into a port without the approval of the admiral, the captain, and the crew of the vessel.

He shall swear an oath to fulfill all these things; and in addition, he shall not keep secret anything, because of his friendship for the admiral or the captain or anyone else, that should be done, that he shall not suggest that useless things be done, and that he shall do and order everything done that will be beneficial to the ship. Should he be unable to do this, he shall inform the admiral and the captain about

256

about this matter, and they shall help him in all matters that will benefit the ship. Should they refuse to help him or fail to keep their promise, he shall not be liable to them in any manner.

The navigator has the following authority aboard the ship, that after a consultation with the admiral, the captain, and the other officers aboard, he will have the right to order that the sails be raised and unfurled at any moment he considers proper in his judgment.

The navigator takes command of the vessel from the moment it begins to sail out of a port until it is on the open waters.

In addition, in all situations when it becomes necessary that the ship hover about, the navigator shall issue all orders regarding the proper setting out of sails, from the deck of the ship.

In addition, should he decide to hover about, he shall ask the advice of the admiral, the captain, and the officers of the foredeck, and if they agree, he shall hover about.

In addition, after entry into any port the navigator shall be in command of the ship. After both of the anchors have been cast he will surrender the command of the ship to the party whose turn it is to take over the command.

In addition, if he decides that the mainsail shall be furled or unfurled or trimmed, he shall issue such orders. If it should be necessary to wind up or realign a sail, he may do this without asking anyone about it.

In addition, no anchor shall be put aboard the ship if the navigator did not order or demand it.

In addition, if it shall be necessary to shorten the cable or to cut it, the navigator may do it.

In addition, the ship shall not be allowed to hover about without the approval of the navigator, nor shall its anchor be hoisted or its mooring lines pulled in without his consent.

During the night none of the ship's jolly-boats shall leave its vicinity without his permission; if, however, this was done, the captain shall be notified. The navigator shall set the succession of command among his co-navigators, and they shall report to him everything that they had undertaken.

The navigator shall participate in the division of spoils, because he knows the sailors. He shall also pledge an oath that he as well as those under his command shall faithfully make their reports.

The chief navigator shall be relieved from the responsibility of vouching for the person he hired after the latter has served aboard for a month, for he hired him in the name of the ship.

The navigator may change his weapons for others, if after capture of a vessel better weapons are found, and he may keep such weapons until the completion of the journey, after which he shall return it to the crew of the ship; he shall, however, always be armed while on the deck; and one of the weapons shall belong to him.

In addition, the navigator receives food rations one quarter share larger. For every vessel that pays ransom he shall receive ten bezans, and if the vessel is small, he shall receive five bezans.

In addition, from each sail divided among the other navigators he shall receive a share and a quarter; and from each captured vessel whether a large or small he may demand a payment of one bezan for a drinking toast.

The navigator is required to remain aboard the ship until all the rest of the crew has left the ship, and he shall not leave the vessel until the vessel is secured and the journey is completed. After this has been done, the navigator may leave the ship, if the majority of the crew has left it and he desires to do so.

333-Consuls

The consuls should take an oath in the presence of the crew of the vessel, the navigators, the outfitters, the sailors of the prow, the crossbowmen, and other armed personnel that they shall not be influenced by any means in dealing with anyone aboard the ship, that they shall not be partial to any relatives or anyone else, and that they shall act faithfully in accordance with their best knowledge and good will, and that they shall always act with the advice of all those who shall give their advice, and that they shall not be deterred from this course either by bonds of blood, offers of money, or any other reason.

They shall watch very carefully that everything sold aboard the vessel, whether wine or anything else, shall be honestly measured. They shall also have a clerk; and each of the consuls shall be paid fifteen bezans; and they shall give the captain from the share they received of all the fines imposed aboard the ship one third of the amount and to the clerk also a third of the amount.

In addition, they shall receive half of the imposed fines. They should also receive one rug from each captured vessel.

In addition, they shall receive two bezans for each of them for every person captured aboard the vessel taken, because they arbitrate disputes between the people.

In addition, every consul is to conduct his affairs faithfully and impartially, and should he tolerate any evil acts, he shall be deprived of his office, shall forfeit his shares in the booty, and shall be branded on his forehead.

The guards who are bailiffs or major-domos[115] should take an oath that they shall honestly distribute the food rations among all aboard, with the exception of the admiral who shall receive three portions, and the captain and the chief navigator who shall receive one and one-quarter portions. They shall not be allowed to give a larger portion to either a large or small member of the crew without the consent of the admiral, the captain, and the clerk.

The guards shall receive the hides of the animals eaten aboard the ship. They shall also receive bags and bread baskets, if their ship takes booty.

In addition, for every Saracen captured they shall be paid four millares; they shall, however, be required to watch them, chain and unchain them, and if these Saracens should be able to give ransom, they shall be paid one bezan each.

In addition, the guards shall receive as large a share of the spoils as will be available. Should the Saracens escape, however, they shall be held answerable.

334-Who Is Entitled to One-Fifth of the Booty

Whoever outfits a vessel, whether large or small, or a galley, or some other unit of the armada, at the cost of ten thousand soldinos,[116] more or less, and such unit should capture a prize, after deducting two fifths from the booty, one fifth shall accrue to the admiral, one fifth to the navigators, and one fifth to those who had outfitted the vessel.

In addition, if any person has outfitted a vessel and has failed to make any profit on such a venture and shall withdraw his investment, from this sum shall be taken two fifths and divided in the manner prescribed above.

In addition, if anyone has outfitted a ship but has not made any profit nor withdrawn his investment, from whatever is left of this sum, whether it be much or little, two fifths shall be taken and divided as had been stated.

In addition, if some navigator had secured the means with which to

---

115. In the original manuscript, *senescalchus*. Special guards in charge of protection and distribution of food aboard the ship.

116. *Soldo, soldino*, a shilling. A silver coin minted during the reign of Henry VI at the close of twelfth century. Those minted in Milan contained 1.25—1.30 grams of pure silver; there were also large coins containing 2.06—2.20 grams of silver.

procure his position from a third party upon the condition that they shall mutually share the losses and also equally divide the booty, should the ship upon which he is sailing capture a prize, the profit accruing from the money raised by the navigator shall be added to the share of the booty that shall be due him and the whole amount shall be divided between the two of them. If the ship failed to take any booty, the navigator above mentioned shall be required to pay the party who had advanced him the money half of the wages received by the navigator.

In addition, if the party mentioned above advanced such money accepting all the risk personally, the profit made from such money, if the ship had taken any prizes, shall belong exclusively to the party who had advanced this money, while the income that will accrue to the navigator due to his position aboard the ship shall belong to him in entirety. Thus the party that had provided the original sum of money shall not be liable in any manner to the navigator, nor shall the navigator be obligated in any way to this party, regardless of whether the ship takes any prizes and makes a profit or should incur a loss, and this is due to the fact that the money was advanced on the basis mentioned above.

In addition, a fifth of the spoils is collected in this manner, that if the whole amount to be divided equals ten thousand soldinos, four thousand soldinos shall be set aside for those who are to receive the fifth of the spoils. If the sum should be lower or higher, the same procedure should be followed in designating the fifth share.

At this point we come to the end of the book commonly called the Consulate, in which have been incorporated the various articles, laws, and accepted customs that our forefathers had ordained in matters marine and commercial and in privateer and naval expeditions.

These laws and these articles have been proclaimed, signed, and promulgated by the authorities listed below.

Proclamation

In the year 1075 after the Birth of Jesus Christ, Our Lord, in the month of March, they were proclaimed by Romans, in the city of Rome, in the monastery of St. John the Lateran, that they shall be observed for all times.

In the year 1102, in the month of September, they were proclaimed in the city of Accra, on his way to Jerusalem, by King Louis, and Count of Toulouse, that they be observed for all times.[117]

---

117. King Louis VI (The Fat) 1081-1137 of France.

In the year 1102 they were proclaimed at Majorca by the Pisanians, that they be observed for all times.

In the year 1118 they were proclaimed in the city of Pisa, at the church of Saint Peter, Patron of the Sea, during the reign of Podesta Ambrose Mils, that they be observed for all times.

In the year 1162, in the month of August, they were proclaimed in the city of Marseilles, at the Hospitality building, during the reign of Podesta, His Mightiness Jaufre Antor, that they should be observed for all time. [118]

In the year 1175 they were proclaimed in Almeria by the good count of Barcelona and Genoa, that they shall be observed for all times.

In the year 1186 they were proclaimed in the city of Genoa, during the reign of Podesta Pinell Milrs, and the tenure of city Elders, Peter Ambroise, John de Sent-Donat, William de Carmesi, Baldoni and Peter Desarenes, and the oath to observe these ordinances was taken by those entering the port.

In the year 1187, in the month of February, they were proclaimed by King William in the city of Brindisi, that they be observed for all times.

In the year 1190 they were proclaimed and sworn to on the Island of Rhodes, that they be preserved for all times.

In the year 1200 they were proclaimed and sworn to by the Prince of Morea, that they be observed for all times. [119]

In the year 1215 they were ratified by the Venetian Commune in Constantinople, and were signed by King John, after the defeat of the Greeks, in the church of Saint Sofia, that they shall be preserved for all times.

In the year 1224 the Count of Germany proclaimed them, that they be observed for all times.

In the year 1225 they were ratified and sworn to in the city of Messina, in the new church of the Most Holy Virgin, in the presence of the Bishop of Catania, and Frederick, the Emperor of Germany, that they be observed for all times.

In the year 1250 they were ratified by John de Balmont in the spirit of the King of France, who at that time enjoyed good health, in the presence of the Cavaliers of the Army, Knights of Templar, Hos-

---

118. Podesta, Chief magistrate of a region comparable to Lt.-Governor of a province.

119. Morea, modern Peloponnesia.

pitalers, and an Admiral of the Levant, that they be observed for all times.[120]

In the year 1262 they were proclaimed in the city of Constantinople, at the church of Holy Angel, by the Emperor of Pellonnesia, to be observed for all times within his domain.

In the year 1270 they were proclaimed by Frederick, King of Cyprus, in Syria, and in Constantinople, by Emperor Constantine, that they be observed for all times.

In the year 1270 they were proclaimed and ratified by His Most Royal Majesty, James, by the Grace of God, King of Aragon, Valencia, and Majorca, Count of Barcelona and the city of Urgel; and it was His Majesty, King James, in the city of Valencia, who appointed the consuls in the manner prescribed above.

The Lord be praised

The printing of this work was completed July 14, 1494 in Barcelona, at the shop of Peter Posa, priest and printer.

---

120. Hospitalers (Knights of St. John of Jerusalem) a religious Order established for the care of sick and wounded Crusaders.

PART IV

RELATED DOCUMENTS

Ordinances of King Peter[121]

We, Peter, by the Grace of God, King of Aragon, etc., etc., send greetings, to our gentle and highly prized procurator, our Governor-General of the Kingdom of Sardinia and Corsica, as well as to other officials of that kingdom, to Lieutenant-Governor-Generals of Catalonia and the Kingdom of Valencia, to Vice-Regents, Assistant Regent and Governor-General of Barcelona, as well as other Vice-Regents, Judges, Elders of the Sea Guild, Mayors, Jurymen, as well as other Governors-in-Chief and Governors Ordinary, of all the territories of Aragon, Valencia, Sardinia, and Corsica, the Earldom of Barcelona, as well as Consuls, wherever they have been established, and all other officials, to all of them collectively and individually, who are in our service at present and who shall be appointed in the future.

Human intelligence and the knowledge of past events make it possible for us to anticipate the probabilities of the future and to help us to cope with such problems more expeditiously.

Since it is known to Us at present from the experiences of the past that vessels, large and small and other sea craft, the less they are under controls the more damage and loss of property would result, and would lead to sudden and unexpected death to a large number of persons, therefore, we wish to make it known that as far as it is within Our power to protect the safety of marine commerce, of persons and property, we promulgate and initiate the following sentiments in the articles to follow.

Firstly, every sailor, crossbowman, servant, or anyone else who will enlist aboard a vessel, galley, or any other craft is required to fulfill all the commitments and to perform all the tasks agreed to at the time of his enlistment.

---

121. Part Three in the original manuscript lacks consecutive pagination. It contains original royal and communal proclamations, charters, and ordinances that were added to or supplemented the well entrenched body of contemporary customs regarding marine commerce.

Likewise, if a sailor, crossbowman, or any other member of the crew accepts wages or even a token payment from the master of a vessel or his representatives, he shall be required to complete the journey for which he had enlisted, unless he is prevented from accomplishing this by illness or the necessity of entering into marriage, or has received a legacy after he had undertaken the enlistment. He is required to notify the party who hired him immediately that he is ill or must enter marriage or has become a beneficiary to an estate, and he shall refund the wages or the advance on wages he had received.

Anyone who shall violate the above ordinance shall be imprisoned and must return any wages that he had received from the master, pay a fine of one hundred soldinos and remain in prison for one hundred days; any master of a vessel who would hire or allow such a sailor to enlist aboard his vessel after being notified that this sailor had been hired by another patron shall be fined one hundred soldinos.

The clerk of a vessel shall enter into the register of the vessel any such agreement concluded by the master of a vessel or his representative with any sailor, crossbowman, or a servant.

The above mentioned clerk will before assuming his office pledge an oath in the presence of the Governor-General of Barcelona or his representative, or before the Governor-General of the territory where the clerk was signed aboard the vessel, that he will faithfully perform all the functions of his office.

2. Furthermore, every sailor, or any other member of the crew who fearful of storm or pirate ships deserts or abandons the vessel shall be hanged by the neck until death, unless the master of the vessel or his representative who is in command of the vessel should abandon the vessel first.

Therefore, if the master of the vessel or his representative is about to abandon the vessel, he must before leaving the deck of the vessel announce to the whole crew assembled on the deck that he is abandoning the vessel because he cannot save it and that he releases all the members of the crew from all their responsibilities. If there is a clerk aboard the vessel, he shall execute a proper deposition relating to the abandoning of the vessel.

3. Furthermore, any sailor, crossbowman, or any other member of the crew who will without the permission of the master of the vessel or his representative cut or unfasten the mooring lines in order to wreck the vessel will be hanged by the neck.

4. Furthermore, any sailor, crossbowman, or any other member of the crew who will desert after the vessel sails from the shores of Barcelona or any other place where he had enlisted as a member of

the crew, and has failed to serve the agreed period of time, will be required if apprehended to refund everything that he had received from the vessel, will forfeit all his wages due him for the time he had served aboard, and these wages shall be kept by the master of the vessel, and in addition he shall pay a fine of one hundred soldinos, and will be imprisoned in a fortress for one hundred days.

5. Furthermore, every sailor, crossbowman, or any other member of the crew, regardless of his position or rank, who is attempting to undermine the morale of the crew, shall be seized by other members of the crew, if this is ordered by the master of the vessel, in the name of His Majesty the King. They shall put him in chains, and he shall be kept in fetters until the vessel reaches its home waters. He shall then be surrendered to the local legal authorities, will be fined two hundred soldinos, and he shall not be paid for the time he had been kept in chains, and this amount shall be retained by the master of the vessel. If the other members of the crew should refuse to take hold of him when ordered, each of them shall be fined one hundred soldinos.

6. Furthermore, every master of a vessel is required to pay the sailors, crossbowmen, and all other members of the crew the amount in wages agreed upon at the time of the enlistment for the time served aboard the vessel, as had been agreed.

To continue: If the master of the vessel discharges any member of the crew before the expiration of the time of enlistment, he shall pay them full wages due, as if they had served the entire period anticipated at the time of enlistment, unless he should discharge them for a theft that had been proved against them, quarreling, smuggling, or disobedience of a superior officer. He may not discharge any of them in the territory of the Saracens.

7. Furthermore, if a sailor or any other member of the crew aboard the vessel is wounded or should become ill, he must be paid for the entire period spent aboard the vessel, same as if he were well, and the master of the vessel is also required to pay not only his wages but likewise to provide him with all other benefits in accordance with the terms of the agreement entered into at the time of enlistment.

Furthermore, if the voyage had taken the vessel beyond the sea,[122] the master of the vessel is required to pay such a sailor all his wages and to keep him aboard the vessel until the vessel shall reach the port where he had enlisted.

8. Furthermore, every sailor or crossbowman carried on the

---

122. Mediterranean Sea.

payroll aboard the vessel is required to equip himself with proper weapons, as follows: a strong chain of mail, helmet, head gear, a broadsword, two crossbows in good condition, a grappling hook, quiver, and two hundred common or feathered arrows, and must use these weapons in defense of the vessel every time he is ordered to do so by the officer in charge. Should he fail to do this and act otherwise, he shall pay a fine of twenty soldinos for each such offense.

If a sailor should fail to bring with himself such weapons aboard the vessel when he enlisted, or if he should fail to use these arms when ordered to do so, he will forfeit the wages for the entire voyage and period served aboard the vessel, and this money will be kept by the master of the vessel.

9. In addition, every sailor or crossbowman who enlisted to undertake a voyage beyond the sea and had received part of his wages, should upon the demand of the master of the vessel or the merchants remain aboard the vessel at night, from the moment the cargo was loaded aboard the vessel. This is necessary in order that one fourth of the armed crew would always remain aboard the vessel at night. Each member of the crew staying aboard the vessel at night shall receive a bonus equal to one month's wages.

If, however, a member of the crew enlisted for a specified amount of money for his service during the entire voyage, he shall be paid twenty Barcelonian pennies for each night he spends aboard the vessel while it is in port, unless it had been agreed at the time of the enlistment that he would sleep aboard the vessel without any additional remuneration. The above provision does not include the nights spent aboard the vessel from the moment it is being readied for departure. Anyone guilty of violating the above provisions shall be fined twenty soldinos for each offense.

10. Furthermore, regardless of the fact whether the vessel began or had not begun to take cargo aboard, information is received that galleys or other enemy vessels are in the vicinity, and that privateers are hovering about, all enlisted sailors and crossbowmen who had received their wages or an advance on their wages, are required upon the orders of the master of the vessel, or the clerk, or any other person commanding the vessel in their stead, to come aboard the vessel in order to defend it. They shall remain aboard as long as they are ordered to do so by the master of the vessel or his representative. Under such circumstances they will be paid their full wages. If any sailor or other member of the crew failed to board the vessel when so ordered, he will be fined twenty soldinos.

11. Furthermore, every sailor, crossbowman, servant, or any other member of the crew is required to obey the orders of the master of the vessel or his representative. If any member of the crew

would knowingly or maliciously refuse to obey the master or his representative, he shall be seized by the sailors and all other members of the crew, fettered in chains, and be kept in fetters until they can surrender him to the proper authorities in the environments where the master of the vessel is resident, which authorities will turn him over to a judge of His Majesty the King, who shall dispose of this matter in accordance with the provisions of the law. The above sailor shall not receive any pay for the period he spent in chains.

12. Furthermore, every sailor and crossbowman shall report aboard the vessel on the day announced by its master as the day that the anchor will be hoisted, and from the moment of reporting aboard the vessel he shall be paid full wages. If any of the sailors or crossbowmen should be found on shore after the vessel had unfurled its sails, he shall be fined twenty soldinos.

13. Furthermore, if any of the sailors, crossbowmen, or servants would disembark or leave the proximity of the vessel without the permission of the master, the navigator, or their representative, he shall be fined five soldinos for each such offense. If he should be unable to pay the fine, he shall be imprisoned in the fortress for five days; should the patron of the vessel prefer, he may keep him in chains aboard the vessel, and while in chains he shall not be paid any wages.

14. Furthermore, if one or several sailors, crossbowmen, or servants should take the leading jolly-boat and leave the vessel without the permission of the master, the navigator, or his representative, each of them shall be fined twenty soldinos; if they left the vessel with one of the other jolly-boats, they shall be fined ten soldinos each. If they should be unable to pay the fine, they shall be detained in the fortress, one day for each soldino of fine.

15. Furthermore, if any of the sailors had agreed with the patron or his representative that he shall remain aboard the vessel when it is moored near the shore or any other place, and subsequently leaves the vessel without the permission of one of the two persons mentioned above, he shall pay a fine of twenty soldinos for each such offense and forfeit the wages due to him to that day.

16. Furthermore, if any of the sailors or other members of the crew fall asleep while on guard duty, he shall pay a fine of two soldinos for each such offense if he is stationed on the stern deck, and one soldino if he is doing guard duty on the prow deck.

17. Furthermore, if any vessel due to stormy seas or violent winds is wrecked and begins to sink, the sailors, crossbowmen, and servants, as well as other members of the crew are required immediately to help in the attempt to save the vessel, equipment, and the cargo aboard the vessel. In such a situation the sailors as well as

the rest of the crew should be paid full wages until they are released from service by the master of the vessel.

If, however, these sailors and other members of the crew abandon the vessel instead of helping in the attempt to save it and the equipment, cargo, and other effects aboard it, not only will they forfeit the wages for the time they had served aboard, but also they shall be forced to return any wages or advance they had already received. In addition, if the latter had refused to help in an attempt to save the vessel, and if the cargo or personal effects they had aboard the vessel had been salvaged, they shall be confiscated in the name of His Majesty the King.

In any event, all the sailors, crossbowmen, and servants who failed to help in the rescue operations shall be imprisoned until they shall refund to the master of the vessel the wages or the advance they had received.

18. Furthermore, a statement issued by the master of the vessel or the clerk regarding the enlistment of any sailor or other member of the crew, wages that will be paid or the advance that shall be given them, or other conditions of service aboard the vessel shall be accepted as conclusive evidence; therefore, it is obligatory upon any court of justice functioning at the locality where the accusations are made by the master or the clerk against any member of the crew for failing to abide by the terms of the agreement concluded should immediately order the detention of such a defendant and should imprison him for such time until the latter will be able to resolve this matter with the master of the vessel or his intermediary all the obligations entered into at the time the agreement was concluded.

19. Furthermore, no sailor or any other member of a jolly-boat crew, or anyone else can dare to take aboard and unload grain or any other cargo at night without the consent of the master or his representative. Anyone violating the above prohibition shall be fined one hundred soldinos for each offense, but not less; in addition, anyone committing such a transgression shall be liable to the patron or his representative for all the claims arising out of such a situation.

20. Furthermore, if any person contracts a construction of a vessel, a galley, jolly-boat, or any other kind of craft on the shores of Barcelona, and purchases the lumber, ropes, nails, cotton, anchors, and other equipment and materials necessary for the construction of such a vessel, and should fail to pay the suppliers and the master workmen for the time devoted to the building of such a vessel, and in the meantime the party who ordered the construction of the vessel should die or leave the vicinity, the finished vessel shall not be allowed to sail and shall be sold. In such circumstances the creditors who had furnished the lumber, nails, ropes, cotton, anchors, or

other essential materials for the construction of the vessel, or those who have a claim for the wages due them for the labor in constructing the vessel, they together with the other investors have the priority claim to the money from the sale of the vessel. Thus, neither the wife of the party who had ordered the vessel constructed nor any other of his creditors can have prior claim to those mentioned above, but only if the vessel had not left the locality where it was constructed without the agreement of the individuals who had the previously mentioned claims upon the vessel.

If the vessel had been allowed to sail without any opposition of the original creditors and was subsequently sold, the original suppliers mentioned will be paid from the proceeds of the sale of the vessel only after the shareholders of the vessel who had provided the initial capital will be repaid, that is, before any other interested party in the construction of the vessel.

21. Furthermore, no commander of a jolly-boat should dare to remove from the vessel any sailor or other member of the crew without the consent of the master of the vessel or his representative. Anyone guilty of violating the above shall be fined one hundred soldinos.

22. Furthermore, no skipper, fisherman, or any other person shall dare to cast nets weighed down with stones and equipped with buoys nearer than twenty-five paces away from the shore, that is, from the walls of the arsenal and the signs posted at the walls of Saint Daniel's. Anyone guilty of violation of this ordinance shall pay a fine of one hundred soldinos, and any master of a vessel or his representative and the sailors who come upon nets placed in such positions, in the area between the walls mentioned, may take or cut the nets without being subject to any kind of punishment.

If, however, any fisherman or skipper or anyone else would wish to drop his nets in the waters described above, he may do so provided the nets are weighed down with bags of sand.

23. Furthermore, a gondolier or other person engaged in using of boats for transporting of merchandise cannot have or maintain in his establishment more than two slaves for labor aboard his boat; he is also forbidden to use more than two slaves for loading or unloading his craft, and these two slaves shall be his personal property and not the property of some other person. Anyone guilty of violation of the above provision shall be deprived of any slaves in excess of the number used as laborers aboard his craft.

24. Furthermore, no patron or a financier or anyone else entrusted with command by the owner shall be allowed to negotiate loans using as collateral the investment the shareholders have in the vessel, if these shareholders are not present in the locality where such loans

would be negotiated. Any such loan-maker will be unable to present any claims for the repayment of such loans, even if the agreement indicated that the loan was negotiated for the procurement of essentials for the vessel, unless such a loan was made with the express approval of the mentioned shareholders.

25. Furthermore, each shareholder on the strength of his investment in the vessel can bring about the auctioning off of such a vessel and all the equipment aboard it at a public marketplace and may accept the sum bid for it, and subtract the amount of his investment from the price received for it, and the master of the vessel cannot deny him the right to do this; as a matter of fact, the patron of the vessel shall be forced to agree to the sale of the vessel upon such demand. He shall also be forced to approve such sale and accept the remainder of the proceeds after the shareholder has subtracted the amount of his investment, and such sale may be conducted anywhere except in the territory of the Saracens.

However, the purchaser of such a vessel shall complete the voyage that the vessel was engaged to undertake before it was placed on sale.

26. Furthermore, if a party enters into an agreement with another party relating to the construction of a vessel, specifying that the party of the second part shall accept and pay for a share in the vessel, and the two parties had agreed upon the size of the vessel, the party who had agreed to invest in such an undertaking shall be forced to take the necessary amount from his possessions and invest it as promised.

Under such conditions, the Governor-General of His Majesty the King should force the former party to raise the amount he agreed to invest in the vessel. If, however, the size of the vessel was increased without the knowledge of such an investor, he shall not be required to invest the amount he had promised.

27. Furthermore, if the vessel took on cargo or some other merchandise and while under sail to its port of destination, it will be necessary to throw overboard part of the cargo due to stormy seas or violent winds, or in order to escape the pursuit of enemy ships or vessels, or in order to save those aboard or the vessel itself, the master of the vessel or his substitute should not proceed with this unless he had received the approval of the majority or all of the merchants or their representatives who are aboard the vessel and are the owners of the major portion of the cargo or the merchandise carried aboard the vessel.

If it is necessary to throw some cargo overboard in order to prevent a greater tragedy, and there are no merchants aboard the vessel, the master of the vessel can only do this with the consent and demand of the majority of all the sailors present on the deck of the vessel.

It is further stated that if there is an actual necessity to throw some cargo overboard, and this was actually done, all the personal effects, cargo, money, all the silver whether in coins or tablewear, jewelry or other valuables, all the bills of lading and other papers relating to the vessel or the cargo aboard, pearls, gold brocades, silks, and all other merchandise shall be assessed to pay the damages, except sea chests, that is the wood from which they are made, weapons, clothing, and bed linens of all the persons aboard the vessel, regardless of the fact whether the formerly mentioned property was above or below the deck.

28. Furthermore, all the personal property and merchandise that had been thrown overboard shall be evaluated at the price these items would bring at the port of destination where this property was to be unloaded.

29. Furthermore, the vessel itself shall be assessed at the value it will have after the incident had taken place and after it has reached the port where it is to be unloaded; the vessel shall share in the losses suffered up to half of its value ascertained in the manner above.

30. Furthermore, the owner or the patron of the vessel shall be required to share in the loss of the cargo that had been thrown overboard to the full extent of the lading fees he had received, both for the cargo salvaged as well as for the cargo that had been lost, because the patron is entitled to receive lading fees for all of the cargo that he had taken aboard. The patron shall be able to deduct from the sum he had received from the lading charges, after taking inventory of all the leases, the amount due to the crew in wages, and no one shall be permitted to prevent this.

31. Furthermore, if the master of the vessel or the party representing him had put aboard the vessel any cargo or merchandise of the merchants without their consent, and if due to the circumstances described above it shall be necessary to throw this cargo overboard, the master of the vessel and not the merchants shall be held liable, unless the merchants had specifically agreed that such cargo could be stored on the deck; it should be stated that the cargo loaded below the deck or any other merchandise mentioned above shall not be assessable for the damage of the cargo stored on the deck.

It should be further stated that the cargo stored on the deck shall be thrown overboard before any cargo stored below decks, the latter cargo being liable for assessment in case the need to throw some of it overboard shall arise.

32. Furthermore, it should be further stated that the cargo carried below the deck shall not be liable for the assessment to pay the claims

for any cargo carried on the deck unless such cargo was carried
packed in chests.

33. Furthermore, the patron of the vessel or his representative
may take the necessary amount from the caro carried aboard to pay
for the lading fees and for the loss occasioned by the necessity of
having to throw some of the cargo overboard, or for either of these
two purposes.

34. Furthermore, should the vessel be captured by privateers,
enemy vessels, or some other vessel and is allowed to ransom itself,
the sailors aboard shall be required to share in the payment of the
ransom in the amount due them in wages.

35. Furthermore, if any vessel, galley, or other larger craft
owned by the subjects of His Majesty the King is intercepted while on
the high seas by a galley, ship, or any other armed unit of the enemy
or enemy privateers, and the master of the former vessel decides to
defend himself, he shall be able to destroy and sink any of the other
galleys, barques, jolly-boats, or other craft sailing with him in convoy in order to save his own ship, provided he had consulted with the
majority of the personnel of these barques, galleys, jolly-boats, and
other craft, and provided he had notified all of them in writing prepared by his clerk that he will undertake such action in order to save
himself and his vessel. Should the patron of the flagship proceed in
this manner, he shall not be liable for damages of the mentioned galleys, barques, and the cargo that they had carried.

To continue: If such craft, jolly-boats, and other smaller units
were at anchor adjacent to the galley or a large vessel and the enemy
vessels or privateers came upon them, and the flagship wanted to defend itself, its master is allowed to sink the enumerated smaller
units after notifying the commanders of these boats, jolly-boats, and
other units, should the action he is planning to undertake be necessary
to safeguard his own vessel.

Under such circumstances the large galley or other type of large
vessel as well as the cargo aboard such a vessel shall be liable for
the damages wrought to boats, jolly-boats, and other small craft proportionally to the number and value of such craft, and the amount
such smaller craft would be assessed at in case cargo from the flagship had to be thrown overboard.

36. Furthermore, the patron should sail to such destination with
the crew and equipment as had been agreed to with the merchants
when they had leased the vessel. If the master of a vessel loaded the
cargo of the merchants aboard his vessel but failed to carry out the
terms of their agreement, the merchants may file charges against
him before the judge if they so choose, and the judge will punish him
in the degree decided mutually by the merchants and the patron of the

vessel when they had reached an agreement relating to the shipment of the cargo. The patron of the vessel shall have equal right of making such claims against the merchants, according to the agreement concluded between them.

37. Furthermore, an alien who is not a subject of His Majesty the King is prohibited from cutting, using, or taking away from the domain of His Majesty any common oak or evergreen oak. Anyone guilty of violating the above provision shall be fined one thousand soldinos, and the wood he had taken shall be confiscated in the name of His Majesty the King; in addition, any master of a vessel or a barque who had attempted to export such lumber shall be fined one thousand soldinos.

Let it also be known that the clerk, navigator, and the head guard are authorized to act in the name of the master of the vessel if he should not be personally present. A like responsibility rests upon the shoulder of any person appointed master of a vessel by its owners, whether such craft be a barque or any other type of watercraft.

38. Furthermore, His Majesty the King, his officers, and all other officials have the authority to summon, question, and assess fines against all persons, sailors, crossbowmen, or any other persons, as had been mentioned above, but only under the condition when the charges are made against such persons by the patron of the vessel, his representative, or the clerk. From all the fines and other monetary assessments levied against all parties, the judge or the court that had adjudicated the issue shall retain two thirds of the amount while the accuser shall receive one third of the amount collected in fines.

All the officials of the King as well as the consuls are required to carry out the above provisions in a manner that will enforce these provisions in conformity with the will of His Majesty the King.

Thus we order and instruct all and every individual that they adhere to all the above mentioned articles and ordinances contained therein, which We ordain for the common good (as had been previously stated). We hereby proclaim that they be faithfully and in all details carried out.

Given at Barcelona, on the tenth day of December, in the year of Our Lord, 1340.

Ordinances of the Councilmen of Barcelona Regarding Consuls Stationed in Sicily.

1. In the presence of all merchants and masters of vessels as well as other types of watercraft summoned specially for this purpose, the Councilmen and Elders of the City of Barcelona decree that a consul appointed to serve at Messina, Syracuse, Palermo, or Trapani shall be required to pledge an oath that he will observe, administer, and enforce to the best of his ability all the rights and privileges that the cities of Barcelona and Majorca and the inhabitants thereof enjoy in Sicily, and that he will also protect and defend all the merchants and masters of vessels as well as all other subjects of His Majesty the King of Aragon and the King of Majorca, regardless of the social status of persons involved, that he shall defend them in all litigations in the courts of law, in all disputes with the customs authorities, or with any other instrumentalities of the government, if they should be treated unjustly or should have suffered any damage.

2. Furthermore, they decree that all merchants, masters of vessels, and all sailors pledge under oath before the consul that they will report to him how much money they had spent and what type of cargo they had sold in the territory within his jurisdiction, and that they will pay the consul his fees based on the circumstances listed below; full credence shall be given to each interested party upon a deposition made under oath.

3. Furthermore, they decree that all the merchant subjects of the King of Aragon or the King of Majorca, arriving at Messina, Syracuse, Palermo, or Trapani, are required to pay the consul on all the cargo imported on the basis of one twelfth of an ounce for each ounce of cargo, and the merchant's estimate of the amount of his cargo shall be accepted under oath.

If any merchant should be unable to sell his cargo anywhere in Sicily and will be forced to take his cargo somewhere else, he will be required to pay the consul three fourths of a gram for each ounce of his cargo and no more.

4. Furthermore, they decree that if a merchant or anyone else brought to Sicily money or bills of exchange and used them there, he

shall be required to pay the consul a fee equal to one and one-half percent of the amount involved, as had been stated before.

5. Furthermore, they decree that every master of a single deck vessel pay the consul a fee of five thalers per each deck on every vessel or any other kind of sea craft; it should be understood that this fee is payable each time a vessel delivers and picks up a cargo, on every voyage made.

6. Furthermore, every sailor arriving from any point outside of Sicily shall pay the consul for each voyage completed by the vessel one salut.[123] If any of the sailors had merchandise valued above seven ounces of silver, he shall pay the consular fee on the merchandise but not on his own person.

7. Furthermore, they decree that no master of a vessel shall be required to pay the consular fee for his own person but that all others shall pay such fees. However, should the patron of a vessel bring money or bills of credit, he shall pay in the same amount as do the merchants.

8. Furthermore, they decree that all masters of vessels, all merchants, and sailors pay the consular fee no later than three days before their vessel leaves the port or the shore of the area.

9. Furthermore, they decree that every master, merchant, and sailor pay the fees due to the consul at the locality where the vessel is berthed. If the cargo had been unloaded at some other place in Sicily, the consular fees shall be paid where the cargo was unloaded, if the cargo was sold there. The consul shall issue a proper receipt for the fees paid, and no other fees shall be paid anywhere in Sicily on this same cargo at any other place, because the receipt will show that these fees had been paid at the location where the cargo was sold.

10. Furthermore, they decree that if any merchant or any other person by the will of God should die in Sicily without leaving a partner who would be able to conduct the affairs of the deceased, the consul with the Elders of the Merchant Guild will take control of such property and interests of the deceased, will make an inventory of his possessions, see to it that these possessions are safeguarded, and deliver them to the friends of the deceased or to the Councilmen.

11. Furthermore, they decree that in the event the partners of the deceased take control of his property in Barcelona or at Majorca or at any other place, and a dispute develops between them so that one of

---

123. *Salut* or *carlin,* a silver coin, also coined in gold, from 1278 in Naples by the King of Anjou. The gold salut weighed approximately 4.4 grains while the silver salut weighed 3.34 grains.

them cannot agree with the other and will want to take part of the cargo to be sold somewhere else, with the exception of Barcelona and Majorca where they had taken control of such property, and the other partner shall not agree to this and will take the matter before the consul, asking that the consul should not agree to the demands made by the first partner, but should decide in favor of the second partner who will take the property to the place where they had originally taken control over it, if the consul shall decide in favor of the latter, he shall make certain that the property will not be transported to some other place not designated by him.

12. Furthermore, they decree that in the event the consul and the Elders of the Merchant Guild discover and are able to prove that a particular merchant who had accepted control over a cargo of another is gambling, carousing, or wasting it, the consul and the Elders are commanded to take away all moneys found on his person as well as all the merchandise in his possession. After a consultation among themselves, they shall dispose of the cargo as has been suggested, and they shall take the cargo and the party who had accepted control over it and place them aboard a vessel bound for Catalonia or Majorca.

In the register kept by the clerk aboard this vessel, there shall be an entry made to the effect that this person cannot sell any of this cargo or dispose of it in any manner whatsoever, but rather that this cargo shall be returned to the persons who had originally entrusted it to his care. If the erring merchant refuses to board such a vessel, the consul and the Elders shall store such cargo in a safe place for the time being, until the parties who had entrusted this cargo to the former merchant will notify them in what manner to dispose of the cargo and until their wishes are carried out.

13. Furthermore, they decree that in the event any merchant or master of a vessel would have to appeal to the consul to leave his place of office in order to protect or defend them, such a merchant or master of a vessel must provide proper transportation and maintenance for the consul, the type to which a man of his rank is entitled to, and the consul shall not demand payment of any fees.

14. Furthermore, they decree that in the event the customs officials or any other functionaries of the King of Sicily, by any of their actions, cause harm to any of the Catalans, and the consul shall be required to go directly to the King in this matter, the consul shall be reimbursed for this effort and for his proper appearance before the King; these expenses shall be shared by all the interested parties, that is to say, such expenses shall be divided among all the merchants and masters of vessels who happen to be present at that locality.

Ordinances of the Councilmen of Barcelona Relating to Marine Commerce, proclaimed on the Twenty-first Day of November, A.D. 1435

Upon the recommendations of Their Highness, William de Sent Climent, Cavalier, Judge of Barcelona, and of Mattheu Dezvall, Governor-General of that city, and each of them from within his own jurisdiction, Councilmen and Elders of the city, and in order to protect and regulate the activities of vessels and other craft sailing the seas, and for the protection of such commerce, ordain the following:

That, from this date on, all patrons of vessels as well as other sailing craft capable of carrying more than five hundred salmo[124] of cargo shall be required to retain the services of a clerk aboard their vessel who had taken the oath of office, from whom they shall demand an oath of office in accordance with the provisions made for the administering of such an oath in the book of the *Consulate*,[125] that he shall also observe the provisions of the ordinances contained herein; thus none of the above mentioned vessels or other craft can attempt to sail without a sworn clerk. Should a patron or clerk of a vessel violate these resolutions, neither of them shall be paid any wages or share of the profit made from such an undertaking.[126]

2. Furthermore, the formerly mentioned Councilmen and Elders ordain that from this date on, all obligations related to loans involving the usual risks of sea commerce will be executed in an official public act, otherwise it will be impossible to enforce the fulfillment of the terms stated within, as had been explicitly stated above.[127]

In all such depositions mentioned above the master of the vessel

---

124. *Salmo*, a unit of weight equal to one eighth-ton. Actually 500 pounds as the contemporary ton was 4000 pounds.

125. Reference is made to Article 57 of the

126. Refers to a clerk who had not been administered the oath of his office.

127. In the original manuscript these ordinances were not numbered. In order to avoid confusion each article starting with the word Item was numbered.

as well as the clerk shall state their consent to such loans and state under oath that all these loans made in pursuance of marine commerce or on the basis of some other agreement that had included the risk clause have been paid off without any attempt at deceit or fraud, and that such loans were negotiated for the needs and purposes of the vessel engaged in a specific voyage. In addition, they must pledge that they shall keep an account of every expense incurred in outfitting and of buying the necessities and supplies for the vessel, which shall be necessary at any place from which the vessel shall depart to continue its voyage, and that all these expenditures shall be entered into the register.[128] All this must be done in order that the loan makers could find within the wording of such agreements made regarding these loans and be able to prove if the need shall arise that the money was used for specific needs, essentials, and expenses, and whether these loans were actually used for the purposes claimed, and if there had been any deceit or fraud attempted by the master of the vessel or the clerks, who are required to observe in most minute detail the intent and meaning of the Barcelona ordinances and the articles of the *Consulate,* and carry them out, each within its proper domain.

If they should violate these ordinances, they shall forfeit their wages and any profit accruing from these enterprizes, and their share shall accrue to the other shareholders of the vessel. In addition, clerks of such vessels shall be punished in the manner prescribed in the articles of the *Consulate.*

Furthermore, masters of vessels violating these ordinances are answerable with all their property for these marine loans and other agreements involving marine risks, even if their vessels should be lost due to any circumstance, unless they can prove that the money had been used to repair damage suffered by the vessel, and the money had to be also used to refit the vessel and expended on other essentials for the vessels or other sailing units.

3. Furthermore, the previously mentioned Councilmen and Elders decree that from this date on, all loans and other agreements concluded that contain the risk clause, which can be ascertained in the manner described above, and indicating that such loans were used for the needs and expenses of the same identical journey and the identical destination, although there was a difference in the time period between the issuance of the loans and completion of the journey, that is, if some of these loans were negotiated earlier and some later, all of

---

128. In the original, *en lo libre de la nau.* In the *Consulate,* *cartolari.*

these loans must be acknolwedged, liquidated and repaid by the owners of the vessel or from their lading fees and profits that they had made, and in case of need, out of the wealth of the master of the vessel as well as from the wealth of the other interested parties in the vessel, and that these loans and other financial agreements should be adjusted and liquidated proportionally to the amount of each of these loans without any other considerations and without claims of priority based on the date such loans were concluded.

4. Furthermore, the above mentioned Councilmen and Elders ordain that from this date, no master of a vessel or anyone acting in his name may pay, apportion, or assign from the amount received or due from the lading fees for a specific voyage, with the intention of liquidating the loans or debts encumbering the vessel that he commands, which would be detrimental to and diminish the amount due in wages to the crew signed aboard for the voyage; should any of them do this, they shall be required to provide out of their own wealth the amount of money necessary to pay the wages of the crew enlisted aboard the vessel.

5. Furthermore, the above mentioned Councilmen and Elders decree that all sailors, servants, and all other personnel aboard the vessel who had been given any loans, wages, or part of their wages and refused to sail aboard the vessel of their enlistment without a just cause, as has been described in the articles of the Consulate, shall not only lose such loans, wages, or partial wages, as had been explained in the Consulate, but shall be required to repay the patrons double the amount they had received in relation to the undertaking of a specific voyage; should any of the members of the crew be unable to repay the patron double the amount they had received from him, they shall be subjected to the whipping post at Barcelona.

6. Furthermore, the previously mentioned Councilmen and Elders decree that sailors, servants, and other members of the ship's personnel who had agreed to serve aboard a vessel and promised to arm themselves appropriately at personal expense shall, if they had been given a loan or had received part of their pay, return on board of the vessel each time when due to the necessity occasioned by bad weather or some other reason it shall be necessary to leave the area where the vessel had anchored during a journey, when the patron or the clerk recall them from the shore or when they are summoned by a blaring of a horn calling them to assemble aboard, under the penalty of a whipping for all servants and the payment of a fine of one hundred soldinos for each such offense committed by sailors or other members of the crew, and all such fines may be subtracted from their wages.

7. Furthermore, the previously mentioned Councilmen and Elders

further decree that all sailors, servants, and other members of the crew are required to serve aboard the vessel of their enlistment during the entire voyage undertaken by the vessel and shall not desert or absent themselves from the vessel, either during the day or night without express permission of the master, clerk, or navigator subject to the penalty of forfeiting their wages. If they had already received part of their wages, they shall be forced to return double the amount they had received. Masters of vessels are authorized to treat such sailors, servants, and other members of the crew who behave in this manner as deserters and can discharge them for commission of such an offense; in addition, all servants guilty of such practice shall be whipped.

8. Furthermore, the previously mentioned Councilmen and Elders further decree that sailors, servants, and all other members of the crew of a vessel returned to the port of Barcelona or its shores upon completion of a voyage shall remain aboard the vessel and perform all the services in accordance with the wishes and orders of the masters and shall not disembark until they have been released by their masters, under the penalty of a fine of one hundred soldinos.

9. Furthermore, the above mentioned Councilmen and Elders further decree that all masters and clerks of vessels or any other sea craft that have been newly constructed or purchased, immediately after such vessels had been constructed or acquired shall settle all the accounts in regard to such vessels and shall make proper entries in the ledger or register of all the details of outfitting and construction of such vessels before any voyage is undertaken. All the accounts and ledgers shall remain in the custody of the shareholders in Barcelona, or in custody of a third party designated by the shareholders in the vessel. Masters of vessels and clerks shall enter in these ledgers or registers all the payments made by the shareholders as well as the amounts still due from each of them.

Should any master or clerk violate any of these provisions, he shall forfeit his wages and the profit due to him for his services in such an endeavor, and cannot submit any demands to the shareholders for any accounting in this issue.

10. Furthermore, the previously mentioned Councilmen and Elders further decree that all masters and clerks of vessels or other types of watercraft are required after the completion of each voyage to make a full accounting to the shareholders of the lading fees received, profits made, any other income or booty acquired by the vessel in accordance with the provisions that are contained in the articles of the *Consulate,* and shall prepare and submit such an account in writing for each of the shareholders in the vessel of their share of the profit, other income and any captured booty, and upon a demand made by

anyone of them to show a detail accounting of the venture to a third party mutually agreed on between them.

In the event they would not or could not reach an understanding in this matter, such a ledger or register, upon the demand of the shareholders, or any of them, should be brought before the consuls or some person designated by them. The consuls or the persons designated by them shall examine these accounts and close the matter, paying the shareholders the amount due to them on their investment in the vessel, and only after this is all done will the master of the vessel and the clerk be able to depart on another voyage, in the hope of making new profit and earning additional income.

11. Furthermore, the previously mentioned Councilmen and Elders further decree that all masters and clerks of all vessels and other crafts are required before starting on a voyage to make their vessel available for inspection by the marine consul or some person designated by him, in order to ascertain whether such vessels are seaworthy and whether they contain sea chests, weapons, and other necessary equipment in good and satisfactory condition. Should they violate these regulations, they shall forfeit all their wages and any share of profit due them for taking part in such an expedition.

In the event that after the inspection had been conducted by the consul, it was discovered that the vessel or any other sailing unit lacks some equipment essential to the safety of the vessel, this can be remedied by following the suggestions made by the Elders who are entrusted with the care, guardianship, and preservation of public welfare.

12. All money fines shall be divided into three equal parts, of which one part shall be given to the officer conducting the hearing, one part to the accuser, and the third part shall be designated for the maintenance of the fortification ramparts and walls of the city.

13. The previously mentioned Councilmen and Elders make this reservation, that if in the ordinances and resolutions herein presented there appeared any ambiguous or misleading statements, they themselves as well as their successors shall be able to change, explain, or interpret them when they shall deem this necessary.

Ordinances

Processes for Recovering of Cargo [property]

Article 23

Merchants and Sailors Who Are about to Undertake a Return Voyage May Not Be Detained to Testify Regarding Depositions Made by Others.

Merchants and sailors who are about to sail out into the sea cannot be detained to give testimony in any litigations that are to commence at that moment, if their vessel, raft, or barque is ready to sail or is on the sea, provided that they give assurance that they shall return to give such testimony upon returning from the voyage.

Article 69

Undertaking of a Voyage to Fulfill an Agreement

If a party agreed to undertake a voyage with a shipment of cargo that he had accepted under his control, neither his wife nor any creditor may institute any legal action against him, or demand that he return the cargo that had been entrusted to his care for that voyage, until the party who had entrusted such merchandise to his care shall not have taken possession of such merchandise or some other merchandise that the former had purchased for the money entrusted to him.

Ordinances of King James Relating to the Same Matters

We, James, by the Grace of God, etc., send greetings to our faithful Judge and Governor-General of Barcelona, etc.

We are well aware of the fact that when merchants of Barcelona undertake a voyage to any place after accepting the responsibility for the care of the cargo of one or several citizens of Barcelona and should die while engaged in such a journey, and their wives take possession of such a cargo and claim it as personal property and use it to pay their own expenses, since such a practice is contrary to all customs, ordain and proclaim that if such an incident should take place in the future, regardless of the claims presented by the wives of the deceased merchants, such cargo shall be returned and surrendered to the party who had entrusted it to the care of the deceased, provided that the owners of such cargo can prove their ownership of such cargo by public documentary evidence or by trustworthy witnesses.

Given at the Court of Barcelona, the second day of August, A.D. 1271.

Ordinances of the Councilmen of Barcelona Regarding Bills of Exchange

Upon the advice of the judge, the Councilmen and Elders of the city of Barcelona with the intent to prevent the great abuses and to avoid all sorts of losses that many people had suffered by using such bills of credit, decree:

Every person in this city, regardless of his status, allegiance, or circumstance, now and in the future, against whom bills of credit are issued by any party, should attend to the person who holds such bills of credit within twenty-four hours after being notified in order to inform the holder of these bills of credit whether he will honor or refuse to accept the responsibility for such bills of credit. If he should refuse to accept such a bill of credit, he shall note the date and the hour such a bill was presented to him on the face of the bill. After attending to this matter in the manner prescribed above, the note shall be returned to the party who had presented it for payment.

If the party to whom a bill of credit was presented for payment shall not reply in twenty-four hours, it can be taken for granted that he had accepted the bill of credit, for no other assumption can be made; the party who had accepted the note shall be responsible for liquidating it within the time mentioned within the note.

Charter of King Alfonso, Issued at Barcelona, on the Twenty-fifth Day of May, A.D. 1432

We herein ordain that any person holding an office of rank, who had purchased any merchandise required in his official capacity, regardless of the fact whether he had actually made such purchase personally or through some other party and should become insolvent, shall be imprisoned personally in the same manner as if he had accepted such merchandise under his care, unless he can prove that the merchandise had been lost owing to ill fate. We further decree that it be forever adhered to in the city of Barcelona that any person who takes anything in the exercise of his office and should fail to satisfy his creditors and is called to appear before judges appointed by Us, shall be declared a bankrupt, immediately cast into prison, and kept in prison in conformity with the laws mentioned above.

Petition of the Consular Court of Barcelona, on the Eighth Day of October, A. D. 1481, Regarding the Jurisdiction of that Court over All Donations for Public Welfare as well as for the Benefit of Widows and Other Unfortunate Persons

In order to relieve the Consular Courts of some matters relating to the various aspects of marine commerce, where these matters are adjusted summarily and instantly, there are often made false and fraudulent legacies as well as other special concessions and agreements to favor certain persons, that is, widows, wards, or other unfortunate persons, which agreements under certain circumstances remove these cases from the jurisdiction of the Consular courts and maneuver such litigation into other courts, and in this manner delay the adjudication of such issues:

The above mentioned Consular Court presents this petition in order that His Majesty the King would at His pleasure order that if any donations, bequests, or other types of agreements of this nature are made to benefit the widows, wards, or unfortunate people are attempted to be withdrawn from the jurisdiction of the Consular courts, they shall be declared invalid if they were withdrawn in order to remove them from the jurisdiction of such courts, and that such cases shall be heard and disposed of in these Consular courts, and that the above should be applicable to all the Consular courts in the principality of Catalonia.

His Majesty has consented to confirm the above petition in principle.

Guarantee of Safe Passage for Those Who Wish to Sail Beyond the Seas or to Return from Beyond the seas

Furthermore, His Majesty the King confirms for himself, his heirs, and successors in substance the contents of this article by his Royal assent, and guarantees safe conduct to all the merchants regardless of their place of origin or territorial jurisdiction, as well as to all other persons, his subjects or foreigners notwithstanding their rank, social status, legal responsibility, condition, or occupation, who may be sailing aboard vessels into the environments of

Alexandria or the Sultanate of Babylon, or be returning from there;[129] and who will be engaged in selling, transporting, and exchanging cargoes, merchandise, and any type of commodities, according to their own disposition with the exception of items and categories of goods forbidden by the general statutes. All the above mentioned parties may proceed to any locality where they may trade more advantageously without any restrictions imposed by His Majesty the King, his officers, or any other persons; they may do this without any fear of displeasure of His Majesty the King, or of any prohibitions that he had issued or might issue, or fear of any punishment that had been imposed or might have been imposed formerly against all those engaged in sailing to the above enumerated territories. It shall not be permissible to demand payment of ransom or use of any type of retribution against the vessels proceeding in that direction; further, in the period of four months from the date of the return of the vessels to Barcelona, they shall be able to proceed to all the lands and possessions of His Majesty the King, safely and peacefully, under his patronage and under his special care and protection; and in these circumstances these vessels shall be free of all burdens and any kind of obstacles and interference, as well as ransom, retributions, payments of any kind, or assessments to the account of His Majesty the King, His functionaries, or any other persons.

His Majesty the King wishes and orders that merchants, regardless of which kingdom they may have come from, when venturing into the environments of Alexandria or the territories of the sultanate, or who are resident there and wish to leave these territories in order to migrate to the southern nations from beyond the seas, may benefit from the guarantees and safe conduct mentioned above even in a situation if they did not arrive aboard the same vessel, and independent of whether the merchants came to reside permanently in the Kingdom, with their goods and effects, or if they just arrived to buy and trade cargo.

His Majesty the King further guarantees that in such cases and in any issues connected with such litigations, He will not order that an investigation be made as to their character and their possessions, nor will He institute any juridical action against them or subject them to any forms of taxation; on the contrary, the King shall protect their property, cargoes, and other possessions, and will on all occasions order that they not be subjected to interrogation or examination, or

---

129. Area described here includes modern Egypt and Syria and territories immediately adjacent.

taxation, or any civil or criminal punishment of ordinary or special nature presently existing or that shall be legislated in the future, as well as any other restrictions applicable to such persons; the above privileges apply to all the prohibitionary statutes of His Majesty the King as well to those that had been decreed by His father the King.

Thus, all persons previously mentioned, individually as well as collectively, for the causes mentioned above or any other reasons, cannot be detained, imprisoned, dispossessed, disturbed, interfered with, or subjected to interrogation because of some accusation made against them, or become objects of any judicial investigation, nor ever be sentenced to any punishment by mut   tion.

Thus, neither the King's functionaries nor His Majesty the King will ever be able to invoke against these persons or their property any ransom payments, measures of retribution, nor will they be able to make any other demands upon them, force them to give up anything, nor will they be allowed to accept anything from them.

Furthermore, His Majesty the King guarantees to the former persons that He will not issue, or agree to the issuance under any circumstances or necessity, even if such a necessity was of an urgent character, any prohibitions, obstacles, or make any demands of any nature regarding their vessels, cargoes, or crew. Under no circumstances can they be delayed or prevented from undertaking their voyage, but on the contrary, any prohibitions or penalties proclaimed by His Majesty the King and his functionaries cannot apply to them, regardless of the nature of such acts, because such vessels, cargoes, sailors, and other persons together with their possessions and properties must, as has been explained, be allowed to complete their voyage without any interference.

His Majesty Don Ferdinand during His long sojourn in Barcelona, in the Year of Our Lord 1493, ordered in Article 2, that all the alcaldes would render to the parties concerned full assistance in carrying out their decisions in all commercial matters, in accordance with the ordinances of Queen Mary. [130]

Ordinances Recently Enacted by the Councilmen of Barcelona Regarding Marine Insurance

The following is to be made public to all by the orders of Their

---

130. *Alcalde,* in Spanish use, a mayor of a town who exercised in addition certain judicial powers.

Mightiness Anthony Peter de Roca-Crespa, Cavalier, Regent, of the Judiciary, and William Poncgen, Governor-General of the City of Barcelona, each within his own jurisdiction.

The Councilmen and Elders of the latter city have decreed the following:

Due to the fact that formerly there had been issued varied ordinances regarding the risks and dangers involved in marine and commercial insurance, affecting and endangering vessels, cargoes, marine loans, other property, and possessions, which due to the passage of time should be amended, changed, and modified, these former ordinances are superseded by the articles given below. All ordinances of this nature issued before are invalidated by this ordinance, which is binding from this moment in all matters of insurance.

Article 1

Firstly, these Councilmen and Elders have decreed that all vessels and all other surface craft owned by the subjects of His Majesty the King, as well as those owned by foreigners, regardless of their nationality, as well as all marine loans negotiated for the benefit of these vessels, as well as all cargoes, possessions, and other property carried aboard such vessels to any destination in the world, regardless of their ownership, that is, whether it be the property of the subjects of His Majesty the King or of foreigners, may be insured in Barcelona, the insurable property of the subjects of His Majesty the King, to the amount seven-eighths of its actual value, and the property of foreigners to the extent of three-fourths of its actual value, and that to the actual value of the objects insured may be added the cost of transportation, and the amount of the insurance premium and other expenses.

Subjects of His Majesty the King who insure their vessels, cargoes, marine loans, and other properties shall assume a risk of one-eighth of the amount of insurance, while those who are foreigners shall assume the risk of one-fourth of the amount of coverage.

If anyone violates these ordinances either arbitrarily or unintentionally, any policy that provides a coverage of more than seven-eighths for any subject of His Majesty the King, and more than three-fourths coverage for any foreigner, such policy cannot be held valid and the claim cannot be paid. However, the insurance brokers shall receive the full premium but will be required to pay claims only up to seven-eighths and three-fourths of the coverage and no more, and no one can assess a higher amount of claim against them.

It is to be understood and it is so agreed that if it was impossible to estimate the actual value of the cargo loaded aboard the vessel in

Barcelona, the value declared at the time the vessel clears the customs shall be accepted.

If there were any marine loans taken out on the vessel, cargo, merchandise, or any other property, the amount of such loans shall be deducted from the assessed value of the vessel, cargo, merchandise, or other property. After the amount of such loans has been deducted, the insured party shall assume the loss for the remainder, that is, a subject of His Majesty the King, one-eighth of the amount insured, and a foreigner one-fourth of the amount covered, as had been stated above.

It should be understood and it is so ordained that if such vessels belonged to enemies of His Majesty the King, or to friendly people who, however, are in partnership with His enemies, such vessels or cargo cannot be insured in Barcelona either directly by its owners or by some intermediary, even if such vessels possessed iron letters;[131] if these ordinances are violated, the insurance policies issued shall be invalidated, and this matter cannot become a subject of any kind of litigation.

Let it be further understood that an insurance broker, before undertaking to provide such risk coverage for such vessels and loans, should have the vessels assessed by a reliable consul with the aid of the Elders, and on the basis of this estimate, which shall be entered into the policy, there should be deducted one-eighth from the estimated value, if the insured is a subject of His Majesty the King, and one-fourth of the value if such a vessel belongs to a foreigner. These portions of the risk shall be borne by the insured party, as had been stated before, and the question of the full amount of the risk involving the vessel can even be limited and reduced to cover the keel of the vessel only.

In case the insurance coverage of a vessel extended only to the hull of the vessel, and such vessel was wrecked, the parts salvaged from the vessel will be assessed proportionally in paying the claim of the wrecked hull. In such cases the salvage parts and the hull will be evaluated as one unit.

Article 2

Cargo Shipped from the Other Side of the Straits of Gibraltar to Flanders or the Barbary Coast Cannot Be Insured

---

131. Iron letters, a letter of safe conduct, similar to navicert issued by modern navy.

Furthermore, the former Councilmen and Elders have ordained that cargo loaded aboard the vessels on the other side of the Straits of Gibraltar, regardless of the location where it was loaded aboard the vessel, and intended for shipment to Flanders, England, or any other territory on the opposite side of the Straits of Gibraltar, or destined for any part of the Barbary Coast, or any other vessels sailing into these waters, cannot be insured in Barcelona, due to the lack of information regarding such vessels and the impossibility of ascertaining the cargo carried actually aboard such vessels; such insurance coverage could not become a basis of any legal action for claims, and all underwriters are hereby released from all responsibilities of any claims.

Excepted from the above restrictions are cargoes belonging to citizens of Barcelona. Such cargoes may be insured, provided that their owners accept the responsibility and liability to the extent of one-eighth of the value of coverage as had been stated above. If the vessels are cargoed on the other side of the Straits, and they are bound for this side, they may be insured at Barcelona, if such vessels do not sail into the Barbary Coast area, under this stipulation, that the party who insured his cargo shall accept the liability of one-eighth of the value, if these parties are the subjects of His Majesty the King, and accept a liability of one-fourth of the claim if they are foreigners, as had been stated before.

Article 3

All Cargo Bound to or from Barcelona Is Insurable

Furthermore, the Councilmen and Elders of the latter city have decreed that all cargo and merchandise regardless of its caliber taken aboard a vessel in any part of the world and destined for Barcelona, as well as any other types of vessels that carry such cargo, and are encumbered with loans that include the usual marine risks, and all cargo and merchandise loaded at Barcelona, and all vessels carrying such cargo, even if these vessels were owned by enemies of His Majesty the King, as well as all loans encumbering the vessels, may all be insured at Barcelona to the amount of three-fourths of their actual value, of both the goods and the bottoms, but cannot be insured for more than their actual value plus the cost of transportation and insurance premiums.

Article 4

Cargo Loaded Aboard at Alexandria May Be Insured According to Its Cash Value at Alexandria or in the Amount Estimated by the Parties

Concerned

Furthermore, the Councilmen and Elders taking under advisement the situation that much of the cargo, merchandise, and other goods taken aboard at Alexandria is purchased on credit, and that a great profit is realized by exchanging such shipment while en route for other cargo and goods, and thus the actual value of such shipments cannot be ascertained for the purposes of insurance, have decreed the following: that from this date on, all insurance negotiations, the declaration of value of all cargo and goods taken aboard be stated according to the cash value such shipment had in Alexandria; thus the insured as well as the insurance brokers will be able to reach an understanding and arrive at an honest cash value of such a shipment.

Article 5

The Degree of Liability of the Insurance Underwriters

Furthermore, the latter Councilmen and Elders decree that in the event the amount of the cargo, merchandise, or other goods aboard the vessel does not correspond to the amount of cargo insured, plus one-eighth, which liability is assumed by the insured if he is a citizen of His Majesty the King, and one-fourth if he is a foreigner, or if the parties concerned cannot negotiate the marine loans, or if the vessels do not undertake the journey, or had failed to return back from a journey, the underwriters in such cases do not receive either a full or partial payment of the premiums, but only to the extent the coverage was effected.

If, however, no cargo had been loaded aboard, or if the marine loans could not be negotiated, or if the vessel had neither left for a voyage nor returned from a voyage, the underwriters under such circumstances are required to refund the insurance premiums that had been paid to them.

Article 6

No One Can Insure His Shipment Anywhere Else for More Than Seven-eighths of Its Value If He Is a Subject of His Majesty the King, and More Than Three-fourths of its Value If He Is a Foreigner

Furthermore, the latter Councilmen and Elders had decreed that anyone who had insured his vessel and its contents anywhere else may buy insurance in Barcelona only in the amount that he will need to reach the amount of seven-eighths of the maximum coverage possible and allowable for a subject of His Majesty the King, and three-fourths of the coverage allowable for foreigners, since he must assume the liability himself for the remainder of one-eighth of the value of the insurable property.

Similarly, anyone who insures himself in Barcelona will be able to insure himself elsewhere only in the amount necessary to reach the maximum coverage of seven-eighths of the total value and assume the liability for one-eighth of the value himself, if he is a subject of His Majesty the King, since he must always assume a minimum liability of one-eighth of the value of the insured property, and if he is a foreigner only enough to reach the estimated value of three-fourths, since he shall always have to assume liability for one-fourth of the cargo.

In the event the above should be violated, it shall not benefit the insured or harm the underwriter, in conformity with what has been stated above; it cannot be a basis for any legal judgment, and the insurance premium shall be paid to the underwriters. The amount of insurance that had been beyond the sum allowable to be insured shall accrue to the underwriters, that is to say, that this amount shall be taken into consideration when claims are adjusted.

Article 7

All Insurance Contracts Are Required to be Executed in the Form of a Notarial Act

Furthermore, the latter Councilmen and Elders have decreed that all insurance contracts executed in Barcelona shall be prepared by a notary in form of an official notarial document, and not in form of an ordinary policy, promissory note, or some other type of an agreement of private contractural nature.

If such insurance contracts were entered into in a form of a policy, a promissory note, or other type of agreement of private nature, they shall be unenforcable and invalid in the eyes of the law, and the underwriters cannot be forced to pay any liabilities, nor can such contracts become a basis of any judicial adjudication.

Regardless of the illegality of all such acts, the underwriters, the insured, their agents, and any third parties involved in such transactions shall be fined, each of those who bought such insurance, in the amount of the policy, and each of the underwriters, in the amount of coverage sold, while any agent or third party involved in such transaction shall be fined ten livres.

One-third of the amount of the levied fines shall be taken by the functionary who conducted the hearings in these matters, one-third shall be given to the accuser, and the remaining third shall be set aside for the charitable activities of the city.

Article 8

Penalties for Violation of These Ordinances

Furthermore, the latter Councilmen and Elders have decreed that any underwriter guilty of violation of any of the above ordinances in any manner whatsoever shall forfeit his office and his property in addition to the penalties prescribed above.

Article 9

Buyers of Insurance Are Required to Make a Deposition under Oath That the Estimate of the Value of Their Insurable Property Is Truthful

Furthermore, the latter Councilmen and Elders have decreed that those who purchase insurance in their own name or on behalf of some other party, or while acting under the power of attorney, or recommend that someone be insured, are required above all to state under oath that the cargo or other goods insured is real and not fictitious, and that the commodities that they wish to insure belong to them or to the party in whose behalf they are acting, or to their partners or other interested parties who have an investment in this insurable merchandise.

In such insurance contracts they are required to state specifically and accurately, as far as that is possible, all essential facts about the goods being insured, such as weight, quantity, value, and price of the insurable items, and if vessels are being insured, the amount at which such vessels have been evaluated, in conformity with what had been stated previously, and finally, they shall promise that these goods have not and will not be insured somewhere else also. If it should happen that these goods had been or would be insured somewhere else, they must agree to notify the underwriters immediately and shall make a note of this action on the bottom of the page of the insurance contract, in which they will state in what manner they were notified and will name the place where the insurance was purchased, giving the date and the amount of coverage bought.

If the insured failed to make such depositions, and the consuls assert that this particular party concluded an insurance contract, even though such a party knew that such goods had already been insured elsewhere and failed to mention this fact, it should be taken for granted that the underwriters were misled and that the contract was invalid. Nevertheless, in all such circumstances the underwriters shall be allowed to retain the insurance premiums they had been paid.

In such cases of attempted fraud, the insured parties shall pay a fine of one hundred Barcelona livres, of which one-third of the amount shall be retained by the official who conducted these hearings, one-third of the amount shall be given to the party who initiated the accusation, and the remaining one-third of the amount shall be set aside for the charitable purposes of the city.

Article 10

Oath of Office Required of Insurance Underwriters

Furthermore, the latter Councilmen and Elders have decreed that insurance underwriters must take an oath before undertaking to sell any insurance that the risk liability they are about to underwrite actually exists and is not fictitious, that they are not taking such responsibility in an attempt to defraud under the guise of protection, and that they are not entering into such contracts in the name of other parties.

Article 11

All Insurance Contracts Written Shall Conform to the Meaning and Intent of the Above Ordinances

Furthermore, the latter Councilmen and Elders have decreed that underwriters and purchasers of insurance should invoke these ordinances in all contracts and abide by them and also promise that in all circumstances they shall be bound by them, that they will in cases under dispute submit the issue to the Consular court and to no other judicial body, and that they renounce all rights to institute litigation in these cases before tribunals that may be partial to their cause. All these matters must be attended to in the manner and procedure believed by the notaries to be most apropos to the insured party.

Article 12

The Right to Challenge the Jurisdiction of Consular Courts

Furthermore, the latter Councilmen and Elders have decreed, in due consideration of the fact that the purpose of liability insurance is to facilitate commerce, it would be improper that disputes arising from this pursuit should be adjudicated in other courts or by other functionaries and not by marine consuls, and appealed to the Judges of Appeal, who are called together with the Elders for the purpose of adjudicating such issues in conformity with these ordinances and the customs set forth in the Consulate:

They have decreed that from this moment no underwriter or purchaser of risk insurance can challenge the jurisdiction of the consular courts, nor be allowed due to his rank or title or any other privilege to take any issue concerned with liability insurance before any other judicial body. If this ordinance is violated, the insured party who appealed to another court, attempting to use some privilege or other reason, will be liable to a fine, to which he had voluntarily agreed when he negotiated the instrument of insurance. He shall also lose all rights to adjudication of this issue, which he had before on the basis of the agreement he reached and which he could use before paying the claim. The insured parties shall be released from all their obligations and will not be required to defend themselves in any legal action brought against them.

If the insured after accepting the claims paid them instituted legal action for additional claims before any but the consular court, under the guise that their rank, status, or some other privilege entitled them to take the case to another court, they shall pay a fine, which they had agreed to at the conclusion of such an agreement and shall be required to refund to the underwriters the amount they had received in claims, and shall be prevented from advancing any other grievances.

If the underwriters should challenge the jurisdiction of the consular court under the pretext that their rank, status, or any other privilege entitles them to other considerations, or should have instituted action in any other court of law, they shall pay the penalty agreed to freely at the time they had concluded an insurance contract, and any action taken against them is automatically allowed, and no attempt shall be permitted to frustrate any such action, in order to be exempt from paying such a fine, nor shall any other attempt to oppose the rights of those insured be allowed. Thus, in this manner they will actually act as their own accusers and subject themselves to the payment of the fine to which they had freely agreed, and they shall also be forced to pay all the claims of the insured party together with all the expenditures the latter suffered in prosecution of that case.

All of the above resolutions shall be rendered more binding by the taking of an oath by the parties concerned and by the relinquishing of the right of appeal to a court that would be partial to their cause, as well as the renouncement of all clauses and stipulations that the notary who had prepared the insurance contract would consider useful and necessary.

Article 13

The Impropriety of Including of Clauses into the Contract That Would Be in Conflict with the Object of This Ordinance

Furthermore, the latter Councilmen and Elders have decreed that in any insurance contract the introduction or incorporation of any clauses or obligations contrary to this ordinance shall be prohibited, nor shall the words "binding" or "not binding" or "there is," or "there is not," be written into the contract, nor finally, to decide that an insurer who is the subject of His Majesty the King will not bear the one-eighth liability of the insured amount, or one-fourth of the liability of the amount if he is a foreigner. Under no circumstances are any deviations from the meaning and intent of these ordinances allowed; as they were enacted for the public good and for common usage, any attempt to deviate from the above shall render all the instruments of insurance void and nonconsequential.

Article 14

Punishment of Notaries

Furthermore, the latter Councilmen and Elders have decreed that any notary who had prepared an insurance contract should first of all administer an oath to the underwriters, and then demand that they make a deposition that their liability is actual and that they are not issuing a policy with the view of deceiving or defrauding anyone, and that they are not accepting this risk to pass it on to someone else, because the other underwriters shall accept the liability in their stead; they shall execute all insurance contracts in accordance with the form prescribed by this ordinance and are not allowed to deviate from the wording of the same.

The notaries should insist that the buyers of insurance sign the policy before the underwriters are allowed to affix their signatures. They are forbidden to include any stipulations in any insurance contract and must not allow either party to such a contract to make any stipulations intended to avoid the acceptance of one-eighth of the liability, or one-fourth of the liability by the party purchasing the insurance, as had been stated above.

Any notary guilty of violating these ordinances shall be required to pay damages to both the underwriters and the purchasers of the policy, because he had failed to live up to the obligations expected of him.

Article 15

Failure to Pay the Premium Invalidates the Policy

Furthermore, the latter Councilmen and Elders have decreed that all insurance policies will be voided and unpayable until the premiums have been paid, and until the underwriters execute and endorse these policies in accordance with the procedure outlined above.

Article 16

Simultaneous Signing of All Insurance Contracts

Furthermore, the latter Councilmen and Elders have decreed that all signatures of parties who had purchased risk insurance that have been affixed to the insurance policy are to be considered as having been affixed at different dates. Thus, none of the signatories have priority of making claim demands, and no court of law may give cognizance to such a claim.

Article 17

Risk Insurance Purchased Fraudulently Is Invalid

Furthermore, the latter Councilmen and Elders have decreed that if an agreement had been reached regarding the insuring of vessels, marine loans, cargo, merchandise, or other property, which had been taken aboard and carried to any place outside of Barcelona, and the above shipment had been lost, and at the time of signing of such an agreement by some or all of the insured, the news of the loss of such shipment could have reached Barcelona, the insurance contract shall be declared voided and nonexistent. The underwriters, however, cannot retain such a premium and must refund it to the purchasers of the policy, regardless of any charges that would be made against them; the underwriters cannot be hailed before a tribunal under any pretext in an attempt to force them to assume the liability and to pay the claim, and they cannot be found guilty of any charges.

In order to remove all uncertainty as to the actual date that such information could have been available, the Councilmen and Elders have decreed the following: that if the vessel was lost on this side of the sea, that is, in the waters from which the news of the loss of the vessel could have been sent overland without the necessity of it crossing the sea, the minimum time required will be judged to be at the rate of one mile per hour. Thus, it would have taken as many hours for the news to travel as there are miles separating the two places, that is, the exact location and the time the insured property was lost, and for which the underwriters will be required to pay liability to the insured party at Barcelona.

If the loss of the vessel had taken place in waters from which it will be necessary to send news of its destruction by sea or across the Straits, the time estimated for this information to reach Barcelona will be counted from the time this information had reached this side of the sea; from this point it shall be measured at one mile per hour.

If, however, such information is brought directly to Barcelona across the sea, the time estimated for this information to reach Barcelona shall be from the moment the vessel came in contact with the land or was moored; if, in the opinion of the consuls, enough time had elapsed for this information to have reached the policy buyers before they had signed such an insurance contract, in such a case the insurance contract will be voided, in conformity with what had been previously stated.

If it should happen that the policy buyer knew of the loss of the vessel before he undertook to insure it, he will be fined one hundred Barcelona livres, of which one-third will accrue to his accuser, one-third to the official conducting the hearings, and one-third shall be set aside for the charity fund of the city.

Article 18

Insuring of Foodstuffs

Furthermore, the latter Councilmen and Elders have decreed that wheat, oats, vegetables, beans, wine, and olive oil, taken aboard and destined for Barcelona, may be insured at Barcelona, regardless of the above ordinances to the full amount of the value or estimate mutually agreed upon, but only within the wording and meaning conveyed in this ordinance; in all other circumstances all the provisions of the ordinance shall be strictly observed.

Article 19

Payment of Claims

Furthermore, the latter Councilmen and Elders have decreed that the underwriters collectively and individually are required to pay all the claims for which they assumed liability, or such part of it as they underwrite in a period of two, three, four, or six months, depending on the distance, counting the time from the moment the vessel reached Barcelona, and notifying the majority or all of the underwriters with the knowledge of the consuls of the verified information about the loss or damage that the vessel or other insured property suffered; all such claims shall be attended to as quickly as the payment of bills of exchange.

If the underwriters advanced some reasons why they are not liable or if such insinuations appeared well-founded to the consuls, in each instance where the information received about the loss or damages is accepted, and if sufficient time had elapsed as had been determined above, and the insured demand payment of their claims, the underwriters shall be required to pay such claims upon demand, regardless of any insinuations that may be made.

If the underwriters would be able to present clear and indisputable proof that the insured should not and cannot be paid any part of the damages asked for, and if the local court determines that these charges are of such nature that the parties insured, who demand payments of claims, should show and prove the injustice of these accusations made by the underwriters, refusing to honor such claims, in such a case when the insured demands payment of the claims, he shall be required to furnish a guarantor (the expenses of this guarantor will be paid by the underwriters and not by the insured party) whose ability to pay the amount in question will be determined by the Consuls, who will also guarantee to each of the insured parties the damages together with all the expenses and costs incurred, as well as interest at two soldinos per livre per year, if within one year from the day of the payment of the claim, the insured parties cannot get a decree from the Consular court to the effect that the claims they had been paid were justly received.

Due to the fact that some non-God-fearing people had accepted payments of claims, even though such insured cargo or merchandise was actually never loaded aboard the vessel, and the vessel actually never undertook the voyage or returned from one, and the marine loans were not negotiated, the guilty party shall be fined two soldinos for every livre of evaluation for each such offense, and in addition shall pay two soldinos per livre for the amount he had insured his shipment or vessels; the third part of this fine, at the rate of two soldinos per livre shall accrue to the consuls and shall be added to the fees of the court; one-third of the amount shall be given to the underwriters, and the remaining third part shall be given to the charity fund of the city or to the fund of the public marine defenders.

It shall not be permissible for anyone who had concluded an insurance agreement and paid the risk premiums with the thought that he would be paid the amount of the insurance purchased without any additional expenses should have to suffer due to some accusations made by the underwriters, which accusations cannot actually prevent payment of any justifiable claims; the Councilmen and Elders had decreed that such accusations of the underwriters shall be set aside; the underwriters shall be ordered to pay the insured all the expenses borne in order to get a judgment for such payment, as well as the payment of all damages, as had been stated before.

Article 20

When the Insured Unable to Get a Legal Judgment Will Be Required to Refund the Claim Payments

Furthermore, the latter Councilmen and Elders have decreed that in the event the insured were forced to refund the claim payment received due to their inability to get the final decree in accordance with what had been stated above, after returning such a payment each party retains all the rights and legal avenues that may be resorted to in order to resolve the issue if the underwriters shall be required to pay the insurance to the insured. The underwriters shall retain a percentage of the amount and shall not be required to refund this, even if it had been decided that they shall pay upon demand part or all of the claim. The adjustment of such an issue lies within the jurisdiction of the consuls, and in the event an appeal is taken before the judge of appeals, but to no other court whatsoever.

Article 21

When the Insured Agree to Allow the Amount of the Claim under Dispute to Remain in the Hands of the Underwriters until the Final Disposition of the Case Is Made

Furthermore, the latter Councilmen and Elders have decreed that in the event the consuls have decided that the insured should procure a guarantor, as had been stated above, and the latter fail to comply with such a request, but rather allow the underwriters to retain control of all or part of the money due to them in payment of their claims, and subsequently the Consular court orders that the underwriters shall pay the damages to the insured, regardless of any opposition of the latter, the underwriters shall be forced to pay the insured all the expenses in the amount ascertained by the consuls, with an interest of two soldinos per livre per year, for the entire period of delay of the payment.

In regards to the payment of claims and the interest, the underwriters will be required upon the demand of the insured, after posting a guarantee in court, unless immediately after making the accusations and agreeing to furnish a guarantor, they will deposit an amount equal to the amount due in claims with the court.

Article 22

The Underwriters May before the Date Due for the Payment of Claims, Prove the Validity of the Accusations They Intend to Make

Furthermore, they have decreed that before the lapse of time when the claims are to be paid, that is, two, three, four, or six months, depending upon the distances involved, the underwriters present and demand that the accusations that they had made in order to prove that they should not be required to pay the claims, and that the issue be examined and proved, they may do so. If the date of the payment of claims had arrived before the issue was adjudicated, the underwriters shall be required to pay all the claims without any further delay and without any regard to the accusations made, in accordance with the statements made above. After they have made these payments, they may, however, pursue this matter.

Article 23

Time Limitations on Claims Payments

Furthermore, they had decreed that such claim payments shall be made as follows:

In a period of two months, if the vessels were to sail, or the cargo or merchandise was to be shipped and delivered within the territorial boundaries of the Kingdom of Catalonia or the Kingdoms of Valencia, Majorca, Minorca, or Ibiza;

In a period of three months, if the destination was within the territories of the Kingdom of Naples, Sicily, and the Barbary Coast, on this side of the Straits of Gibraltar;

In a period of four months, if the destination was beyond the boundaries of the territories enumerated above, in any direction whatsoever;

In a period of six months, if there is no information available as to the direction the vessel had sailed.

Article 24

All Insurance Contracts Entered into Prior to the Promulgation of These Ordinances Are Not Subject to These Provisions

Furthermore, the latter Councilmen and Elders have decreed that all kinds of risk insurance bought to insure all kinds of goods, property, vessels, or anything else, and entered into in Barcelona before publication of the above ordinances, regardless of the nature and form of such contracts, shall be binding and valid, and neither these nor other ordinances that were issued subsequently can invalidate any such existing contracts.

However, from the moment this ordinance is proclaimed by a public proclamation at the various places in our city customarily used for such purposes, all the insurance contracts must be entered into in the spirit and the procedure set forth by this ordinance.

Article 25

Oath Pledged by the Underwriters and the Parties Buying Insurance before the Consuls

Furthermore, the latter Councilmen and Elders have decreed that all consuls who presently administer and will in the future administer this office are forbidden to issue a decree in any insurance litigation before administering an oath to all the underwriters and the parties purchasing marine insurance, that neither the underwriters nor the policy purchasers had entered into any agreement, orally or in writing, that would be contrary to this ordinance. If they had reached an agreement in violation of this ordinance, the terms of such a contract cannot become a basis of any judicial decision.

The latter Councilmen and Elders reserve to themselves the right of interpretation, correction, and amendment of all provisions in such a contract that may appear to them to be ambiguous or dubious, every time they shall consider this action indicated and necessary.

This ordinance was proclaimed by Anthony Strada, the city summoner, on the third day of June, in the Year of Our Lord, 1484.

At this point we come to the end of all the ordinances relating to marine insurance that have been lately issued.

The following list of Emperors, Popes, Caliphs, and the genealogical charts of the leading ruling houses in the epoch of development, compilation, adoption, and enforcement of the laws embodied within *The Consulate of the Sea*, are included for quick reference. Many of these personages, lay as well as religious, directly or indirectly, played an important role in the introduction and formalization of these statutes.

ROMAN EMPERORS: EAST AND WEST

Constantine I, the Great (Flavius Valerius Constantinus) 311(306)-337
Constantine II (Flavius Valerius Claudius Constantinus) 337-340
Constans (Flavius Valerius Julius Constans) 337-350
Constantius II (Flavius Valerius Julius Constantius) 337-361
Julian, the Apostate (Flavius Claudius Julianus) 361-363
Jovian (Flavius Jovianus) 363-364
Valentinian I (Flavius Valentinianus, in the West) 364-375
Valens (in the East) 364-378
Gratian (Flavius Gratianus Augustus, in the West) 375(367)-383
Valentinian II (Flavius Valentinianus, in the West) 375-392
Maximus (Magnus Clemens Maximus) 383-388
Theodosius, the Great (Flavius Theodosius, in the East, and after 392, in the West) 379-395
Eugenius, 392-394
Arcadius (in the East) 395(383)-408
Honorius (Flavius Honorius, in the West) 395(393)-423
Theodosius II (in the East) 408(402)-450
Valentinian III (Flavius Placidius Valentinianus, in the West) 425-454
Marcian (Marcianus, in the East) 450-457
Petronius (Flavius Ancius Petronius Maximus, in the West) 455
Avitus (Flavius Maecillius Eparchus Avitus, in the West) 455-457
Majorian (Julius Valerius Maioranus, in the West) 457-461
Leo I (Leo Thrax, Magnus, in the East) 457-474
Severus (Libius Severianus Severus, in the West) 461-465
Anthemius (Procopius Anthemius, in the West) 467-472
Olybrius (Anicius Olybrium, in the West) 472
Glycerius (in the West) 473-474
Leo II (in the East) 473-474

Julius Nepos (in the West) 473-475
Romulus Augustulus (Flavius Momyllus Romulus Augustus,
    in the West) 475-476
Zeno (in the East) 474-491

BYZANTINE EMPERORS

Zeno, 474-491
Anastasius I, 491-518
Justin I (Flavius Justinus) 518-527
Justinian the Great (Flavius Justinianus) 527(518)-565
Justin II (Flavius Justinus) 565-578
Tiberius (Flavius Constantinus Tiberius) 578(574)-582
Maurice (Mauritius) 582-602
Phocas I, 602-610
Heraclius I, 610-641
Constantine III (Constantinus) 641
Heracleon (Heracleonas) 641
Constans II, 641-668
Constantine IV (Pogonatus) 668-685
Justinian II (Rhinotmetus) 685-695 and 705-711
Leontius II, 695-698
Tiberius III (Apsimar) 698-705
Philippicus, 711-713
Anastasius II, 713-715
Theodosius III, 715-717
Leo III (the Isaurian) 717-741
Constantine V (Kopronymus) 741-775
Leo IV, 775-780
Constantine VI (Porphyrogenetus) 780-797
Irene (empress) 797-802
Nicephorus I, 802-811
Stauracius (Staurakius) 811
Michael I, (Rhangebe) 811-813
Leo V (the Armenian) 813-820
Michael II (Balbus) 820-829
Theophilus I, 829(820)-842
Michael III, 842-867
Bardas, 842-866
Theophilus II, 867
Basil I (the Macedonian) 867(866)-886
Leo IV (the Wise) 886-912
Alexander III, 912-913
Constantine VII (Porphyrogenetus) 913-959
Romanus I (Lecapenus) 919-944
Romanus II, 959-963
Basil II (Bulgaroctonus) 963(976)-1025
Nicephorus II (Phocas) 963-969
John I (Tzimisces) 969-979
Constantine VIII, 1025(976)-1028
Zoë (empress) 1028-1050

Romanus III (Argyropolus) 1028-1034
Michael IV (the Paphlagonian) 1034-1041
Michael V (Kalaphates) 1041-1042
Constantine IV (Monomachus) 1042-1054
Theodora (empress) 1054-1056
Michael VI (Stratioticus) 1056-1057
Isaac I (Commenus) 1057-1059
Constantine X (Dukas) 1059-1067
Andronicus, 1067
Constantine XI, 1067
Romanus IV (Diogenes) 1067-1071
Michael VII (Parapinakes) 1071-1078
Nicephorus III (Botaniates) 1078-1081
Alexius I (Commenus) 1081-1118
John II (Calus) 1118-1143
Manuel I, 1143-1180
Alexius II, 1180-1183
Andronicus I, 1182-1185
Isaac II (Angelus-Commenus) 1185-1195
Alexius III (Angelus) 1195-1203
Isaac II (restored) 1203-1204
Alexius IV, 1203-1204
Alexius V (Dukas) 1204

Latin Emperors

Baldwin I, 1204-1205
Henry, 1205-1216
Peter de Courtenay, 1216-1217
Robert de Courtenay, 1218-1228
Baldwin II, 1228-1261

Nicaean Emperors

Theodore I (Lascaris) 1206-1222
John Dukas Vatatzes, 1222-1254
Theodore II (Lascaris) 1254-1259
John IV (Lascaris) 1258-1261
Michael VIII (Paleologus) 1259-1261 (1282)*

THE CALIPHS

Mohammed, 622(570)632

The Orthodox Caliphate

Abu Bakr 632-634   Omar, 634-644
Othman, 644-656   Ali, 656-661

*The rest of the Palaeologi kings on chart p. 318

The Omayyad Caliphate

Mo'awiya I, 661-680
Mo'awiya II, 683
Marwan I, 684-685
Sulayman, 715-717
Yazid II, 720-724
Walid II, 743-744
Marwan II, 744-750

Yazid I, 680-682
Abdalmalik, 685-705
Walid I, 705-715
Omar ibn Abdul-Aziz, 717-720
Hisham, 724-743
Yazid III, 744

The Abbasid Caliphate

Abu-l-Abbas al-Saffah,750-754
Al-Mahdi, 775-785
Harum-Al-Rashid, 786-809
Al-Ma'mun (the Great) 813-833
Al-Wathig, 842-847
Al-Muntasir, 861-862
Al-Mu'tazz, 866-869
Al-Mu'tamid, 870-892
Al-Muqtafi, 902-908
Al-Qahir, 932-934
Al-Muttaqi, 940-944
Al-Muti, 946-974
Al-Qadir, 991-1031
Al-Muqtadi, 1075-1094
Al-Mustarshid, 1118-1135
Al-Muqtafi, 1136-1160
Al-Mustadi, 1170-1180
Al-Zahir, 1225-1226
Al-Musta'sim, 1242-1256

Al-Mansur, 754-775
Al-Hadi, 785-786
Al-Amin, 809-813
Al-Mu'tasim, 833-842
Al-Mutawakkil, 847-861
Al-Musta'in, 862-866
Al-Muqtadi, 869-870
Al-Mu'tadid, 892-902
Al-Muqtadir, 908-932
Al-Radi, 934-940
Al-Mustaqfi, 944-946
Al-Ta'i, 974-991
Al-Qa'im, 1031-1075
Al-Mustazhir, 1094-1118
Al-Rashid, 1135-1136
Al-Mustanjid, 1160-1170
Al-Nasir, 1180-1225
Al-Mustansir, 1226-1242

ROMAN POPES

Boniface V, 619-625
Severinus, 638-640
Theodore I, 642-649
Eugene I, 655-657
Adeodatus, 672-676
Agatho, 678-681
Benedict II, 684-685
Conon, 686-687
Paschal I, 687-692
John VI, 701-705
Sisinnius, 708
Gregory II, 713-731
Zacharias, 741-752
Stephen II(III), 752-757
Constantine, 767-768
Stephen III(IV), 768-772
Leo III, 795-816

Honorius I, 625-638
John IV, 640-642
Martin I, 649-655
Vitalian, 657-672
Donus, 676-678
Leo II, 682-683
John V, 685-686
Theodore II, 687
Sergius I, 687-701
John VII, 705-707
Constantine, 708-715
Gregory III, 731-741
Stephen II, 752
Paul I, 757-767
Philip, 768
Adrian I, 772-795
Stephen IV(V), 816-817

Paschal I, 717-824
Eugene II, 824-827
Valentine, 827
Gregory IV, 827-844
John VIII, 844
Sergius II, 844-847
Leo IV, 847-855
Benedict III, 855-858
Anastasius III, 855
John IX, 855-857
Nicholas I, 858-867
Adrian II, 867-872
John VIII, 872-882
Martin II, 882-884
Adrian III, 884-885
Stephen V(VI), 885-891
Formosus, 891-896
Boniface VI, 896
Stephen VI(VII), 896-897
Romanus, 897
Theodore II, 897
John IX, 898-900
Benedict IV, 900-903
Leo V, 903
Christopher, 903-904
Sergius III, 904-911
Anastasius III,(IV),911-913
Lando, 913-914
John X, 914-928
Leo VI, 928
Stephen VII(VIII), 928-931
John XI, 931-936
Leo VII, 936-939
Stephen VIII(IX), 939-942
Martin III, 942-946
Agapetus, 946-955
John XII, 955-963
Leo VIII, 963-965
Benedict V, 965
John XIII, 965-972
Benedict VI, 973-974
Boniface VII, 974
Benedict VII, 974-983
John XIV, 983-984
Boniface VII, 984-985
John XV, 985-996
Gregory V, 996-999
John XVI, 997-998
Sylvester II, 999-1003
John XVII, 1003
John XVIII, 1003-1009
Sergius IV, 1009-1012
Benedict VIII, 1012-1024
Gregory VI, 1012
John XIX, 1024-1032
Benedict IX, 1032-1045
Sylvester III, 1045
Gregory VI, 1045-1046
Clement II, 1046-1047
Benedict IX, 1047-1048
Damasus II, 1048
Leo IX, 1049-1054
Victor II, 1055-1057
Stephen IX(X), 1057-1058
Benedict X, 1058-1059
Nicholas II, 1059-1061
Alexander II, 1061-1073
Honorius II, 1061-1064
Gregory VII, 1073-1085
Clement III, 1084-1100
Victor III, 1087
Urban II, 1088-1099
Paschal II, 1099-1118
Sylvester IV, 1105-1111
Theodoric, 1100-1102
Albert, 1102
Gelasius, 1118-1119
Gregory VIII, 1118-1121
Calixtus II, 1119-1124
Honorius II, 1124-1130
Celestine II, 1124
Innocent II, 1130-1143
Anacletus II, 1130-1138
Victor IV, 1138
Celestine II, 1143-1144
Lucius II, 1144-1145
Eugene II, 1145-1153
Anastasius IV, 1153-1154
Adrian IV, 1154-1159
Alexander III, 1159-1181
Victor IV, 1159-1164
Paschal III, 1164-1168
Calixtus III, 1168-1178
Innocent III, 1179-1180
Lucius III, 1181-1185
Urban III, 1185-1187
Gregory VIII, 1187
Clement III, 1187-1191
Celestine III, 1191-1198
Innocent III, 1198-1216
Honorius III, 1116-1227
Gregory IX, 1227-1241

Celestine IV, 1241
Alexander IV, 1254-1261
Clement IV, 1265-1268
Innocent V, 1276
John XXI, 1276-1277
Martin IV, 1281-1285
Nicholas IV, 1288-1292
Boniface VIII, 1294-1303
Clement V, 1305-1314
Nicholas V, 1328-1330
Clement VI, 1342-1352
Urban V, 1362-1370
Urban VI, 1378-1389
Boniface IX, 1389-1404
Innocent VII, 1404-1406
Alexander V, 1409-1410
Martin V, 1417-1431
Benedict XIV, 1424
Felix V, 1439-1449
Calixtus III, 1455-1458
Paul II, 1464-1471
Innocent VIII, 1484-1492
Pius III, 1503
Leo X, 1513-1521
Clement VII, 1523-1534
Julius III, 1550-1555
Paul IV, 1555-1559
Pius V, 1566-1572
Sixtus V, 1585-1590
Gregory XIV, 1590-1591
Clement VIII, 1592-1605

Innocent IV, 1243-1254
Urban IV, 1261-1264
Gregory X, 1271-1276
Adrian V, 1276
Nicholas III, 1277-1280
Honorius IV, 1285-1287
Celestine V, 1294
Benedict IX, 1303-1304
John XXII, 1316-1334
Benedict XII, 1334-1342
Innocent VI, 1352-1362
Gregory XI, 1370-1378
Clement VII, 1378-1394
Benedict XIII, 1394-1424
Gregory XII, 1406-1415
John XXIII, 1410-1415
Clement VIII, 1424-1429
Eugene IV, 1431-1447
Nicholas V, 1447-1455
Pius II, 1458-1464
Sixtus IV, 1471-1484
Alexander VI, 1492-1503
Julius II, 1503-1513
Adrian VI, 1522-1523
Paul III, 1534-1549
Marcellus II, 1555
Pius IV, 1559-1565
Gregory XIII, 1572-1585
Urban VII, 1590
Innocent IX, 1591
Leo IX, 1605

HOLY ROMAN EMPERORS

Charlemagne, 800-814
Louis I (the Pious) 814-840
Lothar I, 840-855
Louis II (in Italy) 855-875
Charles II, the Bald (West Frankish) 875-877
Charles III, the Fat (East Frankish) 877-887 (crowned 881)
Vacant, Struggle between Guido of Spoleto and Berangar of
    Friuli, 887-891
Guido (in Italy), 891-894
Lambert (co-emperor with Guido) 892-899
Arnulf, 896-901 (crowned by Pope Formosus)
Louis III (of Provence) 901-905(928)
Berengar, 905(915)-924
Hugh of Provence, 926-945
Berengar, 952-962
Henry I (the Fowler, Saxon) 918-936
Otto II, 973-983

Henry II, the Saint (Bavarian) 1002(1014)-1024

Italian Line

Rudolph of Burgundy, 924-926
Lothar III, 945-950

German Line

Conrad I (Franconian) 911-918
Otto, the Great, 936(962)-973
Otto III, 983(996)-1002
Conrad II, the Salian (Franconian) 1024(1027)-1039
Henry III, the Black, 1039-1056
Henry IV, 1056(1084)-1106
Rudolph of Swabia, 1077-1080
Hermann of Luxemburg, 1081-1093
Conrad of Franconia, 1093-1101
Henry V, 1106(1111)-1125
Lothar II (Saxon) 1125(1133)-1137
Conrad III (Swabian) 1138-1152
Frederick I, Barbarossa, 1152(1155)-1190
Henry VI, 1190(1191)-1197
Philip II (Swabian)1198-1208
Otto IV (Brunswick) 1198-1212
Frederick II, 1212(1220)-1250
Henry Raspe, 1246-1247
William of Holland, 1247-1256
Conrad IV, 1250-1254
The Great Interregnum, 1254-1273
Alfonso X of Castile, 1257-1272
Richard of Cornwall, 1257-1273
Rudolph I (Hapsburg) 1273-1291
Adolf I, of Nassau, 1292-1298
Albert I (Hapsburg) 1298-1308
Henry VII (Luxemburg) 1308(1312)-1313
Louis IV (Bavaria) 1314-1347
Frederick of Hapsburg, 1325-1330
Günther of Schwarzburg, 1347-1349
Charles IV (Luxemburg) 1347-1378
Wenzel (Luxemburg) 1378-1400
Rupert (Palatinate) 1400-1410
Sigismund (Luxemburg) 1410-1437
Jobst of Moravia, 1410-1441
Albert II (Hapsburg) 1438-1439
Frederick III, 1440-1493
Maximilian I, 1493-1519
Charles V, 1519-1556
Ferdinand I, 1558-1564
Maximilian II, 1564-1576
Rudolf II, 1576-1612

Matthias, 1612-1619
Ferdinand II, 1619-1637
Ferdinand III, 1637-1657
Leopold I, 1658-1705
Joseph I, 1705-1711
Charles VI, 1711-1740
Charles VII (Bavaria) 1742-1745
Francis I (Lorraine) 1745-1765
Joseph II, 1765-1790
Leopold II, 1790-1792
Francis II, 1792-1806

THE MACEDONIAN EMPERORS

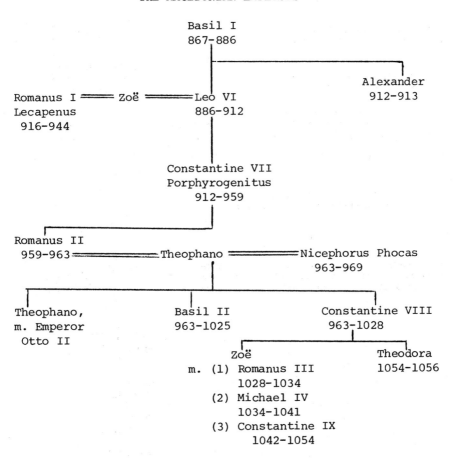

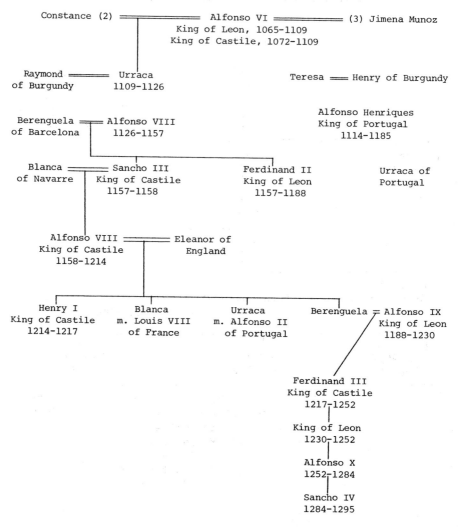

312

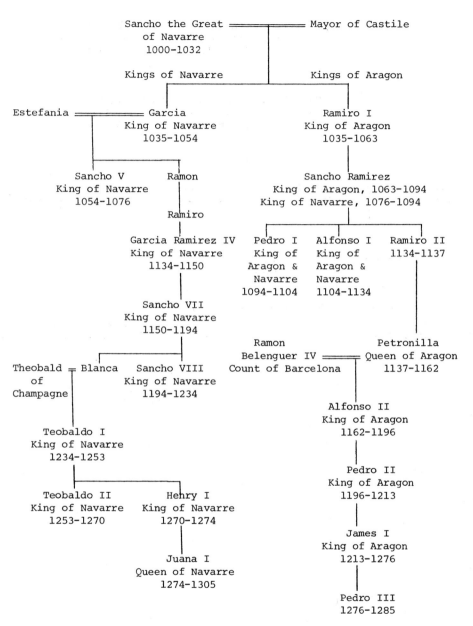

BURGUNDIAN KINGS OF PORTUGAL

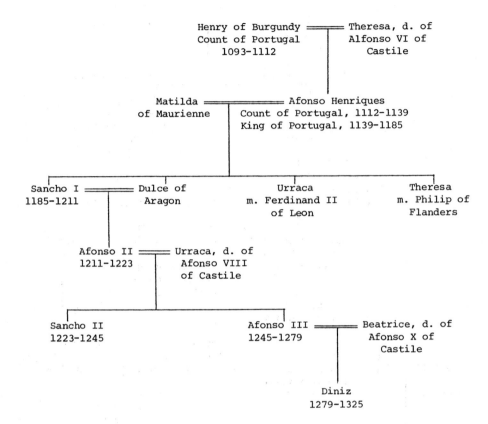

Henry of Burgundy ═══════ Theresa, d. of
Count of Portugal   Alfonso VI of
1093-1112   Castile

Matilda ═══════════ Afonso Henriques
of Maurienne   Count of Portugal, 1112-1139
                    King of Portugal, 1139-1185

Sancho I ═══════ Dulce of   Urraca   Theresa
1185-1211   Aragon   m. Ferdinand II   m. Philip of
                                 of Leon   Flanders

Afonso II ═══════ Urraca, d. of
1211-1223   Afonso VIII
                  of Castile

Sancho II   Afonso III ═══════ Beatrice, d. of
1223-1245   1245-1279   Afonso X of
                                              Castile

                            Diniz
                          1279-1325

314

THE HOUSE OF CASTILE

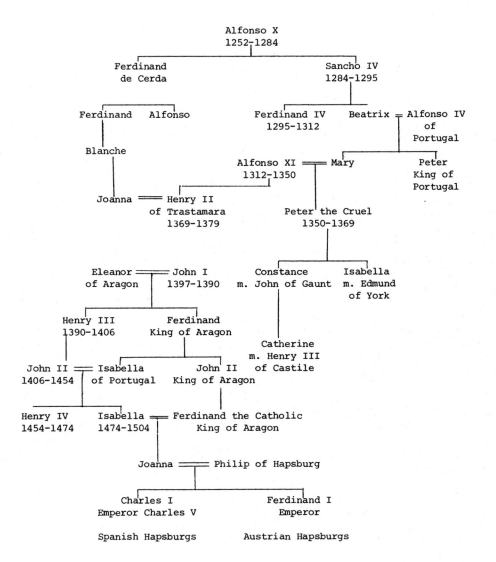

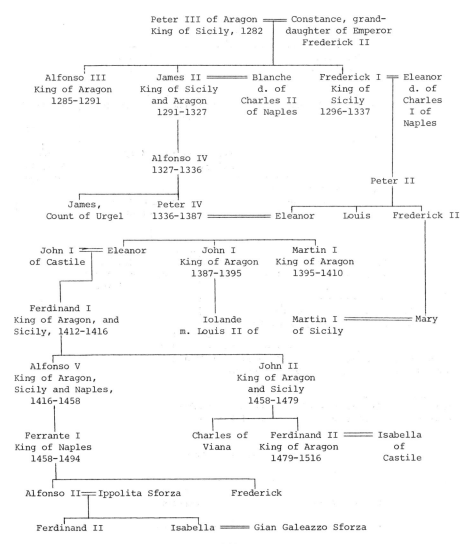

316

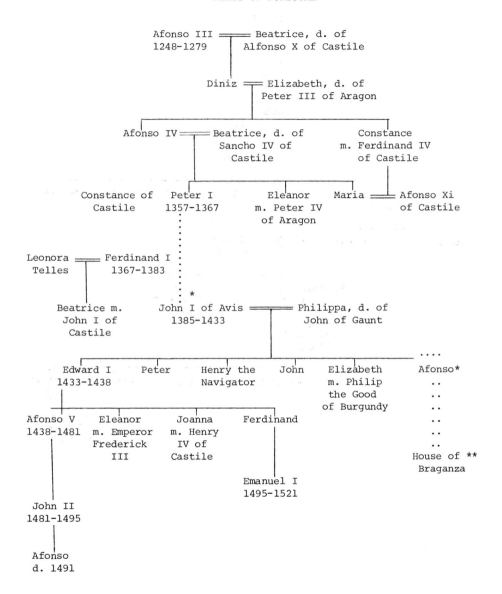

*Illegitimate issue.
**Of another noble family.

BYZANTINE RULERS

THE PALAEOLOGI

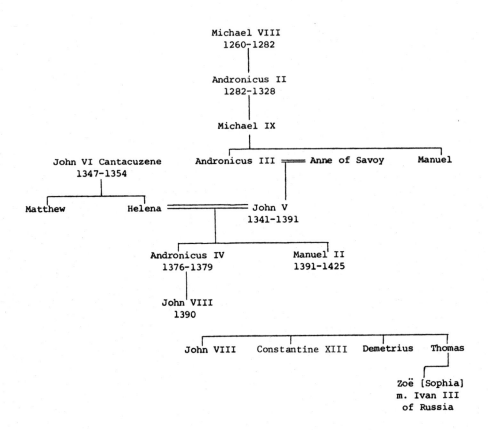

BIBLIOGRAPHY

Azuni, D.A. *Droit Maritime de l'Europe*. Paris, 1805.

Barnes, H.E. *An Intellectual and Cultural History of the Western World*. New York, 1937.

Belli, P. *De re militari et bello tractatus*. Trans. Nuttig, H.C. Oxford, 1936.

Bentwick, N. *The Religious Foundations of Internationalism*. London, 1933.

Boissonnade, P. *Life and Work in Medieval Europe*. N.Y. 1937.

Bonnecase, M. *Precis de Droit Maritime*. Paris, 1932.

Breasted, J.H. *Ancient Records of Egypt*. Chicago, 1906-07, 5 Vols.

Burke, U.R. *A History of Spain*. New York, 1894-95, 2 Vols.

Casaregis, G. *Consolato del Mare*. Bassano, 1788.

Conde, J.A. *History of the Dominion of the Arabs in Spain*. London, 1854-55, 3 Vols.

Cotterill, A.B. *Medieval Italy*. London, 1915.

Cussy, de F. *Phases et causes Celebres du Droit Maritime des Nations*. Lipsk, 1856.

Digeon, J.M. *Systeme universal de principes du droit Maritime de l' Europe*. Paris 1798. 2 Vols.

Dumont, J. *Corps Universal Diplomatique Du Droit Des Gens, 800-1718*. Amsterdam, 1726-1731, 8 Vols.

Fenwick, C.G. *International Law*. New York, 4th Edition, 1965.

Gentili, A. *Hispanicae advocationis libri duo*. Trans. Abbott, F.F. New York, 1921.
De jure belli libri tres. Trans. Rolfe, J.C. Washington, 1933.

Grotius, H. *De jure belli ac pacis*. Trans. Wheewall, W. W. Cambridge, 1853.

Hume, M.A.S. *Spanish People, Their Origin, Growth and Influence*. New York, 1901.

Laurent, F. *Histoire du droit des gens et des relations internationales*. Paris, 1878-1880, 14 Vols.

Marzials, F. *Memoirs of the Crusades*. London, 1908.

Moore, J.B. *International Adjudications, Ancient and Modern*. New York, 1929-1933, 6 Vols.

Munro, D. C., Sontag, R.J. *The Middle Ages, 395-1500*. New York, 1928.

Pardessus, J.M. *Collection des lois maritimes antirieures au XVIII e siecle*. Paris, 1828-1845, 6 Vols.
Dels bons stablimens e costumes de la mar. Paris, 1837.

Ralston, J.H. *International Arbitrations from Athens to Locarno*. New York, 1929.

Rivier, A. *Principes Du Droit Des Gens*. Paris, 1896, 2 Vols.

Scott, J.B. *The Spanish Origin of International Law*. Washington, 1928.

Schaube, F. *Das Konsulat de Meeres in Piza*. Lipsk, 1888.

Thorndike, L. *The History of Medieval Europe*. Boston, 1928.

Twiss, T. *Monumenta Juridica*. London, 1876.

Vattel E. de *Le Droit des gens, ou Principes de la' loi naturalle appliques a la condicite at aux affaires des nations et des souverains*. Trans. Fenwick, C.G., Washington, 1916, 3 Vols.

Victoria, F. de *De indis et de jure belli relectiones*. Trans. Bate, J.P. Washington, 1917.

Ward, R. *Enquiry Into The Foundations and History Of The Law Of Nations In Europe*. Dublin, 1795, 2 Vols.

Wheaton, H. *Elements of International Law*. London, 1836. *A History of the Law of Nations*. London, 1845.